Getting Religion

Getting Religion

*Faith, Culture, and Politics
from the Age of Eisenhower
to the Era of Obama*

Kenneth L. Woodward

Convergent
New York

Copyright © 2016 by Kenneth L. Woodward

All rights reserved.
Published in the United States by Convergent Books, an imprint of the Crown
Publishing Group, a division of Penguin Random House LLC, New York.
crownpublishing.com

CONVERGENT BOOKS is a registered trademark and its C colophon is a
trademark of Penguin Random House LLC.

Selected material in Chapters 1 and 13 originally appeared in the online blog
FirstThings.com, between 2011 and 2015.

Grateful acknowledgment is made to *Newsweek* for permission to reprint
an excerpt from "Has the Church Lost Its Soul?" by Kenneth L. Woodward,
originally published October 4, 1971.

Library of Congress Cataloging-in-Publication Data
Names: Woodward, Kenneth L., author.
Title: Getting religion : faith, culture, and politics from the age of
    Eisenhower to the era of Obama / Kenneth L. Woodward.
Description: First Edition. | New York : Convergent Books, 2016.
Identifiers: LCCN 2016020212 (print) | LCCN 2016026677 (ebook) |
    ISBN 9781101907399 (hardcover) | ISBN 9781101907405 (E-book)
Subjects: LCSH: United States—Church history—20th century. | United States—
    Church history—21st century.
Classification: LCC BR526 .W67 2016 (print) | LCC BR526 (ebook) |
    DDC 200.973/09045—dc23
LC record available at https://lccn.loc.gov/2016020212

ISBN 978-1-101-90739-9
eBook ISBN 978-1-101-90740-5

Printed in the United States of America

Jacket design by Jessie Bright

10 9 8 7 6 5 4 3 2 1

First Edition

For

Luke, Audrey, and Meg
Henry and Hattie Marie

—more bread upon the waters

and

In memory of
The Reverend Theodore M. Hesburgh, CSC

Longtime president of the University of Notre Dame
Longer-time friend
Priest forever

All these things I remember, and how I learned them I remember.
—St. Augustine, *Confessions*

Contents

Part IV

Part V

Getting Religion

Introduction

Being there matters.

As a man who came of age in the 1950s and as a journalist who spent nearly four decades at *Newsweek,* I had the good fortune (or not) of living through the most volatile religious period in American history. There have been other periods of religious enthusiasm and upheaval but none of these, I argue, was so widespread, so wildly diverse in faith and practice, so direct in impact on electoral politics as the one that ranged from the end of the Second World War to the dawn of the new millennium.

How and why this happened, and to what social, cultural, and political effect, is the story I have to tell.

At midcentury, while a student at Notre Dame and later during my apprentice years as a journalist in Omaha, the United States was awash in religious belief. To be American was to believe in God and, when surveyed in those days, 98 percent of Americans answered accordingly. In the Fifties, Americans built more churches and synagogues than at any other time in the nation's history. They regularly worshipped in them as well. Protestant Sunday school was a national institution. By 1960, half of all school-aged Catholics were enrolled in parochial schools. Seminaries thrived. Protestant divinity schools could pick and choose among applicants who might otherwise become lawyers, doctors, or corporate executives. Catholic parents felt spiritually remiss if they did not contribute at

least one son to the priesthood and a daughter to the convent. To
those like myself with memories of that bygone era it seems like
"only yesterday."

Yet, only a half century later nearly one in four Americans
claimed no religious identification. Another 50 percent acknowledged only moderate or intermittent concern for religion. Faith was
no longer a family hand-me-down: parents who sent their children
off to Sunday school or parochial schools watched as a great many
of them, in their maturity, embraced either another religion or none
at all. Long before the new millennium the old Protestant establishment that represented the ruling caste in politics as well as in Main
Street America's largest churches had disappeared, replaced by a
new, rougher-hewn establishment of Fundamentalists and Evangelicals, like Jerry Falwell, who had been waiting patiently offstage for
their turn in the spotlight. Catholics saw Pope John XXIII's promise
of renewal through the reforms of the Second Vatican Council sput-
ter into factionalism and, later, the moral authority of their leaders—
from parish priests to scarlet-clad cardinals—compromised by the
scandal of clerical abuse and hierarchical cover-up. The leading liberal Protestant seminaries remained open only because the mainline
denominations decided to ordain women. Vocations to the Catholic
priesthood declined so precipitously that even the importation of
priests from Africa and other continents could not make up the difference. If former Catholics all belonged to a single denomination,
it would constitute the nation's second largest—after the Catholic
Church itself. The ranks of American nuns, once the face of Catholicism in countless hospitals and parochial school classrooms,
receded to the point of extinction. And American Jews, who had
found new pride in Israel's victory in the Six-Day War against over-
whelming Arab forces in 1967, now faced the certain prospect of
being outnumbered back at home by the more fervent and fertile
Muslim population.

The narrative of institutional decline from the age of Eisenhower
to the era of Obama is only one side of the story this book has to

tell. In the 1960s and '70s, Americans also witnessed an unexpected exfoliation of religious belief, behavior, and belonging. Some historians compared it to the great religious "awakenings" that occurred in the middle decades of the eighteenth and nineteenth centuries, when Americans "got religion" at revival meetings or—like the Mormons, the Disciples of Christ, and other new movements of the day—sought to recover the pure faith and practices of Jesus and His apostles.

But the kinds of religion that the baby boomers got was not like the religions of their parents and grandparents, nor were the new-time evangelizers. Many of them were Hindu gurus and Buddhist *tulku*s preaching salvation from the Vedas and Sanskrit sutras. Others were messiahs of "sacred families" like the Unification Church of Dr. Moon. Still others were secular gurus of "transpersonal psychology" and other techniques of the human potential movement that offered therapeutic solutions to the mysteries of life and death.

This midcentury spiritual awakening is another side of the story this book tells.

And yet neither of these transformations in American religion would have happened—or is even understandable—apart from the cultural and political upheavals that convulsed American society as a whole. Among those addressed in these pages: the migration of southern blacks to northern cities, of whites to the green of postwar suburbs, and the creation of the Interstate Highway System in the Fifties; the expansion of higher education, the relaxation of sexual mores, and the rise of the drug culture in the Sixties; the collapse of bourgeois family structures and the culture wars in the Seventies and Eighties; and the repudiation of constituencies and principles that each of the major political parties once spoke to and for.

Five movements in the second half of the twentieth century were of such consequence for American religion that I have devoted a chapter to each: the civil rights movement, especially in the person of Dr. Martin Luther King Jr.; the antiwar movement, especially in the figures of the Berrigan brothers and their clerical allies; the women's movement, particularly in its efforts to advance a feminist reinterpretation of the Bible and a feminist rewrite of beloved Protestant hymns; the Liberation Theology movement, particularly in its conflict with American foreign policy in Nicaragua and other Catholic countries of Central America; and the Evangelical/Pentecostal movement, particularly as it impacted American politics.

The underlying premise of the pages that follow can be simply put: *how* Americans got religion determined the *kind* of religion they got. For example, in the Fifties, most people acquired a religion through parents, extended family networks, neighborhoods, and the religious institutions nested there. What part of the country you lived in also mattered, as the *Atlas of American Religion* visually attests. Religion acquired this way is what I call "embedded religion."

Conversely, as the civil rights movement took on a momentum all its own, activists, from all sorts of religious beliefs (and none), joined King's crusade. To be in "the movement" was to assume a new group identity as "brothers and sisters" yoked together in "the struggle" for racial equality. Or the struggle to end the war in Vietnam, or the struggle to liberate women from the grip of "patriarchy"— two of the more percussive movements in a menu of Sixties and Seventies causes. Those so yoked just "happened to be" from Detroit or San Francisco or Louisville and just "happened to be" Presbyterian or Unitarian or Quaker. Beliefs, behaviors, and belonging acquired in this way constitute what I call "movement religion."

Although the decades of the last half century unfolded sequentially (as decades always do), the various ways in which Americans got religion, beginning in the late Sixties, occurred almost simultaneously. Hence the chapters that follow are organized thematically and should be read like the leaves of a palimpsest, one overlaying without erasing what came before. After all, most Americans still acquire at least their initial religious orientation from their parents and local surroundings.

Now, why *being there* matters. Many historians have examined segments of this story, the best of them well sourced in the work of journalists who reported events as they happened. History done at a distance in time and place allows larger patterns to emerge, and connections to be made, and I have benefited from books of that kind. But history at a distance often bears the watermarks of a research project. I've attended lectures where speakers discussed events I either witnessed personally or wrote about from files sent to me by *Newsweek* correspondents on the scene. "No, that's not quite the way it really was," I found myself muttering, "not that way at all." Which is why I decided to write this book.

Being there did matter and *being there* does matter. It mattered in Vietnam when correspondents watched napalmed children trying to outrun their own burning flesh. Being there means remembering, as I do here, a Sandinista pilot in Nicaragua offering me his roll of toilet paper while I was deep on assignment, even though that was his allotment for the entire week. Being there allows for "aha" moments like the afternoon I watched Billy Graham watching himself preach on videotape, all the while assuring me that we were not hearing Billy Graham speaking but God speaking through Billy Graham. Being there means feeling the iron grip of the Dalai Lama as he welcomes you into his home in Dharamsala. It makes you realize that Buddhism's doctrinal dismissal of the body as ephemeral doesn't preclude a reincarnated Buddhist deity from daily workouts toning his. In many ways, it is personal accounts that give breath to the body of past events. How things looked and felt, used judiciously, helps the reader understand the way things were and in turn sheds light on why things are the way they are now.

The chapters that follow represent an exercise in what I call "lived history," though perhaps not the kind that some professional historians mean by that term. The reader will encounter lots of *I*'s and *my*'s and *me*'s in passages of memoir and autobiography—plus quite a few stories of the kind that journalists like to tell whenever they gather over drinks. The aim, as I examine the intersection of faith, culture, and politics over the last fifty years, is not to insert myself, Zelig-like, into every scene but to insert the reader into the past as my companion. I want the reader to see what I saw, hear what I heard.

At its most basic level, history can be seen as a collection of stories. The first historians were really storytellers. And telling stories, of course, is what journalists are paid to do. Like other journalists, I had to learn my subject on the job. Inevitably, we journalists became participant-observers—participant because the stories we published mediated to readers the meaning of what we observed. Hence the more personal meaning of my title, *Getting Religion*.

My goal in writing this book is twofold: to provide an account of American religion, culture, and politics over the past fifty years by someone who was fortunate enough to be in the right place at the right time to witness events and people in ways that others never could or did, and to challenge some competing narratives through my personal reflections on what happened and why.

Without *Newsweek* magazine I could not have written this book, or even conceive of it as a book that I could write. Beginning in 1964 as religion editor, I spent thirty-eight years as a writer in its service—longer, I am told, than any other writer in the history of the magazine. Over that span, I reported and wrote stories from five continents, a body of some one thousand articles, essays, and book reviews, including more than seventy cover stories. Fortunately, I've kept copies of nearly everything I've written. Just by rereading them I can readily summon up in an almost Proustian way the circumstances behind each piece. Accordingly, *Newsweek* and its specific newsroom culture are present throughout this book, much like the stage set of a play. Here again, how you got your information can influence the information you got.

A note on endnotes: Any quotations not sourced are taken from my own taped interviews, notebooks, and stories I wrote for *Newsweek* and other publications. I do, of course, source quotes and ideas derived from others. But I have reserved the endnotes mainly for brief additions, amplifications, and asides that otherwise would have interrupted narrative flow. A list of books consulted appears in the Bibliography.

. . .

I want to thank historians Grant Wacker of the Duke Divinity School, Martin E. Marty of the University of Chicago Divinity School, and Philip Gleason of the University of Notre Dame for their comments and criticism of the text. Now emeriti, all three were around when events here revisited occurred. As with my other books, I owe multiple debts of gratitude to my wife, Betty, who makes a few appearances in these pages. Fortunately, in a marriage of true hearts, spouses never achieve emeritus status.

Part I

CHAPTER 1

Embedded Religion

It Goes with the Territory

On the wall of my old *Newsweek* office, next to a window with a narrow view of the changing seasons in lower Central Park, I kept a large map, in a mosaic of colors, of the United States. When you are a writer working in New York City, you need something to remind you of what the rest of the country is like: this was mine. There are no place-names on the map, only the boundaries of the states, and within them the spidery outlines of each county. It's a relief map of sorts: any county in which 25 percent or more of the citizens identify with a single religious denomination is shaded in a color representing that tradition. Counties where more than half the people are of one persuasion—more than half the map—are colored more deeply.[1]

At a glance, the map yields a rough religious geography of America. Across the South, where it sometimes seems there are more Baptists than there are people, the counties are awash in deep red. Utah, Idaho, and Wyoming are solidly gray: the Mormon Zion. There are swaths of Lutheran green in Minnesota and Wisconsin. Belt high from Delaware to central Kansas, especially in rural areas, the map shows streaks and potholes of blue where the Methodists and their nineteenth-century circuit riders planted churches. Catholic purple blankets the Northeast, the Great Lakes region, the Gulf

Coast, and nearly all of California. Like my window onto Central Park, the map afforded a view of America that's closed to most New Yorkers, especially those who regard their city as the center of the universe. When colleagues stopped by my office they'd often stare over my head at the map. "Where are *my* people?" was the usual question. Some Episcopalians, thinking of all their coreligionists elected to Congress and the White House, assumed the nation's capital to be theirs. But the District of Columbia is heavily African American and so it is dyed a deep Baptist red. According to the map, Episcopalians do dominate a half-dozen counties—all of them tribal reservations in North Dakota where the church made converts of the Native American inhabitants. Most Jewish colleagues thought New York City and its environs (home to half the nation's Jews) was surely theirs to claim, but the whole metropolitan area is deep Catholic purple. Jews do own a plurality in one Florida county, Miami-Dade.

Recent demographic studies back up the map's quick visual impressions. Between them, Catholics and Baptists alone account for 40 percent of the American population. Each has its homelands— states where Catholics or Baptists own absolute majorities—and its diasporas, where to be a Catholic or a Baptist is to hold outsider status. In other words, religion cannot be separated from region. And neither can it be separated from ethnicity. Social historians looking at my map would immediately recognize the counties where Dutch Calvinists, German pietists, Scotch-Irish Presbyterians, and Scandinavian Lutherans carved out their ecological niches. In America, even now, religion "goes with the territory."

For me, the map was a visual reminder that religion in America has never been just a matter of personal choice. It has also been about community and connection—to places, to people, and to what religiously convicted Americans have made of the places where they chose to live. Which is to say that religion, as a way of belonging as well as of believing and behaving, is always embedded—in institutions, yes, but also in the landscape. "Habitations," as historian Martin Marty reminds us, "foster habits."

I am a midwesterner—born there, reared there, educated at three midwestern universities, and before I moved to New York and to *Newsweek* magazine I had lived in six of the eleven "heartland" states. In mix of religion, as in mix of population, the Middle West is more representative of the nation as a whole than is any other region of the United States. More important, perhaps, the Middle West is what movie mythmakers have imagined the entire nation to be like when Americans are on their best behavior. From *Meet Me in St. Louis* and *State Fair* through *The Wizard of Oz, The Music Man, Field of Dreams,* and *Hoosiers,* the Middle West has supplied its share of fictive images of hometown innocence, morality, and even magic realism: "Toto, I've a feeling we're not in Kansas anymore," Dorothy says to her dog when they land in Oz. But, of course, they are.

I grew up in Ohio, where, a glance at my office map reminded me, almost every kind of Protestant denomination could claim a town or county as its turf. Even after their children moved on, these immigrants from elsewhere left behind brick-and-mortar evidence of their hegemony in the form of church-related colleges—more of them, when I was college-age, than any other state. The Methodists established Ohio Wesleyan and Otterbein; the Episcopalians, Kenyon College; the Congregationalists, Oberlin and Marietta; the Presbyterians, Wooster; the Quakers, Wilmington College; the German Reform Church, Heidelberg; English Evangelical Lutherans, Wittenberg; the Mennonites, Bluffton, and so on. Students at these small liberal arts colleges not only learned together; they also worshipped together at chapel, and the faculty was hired to ensure that the distinctive character of the founding church tradition was passed on whole and intact. After commencement, graduates married each other, too.

Catholics, of course, had their own colleges on their own urban turf in cities like Cleveland, Cincinnati, and Dayton. There, as in the Protestant colleges, the goal was to provide an education that included solid formation in the faith. For that reason, if a graduate of a Catholic high school wanted to stay near home and attend a nearby

Protestant college—or venture east to Harvard or Yale—he usually had to forward his transcripts himself because Catholic school officials discouraged journeys beyond the pale.

My father was born in the final November of the nineteenth century on what was to become Veterans Day. He was reared among hymn-singing, family-reunion-gathering, Sunday-dinner-making, small-town Ohio Protestants of Welsh and Scotch-Irish stock. An only child, he was never one to talk about his youth. But he did reveal one important detail of his early life: in Youngstown, where he lived, he stepped forward at a revival by evangelist Billy Sunday and at age sixteen declared himself for Christ. It was during the Wobblies' (Industrial Workers of the World) strike against the Youngstown steelworks in 1916, and the conjunction of these two emotional events, I've always thought, is why he was anti-labor all his life. In any case, my job as a religion writer never impressed him more than when, on a Sunday afternoon while my parents were visiting, another evangelist, Billy Graham, called me—at home—just to have a chat.

My mother was from an Irish-Italian family in Detroit. She was the first in the extended Brady-Cauzillo family to go to college—a leap from a one-room schoolhouse to the University of Michigan's vast Ann Arbor campus—and that was the pivotal experience of *her* youth. When we were kids she used to reprise her sorority song for us: it was a sorority just for Catholic coeds. Here's the kind of Catholics my mother's siblings were. Her brother, my only uncle, kept copies of the *Imitation of Christ* by Thomas à Kempis on his desk and passed them out to vendors who called on him for business. It didn't matter whether they were Catholic or even Christian. One sister was a cloistered nun who snuck away from college one day, without my grandmother's permission, and crossed the border to join her friends in a Canadian convent. Two others, both English teachers in mostly black inner-city public high schools and never married, shared a tidy house with a crucifix hung in every room. On a bookshelf they kept a series of volumes by Catholic intellectuals published by Sheed and Ward. Whenever they drove their car, they paused first to dip their fingers in holy water founts mounted on each side of the garage doorframe. On the road they routinely recited the rosary. Even on short trips to the grocery, they measured distances by how many decades they could finish before they reached their destination.

How my parents met and married across religious boundaries was never explained to us. We did know, though, that the ceremony was held in the parish rectory because religiously mixed couples were not allowed a wedding inside a Catholic church. At that time, my father pledged to rear the children Catholic, as the church required, and though he never became a Catholic himself, he never wavered in his pledge.

I have ventured this brief family biography for just one purpose. Growing up where and when I did, I experienced an America that was highly diverse, though not in the ways we think of diversity today. What region of the country you inhabited mattered greatly, and so did ethnic background. But the primary source of diversity in those days was religion. Since this is no longer true, this facet of American social history needs explanation.

The immigrant communities then were mostly white and European. In cities like Cleveland, the place I knew best, each had its own neighborhoods and social clubs, funeral parlors, corner bars and restaurants, as well as churches. At home, adults cooked and talked Greek and Italian, Polish and Slovak, just as more recent immigrants now speak Spanish, Mandarin Chinese, or Arabic. They read and discussed newspapers in Ukrainian, Czech, Armenian, Romanian, and Yiddish. Yes, they were mostly Christian, but that only made differences in church doctrine and tradition more pronounced: Muslims and Hindus are intriguing in their obvious otherness, but none of the religions new to America today challenge Christians like other Christians claiming to be the one true church of Jesus Christ.

In urban neighborhoods, therefore, no less than in small towns, where you worshipped—and how—said much about who you were. Even the ecumenically inclined and the nonreligious observed their social boundaries and kept their social distance. Within all these "ghettos" (though no one called them that), religion was free to form individual and group identities through shared "habits of the heart" and acquired sensibilities. Even in the more open spaces of the sub-urbs, where I grew up, the families you knew best belonged to the same church. But my parents' marriage was proof to me that the boundaries created by religion could amicably be breached. None-theless, among those who took it very seriously, religion remained a powerful symbol system that defined ultimate reality for all who lived in its embrace.

But however diverse Americans felt themselves to be, all of us who would come of age in the Fifties were marked by a single event: the Second World War.

Growing Up on the "Home Front"

I was born in 1935 and passed through childhood while the nation was at war. Unlike the war in Vietnam two decades later, World War II united the nation in common cause. Unlike our more re-cent wars in Afghanistan and Iraq, this war was not fought off-stage by volunteers so that the good life at home could continue uninterrupted. To the contrary, on the "home front" all children were suckled on a culture of sacrifice and restraint—one that linked us closer to the children of the Great Depression (though our cir-cumstances were never so drastic) than to our own children born into postwar affluence. Beginning in 1942, staples of the good life—first sugar, then gasoline, fuel oil, and rubber tires, then fruit juices, canned and frozen food, including baby food, even shoes and clothes—were strictly rationed. As participants in the common "war effort" everyone made do.

My mother dutifully planted a low-yield Victory garden—thin carrots, limp bean stalks, lettuce the size of baseballs. By war's end, 40 percent of the nation's vegetables were harvested from an esti-mated 20 million family plots like ours. At the store, Mother bought meat and butter with red ration stamps from her government-issued "War Ration Book" and soups and dried beans from stamps color-coded blue. Because he was a salesman, and his car was his living, my father got extra ration stamps for gas. At home, he did his civil duty as a suburban air-raid warden: one night a month, when the warning siren sounded, he put a yellow metal helmet on his head and went about making sure the neighbors had turned out all their lights, lest enemy bombers should penetrate the airspace over Lake Erie's southern shore. My older brother and I followed the battles overseas by pasting newspaper headlines in scrapbooks. From inside cereal boxes we collected colorful arm patches worn by the men in uniform, and from strips of balsam wood and glue built models of the airplanes the American pilots flew.

It was a good time to be a child. Despite the separations caused by the war, even young families were remarkably stable. Divorce was rare: most marriages lasted until the death of a spouse. In the families I knew, only the father worked and all the fathers seemed to arrive home in unison by 6 p.m. The mothers not only reared the children and did the housework; they also made the schools and churches hum. Through these community ties they were the marriage partners who decided which neighbors would also be close friends.

Weekends were strung like hammocks between the fathers' Friday evening arrivals and their going off on Monday mornings. In their absence, life on the block unrolled as regular as church ritual. Once a week the iceman delivered a chiseled block to keep our food refrigerated, and cut cold slivers for us to suck. The uniformed milkman delivered full bottles on his scheduled route and took away clinking empties. And when the bread man arrived curbside we rushed inside to inhale the concentrated aroma of fresh-baked jelly rolls and warm pecan buns. Life on the home front was predictable. The war and its restrictions gave even kids a sense of unity and national purpose. Then the war was over. Only later did we learn about the multitude of young men who never came back.

Roots and Horizons

All of us come from a place we mistake for universal. So you should know something of mine. The place I called home was a suburb that mushroomed a century earlier out of farms and orchards and shoreline summer cottages sixteen miles west of Cleveland. Rocky River, as it came to be called, spread out from a tavern overlooking a river (hence the name) that rolls through a deep gorge on a meandering path to Lake Erie. It was our Grand Canyon. A single arch of concrete, once the longest in the world, shouldered traffic east and west, and on a separate wooden trestle, freight trains on the "Nickel Plate Road" (the New York, Chicago & St. Louis Railroad) hustled manufactured parts to assembly plants in Toledo and Detroit. Rocky River had eleven thousand inhabitants then and called itself a city only because it was governed by its own mayor and city council. By my definition, though, a city was a place with a choice of movie theaters and Rocky River had only one: the Beach Cliff.

Like other writers, artists, or journalists who migrated to New York, I brought my hometown with me. Working in New York is what allowed Willa Cather to see her native Nebraska so sharply, Sherwood Anderson his Elyria, Ohio, Willie Morris his Mississippi. As it is with trees, our roots shape our horizons.

My earliest memories are of the water. Our first house was three blocks from Lake Erie, which we reached along a sidewalk lined with blackberry bushes and down a plunge of stone steps, more than fifty of them. Mother took the three of us, Nancy, Bill, and me, to the beach early on summer weekdays, slathering us with oil against the sun and watching as we paddled in the slowly lapping low-tide morning waters. Every day during the summer, the newspaper posted a polio count and when it was high we knew there would be no beach for us that day.

Several times before the age of eight, my best pal and I packed a bag with sandwiches, a cache of our favorite toy soldiers and the stuffed animals we slept with, and set out "to run away from home." We weren't trying to escape; we just wanted to explore what lay beyond the neighborhood, convinced that wherever we went the world would wear a friendly face. Our parents never knew because we always returned in time for dinner. When I tell these stories to my grandchildren they are incredulous. That's because the America they inhabit is a far more dangerous and fearful place.

At war's end we moved to a house farther from the lake on a street that dead-ended in a woods. As soon as spring arrived, I ventured out alone across a marsh of pussy willows, over moldering logs and across the graveled railroad tracks, through thickets of sycamores, elms, and spindly sumacs whose pointed leaves were tipped in red, like my mother's fingernails; then climbed over the fences guarding the city sewage plant and crossed between elegant houses off Lake Road to bluffs that rose up like the cliffs of Normandy. Below was the familiar strip of sand and out along the horizon, if I squinted hard enough, I was sure I could glimpse the shore of Canada. I spent eleven summers on the beaches of Lake Erie as a lifeguard.

If our fathers were incipient Organization Men, as social critics later claimed they were, they never imposed those stringencies on us. For instance, we kids camped out overnight on our own, pitching tents in the woods and warming to fires built and extinguished without the superintending presence of Boy Scout leaders in short pants. Evenings in the fall, we raked leaves to the curbside and burned them, the sweet smell of smoke curling up like incense under streetlights, between the houses and above the trees as if in oblation to some benign suburban deity. Our playgrounds were empty lots where we traced out baseball diamonds and football fields like seasoned groundskeepers, and whenever a new house went up we dangled from the risen joists once the workers left; after dark, we pilfered discarded lumber to build tree huts or to cover secret underground meeting places we shoveled out ourselves. Mounted on bikes, we collected behind the town shopping area at a treeless place we called "the sandpit." That was where the traveling carnival set up its booths and dare-you rides for a week each summer. At other times it became our badlands, our surface of the moon, or our Sherwood Forest, depending on what kind of Saturday serial we had just seen at the Beach Cliff. For spending money we cut lawns, shoveled driveways, and delivered newspapers. From sidewalks to shoreline, Rocky River was one vast neighborhood and, we figured, it belonged to us.

Suburban life as I experienced it, therefore, was open and unfettered and not at all like the caged dystopia I later read about in books. But so was urban life in middle-class ethnic neighborhoods. In the Forties and Fifties, city kids played stickball in the streets, roamed parks till dusk, or gathered under streetlamps on stoops or designated corners at night. Polish and Italian kids from Brooklyn, Jews and Irish from the Bronx, they all felt free to venture on the subway to Yankee Stadium or to midtown Manhattan for the day without parental oversight or fear for their safety. This is not nostalgia speaking.[2] On the contrary, as political scientist Robert Putnam has recently argued, the freedom and sense of security that postwar children enjoyed was based on solid social realities: broad family stability, shared middle-class values, strong neighborhoods and community institutions (for blacks as well as whites), a relatively high degree of economic equality, a strong job market, and upward social mobility.[3] And religion weighed heavily in the mix.

Catholicism as a Parallel Culture

When I was growing up, Rocky River was white, broadly middle class, and mostly Protestant (Jews collected in the more cultured eastern suburbs of Cleveland, blacks in the central city neighborhoods) with a pronounced Methodist flavor: they tolerated the tavern, which had preceded their arrival, but also sustained blue laws that meant only the Beach Cliff was open on Sundays. Decades went by before the first Catholic, Miss Case, was promoted to principal of a Rocky River public school. The Protestant clergy were none too happy, then, when the Catholics built St. Christopher's church and school, right across from the public junior high. The school was especially galling—a divisive breach of faith in the American system of common education. But as first pastor the bishop wisely sent out a gentle Irish priest who looked like God would if He were a grandfather. And when Father Patterson died in 1947, a quarter century later, the local Protestant ministers were his willing pallbearers.

By the late Fifties half of all American Catholic kids attended parochial schools, a figure unequaled before or since. Nancy and Bill and I were three of them. First grade was more than just the beginning of formal education. It was above all an initiation into a vast parallel culture.

As I have already noted, every religious group formed its own subculture, some more closed to the outside world than others. Lutherans, Adventists, and some (mostly Orthodox) Jews also operated their own religious schools. Across much of the South, Southern Baptist majorities effectively determined the moral and religious ethos of public classrooms, as did the Mormons in the intermountain states. But, I want to argue, at midcentury only Catholics inhabited a parallel culture that, by virtue of their numbers, ethnic diversity, wide geographical distribution, and complex of institutions mirrored the outside "public" culture yet was manifestly different. We were surrounded by a membrane, not a wall, one that absorbed as much as it left out. It was, in other words, the means by which we became American as well as Catholic. Call it controlled assimilation.

Catholic education was the key. Through its networks of schools and athletic leagues, the church provided age-related levels of religious formation, learning, and belonging that extended through high school and, for some of us, on into college. Church, therefore, always connoted more than just the local parish: kids experienced it anywhere, including schools, where the Mass was said. In this way, Catholicism engendered a powerful sense of community—not because it sheltered Catholic kids from the outside world, as sectarian subcultures try to do, but because it embraced our dating and mating and football playing within an ambient world of shared symbolism, faith, and worship. In my adolescent years, for example, St. Christopher's transformed its basement on Saturday nights into the "R Canteen," where teenagers from all over Cleveland's west side danced to jukebox music; a muscular young priest from the parish roamed the premises to prevent fights and keep the drunks at bay. Yes, Catholics felt like hyphenated Americans, but nothing in human experience, we also came to feel, was foreign to the church.

In 1971, I looked back on that Catholic parallel culture and tried to capture for the readers of *Newsweek* the contours of a world that was by then already receding into history:

> There was a time, not so long ago, when Roman Catholics were very different from other Americans. They belonged not to public school districts, but to parishes named after foreign saints, and each morning parochial-school children would preface their Pledge of Allegiance to the Flag with a prayer for Holy Mother the Church. When they went to Mass—never just a "Sunday service"— they prayed silently with rosaries or read along in Latin as if those ancient syllables were the language Jesus himself spoke. Blood-red vigil candles fluttered under statues and, on special occasions, incense floated heavily about the pews. Kneeling at the altar rail, their mouths pinched dry from fasting, the clean of soul were rewarded with the taste of God on their tongues—mysterious, doughy and difficult to swallow. "Don't chew the Baby Jesus," they were warned as children, and few—even in old age—ever did.
>
> The Catholic Church was a family, then, and if there were few brothers in it, there were lots of sisters—women with milk-white faces of ambiguous age, peering out of long veils and stiff wimples that made the feminine contours of their bodies ambiguous, too. Alternately sweet and sour, they glided across polished classroom floors as if on silent rubber wheels, virginal "brides of Christ" who often found a schoolroom of 30 students entrusted to their care. At home, "Sister says" was a sure way to win points in any household argument.
>
> Even so, in both church and home, it was the "fathers" who wielded ultimate authority. First, there was the Holy Father in Rome: aloof, infallible, in touch with God. Then there were the bishops, who condemned movies and sometimes Communism; once a year, with a rub from a bishop's anointing thumb, young men blossomed into priests and Catholic children of 12 became "soldiers of Jesus Christ." But it was in the confessional box on

gloomy Saturday nights that the powers of the paternal hierarchy pressed most closely on the soul. "Bless me Father for I have sinned," the penitent would say, and in that somber intimacy, sins would surface and be forgiven.

There were sins that only Catholics could commit, like eating meat on Friday or missing Sunday Mass. But mostly the priests were there to pardon common failings of the flesh, which the timid liked to list under the general heading of "impure" thoughts, desires, and action. Adolescent boys dreamed of marriage when it would be OK by God and the fathers to "go all the way." But their parents knew full well that birth control was not included in such freedom. Birth control was against God's law, all the fathers said, and God's law—like Holy Mother the Church—could never change.

The church, of course, did change, which is why it is worth recalling what it was like before the reforms of Vatican Council II took hold.

Personal Identity and Communal Formation

To be a Catholic child in the Fifties was to imagine yourself at the center of concentric circles of belonging. They included not only the other Catholics that we knew, not only, even, all the Catholics we saw at other parish churches when traveling, but all Catholics who ever were or would be on the face of the earth—plus quite a few saints we knew by name who were now, we believed, with God in heaven but still close enough to talk to because they were always watching over us like grandparents looking down from high front porches. The saint I knew best was Lawrence, my personal patron because his was my given middle name. What I knew about St. Lawrence, a deacon of the early church in Rome, was that Roman soldiers had placed him on a grid, like a hamburger patty, and roasted him inside a fiery furnace. When the soldiers later looked inside they saw he was, miraculously, still alive: "Turn me over, I'm done on this side," he said from the flames. And then he died. The story is legend, of course, but I still like to think of my sainted patron as a martyr with a sense of humor.

In other words, the religious identity we acquired in childhood was a primal identity that absorbed and conditioned all the others. This communal formation began, almost imperceptibly, with the transformation of the seasons.

Like the public grammar school a block away, where my mother often filled in as a substitute teacher, St. Christopher's celebrated the diurnal cycle. In fall, we traced autumn leaves on the schoolroom windows; in winter, snowflakes; and come spring, tulips and other icons of budding nature. But for us October and May were also the Virgin Mary's special months when we prayed the rosary daily. November signaled the arrival of Advent, as well as of Thanksgiving, and so began the liturgical preparation for the birth of Jesus. Lent with its challenge—what should I give up?—followed all too soon in February, and in April the hymns we sang all anticipated the gravity of Good Friday—for me, still the most solemn day of the year—followed by the triumphal music of Easter Sunday and the end of Lenten austerities. In this way, the seasons were subsumed into the liturgical cycle, and our narrative of time recast. And then the cycle recessed for the summer, like school itself, only to resume all over again in fall.

Whatever the season, God was never far away in grade school. St. Christopher's was structured like a U, with the two classroom wings connected by the church. The church was not much larger than a chapel and to get from one wing to the other we had to pass through its silent, sacred space. Each time we entered and departed we blessed ourselves with holy water and genuflected briefly toward the altar. There, behind small gold doors and in the form of Eucharist bread, we knew, Jesus was always present. It was an intimacy easily assumed and not easily forgotten. God's abiding presence, it has always seemed to me, is best experienced in the thickness of silence that precedes and follows those moments when we have our liturgical say.

During Lent and Advent, we attended Mass each morning before school, marching class by class to our assigned pews. On cold days we heaped our coats and metal lunch boxes on the hissing radiators, and before the Mass was over the odor of warming bananas, fruit tarts, and bologna, egg salad, and peanut butter sandwiches permeated the church. Whenever the parent of a classmate died, we all attended the funeral. The casket was always open and one by one we all passed by, glancing sideways at the cushioned body. At funerals, the priest wore black vestments symbolizing death. On martyrs' feast days he dressed in red, the color of spilt blood. White and gold expressing joy were reserved for special "feast" days like Easter. Otherwise, the priest appeared in green, the color of that quotidian virtue, hope. In class, we memorized mantra-like the questions and confident answers printed in our small blue Baltimore Catechisms. But it was from images and sounds and colors that we developed our specifically Catholic sensibility.

Mass of course was said in Latin, a language only priests understood. By fourth grade, however, the boys at least were let in on the secret. In order to assist the priest at Mass, his back to the congregation, we were taught the Latin responses to the priest's prayers; later we followed the entire Mass in our own missals, which provided the prayers in Latin on left-hand pages and English translations on the right. But the Latin I remember best, and still sing sometimes in the shower, were hymns like Panis Angelicus and the Dies Irae and Pange Lingua that we mastered as members of the boys' choir. The choirmaster, Father McGovern, was an exacting musician who stood nose to nose with each of us to demonstrate precisely how each syllable should be formed. By eighth grade, when our voices began to crack, I had memorized each gold filling in his mouth. I have always thought the church's worst disservice to women was not the bar against ordaining them, but the failure to teach young girls church Latin.

In every other way, however, the experience of Catholic grade school was shaped by women. It was the sisters who taught us what to believe as well as how to write script that others could decipher, how to read and do math, and after class how to clap erasers and make black marks disappear from schoolroom floors with scouring pads. They were the ones who knew us, graded us, and then stood aside when the pastor came into class every quarter to hand out the salmon-colored report cards that they had carefully marked with lowercase *a, b, c,* or *d.*

The blue nuns, as the sisters at St. Christopher's were known informally because of the color of their habits, were nothing like the dominatrix caricatures of off-Broadway plays: only once did any of them apply a ruler to my hands. On the playground, these women with their starched wimples and huge rosaries wagging from their waists organized games and comforted homesick first graders by enfolding them in their voluminous skirts. Of course we wondered what color hair they had under their tightly wrapped headdresses, and if they had breasts like other women—who could tell? The blue nuns were wonderfully warm teachers and I cherish nearly every one of them.

But there were also lots of mothers at the school, including mine. She often attended our Lent and Advent Masses—her voice stood out because she liked to sing—and took turns monitoring the basement lunchroom at noon. Around Thanksgiving and Christmas she joined in baking mince and apple and pumpkin pies that we could smell upstairs in the halls. Mothers were the only audience we had for our after-school shows and mine loved the stage. At one time or another she was president of the Ladies Guild at church, of the city's Garden Club, and of the Women's Association at the golf club, where she once won a club championship despite being less than five feet tall. The sisters called her by her first name, Marie, but when in sixth grade she took over my class for a semester, I was embarrassed by this confusion of roles and never did figure out how to address her during school hours. Mom knew all about nuns: every year she took us to visit her sister, a cloistered Ursuline, who ran a school for retarded children (as we called them then) in Canada. The sisters at St. Christopher's lived by more relaxed rules: occasionally Mom would drive them to our house for a glass of wine and one other indulgence. I was always astonished to find on arriving home the odor of cigarette smoke and lipstick-free butts in the ashtrays.

Because St. Christopher's fielded teams in a parochial school league, we were the envy of our friends in Rocky River's public grammar schools, which had no athletic teams. Occasionally in winter we staged impromptu snowball fights between the "Catlickers" and the "Pubstinkers," but in summer neighborhood friendships resumed. One summer, against my vigorous protestations, my parents even abandoned me to a YMCA camp for two weeks. There, around the campfire, we sang songs with lyrics right out of a Baptist playbook:

The B-I-B-L-E
Yes that's the book for me.
I stand alone on the word of God
The B-I-B-L-E.

There was no Latin translation.

In the spring of eighth grade, most of the boys at St. Christopher's took the entrance exam for St. Ignatius High School, where my brother was already a junior. The stakes could not have been higher. Ignatius, a Jesuit school, was for decades the only Catholic high school for boys on Cleveland's west side; not to go there was, in Catholic circles, to risk standing forever on the intellectual sidelines. Besides, my father, a Protestant, had promised to send his children to Catholic schools, as he reminded me, so I had better pass the exam. I did.

More than my leaving home for college, entering St. Ignatius was a major rite of passage. It meant traveling ten miles every morning to a working-class neighborhood where families lived in small frame houses with no grass to cut. The hulking brick Gothic building, erected as a college in the nineteenth century, was full of classrooms and not much else. There was no auditorium, no cafeteria—not even a practice football field: still, Ignatius was a power in schoolboy athletics. The school gym was a small, sweaty box where we played basketball every day and at lunchtime we milled about on a gravel schoolyard like jailhouse inmates. We loved the place.

One of the features of Catholic secondary education at midcentury (a feature often overlooked even by Catholic historians) is the role that Catholic high schools played in integrating children of different social classes and ethnic backgrounds. In Cleveland, a city where east siders seldom met or talked to west siders, Ignatius was the only institution west of the Cuyahoga River that drew students from both sides of this civic divide. They came from blue-collar neighborhoods as well as wealthy suburbs, and included migrants from ethnic parishes named after saints I'd never heard of. We were all Catholics, of course, and we were all white. But ethnically and economically, the student body was far more diverse than most suburban high schools. No one talked of money and those who had it dared not flaunt it. What counted, the Jesuits made clear, was how we handled what they gave us. For four years, St. Ignatius was in many ways the church to us, and our shared identity as Catholics provided the commonality without which a diverse student body is just a crowd. After one semester of commuting mornings with my father to Ignatius and hitchhiking back home in the evening, it was Rocky River and its posh public high school that seemed parochial.

Catholic schooling also offered a valuable rotation in gender influence, though I can only speak for boys. If grade school passed in the company of women, studying under the Jesuits was a thoroughly male experience. Their reputation as educators came presold, though not all of them were effective in the classroom. Besides the priests, the faculty had dedicated laymen who worked second jobs so they could teach at St. Ignatius, where their salaries were much lower than those paid public school teachers. We were also tutored by a corps of Jesuit "scholastics"—apprentice Jesuits barely a dozen years older than we were who coached us, guided our clubs and publications, and occasionally challenged with boxing gloves pugnacious students who got out of hand. The golf coach, Richard McCormick, went on to become a leading moral theologian.

What all these men offered us was the challenge to do whatever we did in later life "Ad Majorem Dei Gloriam"—for the greater glory of God. They did this most effectively by recounting Jesuit lore: right away we were conscripted into a kind of bloodline of Jesuit martyrs and missionaries who had engaged the world on its own terms in order to transform it. The Jesuit mindset is active rather than monastic. And although the thought was then beyond my adolescent ken, I now see a manifestly phallic appeal in their urging us as Catholic laymen to "penetrate" the world for Christ. No priest ever asked me if I wanted to join the Jesuits, nor did they slip us holy cards suggesting that Jesus might be calling us to the priesthood—as the blue nuns sometimes did. They relied instead on their example of the Jesuit way of life to provoke our interest. This was enough to make me think through carefully why that calling was not for me, and for that exercise in imagining a totally different trajectory in life I've always felt grateful.

I wasn't at Ignatius very long before I learned that God is unfair in distributing talent. Many of the best students were also the best athletes. We all studied Latin for four years, but after sophomore year we had to sort ourselves out on separate tracks according to which other foreign language we chose to study. The most promising students were expected to take the Classics Course and study Greek. Next in assigned rigor was the Academic Course, which required French. For those who wanted neither there was the General Course, which featured Spanish. My Latin teacher, who also taught Greek, was close to tears when I told him I had elected French. But twenty years later, I discovered, he was deeply immersed in Latin American Liberation Theology. I trust he learned his Spanish.

Mostly, though, what I thought about in high school was girls. Far from limiting our access to them, being a student at Ignatius only multiplied our opportunities. Cleveland had half a dozen or so Catholic academies for girls and for most of them appearing at an Ignatius dance or football game on Friday nights, plus the beer-drenched parties that followed, was a command performance. To this day, there are Cleveland mothers who tell their daughters they can date any young man they wish, so long as he goes to St. Ignatius.

That's what I call tradition. While we imagined the public school girls were "looser" than the academy girls, my pals in public schools were convinced that Catholic academy girls were lustier because they were more "repressed." We all talked more than we knew.

On the subject of sex, the thumb of the church pressed heavily on our adolescent consciences—and for good reason: sexual sins were the only kind that really held our interest. Even the most tentative explorations in erotic stimulation, it seemed, could imperil our immortal souls. For that reason, the nuns enforced modesty of dress on Catholic schoolgirls (no strapless gowns at proms) and on dates they were to be in charge of controlling libidinous males. Because of this, I fear, some of them entered marriage thinking sex was a nasty business to be endured only for the sake of having children. But for boys like me, the mortal dangers attached to sexual excitement only made the mysteries of our rising sap that much more intriguing. The only question that mattered to us was: "How far can you go?" My parents left it to the Jesuits to explain these delicate calibrations, and were probably relieved to do so. What sticks in mind, though, is not the finely tuned dos and don'ts and whys and why-nots, but the fact that we could talk about all this with celibate priests.

Even so, I don't think Catholic adolescents were all that different from most others who were raised in midcentury America. Though they may have spent Sundays in different churches or none, most adolescents in the Fifties were raised to observe certain sexual limits—just as lovers did in the movies from which we took our cultural cues. Like them, we kissed and groped in the backseats of cars, or at night on the beach, but hardly anyone I knew had intercourse. The thrill of the erotic, we learned, extended all along a line that still fell short of "going all the way."

This mix of social taboo and personal inhibition, I want to argue, was enormously freeing for adolescents, as all good social conventions tend to be. It allowed us to date as adults did, two by two, and to explore our sexuality without "having sex." It also encouraged the serial ritual of "going steady" and breaking up so that by the time we were old enough to marry we had a pretty good idea of the kind of mate we wanted. A generation later, as I watched my own teenagers ripen, adolescents socialized in groups, in large part because by then there were few ritual guidelines, much less social taboos or ingrained sexual inhibitions, that teenage couples dating solo could readily count on. Without them, coping with adolescent sexuality was reduced to a game of all or nothing at all. President Bill Clinton thus spoke a Sixties truth when he said of his White House affair with Monica Lewinsky, "I did not have sex with that woman." We Fifties kids knew better.

In the fall of 1953, I entered the University of Notre Dame. It was a casual choice: I went there because my brother was already there, and he was there because his best friend had decided on Notre Dame—college admissions tests were still in the future. Like most private universities, Notre Dame operated "in loco parentis" (in place of parents) and the rules reflected this assumed responsibility. Freshmen were required to sign into their dorms at 10 p.m. weeknights with lights out an hour later. The seniors' curfew was midnight. Three times a week we had to be out of bed by 7 a.m. for "morning check"—a routine designed to nudge us into chapel (there is one in every dorm) for daily Mass. No one under twenty-one was allowed to drink or keep a car on campus. Across the street was St. Mary's College, but with only five hundred female students—one for every ten males at Notre Dame—freshmen had almost no chance in the competition for dates. By the end of sophomore year I had clocked more than a thousand miles on the road, hitchhiking weekends to party with friends at Michigan, Michigan State, and Purdue—any place where there were girls to meet and drinking beer underage was not punishable, as at Notre Dame, with suspension or worse. This was not what I imagined university life to be—and nothing at all like the Princeton I read about in F. Scott Fitzgerald.

In the long run, though, the regulated life at Notre Dame turned out to be exactly what I needed. I was an undisciplined student, unfocused, and easily distracted. If in those days they had tests for attention deficit disorder, mild dyslexia, and hyperactivity, I'd have aced them all. I devoured books but two weeks later could not remember what I'd read. By junior year, however, I encountered as an English major several teachers who were encouraging mentors. A few of them were accomplished poets who brought a practitioner's keen appreciation to the study of literary texts. Altogether, they introduced me to a lively tradition of Catholic culture—broadly humanistic, rigorously critical, and decisively Incarnational—to which we as students, we came to feel, were the fortunate heirs.

Under their brightening glance, Catholicism became something infinitely more compelling than a way of believing, behaving, and belonging. It was, above all, a way of seeing and coming to understand, and I was dazzled by the possibility that the life of the mind could be integrated with the spiritual life of the church.

It was in the classroom of Professor Frank O'Malley, in particular, that the integration of faith and intellect was made powerfully, even prophetically, explicit. Serious students from the engineering as well as the science and business schools scrambled every year for a seat in his class on Modern Catholic Writers. Under that elastic rubric we read Dostoyevsky, Kafka, Rimbaud, and Joyce as well as identifiably Catholic authors like Graham Greene, Evelyn Waugh, and François Mauriac. To these O'Malley added a long list of distinguished Catholic thinkers like the philosophers Josef Pieper, Étienne Gilson, and Jacques Maritain, whose paperback edition of *Creative Intuition in Art and Poetry* I carried around in my hip pocket like a Baptist would his Bible. Altogether, O'Malley's syllabus of required and suggested books ran to more than three hundred titles. How, I asked him, could anyone get through them all? "Mr. Woodward," he replied—in those days university students had only last names, whereas today they have only first—"to be an English major is a way of life."

I want to focus on O'Malley for a moment because universities no longer encourage teachers of his ilk. Frank possessed a powerful sense of pedagogic mission: he encouraged his students to wrestle with life's big questions and challenged them to live out the answers. Yet he tried not to overwhelm. "The teacher must respect the deli-

cate sacred interiority of each student," he believed; "he must encourage the timid efforts at genuine utterance and integration."

For more than four decades, O'Malley was as influential at Notre
Dame as, for example, Lionel Trilling was at Columbia—and more
accessible to his students. One of a handful of "bachelor dons" who
lived mostly in student dorms, O'Malley had arrived at Notre Dame
as an undergraduate in 1928 and never left. He even turned down a
free ride at Princeton, thereby spurning his chance to earn a PhD.
O'Malley was a brilliant and inspired lecturer, but oddly shy: at the
lectern he never looked up from his notes and so discouraged classroom give-and-take. Yet he memorized each student's name and
where they came from. And if we wanted to talk with him, we were
welcome to attend the "evening colloquia" he held standing up at
one or another of the South Bend bars he frequented almost every
night. O'Malley never took class attendance, either, and regarded
final grades—in which he was always generous—as less important than the copious comments he made on our papers, always in
red ink.

In the Fifties, literature and its criticism defined the work of
public intellectuals as much as politics. In my junior year, for instance, T. S. Eliot addressed a gymnasium crowd of fifteen thousand
at the University of Minnesota on "The Function of Criticism." If I
couldn't be a poet or a novelist, I thought, then at least I could be a
critic and write essays for *The Hudson Review* or *The Sewanee Review*. In his major course, "The Philosophy of Literature," O'Malley
taught us that serious art disclosed truths of human existence and
so required criticism that goes beyond the merely formal, social, or
historical. If Trilling urged on his Columbia students "the moral
obligation to be intelligent," O'Malley urged on us the moral obli-
gations of intelligence illumined by transcendent truths disclosed
by faith. He hated the merely formulaic in both art and religion,
and could be ruthless when he found examples of either in our papers. On the other hand, our best insights sometimes found their
way into his lectures: we were all, he believed, collaborators in an
ongoing communal process he called "the work." When he died
from the effects of alcoholism in 1974, all he left behind in his room

were his books, stacks of student essays, and a drawer stuffed with checks from generations of students who had hit him up for loans. Of course he never cashed them.

Approaching religion through literature proved to be a boon. For one thing, it saved me from reading a lot of bad theology, which for undergraduates was the only kind available. Instead of focusing on church doctrines and their defense, the study of literature attuned us to the theological imagination at work in art and culture, and so to the mysteries of sin and salvation as they are encountered in the messiness of real life. Moreover, we knew that Catholic philosophy was at that moment a lively and fructifying influence in literary theory and critical practice at places like Yale, Princeton, and the University of Chicago. In no way, then, did we English majors at Notre Dame feel like outsiders looking in.

Graduation from Notre Dame was my exit from the Catholic parallel culture, though by then its effects were inscribed in my DNA. My anxiety was what to do next. On the beach at Fort Lauderdale, Florida, during spring break senior year, I had my first date with Betty, a junior at St. Mary's. Immediately I knew she was the woman I would marry. But how would I support her? I won a scholarship to the University of Michigan Law School but one year there convinced me that the law was not my calling. A second scholarship to do graduate work in English at the University of Iowa brought me closer to Betty's home in Des Moines but no closer to a career. I was disappointed to learn that graduate school is a place to study literature, not enjoy it. My pursuit of a doctorate was doomed the day a professor waved off a question saying, "Mr. Woodward, that's a late-eighteenth-century issue and I am, you see, an early-nineteenth-century man."

Betty and I married that summer and went off to Europe on her meager savings. I dreamily imagined that was what all apprentice writers did. Eventually, I put together a job teaching a class on the short story on a U.S. Army base with a stint as a stringer in Germany for *Time*. Betty was the real soldier, though, giving birth at age twenty-four in a foreign land with no family around but me. Back in the States, I reluctantly turned to journalism solely because

I had a family to feed. My start at *Newsweek* was still three years away, and just as well: I had yet to learn how to type.

This, then, is my memory of how Catholicism and its institutions formed me during the first quarter century of my life. The story is my own, of course, but I trust that others who reached adulthood in the postwar era—not only fellow Catholics but also urban Jews and rural Methodists, Utah Mormons and prairie Lutherans, the two hundred different brands of Baptists and three hundred different kinds of Pentecostals who grew up in America's diverse religious subcultures with their boundaries and communitarian loyalties— will recognize elements of their own formative experiences. Not only of religion but of war and rationing, of community ties and childhood freedom, of education as formation, of upward mobility, economic opportunity, and the naive assumption that future generations would enjoy more of the same.

But of course history does not allow for repetition. Which is why I have tried to recapture the feel of an America that only a few of us are left to remember and the present generation cannot recognize. The children and the grandchildren of Fifties parents now inhabit an altogether different world, with local habitations based on secular differences in economic class, educational achievement, political outlooks, and (despite the civil rights movement) persistent racial divides. The engines of this transformation were already at work in Fifties America. To understand them we turn now to the wider social, cultural, and political forces that both sustained and transmuted American religion.

CHAPTER 2

A Fusion of Faith, Culture, and Politics

The Exceptional Fifties

We Americans can never quite let go of the 1950s. Time and again we return to that bygone era as if it represents some kind of benchmark by which we can measure how far society has progressed (race relations, women's rights, gay rights are the usual yardsticks) or, alternately, how far we have declined (religion, family stability, sexual mores are most often cited). Either way, we continue to revisit the Fifties as if through that exercise we might locate where we are today.

According to the genealogy of generations by which Americans tend to identify themselves, I was—and in some ways remain—a Fifties person. My preferences in music, literature, food, and drink—even the cut and fabric of my clothes—as much as in religion, politics, and sports, to name only the basic staples of a civilized life, all betray my roots in the cultural ancien régime. Which is to say that whenever I encounter the trivializing or, what is often worse, the patronizing of the Fifties, I instinctively rise to their defense.

The Fifties, as I think back on them, persisted well into the Sixties: dicing history into decades never made much sense. Minimally, they began with the inauguration of Dwight D. Eisenhower as president in 1953 and lasted through the assassination of President John F. Kennedy ten years later. As a distinct moment in American culture, one could argue, the Fifties embraced the entire twenty years between the end of World War II and 1965, when the first American combat troops arrived in Vietnam. Although Kennedy at his inauguration in 1961 spoke of "the torch" passing to a "new generation of Americans," it was in fact an exchange of leadership between an old hero of World War II and a younger hero of the same war. In foreign affairs, the two political parties were more alike than different.[1] Americans were in a new "cold war" with communism: Russian Sputniks orbited the earth and the threat of nuclear holocaust hung over America's otherwise bright horizon. But at home, Americans were enjoying a period of high employment and low inflation after the recession of the late 1940s, ease of upward mobility, and a level of prosperity they hadn't experienced since the 1920s. It was, as David Halberstam would later put it, an era of "general good will and expanding affluence."[2] In that the Fifties were exceptional.

The Fifties were exceptional for other reasons as well. In literature, the Fifties saw the arrival of novelists John Updike, Philip Roth, and Saul Bellow, now American classics, as well as the blossoming of the slightly older John Cheever, Norman Mailer, Flannery O'Connor, Ralph Ellison (*Invisible Man*), Vladimir Nabokov (*Lolita*), and J. D. Salinger, to cite just a few. And toward the end of the decade the Beat poets and writers emerged with the rebellious instincts of literary outsiders. Altogether, this literary outpouring remains unmatched by any subsequent generation.

The Fifties were also a golden age for American art. First-generation abstract painters like Jackson Pollock, Franz Kline, Willem de Kooning, Jack Tworkov, Mark Rothko, Barnett Newman, Clyfford Still, and Joan Mitchell emerged right after the war along with sculptors Louise Bourgeois and Louise Nevelson. Those who first showed in the decade of the Fifties included Robert Rauschenberg, Jasper Johns, Larry Rivers, and Helen Frankenthaler in New York and Richard Diebenkorn and Sam Francis on the West Coast. No longer was the avant-garde something that originated only in Europe.

In music, newcomers like Dave Brubeck, Sonny Rollins, Chet Baker, and vocalists June Christy and Chris Connor joined John

Coltrane, Miles Davis, and numerous others in a flourishing of jazz, cool as well as hot, bop as well as Dixieland revival. Serious country music arrived in the artistry of Hank Williams. Folk music erupted in the later Fifties and on the pop front rock and roll was born. And of course it was in the Fifties that the nation was introduced to a phenomenon named Elvis. Classical music? In 1955, some 35 million Americans paid to attend classical music concerts—20 million more than the paid attendance at major-league baseball games. And on Saturday afternoons, 15 million Americans tuned in to New York's Metropolitan Opera on the radio, out of a total population of 165 million.[3]

Social commentary was far from bland. I think of the put-down humor of stand-up comics like the wild and profane Lenny Bruce, the in-your-face ethnic barbs of Don Rickles, and the hot-wired monologues of Mort Sahl at the "hungry i" club in San Francisco. By comparison, Jay Leno and David Lettermen were genial late-night jokesters. In the Fifties, too, there was a wealth of public intellectuals who commanded attention and a spread of journals from the *Partisan Review* to *The New Yorker,* where their work regularly appeared. We read them because we felt we had to.

In politics, the early Fifties were dominated by the Korean War and by the search for communists at home, with its attendant blacklistings and congressional hearings. The rise and precipitous fall of Senator Joseph McCarthy was the central drama, although only 10 percent of Americans tuned in to the Army-McCarthy hearings on television. But the more consequential domestic drama was the nation's confrontation with American apartheid.

That drama unfolded episodically: in 1948, President Harry Truman desegregated the armed forces; in 1954, the U.S. Supreme Court outlawed segregated schools, and three years later President Dwight D. Eisenhower would send federal troops to Little Rock, Arkansas, to enforce that decision. Meanwhile, a pair of Negro nobodies, Rosa Parks and Martin Luther King Jr., ignited the civil rights movement with the yearlong bus boycott in Montgomery, Alabama. That was in 1955. My intention here is not to claim the civil rights movement solely for the Fifties, though that is when it began, but to remind the Sixties generation that the burden of confronting their own racism—and the moral challenge to change both laws and hearts—fell disproportionately on their Fifties parents and grand-parents, the more so if they were working-class whites. That is the other, often-neglected side of "the struggle," a subject I will address more fully in Chapter 4.

In short, a Fifties person has good reasons to regard the postwar period as a time of cultural achievement and social transformation. But this is not how the Fifties are usually remembered. According to the now-conventional wisdom, the Fifties was a bland interlude in American history, a period of social complacency and lemming-like conformity.[4] So far as I can see, there are two reasons for the persistence of this cultural stereotype.

The Bogey of Conformity

First, this is how the Sixties generation has chosen to remember the Fifties, and its memory long ago congealed into accepted fact. That generation of American children was the first to be reared on tele-vision, and what they learned there about adult life was shaped by idealized family sitcoms like *Ozzie and Harriet, Leave It to Beaver, The Donna Reed Show,* and *Father Knows Best.* Once the Sixties kids came of age—in unprecedented numbers—this tele-mediated impression of the Fifties as conformist, politically silent, and com-placent became the accepted anodyne to the social and political turbulence that marked their own entry into young adulthood. But whatever the precise mechanism of their transference and the rea-sons for it, the boomer generation has marched into retirement still convinced that everything that happened prior to their arrival on the scene was merely prologue to themselves as history's main event.

Second, the postwar economic boom really did produce some-thing new for thinkers to think about and critics to criticize. Begin-ning in 1946, the number of Americans who achieved middle-class status rose spectacularly: by 1973, the middle class had doubled in size and in real household income—a rare moment in the last half century when income grew more quickly at the bottom than at the top levels of society. As more Americans achieved middle-class status, the more they came to resemble one another in terms of achievement, lifestyle, values, outlook, and—as I will describe—of religion as well. In other words, the Fifties witnessed the flowering of a genuinely bourgeois society—and with it the bogey of conformity.

At least this much of the stereotype is true: Americans in the Fifties, especially those who took their cultural cues from popular magazines and books, were obsessed with the problem of conformity, much as later generations would obsess over diversity and multiculturalism. The loss of individuality—more often, the fear of losing it—is a long-standing trope in American letters, of course. But the engine of anxiety this time around was a series of influential and shrewdly titled analyses of postwar American society that set the terms of what we would now call the "cultural conversation." Most of the writers were left-leaning sociologists who shared the conviction that America, like Europe (though for different reasons), was creating an undifferentiated society of "mass man." And, as we will see, the postwar boom in church attendance was seen by some critics as proof of this mass-mindedness.

The conversation starter was David Riesman's *The Lonely Crowd*, first published in 1950, and shortly transmitted to the wider public via a cover story in *Time* magazine, itself a reliable mirror of enlightened middle-class opinion and concerns. Riesman's superb work, repeatedly revised and much argued over, was followed by two volumes from C. Wright Mills, *White Collar: The American Middle Classes* (1951) and *The Power Elite* (1956). Also in 1956, William H. Whyte Jr. published his widely discussed analysis, *The Organization Man*. In turn, many of these themes found literary expression in popular novels, like Sloan Wilson's hugely popular *The Man in the Gray Flannel Suit* (1955), John McPartland's *No Down Payment* (1957), Cheever's first novel, *The Wapshot Chronicle* (National Book Award, 1958), Richard Yates's *Revolutionary Road* (1961), and, in the Orwellian mode, Ray Bradbury's *Fahrenheit 451* (1953), a fantasy about mass society induced by television and the suppression of books themselves.

Like many other university students in the Fifties, I read these books as they made their way into paperback and their cumulative impact struck me for a time as gospel truth. Collectively, they offered a narrative of decline in what Riesman called "the American character": from a nation of "inner-directed" individualists to "other-directed" conformists. This was particularly evident in the army of white-collar workers who, according to Mills, could no longer find work that gave them personal satisfaction. The reason (Mills again) was that power in postwar America had become concentrated in the hands of an interlocking directorate of military, corporate, and political elites who ran the country. All this led to the emergence of an ignorant and apathetic population (not unlike the "mass society" of the Soviet Union, Mills ventured) that had ceded control over their lives to bloated bureaucracies that, in return, provided them with financial security and a higher standard of living—Whyte's Organization Man.

Thus framed, the world beyond the campus seemed fraught with peril to those of us who were still in college. After all, we wanted to be individualists. Much of what I read seemed refracted in the difference I saw between my father and his father. My grandfather was a self-taught man who understood machinery the way a painter knows pigment. In midlife he was hired away from one manufacturing plant in Youngstown, Ohio, to be foreman of another in Erie, Pennsylvania. His job was to keep a square city block of machines in working order, and everyone from the president of the company on down deferred to the judgment of Will Woodward. My father left Penn State University after two years to become a salesman for the same company's industrial rubber products—a decision that allowed him to ride out the Depression in comparative comfort. My grandfather, I figured, was an "inner-directed" craftsman: at home he made his own tools rather than buy them, and I still have an electric tool-sharpener he fashioned from a discarded washing machine motor. My father, by contrast, was at the beck of customers and could never have enough of them. A fiercely anti-Roosevelt Republican, he saw himself as the personable salesman who carried the entire fortunes of the company on his back. But to me his constant need to please his customers ("Before you can sell anything," he once told me, "you first must sell yourself") epitomized Riesman's "other-directed" man.

The "Greatest Generation" Comes Home to Nest

Of course, history never feels like history when we are living it. Looking back, I want to ask, who exactly were these postwar "conformists" whom writers worried about and intellectuals fretted over? How might their generational experiences have shaped their outlook?

The oldest of them had lived through the Depression, when many families had to pool resources in order to survive. Later, they became beneficiaries of Social Security and other government programs of Franklin Roosevelt's New Deal that were intended as a safety net for the jobless. Many were union members who owed their livelihood to "big labor's" hard-won right to collective bargaining. (In the Fifties, one in three American workers was unionized, compared to one in seven at the century's end.) Younger workers served in World War II, where they were taught to act as a unit if they hoped to survive. A lot of them didn't: some three hundred thousand Americans died fighting in Europe and the Pacific. Of those who made it back home, huge numbers went on to get college degrees only because the government paid their expenses through the GI Bill. When IBM and other postwar corporate giants demanded loyalty, prescribing even what color shirts and suits their representatives should wear, these men saluted. In short, most Americans felt they had good reasons to look outside themselves to the federal government, the labor unions, and especially postwar corporate America for identity and support.

By the Fifties, these young veterans (Tom Brokaw would later hail them as "the Greatest Generation") had settled down to nest—

still another reason why later generations think of them as conformist. Between 1946 and 1956, the average number of births per woman rose to 3.8—the boomer generation that came of age beginning in the second half of the Sixties—and a housing boom to match. The map of America changed as developers bought up huge tracts of land and laid out planned suburban communities—though only white folks could move in. Commercial jets shrank the distance between the coasts and on the ground supermarkets stocked the aisles with fresh and frozen abundance. As average incomes rose and America's war machine retooled for domestic consumption, advertising, with its arsenal of "hidden persuaders," stimulated common consumer tastes. Automobiles grew lower, wider, and longer than boxy earlier models, and many suburban garages sheltered two of them. Television sets appeared in living rooms, though there wasn't all that much to watch, and in more affluent homes summers were cooled by central air-conditioning. Kitchens sprouted amazing new "work-saving" appliances—electric toasters, whirling food mixers, automatic dishwashers, and eventually ovens that cleaned themselves, like cats.

It was amid such American domestic wonders, on proud display at an exhibit in Moscow of a model American home, that Vice President Richard Nixon and Soviet premier Nikita Khrushchev staged their famous "kitchen debate" in 1959. The Soviets were ahead of the United States in the "space race" but well behind—as Nixon knew—in housing and feeding its people. Domestic affluence was our proudest boast. Two months later, Khrushchev traveled to Coon Rapids, Iowa, to inspect the Garst family farm, which the Eisenhower administration had chosen as a prime example of American agricultural know-how. (As it happened, Khrushchev and his entourage were housed in my father-in-law's hotel in Des Moines.) It was a theatrical setup, just like the kitchen debate, and the featured actors played their parts. "You know," Roswell Garst told Khrushchev in a burst of Cold War bonhomie, "we two farmers could settle the world's problems faster than the diplomats."[5]

It is hard to remember now how deeply the cold war between the world's two superpowers contoured the culture and politics of the

Fifties. Both sides called it, euphemistically, "peaceful coexistence," but in fact it was a fierce competition between two ideologies, two very different ways of organizing society, two military powers circling each other like scorpions in a bottle. Above all, political leaders on both sides understood that they represented two radically different belief systems, one officially atheist and the other manifestly religious. And we all knew which side God was on.

America as "God's Footstool"

The Fifties, I want to argue now, were exceptional for yet another important reason, one that David Halberstam's otherwise observant eyes completely overlooked: it was awash in a culture of belief.

No one at the end of World War II anticipated this outbreak of religious belief and belonging. After other wars, and especially among other peoples, victory and affluence often cooled religious fervor. Who needs God when we can provide for ourselves? But here, in the Fifties, the piety that sustained the war effort (and was celebrated in countless postwar combat movies) carried over to the cold war against "godless" communism. Faith and freedom, God and country, were joined at the hip. The motto of my own university neatly captured the nation's mood: "For God, Country, and Notre Dame."

In the course of the Fifties, membership in churches and synagogues reached higher levels than at any time before or since. So did new construction of houses of worship. For Gallup and other hunter-gatherers of the public's opinion, the Fifties became the statistical benchmark against which the religious commitments of every subsequent generation would be measured—and of course found wanting.

In sum, during the postwar era, religion was not only embedded in the landscape—in small towns, urban ethic communities, and the various religious subcultures I've described. It was also woven into the national ethos like the figure in a carpet. Rare was the religious sanctuary, Protestant, Catholic, or Jewish, that did not display the Stars and Stripes. As President Eisenhower famously put it, "Our government makes no sense unless it is founded in a deeply felt religious faith—and I don't care what it is."

In many ways, Eisenhower epitomized the Fifties' fusion of faith, culture, and politics. A nominal Christian from a pietist Protestant background, Eisenhower never bothered joining a church during his long military career. But he did so after meeting the pious millionaires who funded Republican politics and deciding to run for president. Once elected, he assumed a priestly role in the White House by appealing to religion in building a national consensus. It was during his administration that "under God" was added to the Pledge of Allegiance and "In God We Trust" stamped on the nation's currency. "America is the mightiest power which God has yet seen fit to put upon his footstool," Eisenhower declared to a gathering of Protestant church leaders.[6] Seizing the cultural moment, a young Billy Graham called for religious revival, as evangelists always do, but he and Eisenhower were preaching to a national choir. Although some religious leaders objected that the president was endorsing religious indifferentism, and others denounced his fusion of piety and patriotism, no one accused him, as critics later would President George W. Bush, of trying to create an "American theocracy." On the contrary, most Americans barely noticed when, in 1955, the Republican National Committee went so far as to declare that Eisenhower "in every sense of the word, is not only the political leader, but the spiritual leader of our times."[7]

In retrospect, it is obvious that Eisenhower's appeals to religion were part of his effort to build a national consensus against the threat of communism—in China and Korea, as well as in the Soviet Union and its "captive nations" in Eastern Europe. To be American was to believe in God, seemed to be the message. But how was this generalized religious piety related to the specific faiths and boundaried belonging of the nation's diverse religious communities?

Faith in Faith

This was the question Will Herberg set out to answer in *Protestant, Catholic, Jew,* a classic study that, like Eisenhower himself, has shaped our perceptions of midcentury American religion from the moment it was first published in 1955. Although Herberg subtitled his book *An Essay in American Religious Sociology,* he was not a trained sociologist. Rather, he was a theologically inspired social critic who aimed to explain the postwar religious revival in sociological terms that seemed, in effect, to explain it away.

Herberg recognized in the American landscape the footprints of the nation's immigrant communities (he was, after all, ethnically a Jew), each bound by language, customs, and religion. As children from immigrant families assimilated, he argued, their inherited languages and customs gradually eroded so that religious identity became the last surviving expression of the nation's "originating pluralism." Where other intellectuals saw Americans dissolving into a single melting pot, Herberg discerned three kettles of convenience: Protestant, Catholic, and Jew. Under these generic and socially acceptable labels, he believed, the grandchildren of immigrants had found a way of retaining their forebears' sheltering sense of group cohesion even as they merged in a common identity as Americans. In short, the postwar revival of religion could be explained as the way Americans chose to differentiate themselves within the mass of Riesman's "lonely crowd."

Reactions to Herberg's book were swift and various. Jews recognized their own social experience in Herberg's narrative and generally welcomed the parity he accorded them with the nation's Christian majority. Catholics found in his book proof that they had at last overcome the nativist tradition of anti-Catholicism. Protestants, though, worried about the decline of denominational distinctiveness. As *The Christian Century,* the voice of the liberal Protestant Establishment, put it in an editorial, the "domesticated" religion Herberg described threatened to "let us all disappear into the gray-flannel uniformity of the conforming culture."[8]

Of the three, only the Protestants caught the real drift of Herberg's book. To become fully American, he was saying, was to embrace a bogus "civic faith" in freedom, democracy, and prosperity among other "supreme values" of what he called "the American Way of Life." Worthwhile as these values may be, Herberg insisted, they were a pallid substitute for an authentic faith in God. On this point, he waxed passionately prophetic:

> Yet it is only too evident that the religiousness characteristic of America today is very often a religiousness without religion, a religiousness with almost any kind of content or none, a way of sociability or "belonging" rather than a way of reorienting life to God. It is thus frequently religiousness without serious commitment, without real inner conviction, without genuine existential decision. What should reach down to the core of existence, shattering and renewing, merely skims the surface of life, and yet succeeds in generating the sincere feeling of being religious.[9]

"Secularization of religion," he concluded, "could hardly go further."[10]

Herberg was an intriguing foil to Eisenhower and his conflation of piety with patriotism. As a former Marxist theoretician and Communist Party member, Herberg understood that communism was a secular faith with specific beliefs and a demanding personal as well as communal discipline. He expected as much from those who believed in God and belonged to a community of faith. To Herberg, authentic religion was the kind that shook and sustained the biblical prophets, as his reference to "shattering and renewing" makes clear. By evoking the prophetic tradition, he set the bar for authentic religion very high—so high that I doubt that many believers in *any* period of American history could reach it.

Even so, Herberg's lofty perch allowed those of us who read him to see just how much of the Fifties revival was really a "faith in faith" that fostered an instrumental use of religion. For example, one of the signature bestsellers of the Fifties (and still a hardy spiritual perennial) was Norman Vincent Peale's *The Power of Positive Thinking*, which Herberg rightly criticized as a manipulation of Christian language in the service of psychological well-being. The genre is today more robust than ever. Had Herberg included pop music in his inventory of faith in faith, he might well have cited Frankie Laine's lachrymose ballad of 1953, "I Believe," which topped the national hit parade for five months. In this litany of praise for belief in belief itself, the only affirmation of God is "I believe that Someone in the Great Somewhere / Hears every word." You can't be more inclusive or noncommittal than that.

Revisiting Herberg is worthwhile because he was among the first to notice the importance of religious identity as an independent category worthy of sociological analysis. He also helps us see how Americans, even now, can simultaneously be both pervasively secular and persistently religious—still a puzzle to Europeans. And he clearly anticipated the public brooding over the American "civil religion" that erupted in the late Sixties and waxed again during the first term of President George W. Bush. Indeed, when Bush declared in defense of the war in Iraq that "liberty is God's gift to man" he explicitly evoked one of the values that Herberg identified in "the American Way of Life."

But it would be a mistake, I think, to view Fifties religion solely through Herberg's eyes or those of any other contemporary commentator. Certainly he caught the Fifties' drift toward a vaporous kind of religiosity that is with us as much as ever. But, lacking an interest in the empirical, he overlooked the enormous shifts in population created by the postwar economy and the impact these had on American religion. These mass migrations, as much as anything else, disrupted the older, embedded patterns of religious belief, behavior, and belonging, and enlarged the space for more generalized personal religious needs and expression.

Location, Location, Location

Beginning in the decade of the Forties, eight million Americans moved to the West Coast, many of them from small and religiously homogeneous towns in the South and Middle West. It was the largest migration in American history, involving nearly 20 percent of the population. Most of these migrants either toted their religion with them, like household furniture, or found new affiliations that better fit their taste. Either way, religion remained one important way in which they identified who they were, but increasingly that identity was a matter of personal choice.

Another internal migration saw a flow of impoverished rural Negroes from the segregated South move north for jobs in booming industrial cities like Cleveland, Chicago, Milwaukee, and Detroit. In these new locations, many Negroes gradually attained working-class status and, for the first time, enjoyed the right to vote. By 1950, for example, the black population of Michigan had already increased by 112 percent. These migrants, too, brought their religion with them, but found the doors of most northern churches closed to them. So were the doors to inner-city neighborhoods, which often amounted to the same thing. In the Fifties, the urban neighborhoods of the North were mostly Catholic enclaves, divided along ethnic parish lines, each with its own church, parochial school, convent, rectory, and, often as well, its own gym and auditorium—occasionally, even, its own high school and football stadium. These Catholics were not about to abandon these institutions that sustained their dense social networks. Nor were they about to welcome the black folk in. In this way did the maintenance of social distance and communal boundaries take on new and flagrantly racist meanings. Because they were not similarly invested in staying put, inner-city Protestants and Jews more easily could and did split for the suburbs, taking their congregations with them. In Cleveland, which was then the sixth most Jewish urban area, virtually the entire Jewish population relocated to the city's eastern suburbs. For different reasons, those white Catholics and Protestants who stayed behind looked disapprovingly on what one Protestant moralist deplored as "the Suburban Captivity of the Church."

If there really was a domestic "New Frontier" when John F. Kennedy took office in 1961, then surely that frontier was the burgeoning suburbs. Because of the Depression and World War II, there had been virtually no new housing built in the United States for nearly two decades before the war ended. Led by returning veterans, who needed no down payment and enjoyed home loans guaranteed by the government, new housing starts rose almost overnight from "only one per thousand people in 1944 to a record-high twelve per thousand in 1950, a number not equaled since."[11] Nearly all these new houses were single suburban homes, mostly ranch or split-level, each set on its own patch of lawn with a length of sidewalk along the street. Private backyard patios replaced the front porches typical of more communal, less nuclear older neighborhoods. From a nation of mostly city and small-town dwellers, America became by the late 1970s a nation where a majority of Americans called "suburbia" home.

As that word implies, the suburbs were seen by many Americans as utopia for those who never owned a home or thought they never could afford one—an anticipated state of happiness as well as a place to raise a family. In 1950, *Time* took notice of this utopian promise with a cover story, "For Sale: A New Kind of Life," that featured super-builder Bill Levitt, developer of several mass-produced "Levittowns." Four years later, both *Life* and *McCall's* discerned in the child-centered suburbs what *Life*'s editors called the "domestication of the American Male." And at decade's end, *The Saturday Evening Post* suggested that the migration to the new suburban frontier was "motivated by emotions as strong and deep as those which sent pioneer wagons rolling westward a century ago." By this time, idealized images of suburban family life were available every week on television via those sitcoms featuring benignly bumbling dads, forbearing moms, and their cute but devilish offspring. In them, no one (except Mom, in the kitchen) ever seemed to work.

It was myth, of course, as are all utopian dreams. But so, I want to argue, were longer-lasting images of the suburbs as dystopia. According to this counter-myth, the suburbs were cultureless wastelands of personal alienation and social conformity—Riesman's lonely crowd mousetrapped in spiritual and emotional cul-de-sacs. This theme birthed an entire genre of films, from *The Man in the Gray Flannel Suit* (1956) through *The Stepford Wives* (1975) to

American Beauty (1999) and *Pleasantville* (1998), a satire that has two teenagers transported to a fictive Fifties family sitcom. But none of these was more hateful than John Keats's 1956 novel, *The Crack in the Picture Window,* which offered a view of the suburban development as "a jail of the soul, a wasteland of look-alike boxes stuffed with look-alike neighbors . . . a place that lacks the advantages of both city and country but retains the disadvantages of both." Not surprisingly, Keats named his fictive suburban family "the Drones."

In short, the new suburbs of the Fifties became for critics tangible proof that postwar America was becoming hopelessly conformist. It never occurred to them that those who flocked to the suburbs wanted what they got. In the middle of the decade, William Whyte Jr. spent several months examining the inhabitants of Park Forest, Illinois, a "packaged community" of tract homes hewn out of cornfields thirty miles south of Chicago. They were, he felt, perfect specimens of "the Organization Man at home." Most of the families were young and transient: for them, Park Forest was the first of what they expected to be a series of domestic way stops as the husband moved up the organizational ladder. It was also, Whyte reported in *The Organization Man,* "a hotbed of Participation. With sixty-six adult organizations and a population turnover that makes each one of them insatiable for new members, Park Forest probably swallows up more civic energy per hundred people than any other community in the country."[12]

But there are other, more positive ways of describing life in the new suburbs of the Fifties. They offered not only new addresses but also fresh opportunities to create communities where none before existed. This meant forming churches as well as schools, Sunday schools and PTAs, fire departments, Rotary clubs, the Jaycees, and other volunteer civic organizations. In the cities and older suburbs, as well as in small towns, these associations had the benefit of established local habitations and habits—not to mention authority figures like longtime pastors and elders of the congregation. On the new suburban frontier, these human fixtures had to be produced from scratch.

But where, fifty years later, social scientists would have found virtue—namely, the creation of political skills and other "social capital"—in the necessity of Park Foresters to develop civic and communal organizations, Whyte found enforced "belonging" and social pressure to conform. Moreover, where Whyte saw a homogeneous white community of child-centered Organization Men and their homemaking wives, others might have marveled at the religious and (white) ethnic diversity of these migrants, and at their willingness to cross old social boundaries for the sake of building communal institutions.

Even so, Whyte did stumble onto one trend along the new suburban frontier that presaged a long-term transformation in American religion: growing indifference to doctrinal and denominational particularity among American Protestants. If it was not quite the "faith in faith" that Herberg reviled, it was a step in that direction. In his chapter on "The Church in Suburbia," to cite one much-discussed example, Whyte focused on the establishment of the United Protestant Church in Park Forest, a cooperative venture among twenty-two large and small denominations. Since there wasn't enough land to build a church for each denomination, the community was surveyed door-to-door to find out what neighbors wanted in a church. Denominational identity was fourth after minister, Sunday school, and location. This did not surprise Park Forest's "village chaplain." A former chaplain in the Navy, he was experienced in conducting generic Christian services aboard ships. What the survey showed him was a yearning for a useful church that would not let fine points of theology get in the way of forming "a sense of community." "We pick out the more useful parts of doctrine to that end," he said. "We try not to offend anybody."[13] Billy Graham could not have described the effect of his own nondenominational mass evangelism in better terms.

As it turned out, Lutherans and Episcopalians, as well as Catholics, Jews, and Unitarians, all built separate houses of worship in Park Forest. But the idea of creating a Protestant congregation based solely on the members' ascertained wants and needs would eventually become a prized technique among Evangelical Christians in the Eighties and Nineties. It was part of what historian Martin Marty perceived in 1956 as "the New Shape of American Religion," a give-the-customer-what-he-wants attitude that would eventually undercut the denominational diversity and loyalty that Protestants at the nation's founding had created.[14]

In the Fifties, then, religion was embedded in the national culture as well as in the landscape—though, like minerals in the soil, particular religious traditions were deposited at different depths and levels of concentration. Understandably, most historians of American religion have focused on the generalized culture of belief under Eisenhower because that was a feature unique to the postwar era. Historians have also been greatly influenced by Herberg's gathering of religious Americans into the tripartite paradigm of Protestant, Catholic, Jew, which contained a lot of truth. Most Americans *did* identify themselves that way.

At the same time, however, millions of Americans—often the same Americans—continued to identify with particular denominational traditions, living out their lives in communities boundaried by particular beliefs and behaviors that gave them a powerful sense of "place." They rarely prayed with those outside their own fold, and except for weddings and funerals of friends and neighbors, they seldom entered churches not their own. In fact, well into the Sixties, we Catholics were forbidden by canon law to attend Protestant worship services. And even in a town like Grand Rapids, Michigan, where most of the inhabitants were both Calvinist and of Dutch descent (and where many last names began with "Van"), the marriage of a woman from the Reformed Church in America to a man from the Christian Reformed Church was still considered a risky "interfaith" union.

I have stressed the persistence of religion's social distancing not because I miss it—I don't—but because it contradicts the image of the Fifties as exceptionally homogenized and conformist. On the contrary, I would argue, the age of Riesman's "lonely crowd" was yet to come. In the Fifties, the real engines of conformity—mass media, mass advertising, mass markets and consumption, and, yes, mass evangelism—were up and running. But compared to subsequent decades there were still spaces where Americans could be resolutely different. Religion defined one of those spaces. So did region and ethnicity of the originating immigrant European variety to which religion was structurally tethered. On the other hand—and in any era there always is an "other hand"—the erosion of these boundaried spaces was already well advanced. Here I will only point to one event, often overlooked, that as both fact and metaphor divides the America of the Fifties from the America of ever after.

On July 16, 1956, Congress passed a bill that mandated the taxes (four cents on every gallon of gasoline) necessary to build the Interstate Highway System. Like the building of the transcontinental railroad a century earlier, the interstate system was intended to bind the country together for economic, military, and social purposes. Truckers could reach markets faster with producers' goods. The military could move convoys of equipment and troops, just as the Germans had over the autobahn during both world wars. And for the increasingly mobile Americans of the postwar era, the interstate promised greater freedom to "see the USA in your Chevrolet," as Dinah Shore urged again and again on that other emergent transcontinental highway of the Fifties: television.

Like other technological innovations, the creation of the interstate—now nearly forty-seven thousand miles long—birthed unintended social consequences. When I was young and a reluctant passenger in my father's big blue Buick on his salesman's trips south from Cleveland, we would travel two-lane roads that ran straight through every small central Ohio town, linking them like beads on a rosary. We'd stop on Main Streets where my father knew exactly where he could get a savory stew for lunch, or—his favorite—a pig's knuckle sandwich. Most of those restaurants have disappeared, and so have some of the towns.

Today you can travel from east coast to west and never leave the interstate to eat or rest. The food along the way is fast and much the same, and so are the motel rooms. Venture off the highway and you find towns with abandoned centers. The hulking old churches still stand, but there are fewer people in them. The old hotels (the kind my father-in-law ran), the local shops and restaurants that once made each town seem like another country, are mostly gone now, and what little commerce that remains has moved to franchised outlets in anonymous strip malls that long since sprouted up like concrete weeds along the exits from the interstate. Unlike the transcontinental railroad, which created new communities, the interstate system has gutted most of those it has not destroyed. And when, at last, you arrive at wherever you are going, you have the feeling that you've ended up where you began. Only the weather is different.

What I mean to suggest is this: just as the Interstate Highway System bound the nation together by overriding much that once made local communities and geographical regions deliciously different, so did the postwar massification and standardization of consumer products and appetites, of television entertainment and its audiences, of higher education, its curricula and students—even of the way Americans talked and cooked and raised their children—gradually erode the ecologies of localized habitations and habits that had once characterized American diversity. It was inevitable.

But as one set of cultural and social boundaries faded, others—chiefly race—came into sharper focus. Here I want to describe where and how I, a white kid from an all-white suburb, first awoke to the evils of American apartheid. It was a long way from the South. But as Martin Luther King Jr. wrote in his "Letter from Birmingham Jail" in the year of my awakening, "Injustice anywhere is a threat to justice everywhere."

American Apartheid and Me

Before I became a journalist, I had met few Negroes, as they were called then (and will be called here, to preserve the tenor of those times). Growing up, the only black man I ever met was Fletcher, a burly, soft-speaking handyman my mother engaged whenever trees needed trimming, flowers replanting, or any other needed yard work that we kids were too young to do or my notoriously unhandy father couldn't manage. No Negroes lived in Rocky River or, so far as I knew, anywhere else in Cleveland's westward suburbs. Even the "cleaning ladies" my mother periodically employed were white.

Were we racists?

Years later, when I reviewed Norman Podhoretz's *Doings and Undoings,* a collection of his early essays, I was struck by his bravely candid "My Negro Problem—And Ours." In that essay, written in response to the Negro writer James Baldwin, Podhoretz recounted the turf wars between the Jews and the *goyim* (mostly Sicilian Catholics) and the *schwarzes* that made just getting to school and back a fearful experience. Podhoretz was a poor, Depression-era Brooklyn kid and terror was the name he gave to his youthful experience of ethnic "diversity," though there were moments of racial amity as well.

We suburban kids had none of that—no racial taunts in schoolyards to remember, no gang fights in the parks. In our experience of American apartheid, racism was a prejudice that you had to develop from a distance, but for real hatred we had no moving targets. You couldn't grow up hating people with whom you never shared space or time. But you couldn't get to know them, either.

Omaha in Black and White

There were only a handful of Negroes in my class at Notre Dame, and only one on the basketball team, though he was the standout player. There were none (that I can recall) in my law school class at Michigan or among the graduate students in English at Iowa. I did tutor a few black football players while at Iowa, but it wasn't until I went to work with the Sun Newspapers, a string of weeklies in Omaha, that I got to know any Negroes. It was also where I learned the costs of northern segregation.

In 1962, Omaha was a city of 301,000, an ideal size for learning how economic and social structures function. Railroading (Union Pacific), meatpacking (Swift, Armour, Cudahy), insurance (Mutual of Omaha), utilities and construction (Peter Kiewit & Sons) were the major industries. Their leaders served on one another's boards—a perfect local illustration of C. Wright Mills's "interlocking directorates." The social hierarchy was rooted in the Knights Ak-Sar-Ben (Nebraska spelled backward), a faux medieval brotherhood of civic leaders and boosters that even Sinclair Lewis could not have conjured. At their annual ball, the board of governors crowned a member to reign as "King of Ak-Sar-Ben" alongside a Queen (usually a young woman of debutante age) plus a retinue of Princesses, Countesses, and Escorts. The whole apparatus was designed to incorporate ambitious upstarts into its clubby and conformist business circle, and to discourage the sons and daughters of local gentry from migrating after college. There were no Negro Knights, and only a few token Jews. To refuse to join Ak-Sar-Ben, as billionaire Warren Buffett famously did, was to thumb your nose at the Omaha establishment.

In those days Omaha billed itself as "the Gateway to the West"— never the other way around. Politically, it belonged to the western "cowboy" tradition of conservative individualism: personal autonomy, small government, states' rights, free-enterprise capitalism, fierce anticommunism, and a wariness of Washington were its hallmarks. In 1963, Nebraska was Barry Goldwater territory and Republicans Roman Hruska and Carl Curtis were among the most consistently conservative (and intellectually challenged) members of the U.S. Senate. Two of the major events I covered freelance for New York magazines while in Omaha were the Christian Anti-Communism Crusade of Dr. Fred Schwarz, and an investigation into local live television broadcasting by the Federal Communications Commission. Typically, Omaha's daily newspaper, the *World-Herald,* welcomed the first and feared the second as an ambush by the feds.

The *World-Herald,* which was sold throughout the state, was our outsize competition. Its outlook was insular, staunchly Republican, and so conservative that not until 1962 did the editors allow a liberal columnist—James "Scotty" Reston, syndicated by the *New York Times*—to appear on its op-ed page. Other than the *Lincoln Journal*

Star, published in the state capital, the *Sun* was Nebraska's only liberal voice. For those of us who arrived from east of the Gateway to the West, it was hard not to be liberal in a state as buttoned-up as Nebraska.

As the *Sun*'s newest recruit I spent nine months as editor of its North Omaha edition. North Omaha was the one quadrant of the city with no real commercial center or social hub. Breaking news—indeed news of any kind—was hard to come by in my territory, which included poor white communities of East Omaha and Carter Lake. I wanted the *Sun* to be their voice.

A few blocks away, in a two-mile corridor along North Twenty-Fourth Street, was the Near North Side—the city's Negro ghetto. There were twenty-six thousand Negroes in Nebraska at that time, and that's where most of them lived. Malcolm Little—later Malcolm X—was born there in 1926, and in the early Fifties civil rights leader Whitney Young had apprenticed there as director of the Omaha Urban League. The Negro community had its own newspaper, the *Omaha Star,* but the paper's lone reporter, Charlie Washington, graciously introduced me to the clergy and other leaders of the community. I wanted them to be my readers, too.

Some weeks, as I worked the streets, lugging my 4×5 Speed Graphic in search of pictures, it was almost impossible to find a story or picture worthy of front-page display. Eventually, I coaxed white and black shopkeepers to create Pioneer Days, a weekend festival of parades and music and sidewalk booths selling local arts and crafts. It gave me months of stories to print. A decade later, well after I'd moved on, it had expanded into a ten-day community celebration. Ak-Sar-Ben no longer exists, but a version of Pioneer Days is still celebrated every spring.

For the first time in my short life I was mixing regularly with people who were not at all like me. Now and then one of the Negro leaders I got to know would suggest that we and our wives meet for dinner at the Blackstone or one of the other downtown hotels. It never occurred to me then that these social occasions might also be a test: I didn't know that five years earlier some of these establishments had refused to seat Negroes at their tables.

Our favorite couple was Dr. Claude Organ and his fetching wife, Betty. Claude was president of the Urban League and, as a surgeon on the faculty of Creighton University's medical school, something of a pioneer himself. Tall and as physically imposing as Paul Silas, the all-American center on Creighton's basketball team in those years, Claude was at age thirty-four the intellectual match of any man in the city. On one occasion he suggested we drive back for a nightcap at his home, his Betty with me in my car, my Betty alongside him in his. That night, standing in the Organs' splendid house on an isolate bluff above the ghetto, at last it hit me: even this accomplished couple would not be welcome in most white sections of the city, even in our own middle-class neighborhood of modest houses on small lots. Two months later, in fact, when the pastor of our church announced that he had hired a Negro woman to teach in the parish school, he assured the congregation that she would not be looking to buy a house within the parish boundaries.

Omaha was like that, but so was most of the country.

In the late spring of 1963, I was pulled out of North Omaha to write the *Sun* Special, a weekly feature of several thousand words that allowed me to research and report whatever social issue editor Paul Williams deemed worthy of in-depth analysis. Like most of the Omahans I came to admire, Paul was from elsewhere (Kansas) and he examined the city as if he held it under a microscope. Under his direction, I investigated overlapping tax districts, rising health-care costs, children of the affluent, failing schools, and, on occasion, religion. "Lay your statistical base" was one of his mantras, and if that meant spending a week in civic archives, that is what I did. No one then used the phrase "civic journalism," but that is what we practiced.

In the summer of 1963, the civil rights movement that had for so long seemed so far away erupted in Omaha. The city fathers thought it couldn't happen here in the Gateway to the West. There were no Negro members of the City Council to alert them, no black Knights of Ak-Sar-Ben to offer advice, not even any white clergy close enough to the all-black Ministerial Association to warn of insipient militancy. By July a group of Negro clergymen had formed the "Citizens Civic Committee for Civil Liberties" (4CL), promising demonstrations, protests, pray-ins, and other forms of nonviolent direct action advocated by Dr. King. From then until I left for *Newsweek* exactly a year later, civil rights was my primary beat.

Nothing I had read in books about racism taught me more than what I learned by tracking this story. The Near North Side, it soon became apparent, was rather like the black townships I later visited in South Africa: only those who lived there knew much about it. The mayor immediately formed a Biracial Committee in response to the threat of civil disturbances, but its members had no data on Negro employment, education, or housing, the chief concerns of the 4CL. Since neither the *World Herald* nor the local television stations were into investigative reporting, we had the field to ourselves.

It wasn't easy laying the usual statistical base, but over the next few months, here is what we found. There were very few Negroes in white-collar jobs and almost none in the craft and trade unions, where membership was passed from fathers to sons. An examination of the city's public school system revealed only seventy-seven Negroes on its payroll, more than half of them as building custodians and none as senior high school teachers. Part of the problem was lack of education: most Negro high school students never graduated and few of those who did enrolled in college. Creighton University, a Jesuit school with a solid reputation for color-blindness, reported that only twelve Negro students had graduated in the previous five years, and that eight of them had moved elsewhere to find jobs.

Housing was the most flammable issue. In a monthlong study of ghetto real estate transactions, I found that compared to residents of white communities Negroes were paying half again to twice as much for housing relative to value. Many were barely more than shanties, and two-thirds of the buildings, records showed, needed major repair. Most Negroes rented and were at the mercy of slumlords—black as well as white—who thrived on residential segregation. Population density was more than double that of the rest of Omaha. Those who could afford to move couldn't. Where else were they to live? On the ghetto's fringes, where I did interviews door-to-door, neighbors described how real estate agents pressured white homeowners to sell their houses below market value once a Negro family broke the color barrier—a practice called "block-busting." I was a suburban kid getting an urban education.

It was also a moral education. The mayor's committee proposed building public housing on the Near North Side as the answer to ghetto overcrowding. What the Negro clergy wanted, though, was an open-housing law that would ban discrimination by owners as well as by real estate agents. Omaha's Realtors defended what they called a "Property Owners' Bill of Rights," which preserved an owner's freedom to decide whom to sell or rent to. In practice, said the president of the Omaha Real Estate Board, "I would show a house in a white neighborhood to a Negro but I would divorce myself from a sale to a Negro in order to stay in business."

I didn't have to go far to know that wasn't true. As it happened, the Negro teacher in our parish school *did* decide to move closer to her job: she wanted a house for herself and her sister, one with a separate suite for their aged mother. There was just such a house for sale across the street from mine and after sounding out the neighbors we invited the teacher to look it over. But the real estate agent refused to let her even cross the threshold.

Open housing was the one issue on which both the mayor's committee and the black ministers looked to the city's white clergy for moral leadership. Several Jewish spokesmen, who knew all about residential restrictions and gentlemen's agreements, were vocal in support. Among Protestants, however, there was moral dithering.

The most prominent Protestant leader was Dr. Edward Stimson, who had once studied theology in Germany with the great Karl Barth, a boast no other minister in Omaha could make. Stimson was head of the city's Human Relations Board and pastor of Dundee Presbyterian Church, where many of the city's business leaders worshipped. Asked to lead an open-housing initiative, Stimson insisted that "as a Christian minister" he could not in conscience do so—not, he said, without "some means of screening out the morally undesirable." Too many Negro families, he explained, tolerate "a permissiveness in matters we consider moral which would make them unacceptable in most white communities." As an alternative,

Dr. Stimson suggested that "we salt a few Negroes who would be excellent neighbors throughout white neighborhoods."

Most clergymen I interviewed said the issue of residential segregation had never come up in congregational conversations. "I try to gear my sermons to the needs of our members," a Methodist minister explained, "and that need is not pressing enough to supersede other needs." Lutheran minister William Youngdahl, son of a former governor of Minnesota, made a modest proposal: he asked for ten couples willing to meet socially with couples from another Lutheran church in the ghetto. His church debated the proposal for months. The exchanges never happened and in the end Youngdahl was asked to resign. The general pattern was clear: most white Protestant pastors were not going to support an open-housing law for fear of alienating their own flocks.

The Catholic response was more nuanced. The archbishop of Omaha, who labored under no such fear of the laity, thought there ought to be "laws to give equal opportunity for decent housing to every member of the human race." But any concrete action had to come from Father James Stewart, a young, overworked priest who ran the Archdiocesan Council on Social Action. Father Stewart drew up a tough open occupancy law, with possible jail sentences for violators, and presented it to the City Council. It never passed. In the view of the City Council president, the proposed law "bordered on atheism and sovietism."

My last week in Omaha was exactly one year after the civil rights protests began. My last story for the *Sun* summarized the modest progress the mayor's Biracial Committee had achieved: 22 new Negro teachers in the public schools, 116 jobs elsewhere, and no progress at all on open housing. In 1966 and again in 1968 there were riots in the streets. The black clergy were no longer calling the shots. Omaha was now mentioned along with Chicago and other cities as a site of urban unrest. Federal funds were propping up the local economy and the Gateway to the West was now a two-way exit on the interstate.

Father Stewart left Omaha about the same time I did. He went to Notre Dame to get a doctorate, married, and moved on to teach in Minnesota. Before he left, he asked me if I would sell my home to his replacement on the Archdiocesan Council on Social Action, a Negro married to a white woman. My agent refused to let him in the door, nor would he answer my complaints.

In May 1973, the *Sun* won the Pulitzer Prize for investigative reporting, the first weekly newspaper to be so honored. Paul Williams sent me the write-up on page two of the North Omaha edition. But the lead story on page one was about Pioneer Days. And scrawled across the top in red crayon Williams wrote, "You should have stayed." The *Sun* folded for want of advertising three years later. Even the Pulitzer Prize and an infusion of Warren Buffett's money couldn't save it.

I wasn't sorry to leave Nebraska, but I was glad I'd gone there. Omaha was where I learned what journalism is, though I remain a two-fingered typist. It was also a microcosm of all the social tensions, moral challenges, and ambivalent responses occurring all across the country. Never again would my work run so close to any one community's grain. At *Newsweek,* our audience was a nation, our reporting from around the world.

CHAPTER 3

Mediating Religion

Newsroom Cultures

Newsweek is the place where I learned most of what I now know about religion, and where I mediated most of what I learned to others—the millions of readers of the magazine. For that reason alone, I figure, you should know something about my experience of the place.

They told me at *Newsweek* I was the only writer ever to arrive "over the transom." What they meant was I didn't "go down" to New York City from the *Harvard Crimson* or the *Yale Daily News,* like the generations of Oxford and Cambridge graduates who "went down" to London to assume their anticipated careers. Nor was I invited off a major daily newspaper—the other normal route to a newsmagazine—because my bylines had caught the editors' attention. They hadn't. I simply showed up in late May 1964 with a clutch of stories I had written for the *Sun* in Omaha, plus a small cache of book reviews and other pieces I had published in magazines like *Commonweal, America,* and *The Nation.* I was twenty-eight.

Applying for a job at *Newsweek,* a magazine I had never read, was something of an afterthought. I first approached *Time,* the one newsmagazine I did read. I knew a few people there, among them the religion editor, John Elson, who had studied under Frank O'Malley four years ahead of me at Notre Dame. Elson introduced me to *Time*'s chief of correspondents, Richard Clurman, a tall, urbane man distinguished by an eye patch, who offered me a job as a reporter in its Chicago bureau. But *Newsweek,* newly purchased by the *Washington Post,* intrigued me: I was impressed by the fact that they had just hired learned literary critic Richard Gilman away from *Commonweal,* a Catholic magazine I regularly read, to be chief book reviewer. Moreover, from the buzz I heard in New York, *Newsweek* was "a writer's magazine"—that is, a place where the editors, unlike those at *Time,* were more restrained in rewriting stories and not given to imposing an institutional story line. So I gave it a try. Mel Elfin, who later became the magazine's legendary Washington bureau chief, looked over my writing samples, especially my work for Catholic publications. "Can you write about religion?" he asked. I had no idea *Newsweek* was looking for a religion editor to compete with Elson two blocks away at *Time.*

A month later I moved into the Waldorf-Astoria and began my writer's tryout at *Newsweek.* It was soon apparent that none of the magazine's latest Ivy League recruits knew much about religion or cared to write about it full-time. *Newsweek*'s most recent cover story in religion, "The New Missionary," had been a record setter as a newsstand bust, and the fact that I was a Catholic and a graduate of Notre Dame, I began to feel, were to *Newsweek*'s editors my most important credentials. On the biggest religion story of the Sixties, the still-unfolding drama of Vatican Council II, *Time* was outspending, out-manning, and therefore often outperforming *Newsweek*'s two-person bureau in Rome. Curtis Bill Pepper, the Rome bureau chief, had been urging the editors to hire someone with knowledge of Catholicism to write the Religion section. "Do you think you can be fair to the conservative bishops in writing about the Council?" was the only question *Newsweek* editor Osborn Elliott asked me before confirming my appointment. In truth, with two young children and a third on the way, I hadn't given the goings-on in Rome that much thought.

It is difficult to imagine now the cultural authority weekly newsmagazines wielded before the advent of the 24/7 news cycle—especially in religion. Local newspapers published Saturday religion sections, which were mostly parochial in content. Religion occasionally made the front page when there was news of wider public interest. But even at the *New York Times,* religion reporters mainly covered denominational meetings and controversies—even local Sunday sermons—as if "religion" were by definition a subject sequestered in institutions. Jews, Catholics, and Protestants all published opinion magazines that addressed small but intellectually cultivated constituencies. Only the newsmagazines commanded national audiences, and for the interested general reader only *Time* and *Newsweek* consistently covered religion as an important dimension of public life.

Much of the cultural authority ascribed to newsmagazines derived from the form itself. By bundling the week's events into a single package, the newsmagazine presented itself as a distillation of what was most important for the reader to know that week. The editorial voice, especially at *Time,* was that of a single omniscient narrator: "*Time* says." According to the template established by Time Inc. cofounder Henry Luce, the typical newsmagazine article should have the internal consistency, trajectory, and resolution of a good short story. Language and style mattered greatly: every story was to entertain as well as inform. Above all, a newsmagazine story was to tell the reader not only what happened but also what—at least for that week—it all meant. In other words, the magazine judged the news as well as reported it. Often, these judgments were a matter of tone, verbal images, the revealing detail, the snappy quote. Concision was essential, even in a long story. All this made for tightly written sentences and carefully compacted paragraphs intended to convey knowledge and authority. For a writer, especially one with persistent dyslexic tics, it was good discipline.

Those of us who were regarded as "specialists" in areas like science and medicine, the law and religion, bore an extra burden. We tried to please two different audiences at the same time: academics and practitioners knowledgeable in the subject at hand and the vast majority of readers who weren't. It was yet another form of mediation. Insider jargon was to be eschewed. Here the editors positioned themselves as stand-ins for what any intelligent general reader could be presumed to understand, and on religious subjects the bar they set initially was ankle high because the reader's presumed level of knowledge was so low. I first ran into this barrier early in my *Newsweek* career when Pope Paul VI announced the members of the commission advising him on the morality of artificial birth control. In my story I identified the moral theologians and other experts he had picked. But before the story could be published, the editors insisted that in each case the adjective *moral* be excised from the text. Otherwise, they felt, the story implied that the other experts on the commission were immoral.

Every journalistic enterprise generates its own "newsroom culture." By that I mean an implicit set of assumptions about what its collective outlook should be. At *Time,* religion was in the air the editors breathed, and the draft emanating from the top was a broadly Calvinist assumption that God's kingdom was America's burden to spread. *Time*'s Henry Luce, the son of Presbyterian missionaries and husband to the outspoken Clare Boothe Luce, a celebrated writer and convert to Catholicism, was fascinated by theologians and treated the best of them as public intellectuals. Reinhold Niebuhr, Karl Barth, and Jesuit John Courtney Murray, Luce's occasional golf partner, all appeared on *Time*'s cover. It was journalism as if religious thinkers mattered, and what I hoped to do at *Newsweek.*

But it was up to me to make the case. None of *Newsweek*'s top editors was noticeably religious. Religion (let alone theology) was not the sort of subject they were likely to discuss over dinner in Manhattan or on weekends in the Hamptons. Fortunately, the editor of *Newsweek* was hell-bent on beating *Time* at its own game. Oz, as everyone called Osborn Elliott, had been business editor at *Time* and was the man who had convinced *Washington Post* owner Phil Graham to buy *Newsweek* in 1961. Oz exuded the confidence of a well-bred Protestant patrician: more than any of his successors, he was open to Monday morning second-guessing from the staff. If one of us proposed a story on a subject Oz knew nothing about— and religion, God knows, was high on that list—his reflex attitude was "Go ahead, that's what I hired you for."

Newsweek turned out to be a good fit for me. Working there was like having tenure at a university where you were paid to read and never had to teach or grade papers. In time the number of daily newspapers, monthly magazines, and learned journals in my in-box reached more than ninety. *Newsweek* also reimbursed me for any book I wanted for research. In addition, publishers sent me hundreds of new titles each year, hoping for reviews. On Fifth Avenue, Doubleday operated two retail stores where I could exchange any new book for one of my choosing. Within a few years I had amassed at home and office a variegated personal library of more than four thousand volumes. Greed never felt so virtuous.

But the gold mined by my colleagues in the field was richer than what I panned from periodicals or books. Like all writers at the magazine, I had at my disposal *Newsweek*'s vast network of correspondents around the world. If I needed reporting from Rome or Rio or Chicago, I had only to send a query to the bureau chief. Conversely, part of the correspondents' responsibilities was to suggest stories from their area of the world. The *Newsweek* feeding tube of information worked both ways, giving us New York writers the illusion that we were sitting at the vital center of the known universe.

All of which helps explain why the mastheads of *Time* and *Newsweek* were studded over the years with the names of gifted writers who came and eventually went. John Dos Passos, John Hersey, Irving Howe, Dwight Macdonald, not to mention mainstays like James Agee and Whittaker Chambers, all served time in the Luce empire. For shorter terms so did poets like Archibald MacLeish and Robert Fitzgerald, who had taught me how to "versify," as he called it, at Notre Dame. Hart Crane failed a tryout at *Time* and Saul Bellow's lasted just a day.

Among those who were at *Newsweek* when I arrived, Ward Just left to become a superb novelist. Peter Benchley departed as soon as he published his mega-seller, *Jaws*. Michael Janeway returned to Boston and eventually became editor of the *Globe*. Movie reviewer David Slavitt made getaway bucks with a pornographic novel written under a pseudonym, Henry Sutton, and went on to have a distinguished career as a poet, teacher, and translator of Greek and Roman poetry. At different times poets John Ashbery and David Lehman were on staff long after other magazines decided that books of poetry were not worth reviewing. Robert Littell is perhaps the most envied ex-writer for *Newsweek*: he resettled in southern France and became a celebrated author of sophisticated international thrillers. But by far the strangest exit was that of John Lake, our sports editor in the mid-Sixties, whose office was next to mine. One Monday morning we arrived to find his shoes perched on his office radiator, next to his open window overlooking Madison Avenue twelve floors below. His body was never found and an FBI investigation turned up no trace of him.

Not long after Lake's disappearance I got a call from a longtime friend, John Leo, who was then writing for the *New York Times*. Would I be willing to talk to Arthur Gelb, an assistant managing editor, about becoming the newspaper's religion editor? I met Gelb for lunch at Sardi's and listened to his pitch. In turn, I gave him a list of five stories in religion just waiting to be written, and five more the *Times* had already missed. That seemed to impress him. Two days later he called to ask if I would meet with Abe Rosenthal, the *Times'* managing editor. I declined. Gelb couldn't imagine anyone turning down the *Times* and wanted to know my reasons. "Arthur, I'm a thick-paper person, not a thin-paper person," I tried to explain. "I like the idea that my stories reach mailboxes in the Middle West and that the magazine is around all week to be picked up from the coffee table." What I didn't—couldn't—tell him was that I could never write inside an open cubicle in a noisy newsroom. I needed a door to shut. Besides, where would I store my books?

But there was another reason, one that became more justified in later years. I objected to the paper's newsroom culture. The *Times*, I came to feel, was a newspaper with the soul of a church—an established church at that. It had a hierarchy of editors to match the Vatican's, and every day the editorial page exercised its magisterium for all to read. It also had its evangelists in the form of columnists, nearly all of them chosen from within the same newsroom culture. And though they differed one from another, as Peter did Paul, their collective outlook was stridently and pervasively secularist. Assignment editors, too, were typically tone deaf to the religious dimensions of public affairs. It took the *Times* twenty years to recognize the importance of regularly covering Evangelical Christians after their emergence as a political and religious force, and to this day its coverage of education in New York City systematically ignores the city's extensive Catholic and Protestant parochial school systems. Although Gelb struck me as thoughtful and fair-minded, I sensed that the newspaper's editorial hierarchs merely tolerated religion as a beat. So I was not at all surprised that when Arthur published an almost hour-by-hour memoir of his life at the *Times, City Room,* a book of eight hundred pages covering forty-five years, he mentioned religion only once.

In the Sixties, many religion reporters at newspapers were ordained clergymen who regarded their work as a "ministry of words," as one of them liked to put it. For me it was a job, rather like covering the United Nations without knowing quite enough about each member state. Initially, I tried attending a few denominational church meetings, more to get the feel of how different sorts of Protestants think and act in solemn assembly than to report their endless resolutions on this or that. I was on a steep learning curve, like an apprentice anthropologist's first turn in the field. For instance, I'd never before met a bishop who had a wife. The wives of Episcopal bishops, I noticed, tended to knit and chat among themselves during denominational meetings, snapping to attention only when their husbands spoke. But at least the Episcopalians held happy hours where you could cadge a drink. So far as I could tell, Southern Baptists came to their convention every year for one of two reasons: to hear themselves preach, or to listen to those who were better at it. The only really *Newsweek*-worthy Protestant convention I covered occurred in Philadelphia in 1967. There, after years of intense committee meetings, the General Assembly of the Presbyterian Church voted on a new confession of faith. As a Catholic, it had never occurred to me that a church could hold a plebiscite on what it believed. But for Protestants, I was learning, the Reformation is a never-ending process. I was excited, therefore, when an aging

Reinhold Niebuhr agreed to sit down with me and talk. I asked him every question I could think of. Afterward, Niebuhr advised through intermediaries that if I listened more and talked less, I'd get better interviews.

The reason I survived my initiation years at *Newsweek,* though, was yet another church convention: Vatican Council II. The Council turned out to be the most important ecclesiastical event since the Reformation, and *Newsweek*'s editors were counting on me to explain what it all meant. It was also a classic example of what I call "mediated religion."

The Catholic Moment

The early Sixties was for Catholics—and not only Catholics—the era of the two Johns: John F. Kennedy, the nation's first Catholic president, and John XXIII, the pope who was universally loved. Both had immense charm, both inspired optimism, both embodied hope for change. And both died in less than five years of taking office, leaving much unfinished business. The pope's unfinished business was Vatican Council II, and during the four years it lasted (1962–65), all roads really did seem to lead to Rome.

For journalists, the Council was a uniquely Catholic moment. As many as 2,800 bishops participated, making it the largest and most international gathering in the history of the church. By the final session, there were nearly as many journalists in Rome as there were bishops. Initially, reporting the Council was like covering Kafka's castle. The bishops' deliberations were held in secret behind the bronze doors of St. Peter's Basilica and their speeches, called "interventions," were delivered in Latin. Certain ceremonies were open to the media, but then came the announcement, "*Exit omnia,*" ordering nonparticipants to get out. Only summaries of the bishops' interventions could be had at the Salle Stampa, the Vatican press office. But midway through the first session, *The New Yorker* began publishing a series of articles by the pseudonymous Xavier Rynne called "Letter from the Vatican," which described in minute and learned detail the drama unfolding on the Council floor. Clearly, there was a mole inside the Council and many English-speaking bishops themselves followed the Council's weekly proceedings in the pages of *The New Yorker*.

As mediated by the journalists, the story of the Council was framed as a battle between traditionalists centered in the Roman Curia, the Vatican's bureaucracy, and a core of progressive bishops, mostly from northern Europe. It was a facile political trope but one that did in fact mirror how important factions within the Council understood themselves. American readers were particularly interested in the issues of religious freedom, ecumenism, and the church's relationship with Jews and Judaism. On these subjects the lobbying was fierce among the Protestant theologians invited to sit in as official observers and among the delegations of Jewish representatives who kept a lower profile. But as Vatican II progressed, it became evident that the Council fathers were intent on reshaping the way the church would henceforth understand itself and its relationship to the modern world—which is what Pope John had asked them to do.

Theological debates on issues like the relationship between Scripture and church tradition turned out to be grave and timely matters that deserved in-depth reporting and merited front-page display. But few of the media's mediators had the requisite background. Michael Novak, a former Catholic seminarian freelancing for several American journals, was one of the few reporters who recognized what was going on. For too long, he wrote in *The Open Church*, a book published after the first session, the Catholic Church had seen itself as standing outside history as the defender of a "nonhistorical orthodoxy." The Council, as he saw it, was the Spirit-led summons to reenter the historical flow. And to submit to history was to submit to change.

The prospect of change is what brought reporters back to Rome for four straight years, and what kept resident news bureaus busy during the nine months between fall sessions. But the Council's fundamental impact on the media was this: it forced even the most secular of editors to recognize that theological ideas and church history mattered. No one could understand what was going on in Rome, a city anchored to monuments of the past, unless they studied up. The best that most working journalists could do was cultivate enlightened sources from among the four-hundred-plus Council *periti*—the teams of theological advisors and speechwriters who accompanied the bishops. *Time's* Rome bureau hosted a regular weekly session with selected *periti* before filing its reports to New York. *Newsweek,* too, vetted *periti* at restaurant rendezvous over lunch and dinner. Both the news and the interpretation of the Council passed through a placenta of theologians before it reached the public. In short, what readers got were twice-mediated stories of what the bishops said and did.

The Council was already half over when I arrived at *Newsweek*. It wasn't until the fall of 1965 that *Newsweek* sent me to Rome to meet bureau chief Bill Pepper and get acquainted with his contacts at the Vatican. Betty and I had been there once before, in 1960, when, newly wed and poor, we stayed in spartan digs at the YMCA. This time, Pepper had booked a balconied room for us in the Hotel d'Inghilterra, just off the Via Condotti, where the most elegantly turned out women in the world, I came to believe, shopped the world's most elegant boutiques. The Inghilterra would be my home on dozens of future trips to Rome, and every time, Mario, who presided over the hotel's cramped, dark bar, was there to greet me by name.

Pepper picked us up in an American convertible so wide it imperiled pedestrians as he drove through Rome's crowded narrow streets. Along the way, friends of Bill piled on, legs dangling over the fenders until we arrived for lunch at Sabatini's restaurant in Trastevere. There, a dozen of us spent the afternoon outside at a long table drinking Gavi di Gavi and devouring a huge fish that the restaurant called, after Bill, "Pesce a la Pepper."

Bill and his wife, Beverly, a gifted and hugely successful sculptor, were to me the Gerald and Sara Murphy of Rome's journalistic colony. Artists, actors, writers, and film directors formed their primary circle, but it was the mix of priests and bishops whom Bill also befriended that gave dinner parties at the Pepper palazzo an extra edge. It was during one such gathering in our honor that I first met a number of Vatican officials and *periti,* including the elfin Father Francis Xavier Murphy, the man behind the "Xavier Rynne" pieces in *The New Yorker.* Novelist Gore Vidal teased the guests with wicked tales implying that New York's prudish Cardinal Spellman favored young males, as Vidal himself certainly did. As the night wore on, Beverly wiggled outrageously in the lap of the monsignor who served as the pope's English translator. I can still see the perspiration oozing on his forehead. Not long after, he was made a bishop and sent off to a desert post in the Middle East. This was not, I supposed, what the Council fathers meant by dialogue with the modern world, but who could object?

So began my introduction to Rome in the heady days at the close of Vatican Council II. I remember them well because the energy and optimism inspired by the Council were so short-lived.

The Council vindicated the work of a number of European theologians, advocates of the so-called *nouvelle théologie* such as Marie-Dominique Chenu, Yves Congar, and Henri DeLubac in France; Edward Schillebeeckx in the Netherlands; and Karl Rahner and Joseph Ratzinger in Germany. In their roles as advisors to the bishops, these scholars had provided the guiding vision and rationale for the Council's major reforms. Some of them, including the American proponent of religious freedom, John Courtney Murray, had been silenced under the previous pope, Pius XII. Now they found themselves hailed as intellectual heroes by Catholics and treated as media celebrities. The youngest and boldest of them, Hans Küng of the University of Tübingen, whose book *The Council, Reform and Reunion,* had become an international bestseller, quickly made the cover of *Time.*

In the immediate years after the Council, these theologians, together with the Protestant, Orthodox, and Jewish scholars who had worked with them in Rome, formed a kind of theological road show. Listening to them, I realized that there had been an ecumenism of scholarship, especially in biblical studies, that had preceded by years the gathering in Rome. Together, they toured Catholic colleges and

Protestant divinity schools across the United States and Canada, as if the Council experience were now a movable feast. Cardinals and bishops courted them; students and professors sat at their feet. And journalists, of course, plied them with questions. Except for the handsome and expansive Küng, who loved the microphone, these Europeans were mostly reclusive scholars, more at home in small seminars than at press conferences. I remember pushing through a web of reporters' tape recorders at Notre Dame to grab the attention of Karl Rahner, whose writings were notoriously difficult to follow, even for fellow Germans. "Sorry, but I'm on deadline for a story about Jesus," I explained. "So can you tell me briefly, when in your view did Jesus realize that he was God?" Rahner looked up at me with the weary eyes of a bloodhound: "Read . . . my . . . books," was all he said.

Indeed, for me as a Catholic the greatest impact of the Council was not the passel of reforms set out in its official documents, important as these were, but rather the opportunity it gave me to read the books by Rahner and others who made the reforms possible. I read them as I did any piece of good literature, on the lookout for fresh insights and re-renderings of the Christian humanism I'd encountered earlier as a student. As a discrete event, the Council was a journalistic gift that kept on giving: who knew where it would all end? Personally, however, I really wasn't moved by the Council's added definition of the church as "the People of God"—that was already my experience; nor did I need a council of the church to confirm the layman's role in the church—the Jesuits had already done that. I harbored no ambition to assume any of the liturgical roles that would be eventually opened to the laity.

What interested me more was how the lines between Catholics and other Christians were being redrawn. Instead of separate churches, the theologians spoke of different historical trajectories and theological traditions. I was deeply impressed by the mutual respect, camaraderie even, between the Catholic and Protestant veterans of the Council. Clearly, the Protestants had been deeply affected by their experiences in Rome. There they had not only collaborated with Catholics, but prayed with them, sometimes even worshipping together at Mass. "I came to feel that it was our council," Presbyterian theologian Robert McAfee Brown told me. "I went as an observer, became a participant—even a lobbyist. I concluded that if Catholicism was not going to be the same, then Protestantism is not going to be the same either." Conservative Protestants observed the Council from a distance. But after watching what the Council fathers wrought, even a few of these hard-core separationists were moved to second thoughts. Evangelical theologian David Wells concluded that the Council's "change of mind in matters as . . . fundamental as revelation, the relation of the natural and the supernatural, salvation and doctrines of the Church and papal authority has rendered the vast majority of Protestant analysis of Catholic doctrine obsolete. It has also placed on Protestants an obligation to revise their thinking about Rome."[1]

These were changes worth writing about. As late as 1943, Pope Pius XII had taught that the Roman Catholic Church was identical with the Body of Christ, from which it followed that all Protestants were heretics. The fact that Protestant representatives were invited to the Council as observers was a sure sign that the church had already abandoned this negative view. In its Declaration on Ecumenism, the Council recognized that every validly baptized Christian was a member of Christ's body and to that extent was in communion with the Catholic Church as "separated brethren." Indeed, the Council adopted many of the reforms that Martin Luther himself had introduced four centuries earlier—liturgies in the vernacular, greater stress on the Bible in preaching and teaching, emphasis on the laity and "the priesthood of all believers," and above all a firm iteration of salvation as the work of God alone, as Luther had insisted. Without saying so, the Council was acknowledging that on these key points, at least, the Protestants had been there first.

What had yet to be reported, though, was the reaction of ordinary American Catholics to all of this. The American bishops were opposed on principle to church-sponsored surveys of the faithful: on matters of faith and practice, only the voice of hierarchy needed to be heard. Incredibly, no organization had ever polled Catholics to find out what they thought of their church. *Newsweek* was the first. A year after the Council ended we hired Louis Harris & Associates to create a valid random sample from among 4,000 Catholics in 100 selected communities. In personal interviews averaging 85 minutes, each was asked to respond to 160 questions. This was not the sort of cheap and quick survey that would subsequently be commissioned by the media every time a pope visited the United States.

The results were published in my 1967 cover story, "How U.S. Catholics View Their Church," and at the time they seemed shocking. Seventy percent of Catholics wanted the church to lift its ban on birth control and 38 percent said they were already using some form of contraception. A majority stood with the church in opposing abortion, though some said they would make an exception for mothers whose pregnancies were life-threatening. And nearly half thought that priests should be allowed to marry. But there was another side as well. Three out of four reported attending Mass every Sunday and half said their religion was the most important thing in their lives. Some old habits still persisted: more than half (55 percent) felt morally bound to follow their pastor's judgment on what books or movies to avoid, but nearly as many (46 percent) saw no sin in refusing the Eucharist from a Negro priest.

The *Newsweek* profile of American Catholics certainly dispelled the myth of a monolithic church, and many readers who wrote letters to the editor charged the magazine with being anti-Catholic. Some bishops attacked the survey as unrepresentative. In turn, Father Andrew Greeley, a sociologist who had begged the bishops to sponsor a survey of their flock, asked the bishops in his syndicated column why a secular magazine should have to do their work for them. What struck me most, apart from the headline-making results on sex-related issues, was the sheer confusion revealed in the pollsters' personal interviews. The sudden change in traditional dos and don'ts, like abstaining from meat on Fridays, left many Catholics feeling boundaryless. Reading their responses, I remembered what sociologist Peter Berger had said of the Roman Curia officials who had warned of chaos if the Council's liberalizing reformers got their way: "Conservatives have the better sociological noses."

In the five years following the Council, *Newsweek*'s Religion section appeared almost every week, averaging more than a hundred stories annually and, more often than not, producing more letters to the editor than the other ten back-of-the-book sections combined. More than a third of these stories were about the rippling effects of the Council's reforms and initially the tone was relentlessly upbeat.

None was more naively optimistic than our Christmas cover of 1967—"The Nun: A Joyous Revolution" we called it—which described how many religious orders of women were updating their rules at the urging of the Council fathers. At the time, American sisters were 180,000 strong, three times more numerous than the priests. For more than a century they had been the church's most familiar public faces as nurses, hospital and orphanage administrators, and especially parochial school teachers. With every change these "women religious" made, symbolic boundaries between the church and the world outside were breached.

Newsweek's reporters focused mainly on those "new nuns" who were experimenting with more flexible lifestyles—moving members out of the cloister and convent and into inner-city apartments, for example, or taking secular jobs in order to be closer to "the people." Most communities replaced the office of mother superior with elected boards and government by committee. Individual sisters were encouraged to discern for themselves what form of ministry suited their talents. Those who taught in Catholic schools presented bishops with work demands: smaller classes and time off to pursue graduate degrees—a hint of wider gender wars to come. "There are some people," said the superior of one large religious order, "who see nuns as a convenient labor force."

The obvious visual symbol for all this updating was the sudden and widespread abandonment of the nun's traditional religious habit. *Newsweek*'s split-screen cover image showed Sister Corita Kent, a hugely popular artist in the Sixties, in and out of habit. For Corita, whose brightly colored serigraphs hung in New York's Museum of Modern Art, discarding medieval garb was no big deal. Her work, she told me when I visited her in her Los Angeles studio, was sufficient expression of her religious commitment. But to my aunt and many other middle-aged nuns, the religious habit was a precious sign of their vows as virgins consecrated to Christ and (like Muslim women today who take pride in the simple beauty of their hajib) they'd be damned before they'd exchange their veils for frumpy polyester dresses off the rack.

The question of what a nun should wear turned out to be more consequential than a mere change of wardrobe. Fundamentally, it was a matter of personal identity. Neither clergy nor laity, nuns were often and unfairly perceived as asexual women wrapped in swaddling clothes. Upon entering the convent they discarded their family names and took the names of saints. For every Sister Agnes or Sister Mary, there was a Sister Basil, a Sister Joseph, or a Sister Charles Borromeo, which furthered their gender ambiguity.

After the Council, the nuns reclaimed their family names, but among the reformers there was a palpable movement to reclaim their womanhood as well—and with it their sexuality. I woke up to all of this abruptly during a football weekend at Notre Dame. There I was introduced to a stunningly attractive young nun who insisted on controlling her own identity by renewing her vows of poverty, chastity, and obedience one year at a time. She was dressed in a blouse, straight skirt, and a tangerine blazer. But it was her lipstick that caught my eye: the color matched her blazer. It was one thing to see Ingrid Bergman as a nun in *The Bells of St. Mary's,* or Audrey Hepburn in *The Nun's Story.* But to meet a real consecrated virgin so captivatingly turned out was downright disorienting. "Get used to it, Ken," said the priest who was then president of St. Mary's College across the street. "In five years, nuns will be presenting such a new face to the world that their vocational crisis will be a thing of the past."

He was a poor prophet. Within a year, Sister Corita was no longer a "sister." Her religious order, the Sisters of the Immaculate Heart of Mary, splintered into traditional and reformed factions and the latter eventually disappeared. So did a lot of the other communities of nuns. By the end of the Sixties, women's religious orders were reporting defections of up to six thousand a year plus a precipitous drop in new novices. The vocation crisis, at least in the United States, became a steady state of relentless attrition.

The immediate post-Council years also witnessed an unprecedented exodus from the priesthood. Various polls showed that most Catholic priests felt that celibacy should be optional, and thousands of them opted to marry with or without formal dispensations from holy orders. Vatican officials admitted they were receiving more applications than they could handle from priests seeking permission to resign in order to marry. To force the Vatican's hand—and to ensure a faster dispensation—many priests married first and then presented the Vatican with a fait accompli.

Newsweek published several stories on priests who had secretly married and fathered children while continuing to serve as pastors. We also reported on "priests who date," noting how they exploited their attraction to women who were excited by men they saw as forbidden fruit. In 1968, one of the few Catholic bishops I genuinely admired, James Shannon of St. Paul, Minnesota, became the first member of the American hierarchy to resign—the issue was birth control—and he later married.

I tried to find a pattern in all of this but there was no single explanation. I had read the Catholic fiction of J. F. Powers and figured maybe they had tired of the cramped clerical culture he so shrewdly observed. Obviously, some of the priests who renounced their ordination vows had become priests mainly to satisfy their parents' wishes—or to defy them. James Carroll, the son of a World War II admiral, and who became a college chaplain active in the antiwar movement, abandoned the priesthood after only five years, claiming later that once the resistance was over being a priest had ceased to be "fun." Some, like Philip Berrigan, met a nun in the antiwar movement and found a soul mate. Others were Catholic college professors who left, married, and continued to teach theology. A number of pastoral types took off their collars and became psychotherapists.

These, at least, had skills they could transfer to a secular occupation. Most parish priests were not so fortunate. My own pastor, a grumpy monsignor, had been secretly seeing a woman who followed him from parish to parish. Eventually he gave up his double life and disappeared with her. We never heard of him again. Some ex-priests claimed that they were the "healthy" ones—that only the emotionally immature and closeted gay men remained to serve the church. This claim, of course, was self-serving: it supposed that no "healthy" male would choose the celibate life. Personally, I felt betrayed by every priest who left. When I married I had sworn vows to my wife and I expected priests to honor those they made at ordination. In any case, life in a rectory or a convent struck me as poor preparation for the give-and-take of marriage. "Good luck, guys," was the best wish I could muster.

This was not the "open church" that the (then) liberal Michael Novak had so recently celebrated. Words like *crisis* and especially *identity crisis* became routine in headlines on stories about American Catholics. And for the first time Catholics began to talk, usually disparagingly, about something they called "the institutional church." My own attention fastened on the Catholics' sudden loss of confidence in the church's educational system, for which, as I've already made abundantly clear, I felt enormous gratitude. There were, at that time, 309 Catholic colleges and universities in the United States, tenfold more than in the rest of the world combined. Collectively, they represented an enormous achievement by an immigrant and often embattled church. Together with the Catholic grammar and high schools, they educated nearly six million students.

Doubts about the value of this achievement began with the universities. In 1966, the American Council on Education issued a study that failed to uncover a single Catholic university with a "distinguished" or even "strong" graduate department. This prompted Monsignor John Tracy Ellis, the leading American Catholic historian at the time and a tart critic of Catholic intellectual life, to suggest a radical consolidation. "I don't think we should have more than three Catholic universities," he told me in an interview for

Newsweek: "one on the Atlantic seaboard, one in the Middle West and one on the West Coast." Ellis knew it would never happen, given the independence of each university. Even so, his magisterial pronouncement prompted a public-relations contest among them in the hope of surviving the final cut. Fordham, for example, took out a full-page ad in the *New York Times* promising that it would "pay any price—break any mold—in order to pursue her true function as a university."

The mold that needed breaking, according to lay professors on various Catholic campuses, was the control and often arbitrary administration by religious orders. In the late Sixties, conflicts over academic freedom produced a faculty strike at St. John's University, then the nation's largest Catholic campus, in Queens, New York; and another at St. John's Seminary in Boston. Other protests erupted at the Catholic University of America, in Washington D.C., and at St. Xavier's College in Chicago, after the local cardinals banned lectures by the same progressive theologians who were so recently celebrated. At Webster College, a tiny Catholic school for women, Sister Jacqueline Grennan, who had won fame (and a profile in *Life* magazine) as a female New Frontiersman during the Kennedy administration, moved to secularize the college by making theology courses optional. The best-known "new nun" besides Corita, "Sister Jackie" eventually resigned from the religious order that had founded Webster, arguing that a college president should not be subject, as she was, to a religious superior. By 1967, Webster was no longer a Catholic college and Sister Jackie had married, eventually moving on to a tumultuous term as president of Hunter College in New York City. And so it went. The notion that "a Catholic university is a contradiction in terms," as George Bernard Shaw had famously sniped, could now be heard from the mouths of Catholic academics. "The less Catholic it is," declared the vice president of Chicago's Mundelein College (which would disappear), "the better the Catholic college will be." A faculty draft report on academic freedom at the University of Dayton, run by the Marianist Fathers, was more blunt. The purpose of a Catholic university, it claimed, "is to become secularized; for to be secularized means to come of age. . . ."

The assault on Catholic education quickly trickled down to the church's grammar schools. In the mid-Sixties, the most widely discussed book in Catholic education circles was Mary Perkins Ryan's *Are Parochial Schools the Answer?* Her answer, in a word, was "No." The investment wasn't worth it, she argued, since half of the nation's Catholic pupils were in public schools, and there was no way that parochial schools could expand to accommodate them all. But her main argument was that the schools were no longer needed to protect Catholic students from alien religious influences. It was a variation on the theme that American Catholics had "come of age." Instead, Ryan proposed that the church provide after-school catechetical classes and rely on the Sunday liturgy to form the children's religious sensibilities and habits.

Hers was a naive proposal, one that only a liturgical expert would suggest. It presumed that Catholics still lived in urban ethnic neighborhoods where the parish was the center of communal life. In fact, more than half the nation's Catholics had already moved to the suburbs, where, as any amateur sociologist could tell you, the school was now the center around which Catholics formed their connections. Suburban parishes were more like the intentional communities that Protestant congregations had always been, and their vitality depended primarily on the voluntary efforts of that core of parents who sent their children to the parish school. Although Catholics talked a great deal about the importance of "community," they were not well practiced in forming one based solely on Sunday worship— which is what Ryan was proposing.

Also, her timing was bad: the reformed liturgy, in English with the priest facing the people behind a stand-alone altar table, plus congregational singing (never a strong feature of Catholic worship), had just been introduced. These changes were intended to reinforce the idea of Mass as a communal celebration, but at inception it was better described, as one forgotten wit put it, as "the participation of the laity in the confusion of the clergy." Compared to the old Latin liturgy, I found the new Mass about as moving as a freight train. Silence was now a liturgical vice, conscripted congregational responses the new regimen of worship. Pamphlet-thin "missalettes" replaced the thick leather-covered missals with the Latin and English on alternate pages. In a pale imitation of the early Christians' kiss of peace, there was now a scripted pause during which husbands kissed their wives, parents hugged their children, and everyone shook hands with those in neighboring pews. I remember vividly the funeral of the great Catholic apologist Frank Sheed at St. Patrick's Cathedral: swinging round to shake hands with whoever was behind me, I found only a pair of hands holding a limp missalette at arm's length. One middle finger was extended. I shook the finger—there was nothing else to grab—and looked into the disdainful eyes of William F. Buckley Jr. "You SOB," I wanted to say, "I don't like this Rotary Club routine any more than you do."

Buckley's *National Review,* a magazine produced mostly by Catholics, had responded to the church reforms with a question on its cover: "What, in the name of God, is going on in the Catholic Church?" Good question. Defecting priests and secularizing colleges did not affect me directly, but the new liturgy did. In place of my much-loved Latin hymns and chants, the new liturgists bade us sing old Reformation anthems like Martin Luther's "A Mighty Fortress Is Our God." I could not bring myself to join in when the chosen hymn was "Amazing Grace"—in fact, I still refuse to do so. It's a lovely piece, all about getting one's self individually saved, Evangelical-style, but theologically it has no place in the corporate worship of the Catholic Church.

What the liturgists didn't borrow from Protestant hymnals, they conjured up by themselves. Mostly, it was folk music sung to plucked guitars with relentlessly upbeat lyrics about how much a nice God loves us and aren't we fortunate to be his chosen people. There was no awe, no hint of the biblical fear of the Lord in this music, only mildly diuretic self-congratulation. Our children loved it: it matched the treacle they were learning in Sunday school classes, which is why my wife and I pulled them out to teach them the fundamentals ourselves. The church's failure to pass on the faith, through the liturgy or through the classroom, would eventually snip two generations of young Catholics from their own religious roots. Meanwhile, adult Catholics faced a crisis of their own.

Birth Control and the Collapse of a Subculture

Three years after the Council closed, Pope Paul VI issued *Humanae Vitae,* his encyclical reaffirming the church's opposition to contraception. The pope had hoped thereby to preserve the teaching authority of the church, which had long opposed contraception in any form and had only recently, and reluctantly, tolerated the "rhythm" method as a form of spacing births. But his decision had the opposite effect. The negative reaction to the encyclical was so powerful, by clergy as well as laity, that it produced a far-reaching crisis more damaging to the church than even the child-abuse scandal that erupted twenty years later. To understand why takes some telling.

Birth control was not just another issue in moral theology. It was a subject that touched the intimate lives of every Catholic couple. To use a contraceptive, Catholics were taught, was intrinsically evil, a mortal sin right up there with murder and masturbation. In fact, some Catholic moralists called it "intravaginal masturbation." Contraception was also a public issue, one that had for a long time defined an important boundary between Catholics and other Americans. When I was growing up, "rubbers" symbolized what other teenagers did on dates, or tried to. I never found any in my parents' bedside drawers and would have been scandalized if I had. According to church teaching, the purpose of marriage—and therefore of marital sex—was "the procreation and education of children." The attendant physical pleasure experienced by spouses was grudgingly acknowledged, but only as nature's way of allaying concupiscence.

To a lot of married Catholics, this argument for chastity in marriage was one that only celibate clergy could find convincing. It took two births less than a year apart and as many later miscarriages for my wife and me to realize not only that the rhythm method didn't work, but that the reliance on thermometer readings, vaginal tapes, and calendar-keeping to avoid pregnancy was every bit as artificial as latex prophylactics. We were hardly alone. Medical studies found that six out of ten women had irregular ovulation, making rhythm a futile exercise for them.

The early Sixties saw an unprecedented outpouring in the Catholic press of articles and letters from couples describing the baneful effects on their marriages caused by the church's ban on birth control. John Rock, a Catholic gynecologist at Harvard Medical School who helped develop "the pill," thought he had the answer. In 1963, he published a book, *The Time Has Come: A Catholic Doctor's Proposals to End the Battle over Birth Control,* in which he argued that the pill, by helping to regulate ovulation, was morally consonant with church teachings. His appearance on the covers of *Newsweek* and *The Saturday Evening Post,* and on television, plus a series in the *New York Times* and a summary of it in *Reader's Digest,* brought this "good news" to a wide audience. Within five years, half of married Catholic women in the United States told pollsters they were "on the pill," often with the approval of their confessors. In 1965, John T. Noonan Jr., a scholar of natural law at the University of Notre Dame Law School, published *Contraception: A History of Its Treatment by the Catholic Theologians and Canonists,* a magisterial investigation of the church's long and sometimes contradictory teachings on the subject that remains the definitive history. In the end, Noonan argued that acceptance of contraception was now not only possible but necessary given the changing role of women and the growing recognition that procreation is not the single or even primary end of conjugal sex. On this as on other moral issues, he concluded, the church "has grown in wisdom and grace." Noonan's book, too, was widely reviewed in the media.

Noonan's work took on added significance because the author was a consultant to the international commission that Paul VI had appointed to advise him on the issue of contraception. The very existence of the commission suggested that the church's position was not written on stone tablets, prompting many Catholic theologians to rethink the issue on their own. The last papal encyclical on birth control, *Casti Connubii,* had condemned all forms of contraception as contrary "to the law of God and of nature." That encyclical, published in 1930 by Pius XI, had been the handiwork of a single German Jesuit advisor. This time, Paul VI was relying on a diverse commission that grew to include fifty-nine experts in theology, demography, medicine (mainly gynecology), and psychology, plus three married couples and a committee of cardinals and bishops. For four years, the commission met in secret in Rome, and although I knew four of the American members personally, neither I nor any other journalist could spring a leak about their deliberations. Only later, with the publication of several books, did those deliberations—recorded in more than five hundred pages—become public.

The witness of the women turned out to be crucial. Two of the five women, both mothers of large families, were especially eloquent in their personal revelations of how the rhythm method had negatively affected their experience of marriage. Patty Crowley, the cofounder of the Christian Family Movement, augmented her personal testimony with three thousand letters from CFM members, couples with an average of 4.9 children each, who added their own litanies of frustration, depression, and spousal alienation as they struggled to conform their conjugal relations to the church's approved method. It was the first time the committee of cardinals and bishops had heard women speak so openly about their sexual lives—and their first opportunity to consider the issue of birth control from other than a male perspective. From the physicians on the commission the clergy learned that "nature" itself did not support the assumption that every act of intercourse was open to the generation of new life. "Once we learned that," Cardinal Leo Joseph Suenens later remarked, "the breach [in previous church teaching] was made."

But it was the theologians who provided the zestiest intellectual exchanges. Even those who defended the church's ban admitted that there was no basis in Scripture for the church's position. And arguments from natural law proved unconvincing. The only obstacle to change was papal precedent—chiefly *Casti Connubii*. On this point, American Jesuit John C. Ford, who had invested a lifetime in explicating and defending Catholic sexual morality, was unyielding. For Ford, the credibility of the papal magisterium as the divinely inspired interpreter of morality was at stake. To admit that the church had erred on contraception all these years, he argued, would imply that on this crucial matter the Holy Spirit had decamped to those Protestant churches that had already approved of contraception. A Spanish Jesuit, Father Marcelino Zalba, was troubled by an even weightier question, one worthy of Dostoevsky's Grand Inquisitor: "What then with the millions we have sent to hell?" he asked. "Fr. Zalba," Patty Crowley replied, "do you really believe God has carried out all your orders?"[2]

In its final report to the pope, the commission pointed out that the church had seen changes in the papal magisterium before, notably its condemnations of usury and freedom of conscience, and suggested that its teachings about contraception were reformable as well. Marriage, the report recognized, is indeed oriented to the procreation and education of children, but within it spouses were free to determine the number of children and use whatever form of contraception that was not also an abortifacient. Not to change, on the other hand, would mean continuing the harm this teaching caused to Catholic spouses—and to the teaching authority of the church.

Remarkably, the commission was nearly unanimous: 15 of the 17 theologians voted for change, along with 9 of the 12 cardinals and bishops. But among the dissenters were three men with exceptional clout: Carlo Colombo, the pope's personal theologian; Cardinal Alfredo Ottaviani, head of the Vatican's Holy Office, in charge of defending church doctrine; and the resourceful Father Ford. The American Jesuit immediately prepared a dissenting opinion and sent it to the pope. Within days, copies of both documents were leaked to *The National Catholic Reporter* and to *Le Monde* in France. From there news stories turned up on the front page of the *New York Times* and elsewhere around the world, including *Newsweek* and *Time*. Once again, the media were the first to inform Catholics of a major event in the history of their church.

Pope Paul was understandably upset by this breach of secrecy. He felt his hand was being forced. Ford, who had previously sought and received at least two private meetings with the pope while the commission was at work, went to him once more. Later, he would boast that it took him only an hour to dissuade the pope from accepting the commission's recommendations. However it happened, the pope rejected the commission's findings, as was his privilege, and directed Ottaviani to assemble a group of conservative bishops and theologians to write *Humanae Vitae*. Two years lapsed between the commission report and the encyclical's release, years in which, as *Newsweek* reported, a majority of American Catholics changed their views on contraception.

Humanae Vitae was crafted as a direct rebuttal to the commission's report. The key words, the ones most widely quoted, were these: "[E]ach and every marital act must be open to the transmission of life." Why? Because, as footnotes made clear, previous popes had said so, and only the church's magisterium had the authority to interpret natural law.

The encyclical was also a plea for support: from bishops and confessors to enforce the papal teaching, from scientists to perfect the rhythm method, from governments not to sanction artificial birth control, and from Catholic spouses to live by the pope's decision, however much distress it caused them. The pope's fear of noncompliance was evident. But so were his fears that contraception would lead, among other things, to husbands disregarding "the physical and emotional equilibrium" of their wives, thereby reducing them to "being a mere instrument for the satisfaction of [their] own desires." The contrary testimony of women given to the birth control commission was totally ignored.

The swift and sustained opposition to *Humanae Vitae* was historic. Overnight a group of theologians from the Catholic University of America (CUA) issued a ten-page dissent, declaring that Catholic spouses had the right and duty to follow their own consciences. Eventually more than seventy Catholic priests and theologians signed the statement, making the reaction a very public and ecclesiastically messy affair. Almost every bishop had in his diocese dissenting priests to deal with. In the months that followed, the bishops of France, Germany, Holland, Austria, and Canada variously affirmed the right to selective conscientious objection to the encyclical. In the United States there were rallies and protests by lay Catholics as the American bishops debated how collectively to respond. In November, four thousand protestors showed up outside the bishops' meeting in Washington, D.C.—among them Senator Eugene McCarthy, an intellectual Catholic and erstwhile Democratic peace candidate, who read a poem and assured the crowd, "I am not here to start a third party or a second church." It was the day's only light touch.

In *Newsweek,* I wrote several multipage pieces reporting reactions and explaining the issues at stake. In short order they had escalated from academic freedom and the right to theological dissent to the freedom of conscience of Catholic couples and the nature and reach of papal authority. Priests, in particular, were caught between their vows of obedience to their bishops and the needs of penitents in the confessional. An encyclical written to preserve the papal magisterium was now the pretext for challenging it. "Papal authority," declared Father Charles Curran, the boyish leader of the CUA faculty revolt, "needs to be demythologized and brought under limits."

Eventually, I was asked to testify as a representative of the media at a hearing on the dissidents called by the trustees of CUA. The university's chancellor, Archbishop Patrick O'Boyle of Washington, D.C., and his fellow bishops on the board wanted Curran and his dissenting colleagues fired for making public their scholarly dissent. The trustees' position was that if the theologians had kept their dissent private, journalists like me could not have written what we did, and the reaction to *Humanae Vitae* would, presumably, have been more positive. I testified that even journalists read scholarly books and journals, that reporting on theological trends is central to what we do, and that even if *Humanae Vitae* had been met by total silence, we would have investigated the reasons for that silence. "The days when the church informed the press through publicity handouts," I ventured, "were over long ago."[3] Curran kept his job but in 1986 he was fired after a second investigation by the Vatican's Congregation for the Doctrine of the Faith. By then many of the best theologians at CUA had left, several of them to teach at non-Catholic institutions.

The negative effects of *Humanae Vitae* proved to be myriad and far-reaching. Birth control ceased to be a staple of Sunday sermons. On the issue of contraception, both sides of the confessional box adopted a policy of "don't ask, don't tell." Rather quickly, the acute Catholic sense of sin, for so long tied to sexual morality, faded. Parish priests who habitually spent up to seven hours every Saturday hearing confessions found that the serpentine lines of penitents had disappeared. Within a decade, the dark confessional boxes themselves had vanished from most parish churches, replaced by sunnier "reconciliation rooms." So did that special form of Catholic hell-fire preaching, the annual parish mission, which typically homed in on sexual transgressions. For Father Ford, a major battle won had become a war lost. Jesuit seminary students refused to attend his classes. His position as chief moral theologian for *Theological Studies,* the Jesuits' most scholarly journal, was turned over to my former teacher at St. Ignatius, Father Richard McCormick, a trenchant critic of *Humanae Vitae.* In Rome, Paul VI, a pope I personally admired, seemed to lapse into a terminal funk. His reign lasted ten more years but he never issued another encyclical.[4]

In 1971, *Newsweek* again polled American Catholics for a cover story that, with copious charts, went on for seven pages. What we found was a once-cohesive community in disarray; as one liberal monsignor bluntly told us: "the church is one god-damned mess." Nearly as many American Catholics, for instance, said they now looked for spiritual guidance to evangelist Billy Graham as they still looked to the pope. This was the aforementioned cover story—"Has the Church Lost Its Soul?"—and by "soul" this is what I meant: "an integral Catholic subculture with its own distinctive blend of rituals and rules, mystery and manners," which, as I saw it then, "has vanished from the American scene."

Had I that cover story to write all over again, I would have said that the membrane that once separated Catholics from other Americans had been finally rent. The assimilation of Catholics—a quarter of the population—into mainstream American culture and society had been accomplished, though at heavy cost to the institutions of the church. And after *Humanae Vitae* and its fallout, the internal boundaries by which Catholics had differentiated themselves from their neighbors quickly receded. Still, most Catholics clung to their faith, and said they expected their children to do the same. In closing the story I tried to lay a journalistic finger on the reasons. For that I had to look inside myself, and this is what I wrote: "When the Catholic faith runs deep, it establishes a certain sensuous rhythm in the soul, a sacramental sensibility that suffuses ordinary things—bread, water, wine, the marriage bed—and transforms them into vehicles of grace. In these spiritual depths, doctrine and church laws fade in importance."

In fact, conflict over doctrine and church law became central to an enduring Catholic saga, especially after the election of Pope John Paul II in 1978. So much so that for the rest of the century *Newsweek*'s editors never even considered featuring any other Christian denomination on the cover. But however much the reforms of Vatican Council II may have hastened Catholic turmoil, the real causes lay outside the church. In politics as well as in religion, Americans in the early Sixties were inspired by a new if short-lived vision of a robustly secular future.

Part II

CHAPTER 4

When the Secular Was Sacred

Hope in the Secular

The years 1963–68 were, by one reading of events, a dark period in the nation's history. They were bracketed by the assassination of President John F. Kennedy at the start of this half decade and, at the end, by the assassination of Martin Luther King Jr., and of Robert Kennedy just weeks later. In between, we witnessed the murders of Malcolm X, Medgar Evers, and scores of lesser-known victims, both black and white, killed in the Negroes' quest for civil rights. The nation, it seemed, was always in mourning.

And yet, these were also years of exceptional energy and optimism. In January 1964, President Lyndon Baines Johnson introduced the "Great Society," his Texas-sized bundle of federal programs to rebuild cities, improve education, and expand civil rights for Negro citizens. That summer, Congress passed the most sweeping civil rights legislation since Reconstruction. By 1965, Johnson's ambitious "War on Poverty" was up and running. And three years later the first human beings—Americans—were orbiting the moon. It was this second series of events that conditioned the mood of American religion.

In *The Sixties Spiritual Awakening*, historian Robert Ellwood has characterized American religion in the middle of the decade as "the Years of Secular Hope." But in my memory they also register as years of religious "hope in the secular," which is something quite different. Secular hope is what every new president tries to inspire when he takes office—what, in fact, Kennedy did inspire with his appeal to American idealism ("Ask *not* what your country can do for you . . .") and Johnson with his programmatic War on Poverty. "Hope in the secular" isn't just a play on semantics. Rather, it allows room for those aspirations that arise from within religious communities *and* that seek to be realized in a secular fashion. In the mid-Sixties, that hope was embodied in the civil rights movement under the leadership of King.

The struggle to overcome the American system of apartheid was the central drama of the mid-Sixties, though not the only one. Here I want to focus on the impact of this struggle on the white, mainline Protestant churches—the liberal denominations that collectively once embodied "the Protestant Establishment." It was largely because of the civil rights movement, and the political response to it, that the nation's liberal Protestant leadership came to embrace the secular *as* sacred: that is, to assume that if God is to be found anywhere, it is in the secular world, not the church. This was the paradoxical message of the "secular theology" that excited many liberal Protestants in the middle of the decade, and found its most exaggerated expression in the phrase "God Is Dead."

We Shall Overcome

The story of mid-Sixties American religion begins where history dictates it should: with the contagious hope generated by the civil rights movement during its most idealistic years under the leadership of Dr. King. A major question, much debated at the time, was whether the Negroes' quest for civil rights was a secular or religious movement. More precisely, was the hope that animated the civil rights movement secular or religious? How we interpret American religion in the mid-Sixties depends on the answer.

At *Newsweek,* as elsewhere in the national media, the civil rights movement was seen as essentially secular, with black churches serving as its institutional staging ground of convenience. The very word *civil* suggested the movement's secular intent, and King himself, who exhibited grave moral lapses in his personal life, relied more on political strategy than he did on prayer. On this view, King was a civil rights leader who happened to be a minister, and the redress of wrongs he sought was essentially legal. In his speeches, King regularly appealed to the nation's founding documents. "We hold these truths to be self-evident," he reminded us, "that all men are created equal . . . ," thereby grounding his vision of a fully integrated society in secular texts that all Americans recognized as civilly sacred. Moreover, his appeal to conscience was urged on a nation, not just fellow Christians. When, in 1964, King was awarded the Nobel Prize for Peace, it conferred on the man and his movement a secular, not a religious, canonization.

To be sure, King's Southern Christian Leadership Conference (SCLC) was directed by clerical lieutenants like Ralph Abernathy, Andrew Young, and Jesse Jackson. But the SCLC was not the only civil rights organization, and within secular groups like the Congress of Racial Equality (CORE) and the Student Nonviolent Coordinating Committee (SNCC) there were those who resented the clericalism of the SCLC, dissing King himself as "De Lawd." Moreover, King's quest for a racially integrated society was directed against the churches as well as secular institutions. White churches were not the only ones that were segregated. Within the black church establishment—notably the National Baptist Convention, by far the largest black denomination—there were numerous pastors who resisted King's dream for fear they would lose their own power, which depended on a segregated Christianity. And on King's left there were numerous proponents of black power who advanced both racial separatism and violence as the only answer to white oppression. In sum, there were ample reasons to regard the civil rights movement, even under King, as a secular quest.

That said, King always insisted that whatever else he was to others—the list included agitator, troublemaker, and, to FBI chief J. Edgar Hoover, communist—in his heart he remained "fundamentally a clergyman, a Baptist preacher. This is my being and my heritage for I am the son of a Baptist preacher, the grandson of a Baptist preacher and the great-grandson of a Baptist preacher."[1] King's public oratory was laced with biblical language and allusions from the Hebrew prophets and the Gospels. His civil rights rallies were saturated in gospel music and the call-and-response structure of Negro sermons. Even the elements he borrowed from Gandhi, the praxis of nonviolent direct action and a belief in *satyagraha* (the personal force of love and truth), were orchestrated in a Christian key. Above all, King cast the entire black experience in America as a reenactment of the Hebrews' exodus from oppression to deliverance, with himself as a vulnerable Moses ("I've been to the mountain. I've seen the Promised Land. I may not get there myself. . . .").

In sum, Martin Luther King Jr. succeeded where other civil rights leaders fell short because he appealed to black religion—more precisely, to what generations of American Negroes had made of the Christianity that was originally taught to them by white slave owners. African Americans read themselves into the Bible as fully as the Puritan settlers had. Both pinned their hopes on scriptural promise. But where the Puritans found deliverance in their escape to the New World, Negro slaves found only oppression in their transport to the American colonies: their deliverance was yet to come. King appealed directly to this religious hope embedded in black Christianity, a hope that looked mainly to the world to come until King redirected its energy toward goals achievable in the here and now— literally, a hope in the secular. This transformation of hope is well expressed by the movement's signature anthem, "We Shall Overcome." There is no mention of God in the lyrics but it hardly mattered. The anthem grew out of Negro spirituals that resonated with ingrained yearnings of an entire people and helped galvanize their potential for collective action. Black religion, in short, *was* the religion of the civil rights movement for as long as King was its prime spokesman.

A Kairos *Moment*

By the mid-Sixties, it was clear to many in white northern churches that the civil rights movement was a gift as well as a challenge. Jewish as well as Christian leaders recognized in King a prophetic figure in the biblical sense of one who speaks truth to power. "In a real sense, the American Negro, in his travail, is causing the rebirth of the white church," said Episcopal bishop C. Kilmer Myers of Michigan, though most of that travail was then seen mainly as a consequence of segregation in the South. For more than a decade, the National Council of Churches and agencies of the mainline Protestant denominations had been involved in the movement in southern states. But the high tide of northern white clergy involvement was yet to come.

King's last great national success began in March 1965, in Selma, Alabama. King planned a march for black voting rights from there to the state capitol steps, fifty miles away in Montgomery. Like other civil rights marches, sit-ins, and public protests, this march was designed to provoke a violent reaction, in this case from Selma's volatile Sheriff James Clark. King was counting on media coverage to arouse the nation, as it had two years earlier in Birmingham—and to prod the Johnson administration into action. As Rev. Andrew Young explained, "Sheriff Clark has been beating black heads in the back of the jail for years, and we're only saying to him that if he still wants to break heads, he'll have to do it on Main Street, at noon, in front of CBS, NBC, and ABC television cameras."

Sheriff Clark obliged. On "Bloody Sunday," March 7, Negro marchers were met by two hundred state troopers who beat them back with bullwhips, clubs, and tear gas. Mounted troopers pursued them back into the ghetto, flaying them with rubber tubing wrapped with barbed wire—all of which was captured on the evening news. King watched from Atlanta and decided to wait for a federal judge to overturn a state injunction against further marches. Besides, he had amassed a war chest of $1 million to spend on the battle, if necessary, though only he and his most trusted aides knew that.

The march to Montgomery resumed two weeks later. King had spent the interval on the phone, summoning white churchmen who had been waiting for his signal to join the march. For the first time, legions of Catholic nuns from the North showed up and in full dress: like the Protestant bishops in their robes, they understood the symbolic power of religious uniforms. One of the Episcopal bishops who answered King's call was Paul Moore, a close friend of *Newsweek* editor Oz Elliott. Because of the white clerical involvement, Oz Elliott sent word that the story was mine to write—and ordered up a sidebar on Moore as part of the package. It was the first opportunity I had since coming to *Newsweek* to write about the subject that had consumed me in Omaha.

Veteran civil rights reporters from *Newsweek*'s Atlanta bureau, like Joe Cumming and Andrew Jaffee, plus Marshall Frady, a new recruit who would later write fine biographies of Jackson and King himself, managed to be everywhere in Selma that week. From their copious interviews and vivid descriptions it was clear that the more than two thousand white northerners in Selma had, for the duration, only one pastor and they all were members of his congregation. King's lieutenants warned them not to venture outside Selma's black ghetto—earlier, a Unitarian minister from Boston, James Reeb, had been bludgeoned to death by white men after he wandered outside the Negro area. Selma's Jewish and white Christian clergy dared not offer sympathy or support to the northerners; in fact, most local clergy regarded them as invaders. In daily orientation classes, black clergy drilled the white volunteers like Army sergeants: "No matter how big a chief you were in your own tepee, when you got to the border of Alabama, you became an Indian." By day, black churches served as the marchers' meetinghouses and dining halls; at night, the northerners bedded down on pews in Negro churches, or in the maternity ward at Good Samaritan Hospital run by the Edmundite Fathers, an all-black Catholic religious order serving Negro patients. "There were many times before that I thought I'd slept with the Lord," one rabbi quipped, "but this is the first time I've ever slept with a bishop."

As my deadline approached, I put the files aside and brooded on what Selma meant. An image came to mind and then a lead sentence that summed it up:

> Like the lame to Lourdes they came—bishops, rabbis, ministers, priests and nuns—several thousand in all, sensing somehow that God was stirring the waters in Selma, Ala.

Then, as now, it seemed to me that the white clergy needed their immersion in the civil rights movement as much as the movement needed the witness of white clergy. The way King framed it, segregation challenged the very core of religious conscience and commitment. Protestant theologians recognized the Negro challenge to American apartheid as a *kairos*—one of those urgent, God-appointed opportunities in the here and now to recognize and do God's will. Rabbi Abraham Joshua Heschel, who strode arm in arm with King and other religious luminaries at the head of the march, articulated what many of the white clergy experienced in Selma. He was, he said, "praying with my legs."

It took five days for the marchers to reach Montgomery. By then their numbers had swollen to twenty-five thousand, most of them Negroes. Alabama governor George Wallace watched through binoculars from his office but refused to meet his visitors. It hardly mattered. The audience King wanted was watching on television, especially in the nation's capital. Five months later, President Johnson pushed through Congress a Voting Rights Act that abolished literacy tests, poll taxes, and similar Jim Crow devices that Alabama and other southern states had used to limit the registration of Negro voters. King's "hope in the secular" had been vindicated, at least for the moment. The day after the Voting Rights Act was passed, a wild week of Negro rioting broke out in the Watts section of Los Angeles. Houses and businesses went up in flames. The era of nonviolent protest—the kind that northern churchmen could support as "prophetic"—had peaked. But the effects of the civil rights movement on mainline Protestantism turned out to be far-reaching.

After Selma, veterans of the march would talk of their experience as life changing. It wasn't just a memorable moment: it was also a moral credential. There, Protestants and Catholics and Jews and people of no religion at all had stood with their black brothers in common witness. King would call it a "coalition of conscience," one that crossed old religious boundaries and created new forms of religious belief, behavior, and belonging. Thereafter, where one stood on the issue of public agitation on behalf of civil rights became for activist clergy the measure of authentic faith and commitment.

God's Avant-garde

In the fall of 1965, with Vatican Council II about to adjourn for good, I proposed that *Newsweek* devote its Christmas cover story to a meanwhile-back-on-the-ranch examination of American Protestantism. My premise going in was simple: now that Catholicism had changed, how would American Protestantism respond?

At the time, two-thirds of adult Americans identified as Protestants. But beyond that self-identification they did not have a lot in common. A 1965 sociological study of Protestant laymen from all major denominations found that on bedrock beliefs like the nature of God, the divinity of Jesus, and what one must do to be saved, there was more disagreement than agreement. "Protestants can no longer sing 'Christ crucified, risen and coming again,' with one voice," the study concluded, because less than half "really believes it's true." The half that did was mostly Fundamentalist and Evangelical. But from where I sat in my office on Madison Avenue, they were still a distant and disorganized fringe.

By "Protestant," then, I meant the denominations associated with the National Council of Churches (NCC) and the editorial outlook of *The Christian Century* magazine. These were the ecumenical, mostly northern Protestants who officially supported the civil rights movement, who produced the publicly prominent theologians, who sent official observers to the Council in Rome, and who had long been recognized as the nation's Protestant Establishment. Episcopalians, (northern) Presbyterians, Methodists, American (northern) Baptists, Congregationalists (United Church of Christ), most Lutheran denominations, and the Disciples of Christ—these were the Protestant denominations whose members got elected to Congress and theirs were the churches, usually with "First" or "Second" in their names, clustered along the Main Streets of America. Such was the fellow feeling among the mainliners that in 1962 there was a formal effort to unite several of the largest Protestant denominations. "Think of it this way," explained an ecumenical Presbyterian in a sermon I happened to catch on my car radio: "Protestant Christianity is like organ music and we Presbyterians must recognize that we are just one pull on God's organ." (I think "stop" was the word he was looking for.) In this analogy, the studious Presbyterians were Protestants who did the thinking for the Methodists, and the emotional Methodists were Protestants who did the feeling for the Presbyterians. The only differences were matters of history and temperament.

By the fall of 1965, however, events more urgent than ecclesiastical mergers and acquisitions had captured the attention of mainline church leaders. First was the realization that Catholics, now properly reformed, were to be embraced rather than feared. As one Methodist observer in Rome neatly put it: "You fight your father for years, and then one day he says, 'I agree with you.' Protestantism has got to say in a fresh way what it is." Second was the challenge of Dr. King, who had demonstrated the power of black religion to effect social change—something the liberal mainline churches, with their background in the nineteenth-century Social Gospel movement, had hoped to do themselves. The third was a felt imperative to rethink the relationship between the church and the secular order. If the primary purpose of the church was no longer to convert the unbelieving, as many liberal clergy now believed, what was it?

My first problem was choosing a representative Protestant figure to put on the cover of *Newsweek*. The age of the great theologians was over: Reinhold Niebuhr was an old man, Paul Tillich was dead and Karl Barth soon would be, and none of their younger disciples commanded similar national recognition. What we needed, I thought, was someone who embodied mainline Protestantism on the move.

Eventually I settled on Robert McAfee Brown, an ecumenist, a veteran of civil rights marches, a professor of religion at Stanford, and a prolific writer. His just-published book, *The Spirit of Protestantism,* was one attempt to say afresh what "Protestant" means. At age forty-five, Brown belonged to the last generation of well-bred, well-educated American Protestant clergy who, if they hadn't chosen the ministry, would have become doctors or lawyers or business leaders. Besides, he looked good: with wavy silver hair and a square Dick Tracy jaw, Bob was a rare sort among Presbyterian ministers I'd met—a Calvinist with a lively sense of humor.

Bob had to come to me because there was no way I could get to him. The only time he had to sit down for an interview was during an overnight stop on his way from Rome, where he was an official observer at Vatican Council II, to Delano, California, where he was leading an interfaith group of clergy trying to mediate a strike by migrant Mexican grape pickers against fruit growers in the San Joaquin Valley. Our sit-down was at the kitchen table in the new house we had just built in Westchester County. The stove and refrigerator had yet to be delivered and there were our three children, aged five, four, and six months, to attend to. Pizza and beer would have to do.

Bob sketched his religious trajectory in quick strokes. He had been a Navy chaplain, a pastor, a colleague and disciple of Niebuhr at Union Theological Seminary. His introduction to Catholic America was through Senator Eugene McCarthy and the Benedictines at St. John's Abbey in Minnesota, where he had spent his ninth wedding anniversary in a monk's cell. His migration to Stanford was for him the final leg of a journey out of the cloistered world of Protestant "clericalism" and into the secular classroom, where, he believed, the Christian faith can engage "the modern mind." He no longer wore a clerical collar except in Rome, where it was expected, and on protest marches, where it was symbolically useful.

"If you're going to be on the cover of *Newsweek,* you're going to have to show the collar," I insisted over Bob's objections. "We've got to signal the reader visually that the cover story is about religion." And, I added, "It'd be nice if you could find something that also symbolized Presbyterianism." "Presbyterians don't go in for symbols," he reminded me, and besides, denominational differences were passé. Reluctantly, he came up with a three-inch stone Celtic cross that he always carried with him. Magnified by our art department, it loomed over him on the cover of *Newsweek* like a cemetery monument.

Brown wanted me to know that the age of the Protestant Establishment was over and that he for one was relieved. Making room for Catholics meant Protestants no longer had to "assume responsibility for everything in our culture." Thus unburdened, Protestants would be free to regroup as a "prophetic" minority, much like the black clergy under Dr. King. To make this happen, he said, mission boards, Sunday schools—the entire structure of Protestant denominations—would have to be ruthlessly reformed. A new Reformation was at hand.

Brown was hardly a voice crying in the wilderness. Every mainliner we interviewed seemed to be imbued with contempt for American Protestantism in its current suburban flourishing. Colin Williams, the NCC's secretary for evangelism, derided the mainline Protestant churches as "sick with self-concern." By that he meant concern for recruiting new members and building ever bigger churches to accommodate them. For Paul Stagg, evangelism executive for the American (northern) Baptist Churches USA, the question facing Protestants was not "whether the church can convert the world, but whether God can convert his church."

It seemed to me that one difference between Evangelical and mainline Protestants was this: when Evangelicals saw the churches going to hell they preached another revival, while mainliners in the same mood called for a reformation of church structures. Albert Outler, a wise and gentle Methodist scholar who was also just back from witnessing the reformist spirit at work in Rome, tried to help this Catholic journalist out. "There's something you don't yet understand, Ken," he explained. "Deep down, we Protestants distrust the church structures we've created. But for Catholics, even the most liberal among them, 'Holy Mother the Church' is always 'Holy-Mother-the-Church.'"

I knew what he meant about Catholics. He meant what Lenny Bruce meant when he famously asked: "Why is the Catholic Church the only *the* church?" We Catholics did not think of our church as just another Christian "denomination." But I was just beginning to realize that for Protestants, "church" primarily means the local congregation that individuals voluntarily join, the place where families worship on Sundays, study the Bible on weeknights, and find "fellowship" with other believers. On this view, Protestant denominations, while often family-like in feeling, were perceived as essentially provisional bodies whose directives and decisions could be and frequently were ignored by local congregations. "Seats at church conventions are considered a reward for twenty years of being a nice guy," explained Yale theologian George Lindbeck, a Lutheran. "And so the conventions try to avoid dealing with any fundamental questions for fear that a great scandal might issue out of a public debate on unresolved problems." Lindbeck was another Protestant observer at Vatican Council II and had been hugely impressed by the role theologians had played in its deliberations. I thought he was being hard on his Protestant brethren. "Protestants are always holding church conventions," I pointed out. "Vatican II was the Catholics' first council in a hundred years."

Among the structures targeted by mainline Protestant reformers, first on the list were their own suburban churches. The problem with suburban congregations, in the reformers' collective view, was their insulation from the plight of the urban poor—that part of America that President Johnson focused on in his Great Society programs and that King had spoken for when he launched the Poor People's Campaign just months before his assassination.

The reformers' strategy was to expose Protestant youth groups from suburban parishes to the effects of segregation, unemployment, and urban poverty by busing them into the nation's inner cities on weekends. Teenager Hillary Rodham was one such student who, as she later wrote, found these weekend exercises in urban exposure to be life transforming. Gibson Winter, one of the leaders of this back-to-the-city strategy, was very candid about its intent: "We take laymen from their [suburban] parishes and soon they find that they are no longer interested in normal church organizations; we destroy them for [conventional] parish work." The assumption was that suburban Christians, being white and usually well-off, had no real problems of their own.

In place of the old model of the residential church, where members bracketed secular concerns to worship God on the Sabbath, the reformers proposed a new model of the "servant church," one geared to assist God in whatever they believed God was up to in the secular world. And "secular" usually meant "inner-city," where most Protestants who lived there were black. Thus the mid-Sixties saw the creation of urban missions by mainline churches and funded by foundations created by the Ford and Rockefeller families, whose boards were controlled by liberal mainline Protestants. Among them was Chicago's Urban Training Center for Christian Mission, which used black ministers to orient white Protestant seminarians and newly minted clergy in service to black communities. The point was to convert clergy of the Protestant Establishment into "prophetic" ministers of the Gospel. "The church is God's avant-garde," Rev. Archie Hargraves often told his clerical wards at the center. "And its function is to be where the action is, out in the world."

Unlike Hargraves, a black Congregationalist who went on to become president of Shaw University, most white mainline Protestant leaders felt more like God's rear guard. The mantra most often heard from their ranks was "Let the world set the church's agenda." This was the servant church asking for directions, and none was more blinded by white guilt than the Protestant Episcopal Church.

Because of its image as the church of the carriage class, the Episcopal Church was especially self-conscious and self-critical. In the mid-Sixties, about 6 percent of Episcopalians were black, most of them of Caribbean descent; there were 253 black priests, now with their own black caucus, but as yet no black bishops within the

United States. In 1967, Episcopal leaders called for a special General Convention, only the second in its history, to confront its social sins and reform its structures. Optimists hoped to accomplish in six days the kind of changes that had occupied the Church of Rome for six years. The convention is worth recalling for what it tells us about the posture of the mainline at the close of the 1960s.

By the time the convention opened in summer of 1969, on the University of Notre Dame campus, the original agenda had been essentially scrapped. In addition to elected delegates, each diocese was directed to send three outsiders—preferably black, preferably poor, preferably female—to tell the church what its mission ought to be. In the view of the bishop in charge of the program, this new agenda was designed to jolt complacent white delegates "who have the money and the time to spend on the church" through a process that he described as "planned mayhem."

By 1969, however, the civil rights movement had changed as well. King was dead and black power, with its attendant racial anger and threats of violence, was ascendant. In May, former SNCC executive director James Forman issued his Black Manifesto, demanding $500 million (eventually upped to $3 billion) in repatriation to blacks from the nation's white churches, synagogues, "and all other racist institutions." Already Forman had shown up at various denominational meetings, even crashing the sedate annual conference of Christian Scientists in Boston, demanding cash up front for his new organization, the Black Economic Development Conference (BEDC). (The faith-healing disciples of Mary Baker Eddy politely received him, and just as politely ignored his demands.)

The only fear among planners of the Episcopal convention was that Forman might *not* show up. He didn't, but surrogates did. Just a few minutes into his opening talk, Presiding Bishop John Hines had the microphone wrested from his hands by a group of his own black clergy who demanded $200,000 for Foreman's organization. Since the church had already committed $9 million to combat the nation's urban crisis, the extra tribute was not the issue. The question that bothered conservative delegates was whether the church should fund an organization that threatened violence to achieve its goals. In a compromise, the money was handed over to the church's black caucus—a move that placated conservatives—which then delivered the check to Forman, pleasing the liberals. In this way, the BEDC wrested its first "donation" from a mainline Protestant denomination. If Forman got what he wanted, the convention's planners also got what they hoped for: six days of searing group therapy. But for all the "planned mayhem," the delegates left Notre Dame as confused and divided as when they arrived. Those who wanted a theological vision of what the church is and where it was headed would have to look elsewhere for guidance.

Secular Theology

They didn't have far to look. In the middle Sixties, a small but influential group of Protestant thinkers sought to ratify the move from church to world by formulating various "secular theologies." Matching the mood of the times, they were wildly optimistic about "the world," considerably less so about the church. Never more than a half-dozen in number, they nonetheless set the terms of conversation through which liberal American Protestants struggled to locate God in both.

Secular theology presupposed what social scientists call "secularization theory"—the notion that Western societies had already undergone a process in which the authority of religious faith and institutions declined as these societies became more rational, more compartmentalized, more focused on this world (the *saeculum*) than on the next. Max Weber saw secularization as the progressive "disenchantment of the world" that occurs when science finds answers to questions that were previously considered religious mysteries. As the space allotted to the sacred—that is, to God and His Providence—waned, the secular waxed, pushing religion to the margins of human concerns. Most secular theologians were Americans who looked upon this process and pronounced it not only good but also the long-delayed fruit of the sixteenth-century Protestant Reformation.

Ironically, the most influential secular theologian in the mid-Sixties had been dead for twenty years. Nor was he American. Dietrich Bonhoeffer was a young Lutheran pastor and precocious German theologian who left the safety of a teaching post at Union Theological Seminary in New York City in 1939 to join the anti-Nazi Resistance. Shortly after, the Nazis imprisoned him for his complicity in a failed plot on Hitler's life. He was executed at the age of thirty-nine, just months before the German surrender in 1945. While in prison Bonhoeffer wrote a number of letters that, together with some of his papers, were posthumously published. By 1965, an English translation of his *Letters and Papers from Prison* was selling by the thousands on seminary and college campuses. Many Protestants regarded Bonhoeffer as a martyr. Indeed, shortly after Vatican Council II a group of Lutherans went to Rome to inquire whether the Catholic Church might consider canonizing him.

American theologians were drawn to certain enigmatic phrases and tentative theological probes in Bonhoeffer's prison meditations. Toward the end of his life, Bonhoeffer spoke of a "world come of age" in which men would solve their problems and go on with life without need for or reference to religion, as was already happening in Europe. He imagined a "nonreligious Christianity" that dispensed with the traditional myths and metaphysical ideas about God's transcendence. Under such conditions, if God were to be found at all, it would have to be in the midst of secular concerns—again, where the action is. And Christ? If he were to be acknowledged at all, it would be anonymously as "the man for others."[2]

Read in the context of Nazi Germany, Bonhoeffer's prison musings (they were no more than that) made a certain sense. He saw that the German churches that failed to confront Hitler had proffered "cheap grace" to believers, while men of no faith recognized and resisted evil and died for what they did. Many Americans who studied Bonhoeffer saw a direct parallel with the civil rights movement and read their own experiences into his. Bonhoeffer's more enthusiastic followers, however, used his prison writings as starting points for creating a full-blown "secular theology."

I said at the outset of this chapter that the mid-Sixties was a period of enormous optimism for mainline Protestantism; we are now at a point to consider the textual evidence. Between 1963 and 1966, a blizzard of books inspired by Bonhoeffer appeared and, however different from each other, bespoke his peculiar form of "hope in the secular." Among them: *The New Creation as Metropolis* (Gibson Winter, 1963); *Honest to God* (John A. T. Robinson, 1963); *The Secular Meaning of the Gospel* (Paul Van Buren, 1963); *The New Reformation* (Robinson, 1965); *The Secular City* (Harvey Cox, 1965); *Secular Christianity* (Ronald Gregor Smith, 1966); *The Gospel of Christian Atheism* (Thomas J. J. Altizer, 1966); *Radical Theology and the Death of God* (edited by Altizer and William Hamilton, 1966). This list does not include the books about these books—titles like *The Honest to God Debate* and *The Secular City Debate*.

Cox's *The Secular City* was the most ambitious of the bunch and by far the most successful—an international bestseller in fourteen languages, something altogether new for a serious young theologian. *The Secular City* brimmed with optimism, beginning with its jaunty subtitle: *A Celebration of Its Liberties and an Invitation to Its Discipline*. Parsing Bonhoeffer, Cox defined secularization as "the liberation of man from religious and metaphysical tutelage, the turning of his attention away from other worlds and towards this one."[3] Like Gibson Winter, Cox saw a "new creation" in the making, which he called "technopolis," with a new urban style, at once secular and profane, which he identified with the can-do idealism of the late John F. Kennedy. Secular or technopolitan man does not waste time pondering the meaning of life: he is a problem solver.

In this new cultural surround, Cox argued, the church was called out from its old and "crippling structures" on the margins of the secular city. It was to become "God's avant-garde," discerning within the secular city the signs of God's coming kingdom and working for its realization. Like the Israelites in the desert, Cox believed, properly secular Christians were a people on the move with no time or temptation to worship static religion's false idols. They would follow Jesus into the world, working anonymously at his side in a secular fashion while history moved ever onward and upward under the hidden hand of God.

Although Cox's celebration of the secular seemed revolutionary, his ideas actually reconfigured a thoroughly American, wholly Protestant, and specifically mainline vision. Cox himself had been an Evangelical Baptist from Pennsylvania newly recruited by Harvard Divinity School. Like the Puritan John Winthrop's imagined "city upon a hill," Cox's secular city was the latest iteration of a persistent Protestant dream—albeit one that in its details looked a lot like Lyndon Johnson's Great Society. Behind it lay the nineteenth-century Protestant ambition to transform the United States into a righteous empire and the early-twentieth-century Protestant Social Gospel movement's emphasis on taking the church into the world, building there a new Jerusalem fit for Jesus' promised return. Where the mainline Protestant establishment once saw itself as the conscience and institutional custodian of American culture, it would now perform the same role (albeit in concert with like-minded Catholics and Jews) as the disestablished but discreetly embedded conscience of the emerging secular city. Liberal mainline Protestants had nothing to fear from the secular city: as its prophetic avant-garde, they would still be custodians of its conscience.

One measure of the thoroughly Protestant character of Cox's vision was the distance between his secular city and the urban experience of American Catholics. Inner-city Catholic parishes defined neighborhoods where community rather than autonomy or anonymity—Cox's prized virtues—was cultivated. The anonymous city folk that Dorothy Day and her Catholic Workers served—and, for that matter, the Salvation Army and other Evangelical storefront missions—were the utterly poor and uprooted: Manhattan's underside, not the affluent Upper East Side, where Cox's secular city was more clearly visible. Moreover, Catholics still inhabited an "enchanted" world shaped by the very myths and metaphysics that secular theology rejected. God may indeed be active in the secular world, but Catholics were not about to ignore the Christ whose sacramental presence they encountered and liturgically celebrated in churches.

For a handful of Protestant theologians (never more than three or four) Cox's celebration of secularity was not radical enough. Taking as their own Nietzsche's adage that "God Is Dead," they insisted that the transcendent Deity really had died in our time—and that the world was now an immensely happier place for it. In *The Gospel of Christian Atheism,* Thomas J. J. Altizer, a professor of religion at Emory University, called on Nietzsche, Hegel, and especially William Blake's prophetic poems as witnesses to the death of the traditional God—a God who had inspired alienation, sin, and guilt. That God, he announced, had so emptied himself of divinity when Christ died on the cross that he was now wholly immanent in history. For Altizer that was Good News indeed. Abstract, apocalyptic, and wholly idiosyncratic, Altizer's work owed more to the emergent counterculture than it did to Christian theology, and it might have gone unnoticed had it not appeared as part of a wider effort to announce the death of God while affirming the continuing relevance of Jesus.

If Altizer was the prophet-seer of the death of God, William Hamilton of Colgate-Rochester Theological Seminary was its pleased and plainer-speaking funeral director. Although he labeled his work theology, his essays were really sweeping readings of American cultural trends, engagingly but superficially put. Everywhere he looked, Hamilton saw release from postwar angst and the introspective conscience of classic Protestantism. The old God associated with that conscience had died, he concluded, giving Americans a new birth of freedom from tragedy and restraint. Significantly, Hamilton pointed to the civil rights movement and its "We Shall Overcome" anthem as his "most decisive piece of evidence" that a new age of secular optimism had arrived. "That there is a gaiety, an absence of alienation, a vigor and contagious hope at the center of this movement is the main source of its hold on the conscience of America, especially among the young."[4] Ripped from its roots in black religion, the civil rights movement had become in Hamilton's version of secular theology the prime example of an ecstatic "hope in the secular" once God no longer exists.

Except for Altizer, secular theology was easy to read, provocative, and flush with taunting paradox—low-hanging fruit ripe for picking by newsmagazine journalists keen on discerning trends. *Time* seized the moment with the magazine's most memorable cover image: "Is God Dead?" printed in red letters against a funereal black background and published as the Easter issue in 1965. The story inside ran to nearly six thousand words and featured a potted history of God from ancient Babylonia forward. Writer John T. Elson read forty books in preparation for his piece and thirty-two *Time* correspondents around the world contributed some three hundred interviews with experts as well as believers off the street. It was a splendid example of magazine journalism's version of the full-court press, bringing to the general reader's attention news of an important obituary they might otherwise have missed.

Countless clergymen entered the pulpit that Easter Sunday brandishing copies of *Time* and preaching in God's defense. Universities sponsored teach-ins on the Death of God and defiant bumper stickers proclaimed "My God's Not Dead—Sorry About Yours." Like a sudden summer storm, the Death of God came and swiftly went, more media event than movement. But for one brief moment it almost cost me my job. At *Newsweek,* senior editor Ed Diamond, the man who edited my articles, read the *Time* story and concluded that religion, while occasionally interesting, was no longer a subject deserving of its own weekly niche in the magazine. Not enough Americans really believed in God, he argued in a confidential memo to the top editors. In place of religion, Diamond proposed running a regular section devoted to philosophy, a subject he knew even less about. It was a proposal I could challenge only with burlesque: "You're right, Ed," I told him. "There's a huge congregation of neo-Kantians out there and devotees of Wittgenstein just waiting for *Newsweek* to weigh in every week." Eventually, *Newsweek* did institute a new section of the magazine, "Cities," in part because by the end of the Sixties so many of them had been trashed in inner-city riots.

Secular theology, it should be noted, was not addressed to secular Americans—who in any case paid little heed. Nearly all the writers I've mentioned were ordained ministers writing for a Christian audience of mostly mainline Protestant readers. Cox's *The Secular City*, for example, was commissioned for a conference of the National Student Christian Federation. But it wasn't just optimism about the secular world that distinguished the secular theologians from their more distinguished predecessors like Niebuhr, Barth, and Tillich. Even more pronounced was their dismissive approach to classic Christian doctrines and their blithe disregard of the historic Christian church.

What we have yet to examine is how secular theology affected those who represented mainline Protestant churches. Here, by way of example, I turn to the life and career of Episcopal bishop James A. Pike, easily the best-known mainline Protestant churchman of the Sixties. Following his career was like watching a weathervane register every new breeze blowing from the zeitgeist.

Pike's Pique

On the second Sunday of September in 1966, Episcopal bishop James Albert Pike strode down the center aisle of San Francisco's Grace Cathedral, doffed his miter, lowered his scepter, and climbed one last time into the pulpit, his brown leather penny loafers barely visible under his buff-colored robes. His parting sermon before resigning as bishop of California was titled "What a Man Can Believe." It wasn't much. Having jettisoned the Incarnation, the Trinity, and other doctrines of the Christian faith, Pike affirmed his belief in an afterlife based on his séances with mediums, endorsed love—"I-thou relationships are tops," he offered—and urged his 2,500 well-wishers to continue to praise God as "that which is in, and under, and beyond all this and maybe continuous with it—I don't know."

Had he not been a bishop, no one would have cared what James Albert Pike did or did not believe. But as a bishop he was the most visible mainline Protestant churchman of his era, a man who insisted that the media pay him heed and then returned the favor by proceeding to come apart before our very eyes. In life, as in his religious views, Pike was tumbling tumbleweed, always moving on, always reinventing himself according to what's happening. In this sense, he provides us with a parable of liberal Protestantism in the middle of the Sixties—"the years," as essayist Joan Didion, a fellow Episcopalian (and fellow Californian), later wrote, "for which James Albert Pike was born."[5]

Pike was born in 1913 in Oklahoma. Two years later his father died and his mother moved to California. She was Catholic and as a boy Jim imagined becoming a priest. But during his sophomore year at the Jesuits' Santa Clara College young Jim lost faith in the Catholic Church. Papal infallibility and birth control, he later claimed, were the issues that drove him into religious indifference, though like many of his assertions this seems like retrospective editing: at that time, most Protestants no less than Catholics opposed birth control. Pike's intellectual formation was in the law, first at the University of Southern California and then at Yale, where he earned a doctorate in jurisprudence, a secular credential. In 1938, he married for the first time and went to work at the Securities and Exchange Commission in Washington, D.C. In 1940, his wife divorced him. While serving in naval intelligence during the war, Pike occasionally attended liturgies in the National Cathedral. "It looked like a church ought to look,"[6] he thought, and he liked the enlightened elasticity of Anglican theology. Besides, as he wrote to his mother at the time, "practically every churchgoer you meet in our level of society is Episcopalian, and an RC or straight Protestant is as rare as hen's teeth."[7]

Pike married a second time and in 1946 was ordained an Episcopal priest. In taking holy orders, he liked to say, he remained a lawyer who merely changed clients. Pike's approach to matters theological, first as an apologist for traditional Anglicanism and then as orthodox Christianity's prosecuting attorney, was always essentially forensic. He liked to sift the evidence for this or that belief.

It took Pike just nine years to move from small-town church rector to chaplain at Columbia University (where he also upgraded its meager Department of Religion) to Episcopal bishop of California. His key career boost occurred in 1952, when he was appointed dean of New York's Cathedral of St. John the Divine, an edifice larger, if not more grand, than the National Cathedral.

As dean, Pike quickly assumed the role of the unofficial voice of the Episcopal Church. He wrote a half-dozen small books explaining and defending the Anglican middle way between the Anglo-Catholicism of the liturgy he celebrated and the Protestantism he preached from the pulpit. It was easier to chant doctrines you didn't believe in, he would later say, than to recite them in a creed. Pike hired theologians for his staff, hoping to make his cathedral a center of Anglican scholarship. Although Catholics had the larger numbers in New York, Pike believed the Episcopalians attracted the more sophisticated crowd. One of his first acts was to register the corporate title of "The New York Cathedral" with the state, thereby denying legal use of that title by the Catholics' St. Patrick's Cathedral. He especially enjoyed jousting with New York's Cardinal Francis Spellman over issues like birth control, the cardinal's penchant for condemning "dirty" movies, and Spellman's ardent anticommunism. Pike was no left-winger but he believed the Church of Rome was soft on fascism. When John F. Kennedy geared up his run for president of the United States, Pike wrote a book arguing that the senator's allegiance to the Catholic faith made him unfit for the nation's highest office.

Pike drew attention to his views by writing for secular publications like *Look, Vogue,* and the Sunday newspaper supplement *This Week*. In 1955, the ABC television network gave him his own weekly program, *The Dean Pike Show,* which put him in direct competition with another media favorite, Catholic bishop Fulton J. Sheen. Pike liked to display his wife and four children on his program to show that a bishop can be a family man as well—though in fact these on-camera sessions were often the most time Pike spent with his family each week.

By the late Fifties, then, Pike had become mainline Protestantism's ablest—certainly its most recognized—public apologist. But in this role, his most enduring credential would turn out to be his refusal in 1953 to accept an honorary degree from the University of the South in Sewanee, Tennessee. The university was supported by seven southern Episcopal dioceses and included a seminary that would not accept black students. When several teachers at the seminary challenged this segregationist policy, Pike supported them by refusing the university's offer to honor him, saying he didn't want "a degree in white divinity." This was two years before the rise of Martin Luther King Jr. and burnished Pike's later image as a "prophetic" churchman.

The California Pike returned to as Episcopal bishop was not the distant cultural outpost he had left a quarter century before. Whatever California is now, it was said, the rest of the country would soon be. The hippie counterculture, the Free Speech Movement, the gay rights movement—all of which Pike progressively embraced—made him feel at the cutting edge of social change. Grace Cathedral, his Episcopal seat, hovered like a vaulted spaceship above the genteel neighborhoods on Nob Hill, rivaling in magnificence those in Washington and New York. From there he traveled widely, giving lectures and sermons and turning up wherever there was a rally or protest march. As a churchman, Pike had reached his peak.

If Pike feasted on public attention, he also watched the market. In the first phase of his church career he had addressed those Americans who were personally not religious but lived vicariously off those who were, and who expected churchmen like himself to maintain institutions and traditions: after all, everyone needs a fit place to marry and to bury. Now he was tired of that role. In 1960, Pike began to air his private doubts. The Trinity, the divinity of Jesus—the whole carapace of Christian doctrine, he had come to believe, was now so much "excess baggage" that had to be jettisoned in the name of "Christian candor." By going public, he hoped to rally those *within* the church who, like himself, enjoyed the liturgies, the music, the belonging, but personally could not accept the doctrines that these rituals presumed and expressed. Who better to shoulder the burden of vicarious disbelief than a bishop?

Pike himself was not a theologian, though this was now what he wanted to be. His gift was playing middleman, adept at retailing the thoughts of others. Although he owned a bachelor's degree in divinity (magna cum laude) from New York's Union Theological Seminary, his exposure to systemic theology was limited to a pair of seminars with Paul Tillich. Tillich became his close friend and chief inspiration: from him, Pike borrowed the idea of addressing God as "the Ground of Being," a title about as compelling as Aristotle's "unmoved mover." Tillich also inspired his former student to live "on the boundary" of Christian faith—including the boundary of Christian marriage. Both were notorious philanderers, and neither went to church unless he was the preacher. From Bonhoeffer, Pike appropriated the servant image of Jesus as the humble "man for others." And from *Honest to God* he swallowed whole author John A. T. Robinson's program (itself a distillation of others' thoughts) for demythologizing the Christian faith. In this way, Pike became the ecclesiastical spear-carrier for the gathering secular theology. *Time* noticed and put him on its cover.

I first met Pike in the summer of 1964 when he frequently came by *Newsweek* for lunch. He had just joined Alcoholics Anonymous— "Make it a Virgin Mary," he would tell the waiter—and chain-smoked nervously through the meals. His face was lined like a tobacco leaf, making him look a dozen years older than he was. The bishop was by then well into a series of sermons at Trinity Church, Wall Street, culminating in one that famously dismissed the Trinity itself: "Sounds like a committee God," he said.

Pike was spoiling for a fight with his own church. He wanted to test its vaunted reputation for tolerance in matters theological. A group of twenty-seven Anglo-Catholic bishops from southern dioceses eventually took him on, demanding that he be tried for heresy. Pike was not on trial, the church was: if a bishop need not accept the basic doctrines of the Christian faith, then all members of the church were free to believe what they wished. The outcome,

I felt, held important implications for the future of all the mainline Protestant churches. What exactly were the truths to which they were bearing witness?

"The Bishop Pike Affair," as it came to be called, crested at a meeting of the Episcopal House of Bishops in 1966. Most of the bishops wanted to avoid a heresy trial, which they felt was anachronistic— even medieval—for so modern a church. A committee created to resolve the issue voted to censure Pike for his flippant ways with historic Christian doctrines, but judged that his "often obscure and contrary utterances" did not warrant the time and effort and wounds of a trial. The church, the report concluded, "had more important things to get on with."

And what were these more important things? A minority report from the church's more liberal bishops was quite clear: "We believe that it is more important to be a sympathetic and self-conscious part of God's action in the secular world than it is to defend the positions of the past, which is a past that is altered with each new discovery of the truth." Chief among God's actions was, of course, the civil rights movement. "Why is it," asked Bishop Paul Moore, "that the House has not censured any of the rest of us who have not spoken out and allowed to occur within our own dioceses greater blasphemies. . . . I speak of church doors closed against members of another race, clergy denied backing by their bishops because of their Christian social views, and the public impugning of the motives of fellow bishops." This was a less-than-veiled reference to Pike's southern accusers, whose timidity in supporting the civil rights movement was, in the mind of Pike's defenders, more heinous than the flippancy of their resident Doubting Thomas.

Pike's very public non-trial was the strongest signal yet that civil rights had emerged within the mainline churches as the index by which fidelity to Christ's teachings was to be judged. There would be others, notably the war in Vietnam and women's liberation, and woe to those who did not properly discern what God was doing in His secular manifestations. For Bishop Pike, though, there would be other trials and other personal transformations.

When Pike retired as bishop of California, his private life was a mess. His second wife was preparing to divorce him for his repeated infidelities over the course of their marriage. He also had a mistress, Maren Bergrud, who would soon commit suicide in their shared apartment—an act in which the bishop was partially complicit and, as it turned out, one that he illegally tried to cover up. Also, the very week *Time's* cover appeared, Pike commenced a sexual relationship with a third woman, Diane Kennedy, a student twenty-four years his junior in a class he was teaching on "The New Morality." Although Pike remained on the wagon, Bergrud was into drugs. So was his semi-estranged son, Jimmy. A week after his twentieth birthday, Jimmy sat alone on the bed in a London apartment and blew his head off. His grieving father turned for help to spiritualist mediums, and in a series of séances claimed consoling contact with his son's wandering spirit. One of these sessions was aired live on Canadian television and became part of yet another book from Pike's hand, *The Other Side,* which used his experiences with psychic channelers as evidence of a hereafter. After his divorce and the suicide of his mistress, Pike married Diane in December 1968. When the local Episcopal bishop refused him a liturgical marriage, he resigned from the church. Typically, his leaving and the reasons for it were announced in an article he wrote for *Look* magazine.

Throughout his tumultuous final years, Pike wrote short letters updating me on his doings, just in case I hadn't noticed. So I wasn't surprised when he called me early in September 1969 to say that he and Diane were going to Israel to visit the desert ruins at Qumran, where the Dead Sea Scrolls had been discovered. The journey, he said, was part of his new interest: investigation of the historical Jesus, a subject about which he planned to write several books. It was a field trip of sorts. He wanted to get a firsthand feeling of the barren Judean desert, unchanged since days when Jesus went there to fast and pray before taking up his ministry. There, Pike believed, he might somehow make contact with the earthly Jesus the way that psychics claim they can pick up spiritual vibrations from past events just by visiting the places where they occurred. His hoped-for experiences would be one more set of empirical facts to bolster his belief in an afterlife.

"Do you fear death?" I asked him on the phone. "I guess all men fear death," he replied. "But to me death now is like going to a new country to live. Frightening, maybe—but exciting, too." It would be yet another transformation. I think that was the last conversation he had with an American journalist.

Pike died in the desert wilderness. He had taken a wrong turn driving out of Bethlehem and soon got lost. Diane set out on foot alone seeking help, leaving her exhausted husband resting in a cave. She was found by Bedouin workers and carried back to Bethlehem. The next day the Israeli army launched the largest manhunt in the young nation's history, deploying planes and helicopters and more than two hundred troops to scour the desert's rough wadis and cloven hills, but to no effect. On a hunch, I cabled *Newsweek*'s London bureau to call on Ena Twigg, a famous psychic and pious Anglican whom Pike had often consulted. Maybe she had a clue. Twigg said she had been trying to reach him for days. Her visions placed him in a cave but that was all she could see. Besides, she complained, *Newsweek* reporter Kevin Buckley had brought with him an interposing shade from the other world, whose features she described in detail. His presence, she complained, was blocking her channel to the beleaguered Pike. "What she described resembled my dead grandfather," Buckley cabled back, "so please don't send me out to her again."

Eventually, a volunteer search party found Pike's body: he had tried to follow after his wife and fallen seventy feet onto a subterranean ledge. The news of his death was broadcast while the Episcopal bishops were convened at Notre Dame for their previously noted special General Convention. It was the first such meeting in years that had not been dominated by Pike. The bishops promptly hailed him as a "prophet," but it wasn't clear of what. Ironically, although Pike had left the church, technically he was still a bishop.

Bishop Pike reflected all the crosswinds coursing through mainline Protestantism in the middle Sixties, albeit in a convex mirror. Like other churchmen, he really thought he was witnessing a new Reformation, and as a bishop he tried to urge it into existence. Like the secular theologians, he supposed the church could be reformed by accepting the outlook of a putative secular man. Indeed, though the church provided Pike with a career and institutional platform, it was not a community of faith he loved or trusted as a source of wisdom, much less truth. "I never became disenchanted with the church," he said toward the end of his life, "because I never was 'enchanted' in the first place." He might have said the same about the Bible, which he approached with lawyerly suspicion. In short, he was a church careerist without religious convictions or commitments. Still, Pike remained absurdly enchanted by the figure of Jesus. He thought he could encounter Jesus, one-on-one, somewhere beyond the community of faith, beyond the Bible, beyond time itself. In this quixotic gnostic quest he prefigured a whole generation of younger spiritual drifters, church "alumni" like himself, who would follow in his wake.

Endgame for the Mainline

History doesn't turn on a dime nor does an era end with an exclamation point. Still, anyone who was around when Martin Luther King Jr. was murdered on Sunday, April 4, 1968, realized, if it was not already apparent, that the hope placed in the secular had been naive. Hours after the news of King's assassination flashed across television screens, the National Guard was called out to stanch rampaging black Americans in Chicago, Detroit, Pittsburgh, and Baltimore. In Philadelphia and Boston, too, Guardsmen were put on alert—and that was just in the North. *Newsweek* reported that Washington, D.C., looked like "the besieged capital of a banana republic": mobs of black youths smashed windows, torched buildings, and looted stores—the havoc went on for days. Helmeted combat troops with fixed bayonets guarded the White House. Stokely Carmichael, who loathed King's nonviolent ethic, stood near the Capitol steps preaching mayhem: "Go home and get your guns!" he shouted. "When the white man comes he going to kill you!" More than four thousand rioters were arrested in Washington, D.C., alone.

With the death of Dr. King, the civil rights movement lost the compelling moral vision that had energized white as well as black churches. The murder of Robert Kennedy two months later seemed to snuff out what optimism remained in American politics. I used my press credentials to attend his funeral at St. Patrick's Cathedral, where I lingered for an hour after the service had concluded, the smell of incense still heavy in the air over the center aisle where his coffin had been. I was hardly alone in feeling that something was over, finished. The rioting at the Democratic National Convention in Chicago that summer seemed a final confirmation. Nineteen sixty-eight was a year like no other, a rupture in time that Americans would not again experience until the attack on the twin towers on September 11, 2001.

Here, though, I want to use 1968 as a kind of close-parenthesis on mainline Protestantism's long reign as the nation's religious establishment. By then there were already signs of decline in both the membership and influence of the mainline churches. In 1967, the Southern Baptists overtook the Methodists as the nation's largest Protestant body. Year by year, the mainline statistics showed erosion. By 1984, the Methodists had decreased by 16 percent, the United Church of Christ by 17 percent, the Episcopal Church by 19 percent, the Presbyterian Church (USA) by 27 percent, and the Disciples of Christ by a whopping 40 percent. By the end of the century, no more than one in five Americans belonged to a mainline Protestant denomination.

What went wrong? That was the question *The Christian Century* posed at the end of the Sixties in a series of articles, and that sociologists probed in books. There was more than one answer. Some analysts saw the decline in membership as a proper winnowing from church rolls of those who had joined in the 1950s, when going to church was socially expected. In this view, that decade's surge in religious belonging was a brief and aberrant demographic bulge in a longer history of drift from organized religion. What the churches gained in the Fifties, according to one sociological study published in 1968, was a larger "audience," but few committed believers. In economic terms, American religion was experiencing a cyclical "market correction."

Some activist clergy on the left interpreted the decline in a more positive light—good riddance to those members who refused to embrace the churches' prophetic role, especially on civil rights, but also the mainline leaders' opposition to the Vietnam War, which will be addressed in the next chapter. There was some evidence for this view. As in 1960, so again in 1964 and 1968, white Protestants were more likely to vote Republican than Democrat, and did so overwhelmingly in 1972 when Senator George McGovern ran on an anti–Vietnam War platform. During this period, the leadership of the mainline churches moved to the left, embracing or at least tolerating racially separatist "black power" movements represented variously by James Forman, Malcolm X, and theologian James Cone. In a series of books beginning in 1965, Cone articulated a Black Liberation Theology that identified God with the goals of the black community: "If God is not for us and against white people," he wrote in one typical passage, "then he is a murderer and we had better kill him."[8] This was death-of-God theology in the key of racial contempt, but it was a measure of mainline Protestant guilt that Cone was given a faculty position at Union Theological Seminary, where his critique of white religion was celebrated as—of course— prophetic.

Even so, later studies showed that mainline Protestants did not abandon their congregations because of their denominational leadership's support for radical movements. That only increased the inherent Protestant distrust of denominational structures that Albert Outler had alerted me to, and further isolated the National Council of Churches and its agencies from grassroots constituencies. Protestants could and did remain mainline in membership on the congregational level while withholding funds and support for denominational programs with which they disagreed. One such program was the defense fund to which mainline leaders contributed on behalf of imprisoned black militant Angela Davis, an avowed communist who had been on the FBI's "Ten Most Wanted" list on charges of murder, kidnapping, and criminal conspiracy. She was found not guilty in 1972, but by then it was clear that the mainline leadership had lost much of its followership.

That same year, Dean Kelley published a widely influential book, *Why Conservative Churches Are Growing*, which was chiefly about why the liberal mainline churches were not. Citing the Mormons, the Southern Baptists, Orthodox Jews, and similar groups with recognizable boundaries against secular influences, Kelley argued that "strong" religions such as these thrive because they provide firm beliefs about the meaning of life, make high demands of their members, and in return elicit strong commitments from them in the form of time, enthusiasm, and financial support. In contrast, Kelley found that the liberal mainline denominations were declining because they had lost all the "traits of strictness" necessary to strong religion. Unless a religion "makes life meaningful for its members," he insisted, no amount of social action, welfare services, or patriotic preaching could take its place—nor would these substitutes benefit the larger society as much as providing meaning for its own membership.

Kelley's sharp critique of liberal Protestantism was all the more arresting because he himself had spent most of his professional life in the service of the National Council of Churches as its church-state expert, and was an ordained minister in the United Methodist Church, which owned the council's deepest pockets.

Kelley's book, though contested, provoked further denominational self-scrutiny. If the institutional test of any religion is its ability to pass on the faith to subsequent generations, then liberal Protestantism was indeed in trouble. The Presbyterian Church in the USA, for example, found that 45 percent of children reared as Presbyterians do not grow up to become adult Presbyterians: rather, they become something else or, just as often, nothing at all. Why? One telling answer was this: those who remained Presbyterians did not differ significantly in beliefs or behavior from those who dropped out. They had no compelling or coherent answer to the question, "What do Presbyterians do that make them different?" For the Presbyterians, as for the rest of the mainline churches, the problem was that the boundaries between themselves and the world in which they moved had effectively vanished.

Where Kelley pointed to internal institutional factors to explain the mainline's decline, other investigators found equally compelling external reasons. Chief among these was demographics. Mainline Protestants had fewer children than conservative Protestants, and were more apt to use birth control and to marry at a later age. Moreover, mainline Protestants tended to live outside the Sun Belt states, where the population was growing and where Sunday churchgoing was expected in ways that it was not in the more urban North. Nor were they as aggressive as conservative southern churches in trying to "grow" their congregations. Hanging out a sign that says "The Episcopal Church Welcomes You" is not nearly as effective as knocking on doors and inviting strangers to join your fellowship. As chaplains to the nation's established leadership, mainline clergy expected others to come to them.

For all these reasons, then, the close of the Sixties signaled the long withdrawing roar of liberal American Protestantism. For decades, liberal Protestants assumed that history's gravitational pull worked in their direction. A professor at Union Theological Seminary described it this way: evangelists like Billy Graham would convert sinners, whose children would eventually migrate upward from strict conservative to more relaxed mainline churches, and whose gifted grandchildren would then enroll at Union, where they learned that religion was mainly applied ethics and that God was best thought of as an expression of Ultimate Concern. At the close of the Sixties, this trajectory was no longer operative, if it ever was. Instead, as conservative Christians moved up the social and economic ladder, they took their churches and schools with them, sprinkling the suburbs with Pentecostal and Adventist, Southern Baptist and Mormon congregations.

As it turned out, my story on "The Protesting Protestants" was the last time *Newsweek, Time,* or any other general-interest magazine featured the mainline churches on its cover. Moreover, by the end of the decade, I had come to the conclusion that whatever residual group identity mainline Protestant denominations retained, denominational labels had ceased to be reliable indicators of what their members believed or predictors of how they would behave. Some combination of ecumenism, indifference, and loss of historical memory had made such labels moot. If I were to continue writing about American religion, I would have to find more descriptive categories to distinguish one form of belief, behavior, and belonging from another.

CHAPTER 5

Entrepreneurial Religion

God's Self-Starters

In one of those deft phrases, of which he is a master, historian Martin Marty once described Evangelical Christianity as "the religion you get when you get religion." Marty was referring to the soul-saving, convert-making style of American Christianity identified with the Great Awakening of the eighteenth century, the circuit-riding Methodist preachers of the nineteenth century, and the itinerant revivalists of every stripe who laid across the hinterlands of America a sawdust trail that eventuated in the minutely managed urban crusades of Billy Graham. Marty's pithy definition, adopted from a line by journalist H. L. Mencken, captures Evangelical religion as experienced individually by those who come forward to "get saved" or be "born again," but it leaves out the nature of that religion as organized and marketed by the convert-makers themselves.

From that angle, Evangelical religion is essentially an entrepreneurial religion. This is not a theological definition, nor is it how most Evangelicals today would understand themselves. But it is, I would argue, a definition that captures Evangelicalism's distinguishing feature. There would be no Evangelicalism without evangelizers and their organizations. But what kind of organizations are they?

Those evangelists who care about pedigree trace their genealogy back to George Whitefield, an itinerant Anglican priest whose
New England revivals in the 1730s and '40s lit the fires of the First
Great Awakening. Whitefield's operative words all began with *re—
revelation, reform* (as in the Reformation), *regeneration,* and, especially, *rebirth.* "My one desire," he said, "is to bring poor souls to
Jesus Christ," the baptized no less than the nonbaptized. But his
method—preaching outdoors to massive crowds—was new. (His
biggest draw was twenty-five thousand, in Philadelphia.) So was his
disregard of established churches and denominational differences.
He would share his platform with anyone who believed that the only
thing that made a Christian a Christian was her (Whitfield's audience was preponderantly female) experience of personal conversion,
or "new birth," and the subsequent power to lead a holy life. In the
Second Great Awakening, just prior to the Civil War, the message
was essentially the same. What differed for those preachers and for
their twentieth-century successors were the medium and technique.

The genius, the energy, of Evangelicalism lies in its protean drive
to fashion ever-new ministries and movements in order to segment
and target new audiences as markets for spreading the Gospel and
converting individuals to Christ. It is this entrepreneurial character
that makes Evangelicalism an especially American form of Christianity, and helps explain the strong affinity between Evangelical
Protestantism and free-enterprise capitalism, as manifest in the
sudden rise in the late 1970s of the "New Religious Right."

In the Seventies, as in the previous two decades, Evangelical
Protestantism was identified most prominently with evangelist Billy
Graham. "If you want to know where the center of Evangelicalism
is," so the saying went, "look to Billy Graham. And if you want to
know where Evangelicalism is headed, keep looking to Billy Graham." At any given moment, Graham and his associates defined
where Evangelicals stood in relation to the narrow Fundamentalism
out of which they grew, and to liberal Protestantism, which functioned as their foil, and to American politics, a place where Graham
had firmly planted his personal flag as friend and unofficial pastor
to successive occupants of the Oval Office.

That Graham was an evangelist by calling and by trade suggests just how deeply Evangelicalism itself is wed to the entrepreneurial spirit. The classic stand-up evangelist is an itinerant preacher, not the pastor of a church. People go to church, but evangelists take religion to the people. Theirs is a mobile ministry in the manner of the Apostle Paul, for which the closest modern secular analogue is the traveling salesman. Selling Jesus one-on-one and marketing him to millions through revivals and latterly through the media is what evangelists do.

But unlike Paul, modern American evangelists do not travel alone, much less on foot. All successful evangelists create their own business organizations that seek venues, sign television contracts, promote, advertise, sell (Bibles, books, audios, videos, T-shirts, and sometimes even healing cloths and tiny plastic communion cups), and in general see to it that the donations keep coming in. In this respect, the modern evangelist epitomizes the self-starting entrepreneur, and as such is apt to imagine that Jesus was one, too. The connection was established in 1925 in *The Man Nobody Knows*, the huge bestseller by advertising genius Bruce Barton. Barton marveled at the way a humble carpenter "picked up 12 men from the bottom ranks of business and forged them into an organization that conquered the world."

Not all evangelists are ordained ministers and of those who are, most in the past took up the call with no formal theological education. Among the most successful lay evangelists in the last decades of the twentieth century were Bill Bright, founder of Campus Crusade for Christ; James Dobson, a pediatric psychologist who established Focus on the Family; Chuck Colson, the former Nixon White House aide who created his own prison ministry after serving time himself as a convicted Watergate conspirator and felon; and Pat Robertson, the religious broadcaster and onetime candidate for the Republican presidential nomination. A complete list of all the evangelistic "outreach" organizations and their missionary affiliates formed since the Fifties does not exist. If it did, it would be thicker than most yellow pages.

Evangelicalism is also entrepreneurial in its theology. Although the message comes from the Bible, the interpretation is up to the preacher, whose challenge is to find fresh ways to sell his message. These preachers do not, as a rule, subscribe to formal creeds or honor denominational distinctions. Their job is save individual souls, something that can occur quite independently of churches and usually does. Not surprisingly, entrepreneurial religion measures its success by the number of converts it makes. Even local churches that call themselves Evangelical "count the house," and a growing church is, by Evangelical accounting methods, a sign of God's favor.

Indeed, if you read the biographies and autobiographies of some of the better-known Evangelical pastors, their stories go well beyond the conventional conversion narratives of the eighteenth century: they reek of Horatio Alger. The theme of the self-made man is what united in the 1970s and '80s a Fundamentalist like Rev. Jerry Falwell with a therapeutic megachurchman like Rev. Robert Schuller, the founding pastor of the huge Crystal Cathedral in Orange County, California. Schuller, who was educated in a Calvinism he no longer preached, started his first church by preaching solo in a defunct outdoor movie theater. Falwell started his in an abandoned bottling plant. Even today, at schools like Liberty University, founded by Falwell, graduates who go into the ministry are expected to set out on their own and "plant" new churches; they do not, as mainline Protestant clergy do, begin by taking a junior position in an established congregation. And it works. Independent churches—that is, those with no denominational ties or creedal identity—represented the fastest-growing segment among Protestant congregations in the second half of the century.

Today, Evangelical Christianity has developed well beyond the originating characteristics I've just described. But in the Seventies, its entrepreneurial style was its glory and its boast. I did not learn this just by reading about evangelists or attending their revivals but by meeting them face-to-face.

The Great Commissioner

The evangelist I saw most often, apart from Billy Graham, was Bill Bright. He and one of his aides came calling on me at least once a year to pitch the latest venture of Campus Crusade for Christ. Bright founded CCC in 1951 as a proselytizing ministry at the University of California, Los Angeles, using students trained by him to "witness" to fellow students. Soon it spread to hundreds of other campuses and eventually went international. Bright saw himself as the kind of man the risen Christ had in mind for His Great Commission: "Go therefore and make disciples of all nations. . . ." Although Bright founded and controlled Campus Crusade, he was not, like Graham, the medium of his message. His gift was training others to be effective evangelizers. Bright's own training was in sales and he employed the lingo—sales force, sales tools, memorized sales pitches, and tips on how to close a deal, meaning getting someone to come to Christ. Fraternity presidents, student body officers, cheerleaders, and star athletes were his prime targets. His evangelizers worked the cafeterias, library steps, and student lounges. Trouble was, his youthful recruits were not steeled salesmen accustomed to rejection. Many students disparaged them as "Christers."

Bright's first big breakthrough came after he simplified his pitch by writing a short pamphlet called *The Four Spiritual Laws,* which his evangelizers could read to students and leave for them to ponder. Based on the idea that God has a plan for every human being, the four laws became the stripped-down summary of the Campus Crusade theology. The second was Bright's eventual decision to require his staff to raise their own salaries through donations, freeing Bright himself to concentrate on donors with deep pockets for his new and ever more ambitious projects. Among the latter were giant youth gatherings like "the Berkeley Blitz," which was his planned invasion of the campus where the Free Speech Movement had started. He was determined to create a Christian youth culture to counter the Sixties counterculture. It was another of these extravaganzas, "Explo '72" (short for "Spiritual Explosion"), planned for Dallas, that brought Bright to New York a year ahead of time to pitch the media. He predicted the event would attract one hundred thousand young people and it almost did.

Whenever evangelists came calling, I told them they would have to pitch me over lunch—on them. I picked the restaurant, always a good one, and routinely ordered two Jack Daniel's as bracers while they talked. It was a taunt, I suppose, but I wanted them to know at least that much about where I stood. Bill Bright was a short, somber, rather unctuous undertaker kind of man whom I imagined as T. S. Eliot's Eternal Footman sans the snicker. He was not at all like the cheerful, sociable southern evangelists who came round and right off called me Ken. At lunch, Bright told me how he had felt a personal call from God to "win the entire country for Christ by the year 1976," the nation's bicentennial. Dallas was to be the first step. His next goal was to evangelize the entire world for Christ by 1980. Being in the business of saving souls, all evangelists tend to identify their goals with God's own. But Bright was the only one who also assigned God a timetable.

As at lunches past, I could see behind Bright's salesman's eyes that he was wondering about the state of my own immortal soul. This time I thought I'd tease him with a glimpse. I told him how my father had been saved by Billy Sunday as a youth. Bright's eyes brightened.

"And you, did you follow in your father's footsteps?" he asked. "Have you accepted Jesus Christ as your personal Lord and Savior?" In all the years I'd known him, Graham had never asked me that. But Bright had slipped into witnessing mode and I thought I'd witness back.

"No," I said. "I don't want a personal Lord and Savior. I prefer the one everyone else has." I'd been waiting for years to tell an evangelist that.

I knew what he meant, of course. But the idea of pushing Jesus as my personal savior rankled, as if Bright were recommending a personal trainer. The Jesus I knew had been mediated to me by others, a rather old and large community of others at that. And as I understood the Gospels, Christ was to be encountered through a community of faithful, not just in that deceptive inner space we call the heart. Bright, too, was offering me a socially constructed Jesus, one mediated to him by others, though he was blissfully unaware of that.

Explo '72 nearly fizzled until Billy Graham agreed to serve as honorary chairman. He even predicted it would be a "Christian Woodstock," a prospect that unsettled some conservative folks in Dallas. Bright took the hint and turned the final night into a "Jesus music festival" headed by Johnny Cash and Kris Kristofferson. An estimated seventy-five thousand kids turned up, proving, according to one of Bright's biographers, that there really was a Christian youth cohort out there that dressed counterculturally but was religiously and politically conservative at heart. Working through Graham, President Nixon let Bright know he'd accept an invitation to address the crowd. That very year Nixon had been named, improbably, "Churchman of the Year" by a private foundation called "Religious Heritage of America": this for a man who, on Graham's advice, attended religious services only downstairs at the White House. But 1972 was also an election year, and Bright's aides convinced him not to make his Explo '72 *overtly* partisan. In any case, Explo' 72 turned out to be an organizational success: with hyperbole typical of evangelists, Graham generously dubbed it "the greatest religious happening in history." (So much for Pentecost.) Bright was the real winner: Campus Crusade attracted so many new recruits that he was able to double his staff to three thousand.

By 1974, Bright could no longer resist political temptation. As conservative in politics as he was fundamentalist in theology, he opened "the Christian Embassy" in a splendid mansion purchased from the Catholic Archdiocese of Washington, D.C., for $550,000—a huge sum at the time. The purpose of the embassy was to provide prayer, worship, fellowship, and counseling to legislators and government officials. But if the art of evangelism is based on personal contact, so is the art of politics, and Bright was soon a familiar figure in conservative Republican circles. Two years later, he covertly joined forces with a movement led by Arizona congressman John Conlan, an ex–Catholic priest married to a former nun, that planned to go precinct by precinct organizing "real Christians" (a designation that excluded all but Fundamentalist and Evangelical Protestants) behind conservative politicians. One publisher involved put out a "Christian Index" ranking members of Congress according to how they voted as measured by a conservative reading of the Constitution and "God's law." The index was put together in Conlan's office and—no surprise—his name topped the list. All this took place years before anyone had heard of Rev. Jerry Falwell, the Moral Majority, or the Religious Right with its voters' guides.

It was Billy Graham who tipped me on what Bright was up to. In May 1976, he sent me a copy of a letter he had sent to Bright outlining his disagreement with the latter's political activities. I sat on it until a story on Bright's maneuvers appeared in *Sojourners,* a youthful, left-leaning Evangelical magazine edited by Jim Wallis, one of the truly gifted Evangelical ministers of our time. I immediately asked *Newsweek*'s Washington bureau to follow up. Meanwhile, I phoned Billy Graham, who reiterated that he was "opposed to organizing Christians into a political bloc" and that he was furious with Bright. "Bright has been using me and my name for twenty years," he grumbled, promising to have it "straight with him" that very week. Graham went on to list a series of differences he had lately had with Bright. By recruiting evangelizers from among those he converted, Graham said, Campus Crusade "has become almost a denomination by itself, in competition with the churches."

The rebuke from Graham stung Bright and threatened his future fundraising efforts. But he had every reason to believe that Billy would support his venture into political mobilization: in his own way, Graham had been doing the same thing for decades.

Graham's Secret Effort to Stop JFK

The most egregious example, long suppressed by Graham, occurred during the Kennedy-Nixon contest in 1960. Graham wrote his close friend Lyndon B. Johnson, Kennedy's running mate, assuring him that he would remain neutral in the race and in fact was sitting it out in Switzerland. On the contrary, three months before the election, Graham summoned about two dozen Evangelical leaders to a relative's home in Montreux where he often vacationed. There they discussed how to mobilize American Protestants against Kennedy. They deeply feared having a Catholic in the White House. Among them were Norman Vincent Peale; L. Nelson Bell, editor of *Christianity Today* and Graham's father-in-law; Harold Ockenga, a leading Evangelical theologian and rabid anti-Catholic; J. Elwin Wright, cofounder of the National Association of Evangelicals (NAE); and Glenn Archer, head of Protestants and Other Americans United for the Separation of Church and State, a vocal anti-Catholic organization.

After the meeting, both Graham and Peale wrote Nixon, explaining their plan. Under the auspices of an NAE spin-off called—ironically—"Citizens for Religious Freedom," they would hold a conference at the Mayflower Hotel in Washington, D.C., to brief 150 other Protestant leaders and pastors on how to stop Kennedy. Billy stayed in Montreux, though he advised Nixon by letter on the campaign, and Peale agreed to front the meeting, where several of the Montreux group spoke. Peale warned that "our American culture is at stake" and Bell declared that "the antagonism of the Roman church to Communism is in part because of [their] similar methods." Two reporters slipped into the session and took notes on the rabidly anti-Catholic discussion, and passed on what they heard to their colleagues. When Peale held a press conference afterward, he took such a drubbing from the reporters that the plan never got off. In fact, the entire effort undoubtedly bolstered Kennedy's election. The Democratic candidate read about the meeting while campaigning in the West. He already had in his pocket an invitation to address the Greater Houston Ministerial Association and decided right then to accept it. That address, of course, is now history.

Publicly embarrassed, Peale went into severe depression and hiding, offering to resign his post as pastor of New York's Marble Collegiate Church, the editorship of his magazine, *Guideposts*—even his membership in the New York Rotary Club. Privately he felt that Graham, by hiding his central role in the project, had let him suffer the consequences, though he never said so publicly. Graham never did own up to his role in the stop-Kennedy cabal, telling JFK that his vote was *for* Nixon, not against him. The entire episode gets only a brief, bland summary in Graham's grandly misnamed autobiography, *Just as I Am.*[1]

Bright's "Ministry of Giving"

By 1974, Graham had become a wiser man. Eventually he and Bright reconciled. But in airing his differences with Bright, Billy had done his fellow Evangelicals a favor. The biggest problem Campus Crusade posed to others in the Evangelical camp—Billy excepted—was Bright's ability to corner the market on major donors. Increasingly, he relied on the financial support and referrals from deep-pocketed political reactionaries like the Hunt brothers of Texas. "Wherever I go and meet a wealthy person," complained David Hubbard, president of Evangelicalism's flagship school, Fuller Theological Seminary, "I find that Bill Bright has been there first." Undeterred, in 1977 Bright set a budget of $1 billion for his biggest entrepreneurial effort yet, "Here's Life World," through which he hoped to make good on his promise to preach Christ to the entire globe by 1980. He failed, of course, but it was just a marketing plan anyway. Just six months before his deadline, Bright established "History's Handful," a gimmicky effort to raise $1 billion from 1,000 donors willing to give or raise $1 million each. Part of the strategy was to convince donors to go into debt, if need be, in order to support his effort. Bright assured them that they were participating in a "giving ministry" that would result, among other things, in their "eternal salvation." Martin Luther would have condemned this as salvation through good works. But Bright saw it as the fiduciary obligation a Christian acquires once he knows he is saved. In Bright's hands, theology was always fungible.

Campus Crusade turned out to be a classic example of Evangelicalism's inherently entrepreneurial spirit. "A man's gotta dream," as was said of Willy Loman at his funeral, and in pursuit of his, Bill Bright raised and spent at least a billion dollars. In addition to his ministries targeted to college and high school students, he added Evangelical training organizations for families, single young adults, and military personnel, plus media ministries. By acquiring Athletes in Action (AIA), he was able to penetrate college and professional locker rooms, recruit coaches, and even field a barnstorming AIA basketball team composed of former college players who witnessed to their faith at halftime.

In his battle with the Sixties counterculture, Bright emerged the twelve-round winner on points. His evangelizing of the young proved to be more populist and more enduring than the counterculture's immersion in acid and alienation. History has to give him that much. Bright never did manage to fulfill the Great Commission, but organizationally, at least, he achieved a salesman's success. At his death in 2003, Campus Crusade was an international big tent with thirty different ministries and a staff numbering half a million.

The "Chairman of the Board"

In the world of entrepreneurial religion, there was only one organization that surpassed Bill Bright's in global reach and clout. The first name of the man that organization answered to was also William, but everyone called him "Billy." He had an immediately recognizable voice, magnetic personal charisma, a powerful stage presence, and a buddy in the White House, and among the brethren he was the acknowledged "chairman of the board." For many of us that description denoted Frank Sinatra, but in the world of entrepreneurial religion it was Billy Graham.

From the start of his public ministry Graham determined to avoid the Elmer Gantry stereotype by separating his preaching from the business side of mass evangelism. He was lucky. Unlike Bright, he did not go hat in hand to wealthy donors: they came to him. The alliance between private wealth and big-time evangelists is an old and sturdy one. Dwight Moody had his John Wanamaker and J. P. Morgan; Billy Sunday had his John D. Rockefeller Jr. and S. S. Kresge; and Graham had J. Howard Pew, W. Maxey Jarman, J. Willard Marriott, and many more. This alliance also helps to explain why big-time evangelism has also espoused conservatism in politics. Historian George Marsden has said that "Revivalism has been to American religion what free enterprise has been to the American economy,"[2] but that observation falls just short. Revivalism *was* free enterprise in the service of religion.

If Billy Graham was well connected, he was also well advised. As early as 1950, when his reputation was just ascending, Graham set up the Billy Graham Evangelistic Association (BGEA), taking a modest but always sufficient salary from it, and hired others to handle his ministry's financial matters. In this and in all other ways but politics, his integrity was unimpeachable. Billy was the chairman of the board and very much its CEO, a fact that was usually lost on his adoring public but everywhere evident to the gathering Evangelical movement. Organizationally, Billy Graham *was* the movement.

Through the BGEA Graham established a broadcast division that purchased airtime on radio and later on television for his *Hour of Decision* programs. In 1949, when Graham was still a newcomer on the evangelistic circuit, the BGEA bought out Great Commission Films to distribute movies of his crusades; later, under the name of World Wide Pictures and with a studio of its own in Burbank, California, the corporation produced feature films for distribution around the world. In 1952, Graham and his close aide George Wilson started the Grason Company, which published and distributed books, records, and music used by the BGEA and gave its profits to the BGEA. Another affiliated organization, World Wide Publications, handled wholesale sales. Eventually, the BGEA maintained offices in nine foreign countries.

Even without the BGEA, Graham was financially secure. He maintained a comfortable lifestyle on 150 acres atop a North Carolina mountain where he built his home. Under his name, he distributed a column, "My Answer," that appeared in 1,200 newspapers. Altogether, he authored or authorized in his name more than thirty books, several of them huge bestsellers.[3] In 1960, Graham created his own monthly magazine, *Decision,* which eventually gained a circulation of 42 million.

By 1976, the BGEA could report an income of $28.7 million with a budget larger than that of most Protestant denominations. Graham himself was wary of revealing just how prosperous his organization had become: ordinary believers, too, supported his evangelism with their dimes and dollars, though he only saw them (from a distance) at his crusades. When word surfaced that the little-known Billy Graham World Evangelization and Christian Education Fund of Dallas had accumulated $23 million in stocks and real estate, Billy explained to me that he had kept the existence of the fund quiet for fear of being inundated with requests for aid. It was, he said, a reserve he was building up to realize two personal dreams: to build a training center in North Carolina for evangelists and a Billy Graham Center at Wheaton College. And eventually he did both.

No one called the BGEA "Billy Inc." but that is what it was and had to be if Billy was to preach the Gospel on a worldwide stage. It was at once his support system and the mechanism through which he trained others in the techniques of evangelism. No less than Bright, Graham was driven by the words of the Great Commission.

Even so, Graham's entrepreneurial drive went beyond the BGEA. In 1956, Graham, his father-in-law, and others founded the biweekly magazine *Christianity Today,* with Billy serving as chairman of the board. Through it and its associated publications, Graham and the editors he selected both defined what Evangelical Christianity was and provided the medium through which conservative Christians within the liberal mainline denominations could find common cause and identify with traditional Evangelical churches and denominations. In this sense, Graham's new or neo-Evangelicalism ushered in a new kind of ecumenism and postdenominationalism that both countered and paralleled the ecumenical movement represented by the liberal National Council of Churches and progressive Protestant publications like *The Christian Century.* And for a long time Graham also served on the boards of the three major Evangelical schools: Fuller Theological Seminary in California;

his alma mater, Wheaton College in Illinois; and Gordon-Conwell Theological Seminary in Massachusetts, which, with funding from J. Howard Pew, Billy himself established in 1969. Significantly, he never sat on the boards of Southern Baptist universities or seminaries. Although Southern Baptists claimed him as one of their own, Graham had by 1970 established an identity that was far more encompassing. To his legions of followers, especially abroad, Billy the Baptist had become a generic "Dr. Christian." Like the proverbial pealed artichoke, all that was left of his Southern Baptist identification was the scent.

Preacher-in-Chief

In the spring of 1970, I sent several cover-story suggestions up the editorial ladder, including one on "The Surging Southern Baptists." The denomination was by then the largest Protestant church in the country, with big plans for conquering the North for Christ. I had gone south once or twice to address the editors of the Southern Baptist Convention's state newspapers and had come away impressed by the way in which Southern Baptists had so thoroughly shaped the culture and mores of an entire region. Their age-related Sunday schools and other organizations for Southern Baptist youth were much like the formation apparatus I experienced growing up Catholic. Indeed, some called the Southern Baptist Convention the Catholic Church of the South. The Convention's public information director, a wonderfully affable man with the echoing name of W. C. Fields, plied me with numbers: in ten of the eleven states of the old Confederacy, Southern Baptists constituted an absolute majority, and in Texas alone the Baptist state convention, with 1.8 million members, was larger than all but eleven Protestant denominations. It was a chance to study the country's last and largest religious subculture, one that was still struggling over racial integration of society and of its churches.

Summer was usually a slow time for news, so editor Oz Elliott reluctantly gave my proposal a green light, on one condition: "Just make sure we put Billy Graham's picture on the cover." Oz knew Billy would sell more copies off the newsstands than a story on the Southern Baptists, regardless of their numbers, ever could. By then Graham had personally conquered northerners in a way that the Southern Baptists never would.

As the nation's preacher-in-chief, Billy was at the zenith of his political influence, thanks in large part to his deep friendship with President Richard Nixon. They were each other's enablers: Graham won the president's ear and regular overnights in the Lincoln Bedroom, and Nixon got access to Billy's national following together with his blessings. At the moment, Nixon's need of Billy was the greater. It was an election year and opposition to the Vietnam War was fierce, especially on college campuses. The only universities the president dared to visit during his first term were the military academies—with one exception. He did address General Beadle State Teachers College in Madison, South Dakota, the hometown of conservative Republican senator Karl Mundt. So, as it happened, did I a year later. It was a measure of the president's popularity on campuses that the religion editor of *Newsweek*, hardly a household name, drew the larger crowd.

In May 1970, Billy found a way of ushering the president onto a major campus without his being invited. Graham was due to hold a crusade in Neyland Stadium on the University of Tennessee campus in Knoxville. Like all his crusades, this one was sponsored by the city's Protestant churches, which paid to rent the stadium. Billy invited Nixon to be his personal guest; it was, he said, the first time any president would address a revival. Nixon, in turn, invited a group of Republican officeholders to share the platform: it was midterm election time and Nixon was as hell-bent to aid the party as Graham was to aid Nixon.

As president and preacher took their seats together, the choir sang "How Great Thou Art." Given that the camera was tightly focused on both Graham and Nixon, their eyes shut tight and heads bowed in prayer, it was not entirely clear which "thou" was being addressed. Billy then got up to introduce the president to the crusade's final, youth-night crowd. "I'm for change," Billy said, "but the

Bible teaches us to obey authority." There was some pushing and shoving on the football field between a knot of antiwar protestors and a security line that included a burly group from the Fellowship of Christian Athletes. Nixon took note. "I'm just glad there seems to be a solid majority on one side tonight," Nixon told the crowd, "rather than the other." But of course the Graham organization had seen to that.

Working closely with Chuck Colson, H. R. Haldeman, and other White House aides, Graham also planned a July Fourth "Honor America Day" featuring himself as preacher to the nation from the steps of the Lincoln Memorial. It was billed as a day of national unity, with Bob Hope as Graham's cochairman, J. Willard Marriott as organizer, and appearances by Catholic bishop Fulton J. Sheen and Rabbi Marc Tannenbaum. In fact, it was an anti-anti–Vietnam War rally that heard Billy leading a chant of "Never give in! Never! Never! Never! Never!"

On the Road

With all of this unfolding, I knew we had a legitimate cover story. But I needed to talk to Graham myself. Billy agreed to meet me in Los Angeles, where he had gone to edit the videotape of the Tennessee crusade. I took the red-eye from New York, arriving early on a Sunday morning. Like the outtakes of a movie often are, the insights into Billy I got that day were more revealing than the quotes I garnered for my story.

Graham was waiting at the airport with two members of the crusade "team." All three men were dressed in identical green sport coats that matched the green Chrysler sedan they were driving. It was like meeting a college football coach and his staff, all wearing the team's colors. Graham spent so much of his life on the road, he said, his teammates from the Billy Graham Evangelistic Association had become his second family. Unlike his first family back home in North Carolina, Billy's road teammates were all male. Graham had a rule, a wise one for the world's most recognized evangelist: never be alone with a woman—not even with his female personal secretary, not even in a car.

Driving to the TV studio, where we would talk alone, Graham wanted me to know that the car we were sitting in was the gift of a Los Angeles auto dealer, Graham's to use whenever he was in town. Again, I was reminded of college football, especially in the South, where the coach of the state's team was more celebrated than the governor, and the object of appreciative fans' gifts. Coaches are big, but Billy Graham was in a league of his own. I was thirty-four. He was fifty-one.

"I want you to see this," Graham said, as we pulled into the studio parking lot. Billy opened his wallet and showed me a plastic credit card. It was issued by Marriott Hotels and the name printed on the bottom, in raised letters, read: BILLY GRAHAM WORLD EVANGELIST. "Willard Marriott gave me this," Billy said. "He's a Mormon, you know, but he supports our crusades. This card allows me to stay in any Marriott hotel anywhere in the world and I don't have to pay for a thing." Then he pulled out a card from Holiday Inn, which extended him the same gratuity. Several times over Graham had been recognized as "Salesman of the Year," and just like every traveling salesman I ever knew, Billy relished his perks.

It was nearly noon in Los Angeles and it occurred to me that there would be no time for me to find a Sunday Mass. "Hope I didn't keep you from church," I said to Graham.

"I don't get to church much on the road," Billy replied. I could readily see his dilemma, imagining how disruptive it would be for a local preacher and his congregation to have Billy Graham show up at his Sunday service unannounced. But Billy was on the road two-thirds of the year, as he acknowledged, which meant he rarely spent a Sunday in common worship like other dutiful Christians, except at home, where he accompanied his wife to the Presbyterian church in Montreat, North Carolina. No matter: for an itinerant evangelist like Graham every day in the pulpit is the Lord's Day, and even God rested on the Sabbath.

Even so, Graham's relationship with churches was central to his ministry. His advance team organized local churches to support his crusades, and when newcomers declared themselves for Christ his crusade counselors directed them back to local congregations. No one accused Graham, as some did Bill Bright, of competing with the churches. But Billy's relationship with his own Southern Baptists was a marriage of convenience.

"America's Pastor"

Graham was raised in the Associated Reformed Presbyterian Church, a small, culturally conservative branch of Calvinism. But by the age of twenty he had been baptized more than once. The last immersion was by a Southern Baptist, and it was wholly expedient: without it he could not expect to preach in the surrounding Southern Baptist churches of northern Florida. Once Billy decided that his call was to evangelism he determined to elide the differences that divided his Protestant target audiences—as Whitefield had done two centuries earlier. But he also realized that the Southern Baptists, by far the largest Protestant denomination and one that incorporated an opportunity to get saved in every Sunday service, was the fellowship that was most likely to support his crusades. Yet only in 1953 did he formally join a Southern Baptist congregation: First Baptist Church of Dallas, then the largest Southern Baptist congregation in the world—a "megachurch" before there was such a label. He didn't worship there, but his membership gave him access to a clutch of wealthy and conservative Texans. Moreover, by the time we talked, Billy had moved beyond the turgid Fundamentalism of the church's pastor, Wallie Amos Criswell, and his die-hard support of racial segregation. Compared to Criswell, who regarded his lavish lifestyle as God's reward for his service, Graham's habits—like his salary—were relatively modest.

With this history in mind I asked Graham which church he now felt most comfortable in.

"Actually, Ken, I feel most at home in the evangelical wing of the Anglican Church," Billy told me. On reflection, that made a certain sense. London was the site of his first overseas triumph, in 1954, and he always relished returning there. Besides, he admired scholarly Anglican clerics like John R. W. Stott, who sustained the Church of England's evangelical wing. But I also think that Billy secretly admired the stately Anglican ritual, and there was really only one basic ritual—the sermon and altar call—in Southern Baptist worship. That said, Billy always looked at home in his plain, business-suit Baptist threads—and never more so than when photographed alongside the robed and mitered hierarchs of the Catholic, Orthodox, and Anglican churches.

In any case, Graham had long ago placed himself above denominational differences and group identities. An evangelist can't afford to parse theological differences and expect big crowds. Unlike Martin Luther King Jr., with whom he had an unsteady friendship, Billy spoke neither for nor to a constituency: he only addressed crowds of anonymous individuals as "America's Pastor," in Duke historian Grant Wacker's apt phrase.[4] For me the difference between these two Southern Baptist preachers came to this: with Graham you sang "Just as I Am"; with King it was "We Shall Overcome."

Voice Alone

As the two of us sat in his old studio in Burbank—the same studio, Billy noted, from which he had once broadcast his *Hour of Decision* radio program—he rolled the videotape of his crusade with the president as his guest. I noticed that sequences involving protestors had been edited out. I asked Graham if he didn't think that Nixon had used him for political purposes by attending his revival. Billy seemed surprised by the question. "If Mr. Nixon had been running for election," he countered, "I could understand the charge of politics. But he is the president. I wouldn't think that you'd call the president political." He may be that naive, I thought, but it bothered me that he thought I was, too.

We both turned our attention to the television monitor. There was the familiar figure of Billy Graham preaching his familiar message from the pulpit, a choir of five hundred voices, and Graham's closing altar call (though as in all revivals there was no altar) to the crowd to come down one by one and personally accept Jesus as their personal Lord and Savior.

I remembered how, while covering another Graham crusade, I, too, had responded to his altar call, though not for religious reasons. For me it was an exercise in understanding what moves others: I wanted to imagine as best I could the experience of a sinner in the stands getting saved with one momentous decision, like my father said he did. I even walked down to center stage to make my declaration. To my relief no one actually asked me for one. Instead, a counselor handed me a form in quadruplicate to fill out. It was then that I realized that a modern-day revival is a ritual rededication aimed more at the already saved—though maybe backslid—than at the unconverted. The BGEA's own computer printouts showed that on average only 3.5 percent of crusade attendees made decisions for Christ. It was a ritual like any other, and like any other it required prior initiation to be effective.

Every year, thousands of Southern Baptist and other Evangelical and Fundamentalist youngsters are readied from the time they enter Sunday school for that moment, around the age of twelve, when each will step away from the pew, walk up the church aisle alone to recite "The Sinner's Prayer," and declare himself for Christ. It is, like Protestantism in general, a purely oral/aural experience. There is in a revival nothing to educate the eye other than the body language of the preacher, nothing for either the sense of taste or smell to suggest sacred presence. Voice is everything. If the Protestant Reformation was built on a trinity of "alones"—Christ alone, faith alone, the Bible alone—revivalism added a fourth: the voice alone, addressed to the listener as an isolated "Me alone."

Graham himself was first prodded toward the pulpit on the eve of his sixteenth birthday after hearing a revival preached by a converted Jew, Mordecai Ham. Later, he was told by Bob Jones, whose fundamentalist college Billy briefly attended, "God can use that voice of yours." And when, finally, young Billy Franklin Graham gave himself to the preaching ministry, it was, he has written, because he heard "the voice of God" while walking alone on a Florida golf course. And now, with his own baritone as an instrument, the mature Graham had the gift of making the simplest sentence sound like Sacred Scripture.

Once Saved, Always Saved

Whatever else they may be, evangelists are genuine American performance artists, and in watching Graham on videotape I was witnessing one of the best. I also watched Billy watching himself. "What are you experiencing?" I asked. I expected an analysis of his technique, perhaps some second-guessing of his doppelganger on the monitor. But that is not what I got.

"I get so engrossed, I don't think of the man on television as me," Billy said. "I think of him as another person speaking because the spirit of God begins to speak to me through him."

At that moment I began to understand what makes Evangelical preaching more than just a hortatory exercise. Through his voice Graham was exercising a priestly function. It wasn't just the Bible preached as the word of God that mattered. It was the orchestrated collective experience—the speaking and the hearing and the singing—that made Christ present to the crowd. I was witnessing a verbal sacrament (though Graham would never use that term) in which Christ, "the Word made flesh," became Christ, the flesh made words.

Just by listening to himself on videotape that Sunday in Los Angeles, Billy had made it to church after all.

Once Graham clicked off the monitor I got down to basics. "Billy," I asked, "what's it like to *know* you are saved?" It was the sort of question that perhaps only a Catholic would ask, since Catholics do not believe that anyone can be certain of his own salvation—though a lot of Catholics act as if they are. It was also the sort of over-the-plate question any minor-league evangelist could easily hit out of the park. After all, Graham's whole career was built on getting sinners to repent and thereby ensure their eternal salvation.

"It's wonderful," he said. "Indescribable."

"Well," I pressed, "suppose you're saved, and afterwards you—uh—crawl in the hay with the organist?"

I purposely used the sort of down-home euphemism I thought Graham might tolerate, but for a moment he blushed. "Well, Ken," he replied, "I just wouldn't get as high a place in heaven." Once saved, always saved—this is the blessed assurance that tortured Martin Luther, who never overcame the suspicion that he was unworthy of salvation. But American evangelism was built on providing just such certainty, an insurance policy that never runs out.

Months later, over lunch in the Senate dining room with Senator Mark Hatfield, a very serious and disciplined Baptist whose politics were markedly to the left of Graham's, I recounted this story. I wanted his take.

"Ken," he said, "if I *didn't* know I was saved, I couldn't get up in the morning."

"Mark," I blurted out, "if I *knew* I was saved, I *wouldn't* get up in the morning." Such are the abiding differences between the spiritual sensibilities of Evangelicals and of Catholics.

Unlike Hatfield, however, Billy had a very clear if literal view of his role in the afterlife. He imagined, he told me, that in their resurrected bodies, the saved would look like they did at whatever age they were most comely. "And what will you do when you are in heaven?" I prodded. Billy tapped his soft leather Bible. "St. Paul listed five rewards for real Christians," he said. "And each of them must be tremendous crowns—or maybe planets to rule." This from an evangelist who twice (in 1952 and fleetingly in 1964) considered Republican urgings that he run for president of the United States.

Graham and the American "Civil Religion"

My cover story on Graham was written right after his Fourth of July performance at the Lincoln Memorial. Only fifteen thousand showed up. But many times more would watch the videotape on television. What sort of event was it? was the question my story addressed. Was it civic or religious?

As it happened, I had just read sociologist Robert Bellah's now-classic essay, "The Civil Religion in America." In it, Bellah argued that alongside particular religions Americans had elaborated a set of civic rituals and shrines (the Lincoln Memorial was one) that united the nation and—this was crucial—against which, as in any religion, the American republic expected to be judged. The God of civil religion, in Bellah's view, "is much more related to order, law and right than to salvation and love."[5]

That, I thought, was the religion Graham had appropriated to himself. Yes, his main job was preaching individual salvation, but in his public role he reliably resisted anyone or any movement that threatened, in William Butler Yeats's pungent line, to "hurl the little streets upon the great." Graham could and did show great courage by insisting early in the Fifties that his crusades across the South be fully integrated. In fact, he received numerous death threats for his stand. But in the Sixties, he did not join other religious leaders on Dr. King's march in Selma, Alabama, offering instead to go there afterward to calm the waters. Faced with any moral or civil irruption, Billy instinctively shrank from playing designated hitter: he preferred batting cleanup.

The sources of Graham's law-and-order conservatism were more than temperamental. For one thing, his fierce anticommunism made him wary of any form of social unrest. For another, he preferred gradualism in matters like school integration. It was a defensible position, especially for a southerner. Billy also took literally the Apostle Paul's words that everyone should be "subject to the governing authorities" because "those authorities that exist have been instituted by God." Above all, Billy liked to be liked, especially by men of wealth and power. He was drawn to politicians like moth to flame, and they to him. He was a master at networking because, as his archived correspondence shows, he was for many politicians a network unto himself. Biographer William Martin was spot-on when he titled his 1991 book *Prophet with Honor*. But so, from a different angle, was another biographer, Marshall Frady, a very gifted *Newsweek* colleague, who recognized in Graham a compromised Billy Budd.[6]

But as the Seventies wore on Graham changed. Watergate, which brought Nixon down, was a personal blow to Graham. More so was Nixon's profanity as revealed on the White House tapes, which showed that Billy really didn't know the real Richard Nixon, although Graham always insisted the real Nixon was not the frantic president on the tapes. After Watergate, Graham paid less attention to American politics and more to his role as Dr. Christian to the entire world. Here, too, he changed, but only gradually. For years he had traveled to Asia and other far-off places without ever supposing that Hindus or Buddhists might know something worth learning. As a self-styled "ambassador for Christ," he always arrived equipped to deliver the Answer. Recognizing Christ in others, especially when those others are non-Christians, has never been a trait of entrepreneurial religion.

"I Won't Play God Anymore"

Once Graham gained entry into the communist-run countries of Eastern Europe, his vision broadened. There he met Catholic and Orthodox as well as Evangelical Christians who had long suffered under communist suppression and found in them a Christian commitment tested in ways that those back home had never experienced. His eyes were opened.

The first time he talked about this for publication was in the fall of 1977. He was just back from Hungary, his first preaching tour inside the Soviet bloc. As it happened, *McCall's* magazine asked me to do an interview with Graham about his marriage and his family. The editor agreed that once we covered those subjects I was free to ask him whatever I wanted. Since I saw the interview as a "family" feature for a women's magazine and not news, I ignored *Newsweek's* policy requiring the editors' permission to write freelance articles. I took the pseudonym James Michael Beam, after the lower-shelf Kentucky bourbon.

I met Billy in an undistinguished mid-Manhattan hotel where

he was resting between appointments. The hotel room was small, and standing or sitting, Graham at six feet two looked trapped, like a man in a suit two sizes too small. He was tired, he said, and missed his wife. So we talked about his family, the regrets he had about being away from his wife and children most of the year. No traveling salesman I knew put in those kinds of hours on the road. Indeed, Billy was downright apologetic about being an absentee father.

Then we slid into his favorite topic, his personal relationships with the last five presidents. Again he grew reflective and self-critical. He said he now regretted his political pronouncements from the pulpit and his former tendency to identify Christianity with the American way of life. "I no longer think we are a Christian nation," he said. "We are a secular country in which a lot of Christians live. In fact, after visiting Hungary, I wonder whether Christians don't have a harder time coping with the temptations of our society than the Christians in Hungary have in coping with the difficulties of living under a socialist system."

I asked Billy how many fresh converts he figured he'd made in Hungary. He said he no longer looked at his ministry like a bookkeeper. "I don't even give a thought anymore as to whether five or five thousand people come forward. All I care about is whether I have done the very best I can to explain as simply as I can what it means to be a Christian. The cost of Christian discipleship [a phrase coined by Dietrich Bonhoeffer] is coming more and more into my message now. This is where I think I failed in my earlier ministry—I didn't emphasize enough what it costs to follow Christ. That's something I learned from traveling to other countries and from my American critics."

This was a far humbler Billy Graham than the one I had profiled for *Newsweek* seven years earlier. I'd watched him move away from his earlier Fundamentalism and now, it struck me, he was moving beyond the certainty and triumphalism that I found so off-putting about evangelists. When I asked him how he saw his role today, his answer surprised me. "I used to play God," he said. "But I can't do that anymore. I used to believe that pagans in far-off countries were lost—were going to hell—if they did not have the Gospel of Jesus Christ preached to them. I no longer believe that." Here he was being careful with his words, never mind that they were only for a women's magazine. "I believe that there are other ways of recognizing the existence of God—through nature, for instance—and plenty of other opportunities, therefore, of saying 'yes' to God."

I pressed him: "Are you saying that non-Christians can also be saved?"

"God does the saving," Billy said firmly. "I'm told to preach Christ as the only way to salvation. But it is God who is going to do the judging, not Billy Graham." He was particularly adamant about evangelistic groups like "Jews for Jesus" who target Jews for conversion. "If a person wants to convert to Christianity, that is his own free-will decision. I would never go after someone just because he is a Jew, which is why I have never supported the Jewish missions."

When my *McCall's* article appeared the following January under a cover line declaring, "I Won't Play God Anymore," it provoked an immediate public reaction. Other evangelists upbraided Graham for undercutting the very purpose of evangelism. Among other sins he was accused of denying the Gospel, of succumbing to New Age religion—even of being a Satanist. (These accusations can still be found on the Internet.) Jews for Jesus demanded that he clarify his stand. Billy had indeed made news, and *Newsweek*'s editors asked me if I didn't think there was a story in it for us. James Michael Beam had put me in an intolerable position. I assured them, with crossed fingers, that the controversy would disappear overnight. Billy himself called a press conference to defend himself. It was a classic Billy Graham performance: like his favorite president, Eisenhower, he garbled his answers so effectively that he managed to both affirm and deny what he had said in the interview. The one thing he did not do, though, was reveal who had actually written the story. He understood my dilemma. I owed him one.

Billy and the Pope

The following October, Graham made a preaching tour in Poland (in communist countries he never called them "crusades"), where, for the first time, he was invited to hold evangelistic services in Catholic churches. One of them was in Krakow, where he was invited to have tea with the city's archbishop, Cardinal Karol Wojtyla. Meantime, the cardinal had been called to Rome to participate in the election of a new pope. Graham watched on television as Wojtyla himself emerged on the balcony of St. Peter's Basilica as Pope John Paul II. The pope's first words were "Praised be Jesus Christ!" "Right then," Graham later told me in an interview for a story on the pope, "I saw that he was an evangelist." It took one to know one, I figured, and I thanked Billy for giving me the best one-word description of a very multifaceted pope.

In the years that followed, the mutual respect between Graham and John Paul II evaporated whatever reservations the American evangelist harbored about the Catholic Church. It also burned whatever rope bridges Billy still had to old-line Fundamentalists, who regarded Catholicism as a false religion and its faithful as apostates. In a private meeting at the Vatican, the pope told Billy "we are brothers," and in a published interview with me Graham returned the compliment: "He's the moral leader of the West." He meant it. Billy always hoped that his preaching would ignite a great social revolution like the one the Polish pope helped fuel in Eastern Europe. Still, Graham was also fairly certain who was in second place as moral leader. When, in 1988, Billy was invited to Moscow for the millennial celebration of Russia's conversion to Christianity and the leaders of the Russian Orthodox Church barred John Paul II from attending, he told me: "Ken, I probably was invited in place of the pope." Whatever the reason, Billy got to Moscow first. And when John Paul II died in 2005, the only religious organization other than churches invited to send representatives to the funeral was the Billy Graham Evangelistic Association.

A Tradition Apart from Traditions

By then, Graham's major impact on American religion was already thirty years behind him. Through his personal style and organizational leadership, he reshaped the old Fundamentalism of the early twentieth century and gave currency to a new name plucked from the nineteenth: Evangelicalism. By the middle of the Seventies, Protestants as different in beliefs and behavior as Lutherans, Southern Baptists, and Pentecostals—and even theologically conservative Methodists, Presbyterians, and Episcopalians—began to think of themselves as belonging to a larger if more amorphous identity group called Evangelicals.

But this remarkable inclusion by confluence was achieved at a high price. Through his revivals, Graham advanced a generic form of Christianity that dismissed profound theological differences among the various traditions as if they were so much excess baggage. His was inclusion by subtraction and what got lost were all the ways that Christianity had been embodied in the centuries since the Twelve Apostles. While theologians in the official ecumenical dialogues worked through historic differences on the assumption that all partners had valid insights to contribute, Graham's evangelism leaped over millennia of Christian history and experience to promote an individualized "biblical" Christianity that was, in effect, born yesterday. Much as I liked Billy—most people who met him did—he remained a kindred spirit to the Fundamentalist pastor who chiseled this into the cornerstone of his church:

> The Church of Christ
> Founded in Jerusalem in A.D. 33
> Established in Sweetwater, Texas, A.D. 1928

There are countless cornerstones like this in churches throughout the South and Middle West, each testifying to the conviction, endemic in revivalist Christianity, that not only the individual but the church itself is born anew whenever and wherever a preacher takes a Bible in hand and someone listens. This is a tradition apart from traditions, built on the notion that the Bible is a self-interpreting book. But of course it isn't, which is why Evangelicalism as represented by Billy Graham tried but never achieved more than organizational definitions of what distinguishes Evangelicals from other Christians. Even Billy admitted in 1982 that "I'd have a hard time giving you a definition of what it [Evangelicalism] is today." Some Evangelicals took to calling themselves simply "Christians," as if only they could claim that title. What they all had in common, though, was a personal experience. And for that experience they did have a special name: "born again."

Parallel to Graham's rise as America's Pastor, another form of religion emerged, this time from the streets. Like entrepreneurial religion, it, too, appealed to people of all beliefs and none. It, too, challenged listeners to make decisions, to commit themselves, to take action.

Part III

CHAPTER 6

Movement Religion

"We in the Movement"

On March 11, 1970, Coretta Scott King delivered an address to a Methodist seminary eulogizing her martyred husband as "the eminent twentieth-century prophet," and urging continuation of the movement to eradicate "the evils of racism, poverty, materialism, and militarism." The history of Christianity, she observed, "is filled with lay movements which have grown up within the institutional church and then either been forced out into the world or voluntarily moved out into the world to witness more effectively." Her prime exemplar was the Jesus who "preached in the streets, especially to the poor and the slaves." If the institutional church was to "keep the allegiance of the young," she declared, "it will have to rediscover Jesus the radical."[1]

Rereading that address today, one recognizes many of the tropes and even some of the buzzwords associated with what I call "movement religion." By that I mean the forms that religious activism took once the civil rights movement became the new and accepted model for expressing and mobilizing religious conscience and commitment. I also mean the correlative impulse of secular movements to assume the trappings of a religious crusade or quest. In either form, and often in combination, movement religion was directed as much against religious institutions as it was against the secular establishments.

To become part of a movement was to adopt a new group identity—for example, "We in the movement"—that often assumed precedence over all previous identities. Regardless of the cause, movement people all spoke the same idiom. To be in "the movement" was to support "the struggle," to fight for "liberation," to resist "oppression," to "bear witness," to "speak truth to power"—in a word, to be "prophetic." The evil that movements hurled themselves against was never merely personal: it was always "systemic." The military, the government, the university, the church, the bourgeois family—these and other institutions were oppressed because their very structures were corrupt. Movements, on the other hand, created brotherhoods and sisterhoods, purer bonds of human solidarity. Whatever the cause, history and righteousness were aligned with the movement.

If, as the popular slogan had it, the world was to set the church's agenda, there were plenty of causes around which people could and did form movements. Chief among them was the peace (anti–Vietnam War) movement, followed by the women's liberation movement and a whole menu of other movements on behalf of the environment (the first Earth Day was celebrated in 1970), free speech, gay rights, abortion rights, and later, the pro-life movement. Many of these movements are with us yet. But from the late Sixties through the Seventies, not to embrace one movement or another was to be socially disengaged. It was during this period that slogans first appeared on car bumpers (BAN THE BOMB, MAKE LOVE NOT WAR) and that the young, especially, began wearing T-shirts proclaiming their favorite causes as advertisements for themselves. It was about this time that the term *activist* came into regular journalistic use to describe people who otherwise had no noticeable claim to public recognition. Coincidentally, it was also about this time that New Testament scholars began talking about Jesus and his disciples as "the Jesus movement" to distinguish it from other first-century Jewish sects, and from the early Christian church.

For the White House, the FBI, and other keepers of the public order, "the movement" that mattered most was the antiwar movement. It began on college campuses and appeared at first to be an expression of the wider "youth movement" of the Sixties—as much a protest against the military draft as it was against the war itself. Never mind that the vast majority of draftees came, as they do in all wars, from the ranks of the poor, both black and white, whose children did not have the luxury or the deferment of higher education. There were sit-ins and protest demonstrations by hippies and Yippies and anonymous "peaceniks"—street theater—as well as teach-ins by antiwar members of university faculties. Among intellectuals, opposition to the escalation of the war that began in 1965 provided common cause for members of the Marxist-oriented Old Left as well as the Students for a Democratic Society and other factions of the New Left. And in John Lennon's plaintive refrain, "All we are saying is give peace a chance," the antiwar movement had its populist anthem.

It is worth remembering that until large numbers of American soldiers returned home in body bags, the majority of Americans supported their government, or at least gave it the benefit of their doubts. We were a nation divided. When clergy began to mobilize against the war, they not only added a new rationale for opposing what the government was doing; they also brought a new set of standards by which authentic religion was to be judged.

Ecumenism of the Streets

The first broadly based interfaith organization against the war was born on January 11, 1966, in the apartment of Dr. John C. Bennett, president of Union Theological Seminary. The idea for a national organization of clergy came from Rabbi Abraham Joshua Heschel, who was also celebrating his fifty-ninth birthday the same day. Heschel, Jesuit priest Daniel Berrigan, and Lutheran pastor Richard John Neuhaus were named cochairs of what was initially called the National Emergency Committee of Clergy Concerned About Vietnam. The name was later amended to Clergy and Laymen Concerned About Vietnam (CALCAV), though clerics continued to run the show. Heschel, Berrigan, and Neuhaus were veterans of the civil rights movement and among the first clergymen to demonstrate against the war. But to me the most interesting thing about them was that none of the three belonged to any of the historic peace churches. Nor, for that matter, were they in any conventional sense theological liberals.

On the contrary, each of these men had been shaped by very traditional forms of religious orthodoxy and piety. Heschel was a Hasidic Jew, the sixth-generation descendant of Hasidic rabbis stretching back to his namesake, Rabbi Abraham Joshua Heschel of Apt, Ukraine. Berrigan, forty-five, was one of five sons from a pious Depression-era Catholic family: he had joined the Jesuits at age seventeen and was the product of the staid clerical culture that faded after Vatican Council II. Neuhaus, the youngest at age twenty-nine, had followed his father into the ministry of the Missouri Synod Lutheran Church, the least ecumenical and theologically most conservative of the major American Lutheran denominations. In short, each of them was deeply rooted in a religious community that, unlike liberal Protestantism, maintained strong boundaries between the secular and sacred. And yet each found in "the movement" a fellowship deeper than what they experienced among their coreligionists. Like all forms of movement religion, opposition to the Vietnam War dissolved old bonds of belonging even as it created new ones.

Operationally, CALCAV was heavily dependent on liberal Protestant activists who knew how to get things done. Rev. David Hunter, deputy general secretary of the National Council of Churches, gave the organization an office at the council's "God Box," the Interchurch Center near Union Theological Seminary. Presbyterian William Sloane Coffin, chaplain of Yale, came on board as acting executive secretary to help establish a network of 165 local committees in more than thirty states. Robert McAfee Brown contributed his "ministry of the pen," by writing numerous position papers for the group, including a widely distributed "Appeal to Churches and Synagogues" calling for support.

The link between the civil rights and antiwar movements was formally cemented on April 4, 1967, when CALCAV assembled an audience of three thousand at New York's Riverside Church as a platform for Martin Luther King Jr.'s ringing denunciation of the war. In that speech, King went so far as to liken the Joint Chiefs of Staff to the Nazis and called on all Americans to join a "popular crusade" against it. He spoke over the objections of his own lieutenants in the SCLC, who feared his speech would harm the cause of civil rights. And to judge by the reaction, they were right. The Johnson administration, the FBI, and black civil rights leaders condemned him, and so did much of the media. The *Washington Post* charged him with doing "grave injury to those [like the newspaper itself] who are his natural allies" in fighting racial discrimination. The *New York Times* accused him of "whitewashing" the communist regime in Hanoi and warned that linking the "complex problems" of racial injustice and Vietnam "will not lead to solutions but to deeper confusions."[2]

At the outset, CALCAV adopted a moderate approach to Vietnam, calling for a deescalation of American bombing in the North and a settlement negotiated by all parties, including the insurgent Viet Cong. CALCAV's tactics, too, were moderate: teach-ins, prayer vigils, and nonviolent demonstrations rather than acts of civil disobedience. By stressing their moral concerns as men of the cloth, they were able to gain audiences with key government leaders like Secretary of Defense Robert McNamara during the Johnson administration and National Security Advisor Henry Kissinger after Richard Nixon won the White House in 1968. Both men, ironically, epitomized the kind of can-do pragmatism that Harvey Cox (also a key figure in CALCAV) had celebrated as the style of the new secular man. They were unmoved by the clergy's appeal to morality and prophetic witness. Governments seldom are.

By the end of 1967, many of the clergy were ready for more radical forms of "resistance." University-based clerics like Coffin, Brown, and Berrigan felt a pastoral duty to support students who burned their draft cards: Coffin, in fact, participated in a church service in Boston where the collection was of draft cards; afterward, he took a satchel full of them to Washington and delivered it to the Justice Department, an act for which he and other clergy were indicted. If students were willing to go to prison for breaking unjust laws in support of an unjust war, why shouldn't clergy in the movement do the same? Counseling and mobilizing others were not enough. The time had come for clergy and laity to put their own bodies on the line. Within CALCAV, Neuhaus later recalled, there was even a proposal to change the organization's name to "the Church of the Movement"—an absurd idea that he, Heschel, and Berrigan quickly squelched.

Even so, the incident indicates how much the interfaith movement to end the war had developed into a kind of religious sect whose members felt more intimately connected to one another than to their fellow Protestants, Catholics, and Jews. They prayed together, fasted together, witnessed together—at one point, in fact, Coretta King, Heschel, Neuhaus, and Richard McSorley, a Catholic priest, collectively laid their hands on an Episcopal priest to commission him, the way bishops did with missionaries, to look after American military deserters who had fled to Sweden. This was just the sort of new beginning Dietrich Bonhoeffer had hoped for in 1935 when he wrote to his brother Karl-Friedrich: "The restoration of the church must surely depend on a new type of monasticism having nothing in common with the old but an uncompromising adherence to the Sermon on the Mount in the imitation of Christ." This new monasticism, not surprisingly, was especially appealing to antiwar Catholic priests and nuns.[3]

Resistance as Liturgy: The Berrigan Brothers

On Friday afternoon, May 17, 1968, nine Catholics, including two women and two priests, Daniel Berrigan and his brother Philip, seized some four hundred files from a draft board office in Catonsville, Maryland, a Baltimore suburb, and burned them in the parking lot with homemade "napalm" concocted from a recipe in a U.S. Special Forces handbook. Then they stood fast and prayed, waiting to be arrested. Reporters and a television crew, having been alerted, were there to record the raiders' "symbolic action"—what good is a symbolic act if no one else is there to witness it?

But their daring action confused others in the movement. Coffin said the Berrigans were either "God's fools or just damn fools" and only time would reveal which. Outsiders, including the editors of *Newsweek,* found the brothers' new form of protest simply weird. What was the purpose, they wanted to know, and asked me as the resident Catholic to find out. Through a sympathetic jailer I smuggled in a request for an explanation, and back came this reply from Daniel Berrigan:

> I struggled with this for weeks. I had done everything else, including a short stint in jail, fasting, all the tried—and by now untrue—forms of demonstrating. I had a sense, only just under the skin, that I was at the end of something. I had been to Hanoi and seen the charnel house our military had made of a quite beautiful society. Easter Sunday, I visited a boy in Syracuse who immolated himself in front of the cathedral. He later died. And then there was Martin Luther King's murder. Suddenly, I saw my sweet skin was hiding out behind others marching and resisting and disappearing into kangaroo courts and jails. I was in danger, as good liberals began to nod assent to my noble sentiments, of hooking onto their gravy train. I had to risk my skin to save my soul.[4]

It was Philip Berrigan, a former combat officer in World War II, who convinced his older brother Daniel to join in the Catonsville caper. Seven months earlier, Phil and three others ("the Baltimore Four") had poured blood—a metaphorical conflation of Christ's sacrifice on the cross and the lives sacrificed in the war—on draft files in the first symbolic act of resistance. For that Phil already faced a term in prison. Catonsville was the Berrigan brothers' signal to CALCAV that they were upping the ante for clerical war resisters—and going it alone. From here on in, their public acts of resistance would draw on elements of Catholic liturgy and the specifically Catholic notion of priests as "second Christs" who preside over "the holy sacrifice of the Mass." By personally presiding over the destruction of draft board files, thereby subjecting themselves to prison terms, they hoped to dramatize the connections they saw between resistance to the war and the imitation of Christ's redemptive passion.

The Berrigans' Catholicizing of resistance also contained elements of personal resentment. Phil Berrigan resented the failure of his religious order, the Josephites, to support his civil rights and antiwar activities. Daniel Berrigan felt the Jesuits had lost the life-risking courage that had fired up earlier Jesuit martyrs and missionaries. Both resented the hyperpatriotism of Cardinal Spellman, who enthusiastically endorsed every war his country fought. Both saw the antiwar movement as God's own opportunity to cleanse the temple of Catholic institutions of their unholy deference to a militaristic state.

Catonsville signaled the emergence of "the Catholic Left," a loose network composed mostly of antiwar clergy, nuns, and seminarians, plus laymen and -women associated with Dorothy Day's Catholic Worker Movement and other pacifist groups. Eventually, small knots of them would stage more than a hundred raids, adopting names like the Milwaukee Fourteen and the Boston Five, monikers that suggested outlaw derring-do reminiscent of Jesse James and the Dalton Gang. Most were pacifists of recent vintage. But in listening to their bellicose rhetoric I got the sense that they were as angry at their own bishops' silence on the war as they were at the government for conducting it. Some regarded themselves as members of an "underground church" in which experimental liturgies and resistance to the war were the identifying characteristics. Daniel Berrigan, for one, had already decided to say Mass only for groups of like-minded co-conspirators and never in a church building if he could avoid it.

The recruitment of Daniel Berrigan to "the Catholic resistance," as members of the Catholic Left preferred to think of themselves, ensured that the trial of the Catonsville Nine would not go unnoticed. He was a gifted poet, one of the few the Jesuits could boast of since the death of Gerard Manley Hopkins nearly a century earlier. Dan envisioned the trial as a piece of live theater in which the defendants could make their moral case against the war. The flamboyant William Kunstler offered his services as attorney for the defense, and in Roszel Thomsen the defendants would find a federal judge who allowed them ample time for lengthy moral and religious argument.

The Berrigans and their supporters sent out invitations to war resisters to join them in Baltimore for the event. About two thousand showed up, most of them Catholic clergy and nuns who saw in the Berrigans heralds of a new and socially responsive church. At a rally on the eve of the trial, they crammed into the vast basement of St. Ignatius Church, the city's largest, to hear from several icons of the antiwar movement. Among them were Dorothy Day, Pastor Neuhaus, Rabbi Heschel, and Bishop Pike, who (not for the first time) called attention to himself by daring the FBI sentries in the back of the hall to arrest him there and then for inciting and abetting young men to resist the war. Secular lefties like Noam Chomsky, Rennie Davis, and Howard Zinn also lectured the crowd, and letters of support were read from Coretta Scott King, Ralph Abernathy, Benjamin Spock, Tom Hayden, and David Dellinger. It was barely six weeks since the riotous Democratic National Convention in Chicago, and the Baltimore police were put on alert in case of a similar outbreak of disorder.

The trial lasted four days. Throughout, Dan Berrigan took copious notes and with the official transcripts in short order fashioned *The Trial of the Catonsville Nine,* a play that eventually ran for twenty-nine days on Broadway and became a staple of university repertories. At the trial itself, the defendants were found guilty and sentenced for up to three and a half years in federal prison. Kunstler appealed. When that failed, five of the defendants, the brothers Berrigan conspicuously among them, decided to "go underground" as "fugitives from injustice" rather than go straight to prison.

The Berrigan brothers were immediately posted on the FBI's Ten Most Wanted list and the search began. Daniel Patrick Moynihan once quipped that the FBI was full of Fordham graduates chasing Ivy League graduates in the State Department. Chasing priests was a new experience for Catholics in the bureau, and FBI chief J. Edgar Hoover was especially keen on unmasking the Catholic resistance as a group of traitors to the church as well as the country. Within two weeks, word was sent to *Newsweek* and other news organizations that Philip Berrigan and another of the Catonsville Nine would surrender to the FBI in New York City after an antiwar rally at a Catholic church whose pastor, Father Harry Browne, I knew well. Two FBI men arrested them in Browne's rectory before the rally could take place. Father Browne, who had a longshoreman's way with words, mocked Hoover and his agents—a big mistake.

Hoover let it be known that in his hunt for the Berrigans, he had discovered that Father Browne was leading a double life: besides pastoring a church, running a co-op for low-income families, and teaching college history courses, he also had a wife and three children in New Jersey. How Harry found time for a family stumped everyone who knew him, but the revelation, as Hoover hoped, cast a lurid light on the Catholic underground.

Dan Berrigan eluded the FBI for another four months, relying on a network of sympathizers to harbor him. Many of them, it should be said, were liberals of the kind he and his brother scorned. But as Dan saw it, this was their chance to share in his radical resistance. Berrigan played catch-me-if-you-can with the FBI, surfacing from time to time in his signature black turtleneck sweater and black beret to speak at antiwar rallies and to give interviews with the media—including a filming for a television documentary, *Holy Outlaw.* Then he would slip away, sometimes donning disguises. And so his outlaw image grew: the prophet as inspired imp.

In his time on the lam, Berrigan the writer was extremely productive. *The Trial of the Catonsville Nine* opened in Los Angeles. He also wrote poems and essays; began one book, *The Dark Night of Resistance,* about his feelings of loneliness and separation from God; and worked on another, *The Geography of Faith,* with writer-psychiatrist Robert Coles, who concealed him for a time in his Concord, Massachusetts, home. In August 1970, Hoover's agents, posing as birders, captured Berrigan on Block Island, Rhode Island, at the summer cottage of two other writer friends, Episcopalians William Stringfellow and Anthony Towne, authors of a pair of admiring biographies of Bishop Pike. The picture of a grinning Dan, his manacled hands flashing the peace sign between two stone-faced FBI agents doing their duty, provided yet another iconic image of movement religion.

But Hoover would not be mocked. While Dan was locked up in the federal prison in Danbury, Connecticut, for two years, Philip was serving an even longer sentence in Lewisburg, Pennsylvania. Through a paid informer inside the movement, the FBI acquired letters between Phil and Sister Liz McAlister, one of the Baltimore Eight, in which she discussed a zany scheme to blow up the steam tunnels under the Pentagon and to make a citizen's arrest of Henry Kissinger. The sensational allegations spurred *Time* to put the Brothers Berrigan on its cover. The ensuing trial of the Harrisburg Seven, as they were called, ended in a hung jury. What the letters also showed, however, was that Liz and Phil had become lovers—had, in fact, "married" in a private exchange of vows in an abandoned Episcopal church in 1969. Earlier, Phil had trumpeted the value of monastic celibacy over marriage for those committed to a radical lifestyle, but now he saw celibacy as just another rule imposed by a clerical bureaucracy. In 1972, the couple renewed their vows in Danbury prison with brother Daniel and another radical nun as witnesses, but there would be no effort to legitimate their marriage with the church.

In those days, I routinely met movement priests and nuns who fell in love: shared risks often ignited shared passions other than the spiritual kind. But there was something about Phil and Liz's marriage that particularly offended others who identified with the Catholic Left. The Berrigans and their circle were notoriously critical of lesser mortals who were unwilling to join them in their acts of resistance. They lived by higher moral standards and were quick to judge anyone who didn't share them. But the marriage of Phil and Liz—and brother Dan's celebration of it—demonstrated what could happen when prophets decide which rules do not apply to them.

After the Berrigans' break with CALCAV, their circle contracted into a prophetic brotherhood of co-resisters surrounded by acolytes. Besides Dorothy Day, one of the few Catholic figures Daniel Berrigan looked to for direction was fellow poet and pacifist Thomas Merton, the famed Trappist monk. Merton warned the brothers that symbolic actions do not change minds and he was right. In 1971, when the withdrawal of U.S. troops from Vietnam was already in sight, *Newsweek* published an extensive survey of American Catholics, which found that two-thirds opposed Berrigan-style raids on draft boards as "irresponsible." Both Berrigans were still in prison at the time and disposed, in any case, to believe that prophets are not honored by their own people. But the survey also showed that despite the rapt attention of the news media, 62 percent of Catholics did not even know who the Berrigans were. You had to wonder about the effectiveness of symbolic resistance when even Catholics didn't get it.

At the time, my own views on the Berrigans were powerfully mixed. Although I did not share their apocalyptic outlook or their pacifism, I was challenged by the way they took the Bible's emphasis on peacemaking seriously. Most Catholics were just beginning to read the Bible with fresh and curious eyes—and apart from the comforting interpretations of Sunday sermonizers. The writings of Daniel Berrigan were particularly potent in their penetration of the Hebrew prophets, whose idiom he made his own. I admired the Berrigans the way I admired Dorothy Day. The big difference was that never in my conversations with Dorothy did she insist, as the Berrigans did, that hers was the only way to witness to one's faith. One could be "moved" by the Berrigans without joining "the Movement." Certainly their witness influenced the U.S. Catholic bishops' 1983 pastoral letter on war and peace, which definitively ended the Spellman era of automatic hierarchical support for American militarism. But for the Berrigans and the rest of the Catholic Left, it was not enough that the Catholic Church made room for war resisters. They wanted the entire church to embrace pacifism—in effect, to transform the largest Christian body in the world into a peace church like the Mennonites.

So it was with mixed emotions that I agreed to write a review for the *New York Times* Sunday Book Review of Dan's 1982 auto-biography, *To Dwell in Peace*. By then the fires of the Vietnam era had cooled. No longer a celebrity priest, Daniel Berrigan was working with prisoners and with indigent, terminally ill cancer patients whose bedpans he volunteered to empty. I was hoping to find a tranquil retrospective on his life in the movement. What he delivered was, for the most part, a rant against his overbearing father, the intellectual poverty of his Depression-era teachers, and the "midrash of minutiae" imposed by his Jesuit superiors. "There is," I felt compelled to write, "little that is peaceful—or gracious—in this longer view of his life." I had expected to find words of gratitude, but there were few: it was still Dan and Phil against the world, prisoners of conscience with the lingering feeling of being exiles in their own country. "Alas," he wrote in a passage that was all too typical, ". . . I must often travel amid affluent parasites, whose clothing and credit cards and briefcases and vocabulary of money and comfort and security—all are a converging sign, in the biblical sense, of a dying fall."[5] Alas, the Berrigans never learned how to laugh at human folly, including their own.

Philip Berrigan continued to mount blood-spilling raids against U.S. military installations as a member of the Plowshares movement. His autobiography, published in 1993, was full of bombast against the "crypto-fascist" U.S. government and bloated by prophetic self-righteousness. As both the Berrigans practiced it, prophetic religion eschewed mere politics as inherently corrupt and corrupting. They preferred a purer ethic of expectant futility. Yet it was politics as much as domestic protest that eventually brought an end to the war in Vietnam, and it was through negotiations like the SALT treaties that diplomats eventually curbed the threat of what Dan apotheosized as "Lord Nuke." The Berrigans could not acknowledge that, any more than they could acknowledge a role for religion beyond the prophetic gesture.

Like the civil rights movement, then, the antiwar movement had emerged out of the social unrest of the Sixties. Its bywords were freedom, peace, and justice; its basic methods were public protest and civil disobedience. But the Sixties also saw the rise of a robust conservative movement. Its bywords—personal liberty, economic freedom, and the rightly ordered society—were equally compelling to those Americans who feared the social fabric was unraveling. Movement conservatives also appealed to religion—not for its prophetic power, which they distrusted, but for its equally important functions of providing institutional stability and the structures for passing on traditions that encouraged both personal morality and social restraint. In the career of our second major figure from the antiwar era, however, conversion to conservatism inspired a form of movement religion aimed at reforming both society and the church.

The Pilgrimage of Richard Neuhaus

When Father Richard John Neuhaus died in June 2009, upwards of a thousand friends and admirers turned out for his funeral mass at Immaculate Conception Catholic Church on East Fourteenth Street in Manhattan. It was the church where Neuhaus served as an associate pastor in the last two decades of his life, and where my wife and I used to attend Mass when we stayed weekends at an apartment we rented in nearby Stuyvesant Town. The eulogists remembered Richard as a warm friend and generous mentor, a Catholic intellectual, a close friend of popes, and a writer and editor of conservative theological and political convictions. I was one of perhaps a dozen people in the congregation that morning who knew Richard in his antiwar days, when he was an idiosyncratic Lutheran pastor and self-proclaimed religious radical. His transformation from movement activist in the Sixties to Catholic advisor to President George W. Bush at the century's end illustrates the protean character of movement religion: it could be enlisted for conservative as well as liberal causes.

The conservative movement that brought Ronald Reagan to the White House in 1980 arose improbably out of the Goldwater debacle in 1964 and was associated most prominently with its chief publicist, William F. Buckley Jr., and his colleagues at *The National*

Review. The magazine's editors and writers included a number of former communists turned anticommunists, like Whittaker Chambers, Frank Meyer, Willmoore Kendall, and Will Herberg. Their concerns were primarily political and economic. The religious element in the conservative movement came from the staff's coterie of Catholic laymen—intellectuals like Thomas Molnar and John Lukacs, plus Buckley's brother-in-law L. Brent Bozell and of course Buckley himself. These were personally pious men who valued Catholicism for its antimodernism as well as for its anticommunism. But they did not trust—and felt no need to heed—the church's magisterium when it waxed liberal on social and political issues. That was the laity's specific competence and provenance. Significantly, Neuhaus would serve as the magazine's religion writer during his passage from left to right in the mid-Seventies. He was, as I recall, the *Review*'s only clergyman.

Unlike Rabbi Heschel and Daniel Berrigan, Richard Neuhaus was trained from high school on to minister to a congregation, like his father had before him. His education took place within the parochial school system of the Lutheran Church–Missouri Synod before that denomination became so hidebound that its leaders refused to pray with other Lutherans, never mind Roman Catholics. Richard, though, was an independent-thinking, occasionally rebellious student. In seminary he became a disciple of church historian Arthur Carl Piepkorn, who taught that Lutheranism was from its inception a reform movement within the one, holy catholic and apostolic church—that Martin Luther never intended the movement that bore his name to take a separate institutional form. Theologically, therefore, Richard was something of an anomaly in the movement religion of the Sixties: a theological conservative yet ecumenical Protestant.

Neuhaus was only twenty-five and barely out of seminary when he became pastor of a poor and mostly black Lutheran church in the Williamsburg section of Brooklyn. Soon after his arrival, he took to the streets to demonstrate for better public schools. A few years later he ran unsuccessfully for Congress as a liberal Democrat. A marcher at Selma, he was close enough to Martin Luther King Jr. to call him "Martin," though not as close as black associates like Jesse Jackson, who called him "Doc."

In those early days I knew Richard only as a deep, stentorian voice on the other end of the phone. After a year of conversing this way we finally arranged to meet at a welcome-home party for two Catholic pacifists who had served a term in prison for refusing the draft. The gathering was organized by writer Francine du Plessix Gray, who had been profiling the Berrigans and other icons of the Catholic Left for *The New Yorker,* and took place at her stepfather's elegant apartment on Manhattan's Upper East Side. I immediately identified Richard by his voice, which seemed almost too commanding for a man so slight of build. While other guests laughed and joshed, he held forth in argument with a circle of friendly critics. Even at parties, Richard never enjoyed small talk. I joined those arguing against him and left without identifying myself. The next day he called asking why I hadn't shown up. Richard and I remained friends for decades, but because of his intensity, his contentiousness, and his tendency to preach, I always found our relationship easier to maintain over the phone than in person. Perhaps that's why I always assumed he was much older than me, though in fact he was a year younger, and why he always supposed I was a child of the Sixties rather than the Fifties.

Neuhaus remained active in CALCAV long after the Berrigans had renounced the organization as too timid. Richard, though, was never timid: at the 1968 Democratic convention, which he attended as a delegate pledged to Eugene McCarthy, he got himself jailed for leading a protest march with Dick Gregory after the peace plank they supported was rejected. Six weeks later, in a speech at the pretrial rally for the Catonsville Nine, Richard was full of rage, the veins in his neck pulsing visibly above his tight white clerical collar, as he accused the government of murder, betrayal, and "selling out the American dream of liberty for the mailed fist of repression." Like the Berrigans, Neuhaus evidenced considerable violence in his rhetoric of nonviolent resistance, like a man who tries to kill with words because he doesn't believe in guns. But he never was a pacifist and never quite reconciled his predilection for prophetic religion with his penchant for party politics.

As late as 1970, Neuhaus could and did defend the proposition that social conditions in the United States were so unjust that if they did not fast improve, a violent revolution might be morally justified. The next year, however, he gradually withdrew from day-to-day involvement with the organization, and eventually came to oppose it. In his view, CALCAV had become stridently anti-American, naive about the virtues of Ho Chi Minh's revolutionaries, and much too accepting of the youthful counterculture's anti-institutionalism.

By 1974, the Vietnamization of the war was in full swing and the withdrawal of the last U.S. troops from Saigon was just a year away. Without the galvanizing force of the war, CALCAV lost its vivifying focus. Richard's formal break with the movement came in January 1975, when he and his close friend, sociologist Peter Berger, released the "Hartford Declaration," also known as "An Appeal for Theological Affirmation," which was signed by an ecumenical group of eighteen theologians, including (to everyone's surprise) William Sloane Coffin. In essence, the declaration was a robust repudiation of the Sixties notion that the church should let the world set its agenda. To the contrary, the signers asserted the transcendence of religion in relation to any secular ideologies or causes that channeled or constrained it: "We did not invent God," the declaration asserted. "God invented us."

The Hartford Declaration represented a movement away from liberal movement religion—that is, from the idea that the only way for religion to impact society was to mobilize the faithful in support of secular political and social causes. I also read the declaration as a recoiling from the sexual and other forms of antinomianism of the Sixties counterculture. Yes, institutions can be oppressive, the signers acknowledged, "[b]ut human community requires institutions and traditions. Without them life would degenerate into chaos and new forms of bondage."

For Neuhaus, especially, the Hartford Declaration was the signal that he, at least, was moving on. The Vietnam War had called for radical action, he insisted, "but we are concerned with reexamining some of the excesses and mistakes of the movement." In this reexamination, Peter Berger's influence on Neuhaus was immense. Of the two, Berger was the more consistent thinker. As a sociologist, Berger helped Neuhaus see the unintended consequences of movement religion, especially (in Richard's case) its weakness for "revolutionary" solutions to complex social and political issues. He taught Richard to recognize a democratic society's need for a rich assortment of "mediating structures"—that is, communal institutions such as family, church, and voluntary civic organizations standing between the individual and the state. He also strengthened Richard's growing suspicion that liberal Protestantism's fatal flaw was that it spoke with rather unwarranted confidence about social issues and with too little clarity about God.

But the event that finally spun Neuhaus out of the liberal orbit was *Roe v. Wade,* the U.S. Supreme Court's 1973 decision that found in the constitutional "right to privacy" a legal right to abortion for any reason and at any point in fetal gestation. For him—as for me—*Roe* represented the utter repudiation of liberal values, not to mention the fundamental right to life. For me—as for him—the protection of the unborn was the new civil rights movement. When Richard declared, as he often did, that "I did not leave the Democratic Party, it left me," he primarily meant the party's rapid embrace of abortion on demand paid with federal funds. Again, when he wrote his most famous book, *The Naked Public Square* (1984), the energizing example for his central argument—that the secularization of public life and institutions excluded religious rationales and voices from public discourse—was the abortion issue. Like Christopher Dawson, Richard understood politics to be rooted in culture, and the center of culture was "cult"—that is, religion.

In short, Richard's embrace of conservative politics was never merely political. His personal migration rightward was evidence of a much broader religious realignment that Princeton sociologist Robert Wuthnow adumbrated in his seminal book, *The Restructuring of American Religion* (1988). There, Wuthnow redrew the map of American religion by demonstrating in nuanced and copious detail what is now taken for granted—that the boundaries separating religious Americans had ceased to follow denominational lines but ran right through them. On issues of public morality like abortion, homosexuality, and their relationship to government policy, conservative Catholics, Protestants, and Jews had more in common with one another than with religious liberals of the same persuasion. Richard was witness to this change. Three years later, in another book that made a deep impression on Neuhaus, *Culture Wars: The Struggle to Define America,* sociologist James Davison Hunter broadened the division Wuthnow had described. The great polarity in American religion, he argued, was between "orthodox" believers who appealed to an external, definable, and transcendent authority and "progressives" who tended to "resymbolize the contents of historic faith according to the prevailing assumptions of contemporary life." Although Hunter emphasized that most religious Americans huddled in the middle between these polarities, conservative cultural warriors—among them Richard in his most contentious moments—seized on Hunter's categories by adorning themselves with the "orthodox" mantle. It was the theological trimmers versus the true believers.

On the road from radical to liberal to political "neoconservative," Neuhaus was accompanied by a number of other former liberals, notably the Catholic Michael Novak and the Jewish Norman Podhoretz, the longtime editor of *Commentary.* Together the trio enjoyed considerable intellectual influence in Washington during the two Reagan administrations. Even so, Michael frequently fretted over lost friendships with former liberal Catholics like the editors of *Commonweal* magazine, and Norman, whose stepdaughter Rachel was my devoted assistant at *Newsweek,* often complained to me that his views had made him anathema among his (former) Jewish friends on the literary left. Novak, who once identified himself as a democratic socialist, abandoned teaching for the American Enterprise Institute, where he labored to show that Catholic social teaching was compatible with what he now celebrated as democratic capitalism. Podhoretz, who had been a cold war liberal in the mold of his Democrat friends Daniel Patrick Moynihan and Senator Henry "Scoop" Jackson, worked vigorously to convince American Jews that Republicans were their natural allies, especially in defense of Israel against its enemies in the Middle East.

Neuhaus, however, moved on with barely a blink or backward glance. What he brought with him besides his considerable skills as a writer, speaker, and organizer were an agenda, a self-assurance bordering at times on arrogance, plus a latent talent to attract financial support from foundations on the right. His most consequential move, however, was spiritual rather than political.

Long before his formal conversion, Neuhaus embraced the Catholic Church. It was, he came to believe, the one religious institution in American life that was intellectually prepared and organizationally equipped to counter the nakedness of the nation's public square. When the feisty, fiercely pro-life John J. O'Connor was appointed Catholic archbishop of New York in 1984, Richard took him literally in hand, introducing him to his widening network of conservative opinion leaders. O'Connor, in turn, not only sought Richard's counsel, but also provided him entrée to the Vatican's highest circles. For a Lutheran, Neuhaus felt surprisingly at home among the baroque splendors and labyrinthine ways of Europe's last Renaissance court. And for good reason. He had what only the loftiest members of the Roman Curia enjoyed: access. On visits to Rome, Neuhaus dined with Pope John Paul II, who recognized in this American Protestant cleric eager assent to his own efforts to purge the postconciliar church of liberal theological tendencies. In turn, Richard found the pope a powerful champion of his own convictions about the corrupting influence of secularism within the Catholic Church as well as in public life. Just as President Reagan had proclaimed a new "Morning in America," Richard proclaimed the pontificate of the Polish pope a "new Advent" for the church.

In 1987, when still a Lutheran, Richard published *The Catholic Moment,* and he called me to say he thought it arresting enough to merit the cover of *Newsweek.* His contention was that the Catholic

Church in the United States was uniquely endowed to replace the old liberal Protestant Establishment by assuming "its rightful role in the culture-forming task of constructing a religiously informed public philosophy for the American experiment in ordered liberty."[6] His timing was awful: already there was mounting evidence that the Catholic Church in the United States (and eventually in other countries as well) was about to face the worst scandal in its history with the revelations of juvenile sex abuse by priests and cover-ups by cardinals and bishops. But as a manifesto, *The Catholic Moment* proffered a concise statement of Richard's own career-defining project: the construction of a religiously informed public philosophy with an emphasis on "ordered liberty." To that end, the former movement activist, his hour come round at last, would rally a movement of his own.

In 1990, Richard Neuhaus was formally received into the Catholic Church by Cardinal O'Connor, with Jesuit theologian Avery Dulles, his friend and fellow convert, as his sponsor. A lifelong celibate, Richard was quickly ordained in the Catholic priesthood, but his mission was of his own making. A year earlier, he had founded the Institute on Religion and Public Life and launched a new monthly magazine, *First Things*, with himself as editor in chief. Thanks to backing from conservative foundations like the Bradley Foundation, he now had the financial wherewithal to invite intellectuals of his choosing to seminars on topics of his choice and to entertain them in high fashion at white-glove redoubts like Manhattan's Union League Club. On a few occasions he invited me to join in. The institute was his salon, as much as William F. Buckley Jr.'s Manhattan home was his. But only Richard could promise seminars with guests like Cardinal Joseph Ratzinger, a future pope. This was Richard as I had first met him, presiding as a conductor of robust dialogues, but ever confident that the truth as he had come to see it would eventually prevail.

Richard's main platform was his monthly magazine, *First Things*, patterned after *Commentary* but very much a vehicle for advancing his own intellectual agenda. Through it he fashioned a new and varied constituency of conservative readers and contributors for whom religion was central to their thinking. From the first issue, Richard shrewdly opened the magazine's pages to congenial Jewish, Mormon, and—in much larger numbers—Evangelical Protestant intellectuals, thereby expanding both his circulation and his sphere of influence beyond a merely Catholic audience. An ecumenist of the right, he figured that every religious tradition that put God first (hence his magazine's title) was worth engaging in the war against the secularization of public life and discourse.

Even so, Neuhaus never tired of insisting that "the Catholic Church is the Church of Jesus Christ most fully and rightly ordered through time."[7] Central to that "right order" was the papal magisterium, which he defended with all the zeal of a recent convert. If the Catholic Church was to tutor the nation in rightly ordered liberty, it must first have rightly ordered Catholics. Here again, Neuhaus assumed the role of movement protagonist by promoting a return to orthodoxy within the Catholic Church. For Richard, orthodoxy was not only what the church had always and everywhere taught, the classic definition. On a daily basis it was always and everywhere what a sitting pope taught. When a pope did take stands with which he disagreed—especially on wars that Neuhaus supported—Richard was silent. Unlike liberal Catholic publications, there would be no criticism of papal teaching in the pages of *First Things*.

Richard's regular contribution to each issue was "The Public Square"—never less than twelve thousand words of observations and barbed commentary based on his own prodigious reading. Reading his longer and most considered pieces, I agreed with him as often as not. Unfortunately, Richard also used his platform to conduct a ritual hazing of liberal Catholics and Protestants. His sarcasm was imitative of Buckley's, but without the latter's leavening wit and charm. Cradle Catholics like myself found him presumptuous for so recent a convert. As in his radical days, Richard needed people to oppose as much as he needed people to convince.

In sum, Richard Neuhaus did not abandon movement religion so much as reconceive and redirect its energies toward conservative ends—especially the protection of the unborn. The pro-life cause was always the engine that drove his political and social agendas. At his passing, he was inordinately hailed by friends as a great theologian and public intellectual: Michael Novak, for example, pronounced him "the most consequential Christian intellectual in America since Reinhold Niebuhr." A more modest, and I think more accurate, assessment would recognize him as a gifted Christian polemicist and Catholic publicist whose life and work most nearly resembled that of Orestes Brownson, the most articulate Catholic publicist of nineteenth-century America. Both were converts who created their own constituencies. Both believed, as Brownson put it, that "Catholics are better fitted by their religion to comprehend the real character of the American Constitution than any other class of Americans, the moment they study their own theology." But in his final book, published just after he died, Neuhaus also confessed that he—much like Daniel Berrigan—felt like an exile in his own land. In this life, it seems, radicals get no satisfaction.

If any of "the movement's" major religious figures had a right to feel exiled, it was the rabbi whom both Neuhaus and Berrigan looked to for prophetic inspiration. Yet because of his profound spirituality, he struck me as a man who was always "at home" even under the most trying circumstances. That's why Rabbi Abraham Joshua Heschel was the religious figure who made the most lasting impression on me.

Heschel: "Let Me Tell You a Story"

One of the great anomalies of movement religion was the emergence of Abraham Joshua Heschel as the Jewish figure most readily identified with the civil rights and antiwar causes. Heschel was leader of no religious or communal organization. He had no congregation to support him, edited no publication to trumpet his views. Even within New York's Jewish Theological Seminary he was for most of his tenure more tolerated than respected by rivals on the faculty. All he had was his immense learning, his passionate convictions, his magnificent books, and—above all—the power of his presence and of his words.

To be sure, many Jews were deeply involved in the civil rights and antiwar movements. But most of them were either secular Jews active in New Left groups like Students for a Democratic Society or organizational rabbis associated with Reform Judaism, which on social and political issues typically mirrored the positions of the National Council of Churches. Heschel, though, was an old-world rabbi from Poland, a survivor of a prewar Hasidic community that the Nazis had extinguished. On the front lines at Selma, or at antiwar mobilizations, there was no mistaking the Jewishness of the short man with the patriarchal beard and the black yarmulke pinned to his head of luxuriant white hair. And that, for many American Jews, was the problem. Despite its usual liberal profile, the Jewish community was as divided on the war as other Americans. But a great many of them on both sides worried whenever any Jew played too prominent a role in any radical movement: it was, they feared, a sure incitement to anti-Semites. Worse, it might mitigate U.S. military support for embattled Israel. More than one Israeli official pressured Heschel to desist.

Heschel was accustomed to taking risks. During Vatican Council II, he went to Rome to impress upon Pope Paul VI the importance of passing a strong declaration recognizing the enduring validity of the Jewish faith and absolving Jews of the ancient Christian charge of deicide. He did so despite the criticism from fellow Jews, especially Orthodox rabbis, who thought it beneath the dignity of any rabbi to ask anything of a church that had for centuries persecuted his people.

Heschel's self-assuredness was both inbred and acquired. Within the Hasidic community of Warsaw, where he was born, his family was recognized as spiritual nobility. Even when he was a child, adults acknowledged his genius by rising from their seats whenever he entered the room. He was reared to be a rebbe as his forebears had been in a lineage that went back to the founders of the Hasidic movement in the eighteenth century. Instead, Heschel left Warsaw at the age of eighteen for higher Jewish and secular studies in Vilna, Lithuania, and eventually took a doctorate in philosophy at the University of Berlin with a dissertation on the Hebrew prophets. For a time he taught at Martin Buber's school of Jewish studies in Frankfurt; he composed poetry in Yiddish and by the age of thirty had written in masterful German a monumental interpretation of the medieval philosopher Moses Maimonides. In 1939, he escaped to the United States just six weeks before Hitler's army invaded Poland. His mother and three sisters along with other relatives eventually perished in the Holocaust. So did the intensely spiritual world of East European Jewry that was his imperishable inheritance. Heschel, the survivor, bore the embers of that world within him. They provided, in the words of an old Hasidic tale, "the fire he could light."

Even in America, Heschel remained something of an exile. He was an Orthodox rabbi who taught non-Orthodox students, a Hasid outside New York's inbred Hasidic clans, a Jewish activist whose closest movement comrades were Christians like the Berrigans, Neuhaus, Coffin, and John C. Bennett. Like them, Heschel opposed the war for what it was doing to his adopted country as well as to the people of Vietnam. He had also come to see the necessity of Christians and Jews making common moral witness. For Heschel, of course, working for justice and peace was rooted in the Hebrew prophets. But I also think he saw in the movement religion of the Sixties an opportunity to demonstrate, for Christians and Jews alike, the enduring moral challenge and validity of the Hebrew Bible.

To clergy in the movement, Heschel was the embodiment of prophetic religion. His passionate utterance readily moved the already convicted, but in meetings with government representatives he was sometimes too excitable to be effective. In any case, I was not much interested in what made Rabbi Heschel a movement activist. Like so many others who met him, I wanted to know what made Heschel Heschel.

I myself had just turned thirty when I first encountered Rabbi Heschel in the fall of 1965. He was finishing a stint as the first Jewish scholar invited to teach a course at Union Theological Seminary. By then his theology was more influential in Christian than in Jewish circles. On that occasion I wrote a one-page profile of him for *Newsweek*. Afterward he invited me to visit him whenever I wished. And for the last eight years of his life that is what I did.

Within the warren of faculty offices at Jewish Theological Seminary, Heschel's was the smallest—windowless like the restroom down the hall and not nearly as roomy. Tilting mounds of books rose up like stalagmites from his desk and teetered precariously from the bowed shelves above his head, threatening at any moment to bury him under the texts he so much loved. Although he never mentioned it to me, his cramped quarters were indicative of the rude treatment he experienced at the seminary. He was not permitted to sit in the front row of the synagogue for services, was only rarely asked to give a blessing (*aliyah*) over the Torah reading, and in his twenty-seven years at the seminary he was never asked to deliver a sermon, an honor even students were accorded. Why? Because his Hasidic theology and piety contradicted the post-Enlightenment Judaism of the seminary.

Our conversations always began with a topic of my choosing and his reply invariably began in the same Hasidic fashion: "My friend, let me tell you a story."

Heschel preferred stories because like poetry and parables they provided the insight and inner meanings (*aggadah*) to what the law (*halakhah*) commanded. It was the difference, he wanted me to know, between the letter and the spirit, deed and intention, manner and mystery, reasoning and wonder, the contents of belief and the experience of faith. If his stories amazed, that was the point: "radical amazement," he insisted, was the necessary precondition for those who would know God.

Heschel became my mentor in matters Jewish, but only incidentally. In his books, as in his conversation, his great themes were God's concern for humankind and how we who are made in His image should respond. He refused to separate talk *about* God (theology) from talking *to* God (prayer)—a position that ran counter to the modus operandi at his own seminary. Heschel loathed the tendency of academics to treat religion as "a patient, etherized upon a table" that experts could then dissect with the tools of sociology, psychology, philology, and philosophy. And he was driven to near despair by the Judaism he heard preached in American synagogues and taught in Hebrew day schools. "We are like a messenger who forgot the message. We teach our people either the law or the liturgy," he complained one afternoon. "But we don't teach them that Judaism has an inner dimension. We don't teach them how to pray." As for the American rabbinate, he had this to say: "Too often their sermons deal with the latest survey of Jews or the latest turn of events in Vietnam. We have forgotten that Judaism is a way of thinking as well as a way of doing." This comment was the first of many signals that Heschel was committed to "the movement" but not consumed by movement religion.

Heschel was no less concerned by what he heard from contemporary Catholic theologians, and felt no less free in criticizing them. During a four-day conference at Notre Dame, I watched him in the second row as he listened to lectures by Karl Rahner, Hans Küng, and other luminaries of Vatican Council II. Invited to respond, he rose from his seat and said: "With all respect, your people are asking for bread, and you are giving them stones."

I had heard him say that more than once and this is what he meant: your theology is too abstract, too dispassionate, too redolent of the academy to bring anyone closer to the living God. On another occasion, Heschel reminded me that before the rise of the medieval universities and theology becoming a sacred "science," Christian theology was created by prayerful monks meditating on the Scriptures. More from the Bible, less from Greek philosophy— more of Jerusalem, less of Athens is the way he put it—was what he hoped to find in the Catholics' theological renewal. God was not Aristotle's unmoved mover, he liked to say, but the Hebrew Bible's "most moved mover." Indeed, this "divine pathos," as he called it— the intuition that God is in search of us, even has a need of us—was the controlling insight of Heschel's immense theological enterprise.

It was also the dynamic center of his own prayer life. Listening to Heschel gave the lie to the Christian conceit that only in the New Testament do we find a God of love and compassion.

Despite the thirty-year difference in our ages, what drew me to Heschel, and perhaps him to me, was the understanding we shared of religion as hallowing the everyday. "We Jews have no holy places, no holy monuments," he insisted, "only holy time." His God was the Lord of history who reveals Himself at key moments in time. Jews, he wanted me to know, are called to "sanctify time," through daily prayer, observance of the Sabbath, and prophetic witness. This idea was not altogether different from the parting classroom charge from my first mentor, Frank O'Malley, to "redeem the times"—itself a line from another Jew, the Apostle Paul. Simply put, Heschel understood that our lives are lived in the presence of God. It was an awareness he had absorbed from the religiously patterned communal life in the old Warsaw Ghetto. Growing up Catholic had given me a similar though far less acute awareness of time's religious architecture through the liturgical cycles of the seasons. But the religious cultures that had formed us, him as a Jew, me as a Catholic, were now vestigial: his already gone, mine beginning to evaporate before my eyes. That, too, was something we shared.

The Israelis' victory in the Six-Day War in June 1967 had a profound impact on Heschel, as it did on Jews everywhere. For the first time he could visit the Old City, which he did for a month the following July, and place his hands on the Wailing Wall of the old Temple Mount. On his return he wrote a rapturous book, *Israel: An Echo of Eternity,* which celebrated the "resurrection of the land of the Bible; a land that was dead for nearly two thousand years is now a land that sings." "So Jews have holy places after all," I needled him during a visit. "No," he said. "The land is holy because of the history of what God did there. The prophets made it holy, and now it is up to Jews to again sanctify the land by returning there and securing a just peace between Israel and the Palestinians." That was hope speaking. He never saw it happen in his lifetime nor, I fear, will I in mine.

To his great discomfort, Heschel found that many of his closest Christian friends, including Daniel Berrigan, were supportive of the

Palestinians and critical of Israel's determination to control Jeru-salem rather than cede it to the United Nations as an international city. Movement pacifists, especially, wanted to know how Heschel could challenge his own country on Vietnam but not challenge Is-rael's preemptive strike against the massed forces of the Arabs. But Heschel was not a pacifist, certainly not where Jews were concerned. The Six-Day War caused a rift in Heschel's community of antiwar activists, but with Heschel personal friendships always prevailed.

On a few occasions Heschel invited me into his private life. Un-like Berrigan and Neuhaus, he was married and a father. I was hon-ored when he invited me to attend the bat mitzvah—a ritual novelty at the time—of his only child, Susannah, who has since become one of the nation's most distinguished scholars of Judaism. There I first I met his wife, Silvia, a fellow migrant from Ohio, and some of his dearest friends, like Elie Wiesel, Heschel's fellow Holocaust survivor. On another occasion, he asked me to his home for Pass-over Seder. That year Passover fell on Good Friday. Heschel hadn't noticed the congruence in the two religious calendars. He was as distraught by his oversight as I was to have to decline. Because of his death at the age of sixty-five there would be no second invitation.

As a Christian, I could never fully understand what made Heschel Heschel. But I did come to realize that by virtue of his own deeply rooted yet encompassing spirit, he possessed a rare ability to pass over from his own tradition and experience the holy to the perspec-tive of another. To explain this let me (as he would say) tell you a story.

In 1969, after delivering a series of lectures in Italy, Heschel phoned me in a state of extreme agitation. "My friend," he said, "you must do something. You must write something. Do you know what is happening in Rome?" He was in an emotional stammer.

"What is it, Rabbi?" I asked. Other rabbis I called by their first names, but Heschel was always rabbi, teacher. "They are selling their religious statues," he said. "You see them for sale everywhere on the streets. You must write about how terrible this is."

In my mind's eye I summoned up that opening scene from Fellini's famous film *La Dolce Vita,* in which a helicopter is seen ferrying a huge statue of Jesus across the sky above modern Rome. I tried to explain to him that Rome was awash in statuary, both religious and pagan, and that trafficking in them was a part of the very visual Roman culture. But I could not quell the very real anguish he felt. Now here was a man from a strictly iconic tradition—there shall be no graven images—deeply distraught over what he regarded as the profanation of objects sacred to Catholics. To him this was an external manifestation of an inward loss of piety, a desecration he urged me to disclose and deplore in *Newsweek.*

What I took from that remarkable conversation—indeed, what I drew from my whole encounter with Rabbi Heschel—was that those who have truly given themselves over to God in one tradition are the ones best able to appreciate those who are equally possessed by another religious tradition. This was verified several times over, as when a group of Catholic nuns sought Heschel's advice on whether to discard or continue wearing their traditional religious habits. Or again, when meeting for the first time, he and Thomas Merton fell immediately into a deep discussion in the backseat of the car. Soul spoke to soul, pilgrim to pilgrim, out of their common lifelong quest to discern and do the will of God.

The lesson from Heschel for me was this: although religions separate, that separation is also the condition that makes true spiritual conversation possible. From that point on, I promised myself, I would try to write about every religion from the inside, as if it were my own.

According to Jewish tradition, it is a blessing to die on the day God set aside for rest. For Heschel, the Sabbath was "a foretaste of eternity." And so it happened that my rabbi died sometime between Friday evening and the Saturday morning after a Shabbat meal with his family and some friends. Because it was the Sabbath, the first to arrive and kneel in prayer at his bedside were Christians, notably Pastor Neuhaus and the Berrigan brothers. More than five hundred people, including New York mayor John Lindsay, later turned out for his funeral. Weeping, I remembered my last interview with him.

It was about death and his hope for the afterlife and this was all he said: "I trust the God who made me to do with me what He will."

But it was not until I began to write this book that I came across a final Heschel story. According to Edward Kaplan's fine biography of the rabbi, when Silvia Heschel discovered that Sabbath morning that her husband had died, she placed two books indicative of his life on his bedside table: *The Best and the Brightest,* David Halberstam's incisive critique of Nixon's war cabinet, and the *Keter Shem Tov,* a Hasidic classic. She then removed the less edifying material he actually had been reading: my cover story on his friend, Episcopal bishop Paul Moore Jr., in the Christmas issue of *Newsweek*. It was, I like to think, our final conversation.[8]

"Never Again"

Jews of Rabbi Heschel's generation experienced the three most important events in Jewish history since their forefathers' dispersion from the land of Israel two millennia earlier: the Holocaust, the establishment of the state of Israel (1948), and the Six-Day War (June 1967), which threatened to extinguish the second event and replicate the first. The Israelis' swift and decisive victory profoundly affected Jews everywhere. It was, said Sol Linowitz, the U.S. ambassador to the Organization of American States, "the end of the image of the Jew as a loser. He became a man who resembles David more than Shylock." On the other hand, many American Jews also felt a new vulnerability. The rise of anti-Semitism among militant blacks (especially Black Muslims), the anti-Israel politics of the New Left (especially anti-Zionist Jews), and the unwillingness of many political liberals (especially progressive Protestant churchmen) to rally to Israel's defense when its very existence was at stake forced Jews to reassess the security they felt in America's democratic diaspora. Rabbi Marc Tannenbaum, director of interreligious affairs for the American Jewish Committee, put it bluntly: "Many of us now feel that when the chips are down, only Jews will stand up for Jews."

The two decades between the end of World War II and 1967 had been a golden era for American Jews. Although they represented barely 3 percent of the U.S. population, Jews had prospered to the point where only Episcopalians among religious or ethnic groups reported higher average incomes. A major reason was education. By the end of the Fifties, the last quota systems limiting Jews in U.S. colleges had crumbled. Fifteen years later the proportion of Jewish students in graduate and professional schools was triple that for students in the general population. Social assimilation proceeded accordingly: in 1965, 83 percent of American Jews said they were opposed to intermarriage with gentiles. By 1971, only 41 percent objected—in part because they knew so many kin and friends who had done so. Most Jews accepted the judgments of those sociologists (usually Jews themselves) who studied them: in America, Jews are not defined by adherence to Judaism or by the European sense of peoplehood. They are Americans first, free to identify as Jews or not. As an official of the Jewish Anti-Defamation League put it to me, "The Jew is just like anybody else, only more so."

The 1967 war, however, was a warning to Jews everywhere that they could not choose *not* to identify with fellow Jews. In the United States, reaction to the war also gave birth to new and specifically Jewish forms of movement religion. The most obstreperous organization was the Jewish Defense League, led by the fiery Orthodox rabbi Meir Kahane. The JDL began as a vigilante group for the protection of Jewish shopkeepers and their families in the predominately black sections of Brooklyn. Their militancy expanded to include harassment of Soviet diplomats for their government's brutal suppression of Soviet Jews and, after Kahane's migration to Israel, terrorist raids on Palestinians. The JDL appealed mostly to recent, lower-class émigrés from communist Eastern Europe who openly embraced their *Yiddishkayt* (Jewishness). Their rough tactics were not at all congruent with those of the Jewish Establishment and its agencies like the AJC and the Anti-Defamation League. These organizations represented the wealthier and assimilated American Jews whose cultured forebears had migrated much earlier from Germany. Writing in *Commentary,* Harvard sociologist Nathan Glazer saw in the JDL a rejection of everything that Americanized Jews "have come to stand for: rationality, moderation, balance, toleration." And yet, the JDL's militant war cry—"Never Again!"—articulated the new mood of Jewish defiance more exactly than Glazer's catalog of enlightened Jewish virtues.

More significant was the settlement movement. Between 1967 and 1971, seventeen thousand American Jews resettled in Israel—more than had moved there in the previous twenty years. It was, many of them believed (naively, given the pervasive secularism of Israeli society), the one place on earth where a Jew can live a fully Jewish life. A related cause, to which both militant and establishment Jews responded, was the defense of Soviet Jewry. In 1966, Elie Wiesel described the suppression of Russian Jews in a book with the haunting title *The Jews of Silence.* Since the war, however, thousands of Russian Jews had risked punishment and loss of livelihood in order to emigrate to Israel. Four years later, Wiesel surveyed the international support for the Soviet Jews and concluded, "There are no more Jews of silence."

The movement that captured my attention as a religion editor was the renewed interest in more traditional Judaism manifest among younger Jews immediately after the war. At Harvard, Brown, and other elite universities where Jews now constituted as much as one-third of the faculty, Jewish students created *havorots* (literally: coming together) for prayer and study outside the formal structures of existing synagogues. Influenced by the Sixties counterculture, they were searching for ways to live a more communal Jewish life without going to Israel. In that sense, many of them identified more with the boundaried Jewishness of their grandparents than with the attenuated Jewish identity of their parents and classroom teachers. In particular they were turning their backs on Reform Judaism, the denomination of choice among religious Jews, and the high-church liturgies in synagogues like Manhattan's Temple Emanu-El, where even an Episcopalian could feel at home. In Heschel's enduring phrase, they were insisting on bread instead of stones.

And so in the spring of 1971, with Passover as a calendar target, I proposed a cover story on American Jews. I envisioned a story like those we had done on American Protestants and Catholics, one that would explain to our mostly gentile readers what being Jewish meant to Jews. I knew what being Jewish meant to Rabbi Heschel. But it was clear from our research that religious markers like eating kosher and observing Shabbat, not to mention observance of the full panoply of Jewish laws, left the majority of American Jews unaccounted for.

The latest studies estimated that only 20 percent of Jews were committed to regular worship and to Jewish communal organizations. Another 40 percent maintained nominal affiliation, which meant signing checks to Jewish philanthropies and showing up at synagogue twice a year for the high holy days. In our own Gallup survey for the story, only 43 percent described themselves as religious, a figure that included Jewish Unitarians, Ethical Culturalists, Buddhists, and Episcopalians like Barry Goldwater, the first Jew to run for president; Katharine Graham, owner of the *Washington Post* and *Newsweek;* and Arthur "Punch" Sulzberger, the future publisher of the *New York Times.* Not all American Jews were Zionists, either. Still, it was obvious that the 1967 war had reawakened in Jews of the American diaspora deep-seated attachments to Israel and its beleaguered people. In Genesis, God had promised land and progeny to Abraham and his descendants, and those promises still echoed in the minds of all but the most detached secular Jews.

Inevitably, the cover package turned out to be more sociological than theological. *Newsweek*'s graphics department produced a map of the United States showing the number of Jews living in each of the states. Another chart demonstrated in detail just how far Jews outstripped other Americans in terms of education, occupation (males only), and annual family income. A sidebar identified "The Jewish Establishment" and how it had raised more than $170 million for Israel within weeks of the outbreak of war. The text of my own story asserted that "Jews exert more power in U.S. society than ever before—and are more ready to use it. . . ." The Gallup poll commissioned by *Newsweek* found that 95 percent of American Jews thought the United States should support Israel with military equipment and nearly half (49 percent) said the United States should be willing to "risk war" in defense of Israel. The running story also made it quite clear that the turn toward more traditional forms of Judaism among younger Jews was a reaction against their parents' failure to pass on to them the spiritual values they had received from the previous generation. Because of the Six-Day War, the cover story argued, Americans were experiencing new pride as well as new problems.

The day before the issue was to go to press, Managing Editor Lester Bernstein appeared in my office, a copy of my story in his hands. Of all the Wallendas, as the top three editors were called, Lester was usually the most relaxed—"It's only a fifty-cent magazine," he liked to remind colleagues when they got too uptight. But on this occasion he was not relaxed. "I read this last night," he said, "and I asked myself, as we used to say in the shtetl, 'Can this be good for the Jews?'" It was not the sort of question I had put to myself when writing about Protestants or Catholics. But, as it happened, this was the first time that *Newsweek* or *Time* or, for that matter, any general-interest magazine had published a cover story on American Jews. Just as many Jews worried about anti-Semitism when Heschel appeared at antiwar rallies, Lester feared that my candid look at American Jews—in particular their achievements compared with other Americans', and their pervasive secularism—would incite the same reaction.

Nor was he alone. At that time, mainline Protestants ran the business side of *Newsweek,* the advertising salesmen were mostly gregarious Irish Catholics, and Jews dominated the editorial staff—a division of labor Will Herberg would have readily understood. Beginning with Editor Kermit Lansner, eight of the fourteen editors at the top of the masthead were Jews. This was not something you were supposed to notice, nor was it much remarked upon. But given that only one Jewish editor was in any way religiously observant, it fell to me to be the in-house authority on Judaism, as on other religions. When early copies of the cover art arrived, I felt a certain frisson in the hallways. The cover image was a large Star of David in red, white, and blue, and in the center in large black letters was THE AMERICAN JEW. In the Nation Department, Editor Ed Kosner (who would shortly replace Lansner as editor of the magazine) cut out the

Star of David from several covers and hung one around his neck—and then distributed the rest to each of his Jewish writers. That was Kosner's bumptious way of dealing with his own discomfort at having America's Jews singled out on the cover of *Newsweek*.

Just before the issue went to press, Bernstein told me that he had delegated Executive Editor Robert Christopher to "run the story through his typewriter." This was not good news: Christopher was famous for rewriting stories rather than editing them. Most of what I wrote survived in the published version—except for my conclusion, which was essentially this: if the Six-Day War reminded America's Jews of their Jewishness, absent some commitment to Judaism, sociology alone could not tell them what it meant to be a Jew, much less why it mattered.

This was not the sort of pronouncement the editors were willing to support. Yet the war *did* produce a gradual return to more traditional Jewish practices. Reform Jews reintroduced Hebrew in their liturgies a few years later and by the end of the century a record one-third of American Jews between the ages of eighteen and thirty-four self-identified as Orthodox. This represented a remarkable reversal of expectations within the world's largest community of Jews. But to this day, no newsmagazine has ever published another cover story on America's Jews.

Whether Christian or Jewish or interfaith, movement religion was always a reaction to specific causes. Individuals like a Berrigan or a Heschel could and did find biblical imperatives for their radicalism, and for a time, Martin Luther King Jr.'s evocation of a "beloved community" provided an ideal image of an American Peaceable Kingdom. But what movement religion lacked was a coherent theology. For that, activists in the United States had to turn to Latin America.

CHAPTER 7

Religion and Revolution

The Emergence of Liberation Theology

For those Americans who came of age in the middle of the last century, "Liberation" as a rallying cry in public life did not begin with civil rights, women's liberation, gay liberation, or any of the other movements that invoked liberation as its goal. Already in the 1940s, the war against the Nazis was cast as a crusade to liberate the people of Western Europe. During the cold war, we spoke of communist Eastern Europe as "captive nations," as indeed they were. In Latin America, however, the United States supported an array of military dictators and fascist governments in order to preserve its own hemispheric hegemony. Conversely, the United States opposed liberation movements that threatened the economic, political, and military interests of the American imperium. What we feared most was a communist revolution on this side of the Atlantic.

Thus, when Liberation Theology developed from within the (mostly) Catholic churches of Latin America, it was of more than merely religious interest and of more than merely regional concern. It was a major episode in U.S. as well as Latin American history. For political leaders as well as leaders of the Catholic Church, the success of Liberation Theology as a sociopolitical movement became a test of whether Christians anywhere could join Marxist and other revolutionaries to create a new and more equitable social order. In that context, Liberation Theology was a theology of revolution.

Liberation Theology was the creation of progressive Latin American bishops and theologians in response to Vatican Council II's declaration that the church should immerse itself in the problems of the world. Initially, their goal was to transform the Catholic Church from a conservative organization that catered primarily to the ruling families to a church that would promote the economic, political, and social liberation of the continent's desperately poor, oppressed, and marginalized masses. The church could not evangelize the poor—so the argument ran—unless it became the church *of* the poor.

Like the socialist revolutions in Europe, Liberation Theology was the work of a cadre of intellectuals acting on behalf of the masses. The parallels with Marxist revolutionary theory were many, which is why the movement was hotly contested. But the basic imperatives were drawn from the Bible. That God wills the liberation of His people is as old as the book of Exodus. The other basic imperative—that the Gospel must first be preached to the poor, who are more open than the rich to its reception—is firmly grounded in the preaching of Jesus. In Liberation Theology, the history of salvation is manifest in the ongoing process of human liberation. Like Marx, Liberation Theology insisted that "man" must become the subject of his own history. Also like Marx, Liberation Theology recognized the inevitability of class struggle. But the fundamental link with Marxism was the idea of *praxis:* that is, the critical relationship between theology and practice whereby the one is influenced and transformed by the other in an ongoing dialectic. The purpose of Liberation Theology, like the purpose of Marxism, was not to interpret the world but to transform it. In other words, one must first commit to solidarity with the poor and their liberation before one can construct a theology of liberation.

United States Connections

From the very beginning, U.S. Catholics played important but often-overlooked roles in the development and spread of Liberation Theology. In the Sixties, Latin America was home to half of the world's Catholics: Brazil was the world's largest Catholic country and Mexico was second. But sociological studies showed that no more than one Brazilian in ten attended Sunday Mass or otherwise practiced the faith. A major problem was a critical shortage of priests. Some regions of the continent reported 70,000 Catholics for every priest, compared to an average of 600 for every priest in the United States. In countries like Guatemala and the Dominican Republic, as many as 80 percent of the clergy were missionaries from Europe and the United States. Even so, for Catholics in rural villages, visits from circuit-riding priests were weeks apart and taken up with baptisms, confessions, Mass, and marriages, leaving little time for organized instruction in the faith.

In 1961, Pope John XXIII directed the bishops of the United States to send 20 percent (about thirty-five thousand) of its priests to work among the poor in Latin American parishes. Missionary orders like Maryknoll and the Jesuits made Latin America a priority. Notre Dame and other Catholic universities sent administrators and teachers to bolster Catholic universities in Chile and other countries. In a Catholic version of the Peace Corps, thousands of American laymen and -women signed up to serve as Papal Volunteers for Latin America.

That same year, Monsignor Ivan Illich, a priest of the New York archdiocese, established a think tank in Cuernavaca, a resort town a hundred miles southwest of Mexico City. A polymath European intellectual, Illich conceived the Center for Intercultural Documentation (CIDOC) as a place for scholarly research on Latin American economic and political problems. A major source of CIDOC's income was its crack language school, funded largely by U.S. bishops to train the priests they sent for pastoral work in Latin America. Illich ran the school like a boot camp: if students did not immediately shed their Yankee cultural assumptions, he sent them home. It was there that Yankees like Daniel Berrigan (1964), Harvey Cox (1968), and Richard Neuhaus (1972) came into contact with the first probes in Liberation Theology.

Ivan Illich was one of the most fecund and unpredictable geniuses I ever encountered. An aristocrat by birth and education, he became contemptuous of American middle-class religion and values—and of the institutions that supported them—while serving as a parish priest in the Bronx. I once argued with him that it was precisely the lack of a thriving middle class that made Latin American countries chronically unstable and prone to military dictatorships. But he would have none of it. Illich was vigorously opposed to U.S.-based multinational corporations, arguing that they only benefited Latin American oligarchies and forced Latin American economies to be dependent on the market-driven vagaries of foreign capitalists. Eventually, he came to resent even the priests and nuns sent to him from the United States as "a colonial power's lackey chaplains." Illich never imagined that these foreigners would become far more radical than most Latin American clergy, and that their influx would provide a channel for the introduction of Liberation Theology into the United States.

What I didn't know then was that Ivan Illich was also Liberation Theology's initial organizing genius. Beginning in 1964, it was Illich who brought together the first generation of Liberation Theologians—men like Gustavo Gutierrez from Peru, Juan Luis Segundo from Uruguay, and others for a series of meetings in Brazil, Colombia, and Cuba. Most of these theologians worked with the poor and had given up on the idea of establishing Christian Democratic parties like those in postwar Europe. Many eventually embraced socialism as the only system compatible with the Gospel.

The prospect of a church-based radical movement in Latin America bore important implications for U.S. policy in the hemisphere. To see why, we must locate Liberation Theology in its geopolitical context.

In 1959, Fidel Castro's guerrillas overthrew Cuban dictator Fulgencio Batista and established the first communist government in the Western Hemisphere. Castro's success inspired similar guerrilla movements in Venezuela, Peru, Uruguay, Colombia, and Guatemala. In April 1961, the Kennedy administration tried and failed to oust Castro in the bungled secret invasion at Cuba's Bay of Pigs. The following year, Soviet efforts to build a missile base in Cuba brought the United States to the edge of nuclear warfare with the USSR. At the same time, President Kennedy launched the Alliance for Progress, a political and economic effort to support democratic reform throughout Latin America. The Alliance never achieved the funding Kennedy promised and the project faded as a priority during the Johnson administration's concentration on another war of liberation, in Vietnam.

But there was one lasting legacy: a beefed-up presence of covert CIA operations throughout Latin America aimed at thwarting left-wing revolutions. Monitoring and infiltrating left-wing church groups that espoused Liberation Theology was part of its assignment. These operations continued for thirty years and came to a combustible head during the Iran-Contra scandal under President Ronald Reagan.

As it happened, one of these CIA operatives was a friend and Notre Dame classmate, a tightly wound philosophy major from Florida who, according to his own account, became so unwound by the torture of people he had turned in to the Uruguayan police that he became an agent—through Cuba—of the KGB. From exile in Germany, he later wrote a book describing in brutal but accurate detail how the CIA maltreated suspects in its care. He also blew the cover on several covert agents around the world. They were immediately killed. In this way did Philip Agee become the era's most notorious traitor.

In sum, because of the success of the Cuban revolution, the perceived negative impact of multinationals on Latin American economies, CIA support for repressive regimes, and disillusionment with the Alliance for Progress, partisans of Liberation Theology—including many pastoral workers from the United States—came to oppose U.S. imperialism in Latin America. Cuba's Fidel Castro took note: "The United States shouldn't worry about the Soviets in Latin

America," he told a group of foreign visitors in 1967, "because they are not revolutionaries anymore. But they should worry about the Catholic revolutionaries, who are."[1]

The Papal Connection

In 1961, Pope Paul VI issued a powerful social encyclical, *Populorum Progressio* ("On the Development of Peoples"), which focused on economic development in Third World countries. In it, he gave papal approval to several themes that would become central to Liberation Theology in Latin America. With a boldness and specificity unmatched by any papal document before or since, the pope called for a more equitable distribution of wealth between and within nations. In his denunciations of economic neocolonialism, he made no distinction between socialist and capitalist nations: against both hegemonic systems he affirmed the right of developing countries to "move freely toward the kind of society they choose." On the agitated issue of agrarian reform within developing countries, the pope sent a pointed message to established oligarchies: "If certain landed estates impede the general prosperity," he declared, ". . . the common good sometimes demands their expropriation." Private ownership of the means of production, he insisted, is not an "absolute right."

As the tone of these statements made clear, Pope Paul was calling for social reform by the "haves," not revolution by the "have-nots." Even so, he did legitimate revolution "where there is manifest long-standing tyranny which would do great harm to the common good of the country." To many progressive bishops and clergy in Latin America, long-standing tyranny was exactly what they were up against, and the only choice was between violent and nonviolent revolution.

Astonishingly, many U.S. newspapers overlooked the pope's most radical statements, myopically searching instead for any hints that he might change the church's position on contraception as a method of curbing population growth in Third World countries.

One notable exception was the *Wall Street Journal,* which dismissed the encyclical as "warmed over Marxism." Many Latin American newspapers agreed.

In September 1968, Pope Paul traveled to Medellín, Colombia, to open a crucial meeting of the Latin American Bishops' Conference (CELAM). It was the first visit by a pope to the continent and his mere presence excited crowds to feverish adulation. At one point a rush of campesinos, having already paid a day's wages (about thirty-five cents) for commemorative holy cards, stormed a church hoping to see him in person and nearly crushed the pope as he knelt to pray.

The bishops' meeting was a two-week affair called to formulate the Latin American church's authoritative response to Vatican Council II. The process, which called for the bishops to critically assess economic, political, and social problems of their countries, reflect on them theologically, and propose the church's pastoral response, mirrored exactly the methodology of Liberation Theology. This was no surprise, since the leadership of CELAM and its staff had embraced the movement. Most of the Liberation Theologians had been schooled in Europe and were well versed in the Christian-Marxist dialogue raging there, especially in Germany and France. Marxist social analysis was also the intellectual coin of the realm in Latin American universities. Marxist concepts flavored the bishops' deliberations and free-market capitalism was subjected to withering criticism. But the phrase that epitomized Medellín and became a permanent part of Catholic social teaching was "the preferential option for the poor." This was a declaration that the church's primary (though not exclusive) obligation was solidarity with the marginalized, the outcast, the oppressed. That obligation also entailed the liberation of the poor from the "institutional violence" inflicted by "sinful" social, economic, and political structures. And so, with a little help from Karl Marx, ideas like "structural sin" and "institutional violence" gained ecclesiastical approbation.

To this day, Liberation Theologians regard the documents forged at Medellín as the Magna Carta of their movement. They got what they wanted—official support from the continent-wide conference of bishops—even though some bishops clearly didn't realize what they were approving and some conservative national hierarchies (Colombia was one) refused to ratify the final documents.

As a set of ideas put forward in books, Liberation Theology influenced clergy, university professors and their students, and those radical organizers who looked to religion for inspiration. But the poor of Latin America could not afford to buy books, or understand them if they did. Unless Liberation Theology were grounded in a suitable set of practices for working with the mass of unlettered Latin Americans, it was destined to become just another academic exercise for schooled elites.

As a social movement, Liberation Theology depended on three organizational practices. The first was adopted from the pioneering work of Brazilian educator Paulo Freire. In books like *Pedagogy of the Oppressed,* Freire had demonstrated how literacy education among peasants could be advanced when it was combined with "consciousness-raising" (*concientización*)—that is, helping them recognize the reasons for the oppression they experienced. In Liberation Theology, "consciousness-raising" became a method of making the poor aware of the economic structures behind their personal oppression and, at the same time, of the Bible's message of God's will for their liberation in this life, not just in the next. This was a particularly powerful message in countries like Guatemala, where descendants of the Mayan Indians (85 percent of the population) formed the broad base of a social pyramid that allowed them no hope of upward mobility.

The second method used to reach the poor was the creation of "base ecclesial communities" (BECs) where consciousness-raising could take place. First pioneered by progressive Brazilian bishops, BECs initially were small groups that met in homes or community centers for Bible study and adult education directed by lay catechists. In 1963, Bishop Marcos McGrath of Panama, who had studied at the University of Notre Dame and become a priest of the Congregation of the Holy Cross, invited a group of Chicago priests and sisters headed by Father Leo McMahon to set up in a Panama City slum the first BEC devoted to the praxis of Liberation Theology. McMahon's experiment showed that if priests and nuns moved out of their rectories and convents and into urban barrios and rural villages to build grassroots BECs, they could ameliorate the clergy shortage in Latin America. Thousands eventually did just that, becoming radicalized in the process.

Partisans of Liberation Theology seized on base communities as the vehicle for identifying the church with the struggles of the poor. Base communities offered an ideal setting where teachers of Liberation Theology could reinterpret the basic mysteries of God, Christ, divine grace, sin, and the sacraments through the experiences of the poor. From the perspective of Liberation Theology, the poor of Latin America were not only the new proletariat; they were, through this reinterpretation, truly God's chosen people.

The decade following Medellín saw an eruption of BECs throughout Latin America—and with it, the dispersion of Liberation Theology to its target audience. Brazil alone reported eighty thousand base communities. Although the learned vanguard of Liberation theoreticians like Gutierrez, Leonardo Boff (Brazil), and Jesuit Jon Sobrino (El Salvador) never numbered more than a hundred, they spent much of their time giving workshops for tens of thousands of religious and lay pastoral workers in Peru, Chile, and Brazil as well as the politically incendiary countries of Central America. In this way did the movement metastasize.

Unlike traditional Catholic social action movements in Europe and the United States, Liberation Theology insisted on total independence from the hierarchy and the institutional apparatus of the church. As sociologist Christian Smith has shown, the goal was always "to build coalitions with other militants—labor unions, peasant leagues, Marxist organizations, student groups, guerrilla movements and so on—to produce popular campaigns, organizations, and movements that achieve commonly held goals."[2] In this wholly secular context, Liberation Theology easily mutated into a theology of revolution—including the violent kind. We journalists all heard stories of priests who opted to serve God by joining the revolution. The classic figure was Colombia's Father Camilo Torres, a European-trained sociologist who ran afoul of his bishop after organizing a militant coalition of workers, peasants, and slum dwellers. Rather than give up his work he abandoned the priesthood and joined an insurgent guerrilla movement, declaring, "I took off my cassock to become more truly a priest." Four months later, the priest-turned-revolutionary was killed in an ambush. By the next year, his face had joined that of Ernesto "Che" Guevara on T-shirts as a symbol of revolutionary sainthood.

By no means were all partisans of Liberation Theology revolutionaries. But those who did embrace the movement from the pulpit, the platform, or a base ecclesial community put their lives at risk from the military, right-wing death squads, or (less often) leftist revolutionaries. Indeed, one of the known fruits of Liberation Theology is a modern martyrology of raped nuns and murdered priests and "disappeared" lay church leaders. Bishops were not excluded. Brazil's Dom Helder Camara, for example, survived sixteen attempts on his life. But others were not so fortunate.

A Turning Point: Puebla

By 1978, Liberation Theology had developed indigenous roots in Africa and Asia through networks like the Association of Third World Theologians. But in Latin America, the movement was facing a critical backlash within the Catholic Church. Control of CELAM had passed into the hands of political reactionaries headed by Colombian archbishop Alfonso López Trujillo. With encouragement from Cardinal Sebastiano Baggio, the Vatican official in charge of Latin American affairs, he purged the CELAM staff of Liberation Theology sympathizers. The conservatives' goal was not to repudiate Liberation Theology but to tame and transform it by severing all connections between religion and revolutionary movements. This was to be accomplished in 1979 at the first CELAM meeting since Medellín, held in the Spanish colonial city of Puebla in central Mexico.

In a reversal of Medellín, López Trujillo excluded all but a handful of progressives from the meeting. No Liberation Theologians were invited, either. As an added precaution, he chose as the site for the two-week meeting an isolated seminary surrounded by a ten-foot stone "wall of freedom," as he called it, and posted with security guards. Delegates could leave the compound, but only delegates were allowed in.

But there was one unknown factor: the new Polish pope, John Paul II, the first man from a communist country to head the Roman Catholic Church. Puebla would be his first foreign journey since his surprising election the previous year. Ironically, Mexico was the only country in Latin America that did not maintain diplomatic ties with the Vatican. Moreover, because of the church's opposition to Mexico's 1910 revolution, foreign clergy were forbidden to say Mass and no priests were allowed to wear clerical garb in public. The Mexican government temporarily waived both laws for the pope, but the real question was this: would a pope who had stoutly defended human rights against a communist government in his homeland defend those same rights against repressive Catholic regimes in Latin America? To support Liberation Theology was to risk losing government support for the institutional church, but not to support the movement was to risk losing the continent's masses.

In the course of his seven-day visit, the pope gave thirty-seven speeches before massive audiences totaling 18 million. Not once did he use the phrase "Liberation Theology." The reason, I figured, is that he wanted to unify the bishops, the way that the Polish bishops remained united in the face of communist efforts to pit one against another. He made plain his fear that the base ecclesial communities would become a parallel church competing with the hierarchy, and nowhere did he encourage revolution, even as a last resort. Indeed, from my reading of his speeches it seemed evident that the pope rejected most elements of Liberation Theology—specifically, the use of Marxist theory and analysis, clerical involvement in political movements, and the emphasis on social sin over personal sin. Instead he preached a theology of the cross as the true theology of liberation. Still, it was up to the bishops to formulate their own conclusions.

If media interest is any measure, the Puebla meeting was the most dramatic church event since the close of Vatican Council II. Nearly two thousand journalists from around the world crowded the hotels and bars around the city's central plaza. *Esquire* magazine dispatched the newly liberal Garry Wills to fly from Rome on the papal plane—such was the secular interest in the future of Liberation Theology. Banner-waving demonstrators for and against Liberation Theology marched daily from the central city to the seminary walls. Mixed among the journalists and marchers were agents of the CIA, Cuban intelligence, and their buddies from the Eastern European secret services and, of course, the Soviet Union's KGB. It was quite a party.

Puebla was my first opportunity to observe Liberation Theologians in action. Although unwelcome at the bishops' table, they still found ways to influence the debate. About ninety of them set up shop in a convent three blocks from the seminary. As each committee document emerged from the meeting, a sympathetic bishop would carry a copy to the convent, where teams of Liberation Theologians and social scientists wrote short critiques for circulation inside the conclave. Their strategy was to pepper the meeting's final, official report with enough positive sentences to justify a pro-Liberation interpretation of the bishops' concluding pastoral message.

Equally important, their convent headquarters served as the press center for visiting journalists. With no access to the bishops themselves, reporters had to rely (as happened at Vatican II) on the theologians outside the wall to explain what was going on inside the meeting. Every afternoon we gathered in the crowded convent parlor. The air was scented with the odor of theologians who had worked through the night without the benefit of showers, and from the cigarettes they constantly drew on—odious Latin American brands that made the French Gauloises seem like mild Kentucky Burley. Over and over again, the theologians insisted that the bishops' conservative statements had to be understood in light of other, more liberal statements—which, unbeknown to the reporters, the theologians themselves had written. If opponents of Liberation Theology controlled the agenda, the theologians outside controlled much of what the media made of it.

The bishops' 240-page final document did indeed include many fine phrases supporting Liberation Theology. But the document was so contradictory that neither side left Puebla with a mandate. In fact, 26 of the 187 voting delegates refused to endorse it and another 27 went home before the meeting ended. The real import of Puebla was that neither the Vatican nor CELAM would second any bishop who dared speak out against the terrorism and repression that passed for governing in many a Latin American country. Those who did were fair game for the death squads.

And so it happened that eight months after Puebla, a marksman pulled up outside the open doors of the Carmelite Sisters' hospital chapel in San Salvador, El Salvador. Inside, Archbishop Oscar Arnulfo Romero was approaching the most sacred moment of Mass when a single bullet tore open his chest, spattering blood over the bread and wine. Not since the murder of Thomas à Becket had so prominent a prelate been cut down at the altar.

Romero was an unlikely martyr for Liberation Theology. Conservative, cautious, and wary of leftist mystiques of violence, he had only recently begun to speak out against the murderous military junta that ruled his native country. He had dared to support human rights groups, as the pope was then doing in Poland, and had written to President Jimmy Carter asking—to no avail—that the United States cease its military support for El Salvador's rule by death squads. Only the day before, in his Sunday sermon, he had pleaded with the men in the Salvadoran armed forces: "In the name of God, I pray you, I beseech you, I order you! Let this repression cease."

Romero's death was the preface to seventeen years of civil war that left upwards of seventy-five thousand Salvadorans dead. In 1987, I visited the site of his assassination. Already, the Salvadoran people revered him as a patron saint, but the Vatican had made no move to take up his cause, fearing that a proclamation of his sanctity would signal support for opposition forces. It took more than a decade to prove that Romero's death was ordered by leaders of the right-wing ARENA party, which continued to rule Salvador until 2009. Only after its defeat was Romero's death officially commemorated in Salvador. In 1990, I published a book, *Making Saints: How the Catholic Church Determines Who Becomes a Saint, Who Doesn't, and Why,* that included an examination of the evidence favoring his candidacy for sainthood based on the church's own criteria for Christian martyrdom. Romero's cause remained stalled until 2013, when Cardinal Jorge Mario Bergoglio of Buenos Aires, a Jesuit, became the first pope from Latin America. But in the eyes of Christians everywhere, Romero was already a saint.

Romero was a fine example of prophetic religion in the manner of Martin Luther King Jr. But the problem with prophetic religion is that it arouses a passion for justice without knowing what to do with the oppressed once the oppressor is vanquished. In 1979, the Sandinista National Liberation Front (FSLN) produced the only successful revolution in Latin America after Castro's in Cuba. With its mix of workers, peasants, and artisans, of Marxists, Leninists, and Catholics from the base communities, the Sandinista Front fit precisely the recipe for revolution envisioned in Liberation Theology: it was popular, democratic, and anti-imperialistic. Even the archbishop of Managua, Miguel Obando y Bravo, welcomed the new regime. For me, Nicaragua was the real test of Liberation Theology: after all the books and organizing, what would its partisans contribute to the creation of a new social order?

Priests of the Revolution

In the fall of 1983, downtown Managua was a muddy checkerboard of empty public squares. The baroque Cathedral of Santiago de Los Caballeros was half rubble, the result of a devastating earthquake in 1972 that tumbled 80 percent of the capital's buildings into the streets and left a quarter million (mostly poor) Managuans homeless. In the old city core, the only surviving structures visible above the trees were the Hotel InterContinental, shaped like an Aztec pyramid, and an empty former U.S. bank that would eventually house the revolutionary national assembly. The new city center, the Plaza de Revolución, resembled a blacktopped parking lot with a tiny bus shelter and weathered bleachers set below outsize billboards celebrating the revolution's heroes. Since there were no signs to identify streets, Managuans had no addresses. I thought of what Gertrude Stein had said of Oakland: "there is no there there."

What the quake had not destroyed the Somoza family had plundered for itself during forty-five years of brutal misrule. Beginning with Franklin Delano Roosevelt, who memorably called the first Somoza dictator "a son-of-a-bitch—but he is our son-of-a bitch," a succession of U.S. presidents supported the rapacious Somozas. At one point, the family controlled 30 percent of Nicaragua's arable land—a fiefdom roughly equal in size to the whole of El Salvador— and the twenty-six largest businesses. Now, four years after the last of the Somozas had been overthrown in a popular revolution, President Ronald Reagan was threatening the new, Marxist-oriented Sandinista government by a combination of economic strangulation and not-so-covert military action: several thousand "Contras"— most of them former members of Somoza's National Guard—armed and equipped by the CIA, were staging a counterrevolution along Nicaragua's border with Honduras. The Reagan administration claimed, with no hard evidence, that the Sandinistas were shipping arms to Salvadoran guerrillas. The administration's goal was not another U.S. invasion of this desperately poor country—a gambit that 87 percent of Americans opposed, according to a *Newsweek* poll—but to cripple the Sandinistas' efforts to build a sovereign, multi-aligned socialist society. Reagan did not want another Cuba in the hemisphere.

For a country ostensibly at war with the United States, Nicaragua was full of North Americans. Altogether, about one hundred thousand U.S. citizens passed through the country in the 1980s. Some were intellectuals like my friend Robert Coles, who explained one evening at dinner that he was there to study the effects of war on the young *muchachos*—the teenage soldiers who had spearheaded the revolution. Many more were midwestern farmers and other sympathetic *brigadistas* from the United States who volunteered their labor and expertise while some sixty thousand Nicaraguan workers were conscripted to hold off the Contras. Lay and religious missionaries from Maryknoll were there to teach peasants and help complete what the Sandinistas called "the revolutionary process." On any given night you could always find correspondents from a dozen U.S. publications at the dark, cavelike bar in the InterContinental. No part of the country was off-limits to foreign journalists: the Sandinistas courted world opinion through them. U.S. photographer Susan Meiselas served as a kind of self-appointed advisor to the junta as to which visiting Americans were likely to be sympathetic to the cause.

My goal was to assess the impact of Liberation Theology by talking to priests who either worked for or advised the junta. I had one specific assignment from *GEO* magazine to interview Father Ernesto Cardenal, the priest and much-admired poet who served as the Sandinistas' minister of culture. Eight months earlier, on a brief visit to Nicaragua, Pope John Paul II had publicly admonished Cardenal as the minister doffed his beret and knelt at the airport to kiss the pope's ring. Instead, the pope angrily shook a finger at the priest and ordered him to regularize his relationship to the church. The moment, captured on television and seen around the world, dramatized the pope's increasing opposition to Catholic cooperation with revolutionary movements in Latin America. I had wired Cardenal that I wanted to hear his side of the story.

My own view was that Catholic priests ought not take positions in any political party or government. In 1980, the Vatican had ordered Jesuit Robert Drinan, the only Catholic priest ever elected to the U.S. Congress, not to stand for a sixth term as a representative from Massachusetts. Drinan, a passionate liberal Democrat, always wore his clericals in Congress—"It's the only suit I own," he liked to say—as if this gave his views an extra layer of authority. But I thought his dual role divisive and inherently compromising for a priest: had his politics been as conservative as they were liberal, Catholics on the left would have called for precisely the action John Paul II took. After all, it was not as if Democrats in Massachusetts—or in any other state—were short of Irish Catholic politicians.

But Nicaragua was different. The Sandinista insurgency, as they preferred to call it, was a nationalist rebellion against a hereditary oppressor in a country where most of the people were Catholics.

Unlike Fidel Castro, the Sandinista junta wanted clerical supporters in government posts—not only for the signal their presence sent
that Christianity and Marxism were compatible ideologies, but also
because priests were among the best-educated and internationally
experienced Nicaraguans.

For example, Foreign Minister Miguel D'Escoto Brockmann
was the son of a Nicaraguan diplomat, born in Los Angeles, and
a priest of Maryknoll. I had met him at Maryknoll headquarters, a
mile from my home, where he was the founding publisher of Orbis
Books, which specialized in publishing Third World theologians of
a Liberationist bent. Ernesto Cardenal and his Jesuit brother, Fer-
nando, who was head of the Sandinistas' massive (and massively
successful) Literacy Campaign, came from a large and wealthy mer-
chant family in Nicaragua. Ernesto had studied poetry at Columbia University in the Fifties and spent three years at the Trappist
monastery in Gethsemane, Kentucky, under the spiritual direction
of Thomas Merton. Most of the Jesuits at the University of Central
America in Managua who supported the revolution were also educated abroad and the government was heavily dependent on their
technical expertise. These priests were as eager to talk to a journalist
from the United States as I was to question them.

Poetry and Revolution

When I arrived in Nicaragua, Ernesto Cardenal had just returned to
his home at Our Lady of Solentiname, a contemplative community
he had founded in 1965 on a ripe tropical island in Lake Nicaragua.
Over time it had evolved into an arts-and-crafts colony and then a
rural base ecclesial community where Cardenal led peasant fisher-
men in simplified discussions of Liberation Theology in support of
the revolution. It was the first time since becoming a government
bureaucrat that Cardenal had spent more than a day at his beloved
retreat. He would see me there.

The government chartered a small plane to take me to San Carlo,
on the lake's southern edge. There we were met by a young soldier

wearing a Florida State University T-shirt with an AK-47 strapped to his back. This was a country where 40 percent of the population was under age twenty-one and he had been one of the teenage *muchachos* who spearheaded the revolution. I could hear gunfire near the Costa Rican border a few miles away where the United States had created a second Contra force. From San Carlo a rowboat powered by an outboard motor that frequently gave out took four of us on a choppy forty-minute trip to the island. There the poet welcomed us with a lunch of fresh crab soup, boiled lobster, and cold bottles of white wine around an open fire pit. I pulled a bottle of Jack Daniel's from my bag and we shared a drink.

Like Father Drinan, Ernesto seemed to possess only one set of clothes: a loose white peasant's smock over blue jeans, which he wore in all his photographs. As we talked he squinted myopically behind thin wire glasses, his long white hair bleaching in the sun. Only eight years my senior, Cardenal had long since assumed the bardic mien of Nicaragua's Walt Whitman. Whenever he could, Cardenal curved our conversation back to his relationship with three other well-known poet-priests: Daniel Berrigan, Merton, and John Paul II. As a poet, Cardenal was the best of the lot.

Right away Ernesto wanted me to know that the fuss over priests serving in government was a nonissue. They had secured prior clearance from the Vatican's secretary of state, Cardinal Agostino Casaroli, who, he said, recognized that Nicaragua presented "a special situation requiring an exception to the pope's rule." This news suggested that not all Vatican officials were on the pope's page. Cardenal thought the pope had acted on impulse and in bad faith when he rebuked him, but the incident still rankled. In any case, the priests had agreed not to say Mass or hear confessions for as long as they were government functionaries. As far as Cardenal was concerned, it was the pope who had stepped out of line.

I asked Ernesto how he became a Marxist. It began, he said, with a visit in 1970 to Cuba, where he saw the government "putting the gospel in action." The pope "does not understand Marxism," he insisted—a statement so absurd I let it pass. But when pressed, Cardenal admitted that he himself had not read anything of Marx beyond the early chapters of *Das Capital*. Most of what Cardenal knew of Marxism came from his readings in Liberation Theology, especially Gutierrez, which had convinced him that one could be a Christian and a Marxist at the same time—indeed that Jesus himself was a communist. "I am a Marxist who believes in God, follows Christ, and is a revolutionary for the sake of His kingdom," he explained at one point. It would not be the first time that I would hear a priest in Nicaragua identify the Sandinista "revolutionary process" with the coming Kingdom of God.

Until the Sandinista guerrillas took charge of the insurrection, Cardenal had been a pacifist like Berrigan. Berrigan, he said, was like a brother—Ernesto had visited the Jesuit in Danbury prison. But in 1977, Cardenal embraced violence as a revolutionary necessity, allowing Sandinista forces to use Solentiname as a base from which to launch a failed attack on National Guardsmen stationed in San Carlo. The decision provoked a public falling-out with Berrigan, which Cardenal said had caused him more pain than the papal scolding. Someday, he said, he hoped he could again embrace nonviolence, but not as long as Reagan and the Contras threatened counterrevolution.

The man Ernesto most wanted to talk about was Thomas Merton. It was Merton who had urged him to return to Nicaragua and create a new kind of religious community without rules like those the Trappists followed and open to participation by peasants. It was Merton, too, who had told him to take holy orders: he would have to be a priest if he wanted the community recognized by the church. Motioning me to his straw-covered cottage, Cardenal showed me a cache of sixty letters from Merton, whom he called "the spiritual father of Solentiname." Merton had hoped to join him here on the island, and might have if he hadn't died from an accidental electrocution on a trip to Bangkok in 1968. Indeed, Cardenal had already built a straw house for the spiritually restless Merton to live in.

"Merton would have loved it here," Cardenal mused wistfully. "Nicaragua has more poets per capita than any other country. That's a big part of my job, to teach the people how to make poetry, to paint, make music, cultivate our native crafts. This, too, is part of the revolutionary process, to create a culture of the people."

I found Ernesto as utterly sincere as he was politically naive. He knew nothing of repressive communist societies as they existed in Eastern Europe, Asia, and the Soviet Union. It didn't matter. The Sandinistas, he insisted, were building a new kind of democratic socialism that promised a cooperative way of life rather like that of a monastic community. Communism meant the people working together, praying together, creating together, and sharing the fruits of their enterprise. When he spoke of Nicaragua becoming "a society of brothers and sisters," it was clear that he imagined the future of the entire nation as an enlargement of his vision for the community of Solentiname. All this confirmed my belief that poets—especially poet-priests—are ill-fit for politics: they aim at different things.

As the sun settled into the horizon, Cardenal invited us to stay for dinner and the night. We were glad on several counts: Lake Nicaragua is the world's only inland lake with sharks, and there were no lights on our boat. But the soldier insisted the outboard was now in working condition and that we must make for San Carlo. And so we did. But Marvin, our pilot, refused to fly from there to Managua in the darkness. That meant no dinner for us that night, and no beds, no blankets, no toilets, either. But as we stretched out on narrow wooden benches in a thatched agricultural commune, Marvin reached into his bag and held up a roll of toilet paper, pointing silently to me and then to himself so the others wouldn't notice. Toilet paper was a rationed item, one roll per person per week. Greater love hath no Nicaraguan, I decided, than to share his precious stash of tissues. Ernesto would have loved the gesture.

A People's Church

Solentiname was a dreamscape compared to the Reggio barrio, center of one of the first base ecclesial communities in Managua. The barrio was a vast urban slum, home to some forty thousand Managuans whose makeshift homes were heaped one upon another along unlighted dirt paths. What illumination there was came from the glow of TV sets tuned to U.S. reruns of *Kojak* and *Dragnet*. At the center was our destination, the church of Santa Maria de Los Angeles, for an evening with its pastor, Franciscan friar Uriel Molina.

As a priest and pastor, Molina was Liberation Theology's total package. He had been among the few seminarians from Latin America whose intellectual promise merited study in Rome during Vatican Council II. The bishops' message at Medellín had given him a vision of activist engagement with politics and the poor. While still a professor at the University of Central America he took charge of the barrio parish and then invited his students to come learn from his poor parishioners what liberation meant to them. The aim, as he saw it, was to rid them of their bourgeois assumptions— much as Gibson Winters and the Chicago Urban Training Center had tried to teach suburban students like Hillary Rodham to see the world from the perspective of inner-city blacks. When the revolution came, the people of the barrio gave it their full support.

Unlike the Cardenal brothers, Molina never joined the Sandinista party. But his vigorous support of the revolution was such that the junta offered him the post of Nicaraguan ambassador to Germany. Instead he chose to remain a parish priest. He also created an institute to explore the relationships between Marxism and Christianity, using donations from fellow Franciscans in the United States, the World Council of Churches, and other religious organizations that supported Liberation Theology.

From our conversation it was clear that Molina regarded the Sandinista revolution as the embodiment of "the people's will," with the party serving as the vanguard of that will. Given this new "reality," the clergy's duty was to create a "popular church" that would not only embrace the revolution but also eventually purify and transform the bourgeois institutional church represented by the hierarchy and its leader, Archbishop Obando y Bravo, who had by then turned against the revolution as a Marxist threat to the established church.

Beginning with St. Francis and his embrace of "Lady Poverty," the Franciscans have always harbored a subversive, anti-institutional streak, and there was some of that in Molina's conflict with the bishops. But the squat, plainspoken Obando y Bravo was one of the very few Latin American bishops with a peasant background, and for that reason was much beloved by "the people." Moreover, most of the clergy supported him. And so it was not altogether clear who owned the hearts of the poor, Obando y Bravo or the representatives of the popular church.

But what, exactly, was the popular church? That was the other reason I had made my way to Santa Maria de Los Angeles, a modernist sanctuary mounted on metal girders like legs of a giant grasshopper. Father Molina was to celebrate the Misa Campesina, the much-ballyhooed peasants' mass, composed by musician Carlos Mejia, that had become the most complete liturgical melding of the revolution with Liberation Theology. That evening the congregation was in full throttle, accompanied by guitars and drums. I braced myself for a Nicaraguan version of the tediously keening folk masses à la Peter, Paul & Mary that passed for "contemporary" liturgical music in the United States. Mejia's melodies were more sophisticated and hum-worthy. The real difference, though, was in the lyrics. The God of the Misa Campesina was "the worker God," "the laborer Christ" who is resurrected "in every arm outstretched / to defend the people against the exploitation of rulers." At the Kyrie, the congregation called upon this God not for mercy, as in the traditional mass, but for His support against the ruling classes:

> Christ Jesus identify with us.
> Lord my God, identify with us.
> Christ Jesus be in solidarity
> Not with the oppressor class
> That squeezes and devours
> The community
> But with the oppressed
> With my people thirsty for peace.

This was liturgy as ideology, but the indoctrination did not end with the mass. The Diego Rivera–like murals Molina had commissioned to cover the church walls were a visual celebration of the Sandinista revolution. Though the murals were not yet finished, one could already see in panoramic sequence the history of Nicaragua told as a narrative that begins in oppression—first by Spanish colonizers, then by the Yankee imperialists—leading to the Somoza dictatorship and climaxing in the revolution. Augusto César Sandino, Carlos Fonseca, Ajax Delgado—all the fallen heroes of the revolutionary movement were on display as figures in a modern martyrology. So, too, were Camilo Torres and Archbishop Romero as witnesses to Liberation Theology's wider communion of saints. The panels were arranged, Molina explained, as a contemporary Stations of the Cross celebrating the death and resurrection of the Nicaraguan people.

As he spoke I thought of how the Puritan settlers had read themselves into the Bible by identifying their journey to America as a new exodus of God's people out of bondage and to the New Israel. Here, though, was an even nervier exercise in the appropriation of sacred story: the embedding of a political insurrection in the passion, death, and resurrection of Jesus. If this was the popular church, redeemed and at prayer, I wondered what would happen to it and its liturgy over the long haul if, like most revolutions, this one failed to make good on its promises.

The Jesuits' Economic Plans

I could understand why native Nicaraguans like Molina, D'Escoto, and the Cardenal brothers would want to serve the revolutionary process. But what motivated the Jesuits there, most of whom were foreigners? Drawn to power as much as to the poor wherever they went, the Jesuits had for centuries tutored the children of Latin America's elites, hoping to influence society indirectly through their students. But in response to Vatican Council II, the order's father

general, Pedro Arrupe, issued a public mea culpa for failing to educate the poor. He told the Jesuits they now had "a moral obligation"
to work for "social justice" as the new form of Christian evangelization. With campuses in El Salvador as well as Managua, the Jesuits
at the University of Central America represented a valuable reser-
voir of knowledge and experience of the region and its problems.
What they offered the junta was not theological or liturgical cover
for the revolution but something much more useful: ideas, analysis,
and technical expertise.

The rector of the Jesuit community was a thirty-six-year-old
priest from Omaha, Father Peter Marchetti, who had left Marquette
University for Nicaragua because he thought his knowledge of agricultural economics would be a greater benefit to peasants than to
the sons of prosperous Wisconsin dairy farmers. What he found, he
said, was an economy in shambles, a shortage of staples like bread,
and a market driven heavily by women selling milk and eggs from
their back doors. Even on the larger farms, owners could not accumulate enough capital to buy machinery. To make matters worse,
the Contra buildup on the borders required the conscription of
much-needed farm laborers. "Go back and tell President Reagan
that he is choking a country that cannot feed itself, much less send
troops to Salvador," he said. "Tell him we have about five thousand
foreigners here, most of them from Cuba, and they are not training
soldiers. They are mostly teachers, doctors and nurses, construction
workers giving us services we cannot provide for ourselves because
of Mr. Reagan."

If I wanted to understand the Sandinistas' political economy, everyone told me, I had to talk to Xabier Gorostiaga, easily the most
imposing intellect among the Jesuits of Central America. Like Pedro
Arrupe, Gorostiaga was from the fiercely independent Basque region of Spain—which is why, perhaps, he had chosen to devote his
life to freeing the Central American region from Yankee domina-
tion. His credentials included advanced degrees from Cambridge
and the London School of Economics. While still in his thirties, he
had served as chief economic advisor to the government of Panama
in the negotiations with the Carter administration that led to the

gradual Panamanian acquisition of the Panama Canal. Right after the revolution, the Sandinista junta invited him to come to Managua and draw up an economic plan for the new Nicaragua.

Neither a Marxist nor a member of the FSLN, Gorostiaga nonetheless supported the idea that the peasants and workers who formed the backbone of the revolution had earned the right to have their own—very basic—needs met first. Instead of the "trickle-down" economics of the Reagan administration, in which the boats of the poor were the last to be lifted and the yachts of the rich first, his plan envisioned a "trickle-up" approach that put off till last the richest sector's private accumulation of surplus wealth. Even so, his plan provided from the start for a "mixed economy" of public- and private-sector forces. Government-planned economies, he knew, were notoriously unproductive.

Although the Jesuit described his plan as one called forth by the particulars of the Sandinista political model, it was also, I thought, a very concrete application of Catholic social teachings, which have traditionally favored a vague third way between capitalism and socialism. But Gorostiaga's plan depended very much on development funds from outside countries and international agencies, which the Reagan administration was doing its utmost to block. Indeed, Gorostiaga himself went to Washington to explain to Congress that the administration's policies were forcing Nicaragua to lean on socialist nations when its goal was a nonalignment posture that included relations with the United States, Europe, and Third World countries. He got a hearing—but also an absurd lecture on the errors of Liberation Theology from Vice President George H. W. Bush.

Before I left his rooms, Gorostiaga briefly outlined his long-term scheme for a Central American common market that would, he hoped, bring peace, economic stability, and political solidarity to a region of former banana republics struggling under a staggering collective debt of more than $11 billion. In countries like Nicaragua that bordered both the Pacific and the Caribbean seas, he foresaw the creation of ports facilitating new international trade routes through the region. Listening to him, I was reminded that once before, in the late sixteenth and early seventeenth centuries, the Jesuits had administered most of what is now Paraguay on behalf of the Portuguese crown. The inhabitants then were poor Indian tribes and by all unbiased accounts the Jesuits did an efficient and humane job in building thriving communities. That was real Liberation Theology. But as we now know, there would be nothing commensurable in Nicaragua, or Central America.

The Collapse of Liberation Theology

Here, in brief, is what happened in Nicaragua. The Sandinistas rejected Gorostiaga's plan in favor of a more Leninist program of state planning. In 1985, Daniel Ortega was elected president in one of the freest and most open elections in the nation's history, only to lose five years later to a new coalition of opposition leaders backed by the United States. The Reagan administration's destabilization strategy worked, but it cost the lives of thirty thousand Sandinista and Contra fighters. The war also produced one of the biggest political scandals of the century: the Iran-Contra affair, an illegal and clandestine exchange of arms for hostages in which Colonel Oliver North, Assistant Secretary of State Elliott Abrams, and fourteen other administration officials were indicted on various charges, including lying to Congress. All but one received presidential pardons.

Miguel D'Escoto served several more years as foreign minister but never returned to the priesthood. Ernesto Cardenal eventually broke with Daniel Ortega, charging that he had betrayed the revolution and become just another self-aggrandizing politician. Solentiname became a tropical tourist destination. Uriel Molina was kicked out of the Franciscans but remained a priest. The Misa Campesina survives as a period piece, still available as a recording by Melina Mercouri. The popular church melted into the institutional church, as the pope hoped it might, and Archbishop Obando y Bravo was promoted to cardinal. Peter Marchetti moved on to Honduras, where his pastoral work with the poor made him a target of death squads. Xabier Gorostiaga continued to work in Central America, becoming rector of the university before he died in 2003.

Fittingly, he was buried near the Castle of Loyola, where the founder of the Jesuits, Iñigo Lopez de Oñaz y Loyola (St. Ignatius Loyola), was born. In 1991, work began on a new, $3 million cathedral built between two shopping malls and financed almost entirely by the American billionaire Tom Monaghan, founder of Domino's Pizza, who devoted his fortune to numerous conservative Catholic causes. The Hotel InterContinental still stands but has another name and the bar is no longer a watering hole for foreign journalists. In 2006, Daniel Ortega again won the presidency and a decade later he, his family, and his allies controlled much of the country's land, its major companies, and the media, not to mention the police, the courts, the military, and the Congress—all of which allowed them to live the opulent kind of life the Somoza clan had.

Outside Nicaragua, Liberation Theology ceased to be a revolutionary force within the Latin American church as the bishops who supported the movement died or retired. In nearly every case Pope John Paul II replaced them with conservative men opposed to the movement. A few of the Liberation Theologians were called to Rome to defend themselves against various charges, and in one sensational case, the hugely popular Brazilian Leonardo Boff was silenced for a year. He eventually left the priesthood.

Even so, the Liberation Theologians were right in one respect. The poor of Latin American did crave base ecclesial communities where they could learn the Bible and find a home in an oppressive world. Ironically, however, the communities that prospered were Evangelical—mainly Pentecostal—churches in which even jobless campesinos could become ministers of the Gospel and every believer could experience the power of the Holy Spirit—just the sort of allegedly otherworldly Christianity that Liberation Theology had hoped to eradicate.

My own sense is that Liberation Theology was done in chiefly by geopolitical events that occurred outside Latin America. The collapse of communism in Eastern Europe, the dismantling of the Soviet Union, and the corresponding triumph of liberal capitalism rendered socialism passé as the answer to Latin America's still intractable economic and political woes. And Pentecostalism offered a viable economic as well as religious alternative. By 1989, a number of Liberation Theologians had concluded that Marxism was too crude a tool for analyzing social structures. Gutierrez himself declared, "Socialism is not an essential of Liberation Theology . . . one can do liberation theology without espousing socialism."[3] But without Marx, without socialism, and without associated theories about Latin America's dependence on capitalist countries as the cause of its poverty, Liberation Theology lost its revolutionary edge.

But to the north, another liberation movement was already well advanced. This movement, too, sought to emancipate the oppressed. And as we will see, it owed some of its ideas and techniques to Liberation Theology.

CHAPTER 8

Women's Liberation and the Feminization of Religion

The Secular Initiative

The women's liberation movement—or second-wave feminism, as it came to be called—began about the same time that Liberation Theology did. At first glance their emergence in the early Sixties on separate continents appears to be no more than historical coincidence. For one thing, religion is barely mentioned in the women's movement's founding document, *The Feminine Mystique.* Author Betty Friedan was a secular Jew, as was the movement's later and most visible leader, Gloria Steinem. Neither, in my occasional conversations with them, betrayed a knowledge of or interest in religious questions. Like a great many feminist leaders, the movement *was* their religion.

For another, the women's movement was not, at least at its inception, concerned much with the poor. The women Friedan wrote about were upper-middle-class, well-educated housewives like herself. Their "problem that has no name," as she called it, was the psychosocial malaise that came as a consequence of their thralldom to the "feminine mystique"—the confinement of women's roles to marriage and motherhood in "the comfortable concentration camp" of suburban life. Her one mention of religion was to criticize Judaism and Christianity for sanctifying these confining roles.

When I first read *The Feminine Mystique,* it struck me as yet another journalistic polemic against the flaccid Fifties and the putative emptiness of suburban life. Friedan, who soon divorced and moved back to the city, seemed to know nothing of the corresponding male mystique by which a "working wife" implied a husband who could not live up to a man's duty to be the sole support of his family. Her haughty dismissal of "housewives" as vapid consumerists overlooked the division of labor in which wives managed the household spending from the husband's paycheck. I was certain she had never met the factory worker who turned over his wages at week's end to his wife, and then was handed his allowance for a Friday night at the bar with his buddies from the day shift. Who, in short, was the empowered marriage partner—the one who made the money or the one who controlled how most of it was spent?

But of course I was reading Friedan's book from a man's perspective.

The Feminine Mystique became a feminist classic mainly because so many highly educated, well-provided-for wives read their stories into its pages—much like religious folks read their stories into the Bible. Friedan's timing was perfect: the postwar boom in higher education was producing an educated elite of women with few career options outside of nursing and teaching. Friedan's vision imagined a society of equals, not only in the home but also in law offices, architectural firms, and hospital operating rooms—Smith and Vassar graduates alongside men from Harvard, Yale, and Princeton. It was difficult to justify the higher education of women—and this was Friedan's most salient argument—if most of them ended up trapped like Nora in Ibsen's *A Doll's House.*

As it progressed, the women's liberation movement developed a set of practices much like those I'd seen in Latin American Liberation Theology. Consciousness-raising was the most obvious. Gathered together in homes or other feminist base communities, often around texts like Friedan's, women shared their personal stories and became programmatically aware of the larger, male-dominated structures that oppressed them. Feminists also formed alliances, not only among themselves, like the National Organization for Women (NOW), but also with the Democratic Party, which, especially after *Roe v. Wade,* became the movement's political party of choice. As in Liberation Theology, gaining political power was central to the feminist cause.

The initial goals of the women's liberation movement were modest and practical: equal opportunity in education and the workplace. These were goals that even women who did not identify with feminist ideology could share. But once doors were opened to them in corporations and the professions, women did not change Wall Street, or law or medicine, much less make them more humane, as some feminists had prophesied. Rather, the discipline of the marketplace and the demands of competition changed them, as social historian Christopher Lasch predicted.[1] This would not be the case when religious feminists took on male privilege in the church.

The first hint I got that there was something called feminist theology in the making occurred in November 1971—which may have been the first time Harvard theologian Harvey Cox ran into it as well. Cox had a number of women in his popular class "Eschatology and Politics" at the divinity school. During one class session the female students hooted on party-favor kazoos every time Cox or any of the male students used *he* in reference to God or *mankind* to mean the human race. Cox was usually well ahead of the curve in sniffing out the next trend in theology, but he apparently didn't realize it was happening on his own turf. It wasn't merely "pronoun envy" (as some Harvard anthropology professors slyly suggested) that roused his female students' ire. As one of those students put it in an interview with me, "The education here is geared for males, with a view toward their working in a male-oriented church with a male-dominated theology, male symbols, and a male God."

Sex and Religious Symbolism

This much Cox's students got right: whatever else they may be or do, religions are powerful symbol systems that shape the consciousness of those who live in their embrace. In the myths and stories, images, and rituals of these systems, the polarity of male and female sexuality is deeply inscribed and variously expressed. What Cox's students had yet to understand is that religious symbol systems are not simply mirrors reflecting social norms and structures. Religious symbols can subvert as well as reinforce social hierarchies, which often happens in populist and apocalyptic religious movements. Nor does the worship of female deities make for more egalitarian societies. Athena was the (bisexual) goddess of both militaristic Sparta and democratic Athens, where only men could vote. In Hinduism we find males worshipping female deities and female devotees of male deities with no difference in social norms. As historian Caroline Walker Bynum and other scholars have pointed out, even in male monotheisms, men and women can and do invest the same religious symbols with different meanings.[2] In short, where "God is male," it doesn't always follow that "males are gods," as Mary Daly, an early and hugely influential feminist theologian, insisted.

In the Catholic symbol system, the one that I know best, God is always masculine—"Father"—but the body of believers (men as well as women) is always feminine: "Holy Mother the Church." While Catholicism's most consequential theologian, Thomas Aquinas, was rigorously adversarial (masculine) in writing his *Summa Theologica,* Catholicism's most popular saint, Francis of Assisi, was frankly feminine in submitting himself to God through devotion to "Lady Poverty." In traditionally Catholic cultures, devotion to the Virgin Mary is more pronounced among men than women. There is much sociological truth in the old line about Italian atheists: they will insist there is no God, but will swear that Mary is His mother. Mom rules.

The relationship between gender and leadership is also complex. Men have always exercised institutional authority in the Christian church. In this respect, emergent Christianity echoed the gender norms of the wider society, initially Jewish, then Greco-Roman: there were few Cleopatras in the ancient world in which Christianity spread. On the other hand, Christian marriage accorded women greater dignity than they had in Roman society and protected convert wives from abuse, especially forced abortions and infanticide by the all-powerful and child-averse Roman paterfamilias.[3] With the rise of monasticism, women found in religious orders the space to develop their own forms of power as well as specifically female forms of spirituality. Thus, speaking safely from within her own sphere of influence, a Catherine of Siena could freely criticize a sitting pope—something precious few bishops, even now, would dare to do. And in the nineteenth century a teenage nun behind cloistered walls, Theresa of Lisieux, could compose a spiritual autobiography that would move another pope to declare her a Doctor [*sic*] of the Church. In the pyramidal structure of the Catholic Church, only males can be popes. But in the culture of Catholicism, saints vastly outweigh popes in symbolic power and influence. Over the last nine centuries only five popes have been canonized saints (the last two in 2014)—fewer than the number of women (mostly nuns) canonized annually in recent years. None of this should be surprising in light of the inversion of status that runs through the Gospels: "The last shall be first, the first last."

The Protestant Domestication of Religion

As we saw in Latin America, revolutions in religious structures entail revolutions in religious symbolism as well. In the parts of Europe where the Protestant Reformation took hold, the reformers rejected more than just the authority of the pope and the pyramidal structure of the Catholic Church. They also emptied the monasteries and convents, where specifically male and female forms of spirituality were nourished, and they destroyed the richly symbolic statues and stained-glass windows through which the illiterate faithful were catechized in the stories of Mary and the saints. Martin Luther's marriage to a former nun symbolized the eventual emergence of godly homes—mother-centered households that fathers tutelarily ruled—as a new center of Christian formation alongside the local congregation. This was the domesticated Christianity that crossed the ocean with the Pilgrims. Once the Puritan yoke of minister and magistrate collapsed and church and state were separated, competing Protestant denominations emerged as diverse families of faith and the voluntary Protestant congregation became, in effect, an extension of the home.

Thanks in part to feminist historians like Ann Braude, we now know that from the colonial period forward, women have constituted the majority of religious participants in the United States. Already in the seventeenth century, the great Puritan divine Cotton Mather could complain that "there are more godly women in the world than godly men."[4] In the eighteenth century, the experience of personal conversion promoted during the Second Great Awakening entailed an emotional surrender to Christ that was more attuned to female than to male piety. In the middle of the nineteenth century, liberal Protestant clergy, in league with the female majority in their congregations, elevated women as *the* exemplars of Christian virtue. But there was little that was virile in the virtues upheld. In reaction to this feminization of the churches, thousands of white males retreated to the masculine fellowship and quasi-religious rituals of the Freemasons, the Odd Fellows, the Knights of Pythias, and other fraternal orders. By 1900, notes historian David G. Hackett, there were more fraternal lodges in Boston and other American cities than there were churches.[5]

With the Protestant churches as their base, women formed their own seminaries for training nonordained church workers, their own foreign missionary societies, and interdenominational domestic movements, such as the Woman's Christian Temperance Union, that aimed to reform and purify the nation's unruly, male-dominated public life. Inevitably, the question arose: since women were evangelizing society in all these ways, why shouldn't they do so from the pulpit?

Bodies in Christ

As recently as 1965, it was as rare to see a woman in the pulpit as it was to see one on the train during my morning commute. The American Association of Women Ministers had but four hundred members and the number of fully ordained women graduates of accredited seminaries, most of them Methodist, Presbyterian, or United Church of Christ, was fewer than one thousand—less than one percent of the mainline Protestant clergy. Denominational seminaries were good places for devout Protestant women to meet God-fearing men: as a result, more female seminary students married male classmates than graduated with degrees of their own. And afterward, these wives found that they had effectively married their husband's congregation as well.

Although the Reformation had proclaimed the priesthood of all believers, most Protestants took the Pauline prohibition of women preaching in church to *also* mean that women were not meant to be leaders of a congregation. Women with seminary degrees tended to go into religious education or music ministries or followed their husbands into foreign missions. Those who did get a call to the pulpit faced wives as well as husbands who preferred as pastor a model married man with model children and a model wife to match. Though the rule is unwritten, marriage has always been nearly as necessary for ordained Protestants as celibacy is for Catholic priests. Even now, an attractive young bachelor—never mind an attractive young single woman—is apt to be regarded as an unwanted congregational distraction. In Jewish congregations, the preference for married rabbis was historically even more pronounced because celibacy has no place in Judaism.

But out in rural and other less regimented regions of religious America, there were in the early Sixties another three thousand or so women preachers. Most of them were self-anointed evangelists of a Pentecostal, independent Baptist, or nondenominational bent—women who simply heard a call or found that the Holy Spirit had endowed them with the gift to heal. Like their male counterparts, they created their own constituencies through their personal charisma in the pulpit. Dramatic rather than demure, they embodied the kind of divine power that they offered to those who listened to them.

As it happened, my first encounter with a woman preacher was with one of these. The experience brought immediately to mind what Samuel Johnson had famously (and rudely) said of women preachers, "Sir, a woman's preaching is like a dog's walking on his hind legs. It is not done well; but you are surprised to find it done at all." But then the dyspeptic Dr. Johnson had never met a woman preacher like Kathryn Kuhlman.

The famously flamboyant Kuhlman was well into her sixties when she swept into my office in 1974 to promote her upcoming healing service in Los Angeles. She was slim and enduringly sexy with a flashing smile and radiant red hair set off by a bright blue outfit that shouted Rodeo Drive. Kuhlman was escorted by her musical accompanist, Dino, a handsome Italian stud half her age. The way they giggled and played off each other made me think they might be lovers, too. Kuhlman wanted me to know that she was an evangelist just like Billy Graham, and indeed in her prime she had drawn crowds the match of his. Both were stand-up solo performance artists who augmented their preaching with the language of the body. But whereas the Hollywood-handsome Graham deliberately tried to suppress his manifest sex appeal, Kuhlman acknowledged hers in wispy floor-length gowns that clung just enough to shadow forth a body any model would envy. She healed by touch. Kuhlman knew where her pulpit power lay, and it wasn't just with the Holy Spirit.

Like her equally famous precursor, Aimee Semple McPherson, Kathryn Kuhlman was an outlier among women in the pulpit, able to be both spiritual and alluring in ways that other female pastors could not. Most of the congregations that accepted women as pastors were small—typically fewer than two hundred members—and as emotionally volatile as an intimate extended family. There were boundaries to be maintained, taboos to observe. In an article for *Newsweek,* women pastors told me how they had to watch the language spoken by their clothes. They didn't want to call attention to their bodies, but neither did they want to appear altogether sexless. The challenge was to choose their wardrobe, accessories, and the like (should the pastor wear perfume?) so that they were neither more fashionable than the women in the congregation, nor too plain for their husbands. Above all, they did not want to appear seductive, even on social occasions. "Matronly" with a string of pearls was the safest look. And so, when I began to read achingly tendentious books on "the theology of the body" by feminist theologians who seemed to be just discovering theirs, the one dimension missing from their discourse on the meaning of the female body was the erotic.

In sum, there were a number of reasons why large numbers of women, especially those of an independent feminist bent, did not seek ordination to the Protestant ministry, even after most mainline denominations decided to accept them. The pay was low, the welcome uncertain, the prospects of ecclesial advancement dim. Eventually, some of these disincentives would fade, but not before another, highly symbolic barrier was breached.

Women as Priests

As late as 1970, the one mainline Protestant denomination that still refused to ordain women was the Episcopal Church. It was also the one Protestant church that retained the pre-Reformation concept of the priesthood and the sacramental and ceremonial functions that go with it. On this view, the priest is not just a minister licensed to preach and pastor, but a "second Christ" empowered by holy orders to preside over the Eucharist as Jesus did. Similarly, an Episcopal bishop is not just an administrator but a successor to the Twelve Apostles. Although Episcopal priests usually married, unless they were gay (as, it turned out, a great many were), as celebrants of the liturgy and conferrers of sacraments they were set apart from the laity in the same way as priests in the Catholic and Orthodox churches.

But unlike the Church of Rome, the Episcopal Church is **governed by a two-tiered legislature—a House of Bishops and a House** of Deputies (clergy and lay representatives)—with the power to alter canon law. To change the canons prescribing males-only clergy, however, would not only risk estrangement from the wider Anglican communion, but also rupture ecumenical relations with the oldest and largest Christian bodies in the world. Indeed, it was precisely its claim to continuity with the "fathers" of the early church that gave Anglicans everywhere their distinctive identity as a bridge between Catholic, Orthodox, and Protestant traditions.

To the Episcopal women who wanted to be priests, the argument from tradition only proved that the tradition was inherently sexist, a sin that by the Seventies ranked right up there with racism as a form of discrimination. To them, and to those bishops sympathetic to their cause, the only tradition that mattered was the prophetic, exemplified by Martin Luther King Jr. The barrier they hoped to breach was more than merely canonical: it was the symbolism embedded in the church's sacramental system. To see a woman stand at altars where only men had stood, robed in vestments that only men had worn—in short, to see a female take the place of Jesus at the Last Supper—was to destroy the symbiotic connection between Jesus and gender that privileged males over females in the church. This was something that the ordination of women in the less liturgical Protestant churches could not do, and success would enhance the validation of women clergy everywhere. For all these reasons, therefore, the struggle over women's ordination in the Episcopal Church acquired importance for constituencies far beyond the relatively small (2.9 million at the time) membership of a single denomination.

Adapting tactics from the women's movement, female deacons and other women in the church formed committees and caucuses like Women's Ordination Now (WON, a reversal of NOW) and lobbied progressive bishops who had embraced the prophetic position on civil rights. One of these was Paul Moore, bishop of New York, who personally favored women's ordination. But in 1973, when five women presented themselves to Moore at an ordination ceremony for five men, Moore passed them by. Moore was also a Marine veteran of World War II and to violate laws he was pledged to uphold was something he was reluctant to do. A year later in Philadelphia, however, three retired bishops stepped forward and ordained eleven female deacons to the priesthood. Not surprisingly, the bishops defended their "irregular" ordination ceremony as a prophetic act: "It is our obedience to the Lordship of Christ, our response to the sovereignty of His Spirit for the Church," they said.[6] What they didn't say is that as retirees they faced no canonical sanctions.

The purpose of ordaining "the Philadelphia Eleven," as they inevitably called themselves, was to present the reluctant laity with a fait accompli. As the Bishop Pike affair demonstrated, Episcopalians were deeply averse to public scandals, and the women's ordinations, valid though illicit, threatened schism in the church. To emphasize this possibility, the newly ordained women immediately embarked on a liturgical tour, celebrating Holy Communion in several cities. Against those who found women at the altar symbolically inappropriate, one of the women insisted that it was *men* who were miscast at the altar. "What the priest does," said Suzanne Hiatt in a press interview, "is first of all he dresses up in a long dress and then, in giving communion, he prepares a meal and then he does the dishes."[7] In other words, the Eucharist is just another church supper.

The strategy behind the illicit ordinations was to pressure undecided delegates to the church's 1976 General Convention to change canon law. And that, after much public acrimony on both sides, is what the ordinations accomplished. The next push of the envelope came a year later when Bishop Moore re-won his liberal stripes by ordaining Ellen Barrett, the church's first openly lesbian or gay priest. The consecration of women as bishops followed soon enough and in 2006 one of them was elected presiding bishop of the church.

The ordination of women as Episcopal priests produced powerful reactions outside the United States. After sixteen years of public debate and acrimony the General Synod of the Church of England agreed, by a margin of only two votes, to follow suit. This caught the Vatican's attention: in 1994, Pope John Paul II, responding to the Anglicans' action and to similar demands from within his own church, declared that "the Church has no authority whatsoever to confer priestly ordination on women and that this judgment is to be definitively held by all the Church's faithful."[8] His reasons, based mainly on the maleness of Jesus and of Jesus' chosen inner circle of the Twelve Apostles and the constant tradition of the church, did not convince those scholars who think the gender of Jesus irrelevant or that the early church fathers had suppressed a tradition of female leadership in the early church. As for feminist Catholics, John Paul's effort to settle the issue by papal fiat was taken as yet another example of the male authoritarianism that they considered a consequence of sexism in the church.

My own reaction was that the pope had done the right thing for the wrong reasons, and in the wrong way. The ordination of women would have produced organizational chaos in a church that had yet to absorb all the reforms of Vatican Council II. There is, after all, no precedent for a Christian priesthood composed of celibate males and females, much less for his-and-her rectories. Would women's ordination, then, require a married priesthood as well? That change alone would entail a century of paralyzing retooling and reshaping of an international organization that has long depended on the energy, labor, and evangelical commitment of celibate nuns and priests. These were the sorts of practical issues that proponents of women's ordination refused to address. On the other hand, by refusing any sort of patient research and reasoned discussion of such issues, the pope did the church no long-term favor. Given the continuing crisis in priestly vocations, the time approaches when the survival of the priesthood itself may depend on widening the circle of acceptable applicants.

The battle for women's ordination belongs to the early phase of the women's liberation movement, with its emphasis on equal rights and opportunities. The result was hailed as a victory for "inclusivism." But one had to look inside the nation's seminaries to understand what the ensuing feminization of the clergy meant.

The Minister as Mom

As I noted in Chapter 4, the mainline Protestant ministry once rivaled law, medicine, and business as an attractive option for young college graduates. Students entered prestige divinity schools like Harvard, Yale, the University of Chicago, Vanderbilt, and Union Theological Seminary to become either clergymen or scholars of religion. But every year these elite schools also attracted a cohort of men just back from fighting wars, or hoping to avoid having to, who wanted to spend a year or two deciding what to do with the rest of their lives. Vice President Al Gore was one, and so was another Democratic presidential hopeful, Gary Hart.

Over the next two decades, however, the student bodies at these institutions underwent dramatic change. Gradually, women students outnumbered men at nearly all of them. Women achieved pluralities at many denominational seminaries as well. This trend was in part a strategy for institutional survival. "If we had to depend on the number of men coming to seminary," acknowledged David Ramage, president of McCormick Theological Seminary in Chicago, "we'd be in a bad way." (Even the leading Catholic schools of theology, once males-only enclaves, accepted female theology students and faculty to offset the steep decline in candidates for the priesthood—and to give the seminarians the experience of women as colleagues and teachers.)

The quality of the student body changed as well.[9] Like the men before them, the brightest and most ambitious women went right from college into graduate studies in law, finance, and other high-paying, high-status professions. Of course, some of these gifted female students did opt for a divinity degree instead. But on average, most divinity students were a decade older. That did not mean they were necessarily more mature. Many were seeking second careers, often after having failed to find success or fulfillment in the first. Many of the women, in particular, were divorced. Often they were single moms as well and quite a few were middle-aged. In the Seventies and Eighties, I was occasionally invited to lecture seminary students, and I was struck not only by the number of women in the audience but also by how many seemed to be on a spiritual search. My impressions were confirmed by a number of people who work with seminarians.

From his twenty years of counseling ministerial candidates, psychologist L. Guy Mehl, who was also a Lutheran minister, found that many of the women he saw "had been sexually abused, many had been addicted or come from families in which addiction was present." Even among the healthy-minded women students, Rebecca Chopp, the dean of faculty at Emory University's Candler School of Theology, noted a difference between male and female students. The latter, she wrote in *Saving Work: Feminist Practices of Theological Education,* "come to theological education out of deep changes in their lives and culture." More specifically, they "come for the space and time it gives them and to gain valuable resources for living their lives."[10]

Accordingly, seminaries had changed to accommodate this therapeutic demand. By 1994, psychologist Joseph P. O'Neill, a principal research scientist at the Educational Testing Service in Princeton, New Jersey, found that "most theological schools are 'open admission' institutions that rarely reject anyone who is of sound mind and with a bachelor's degree." Indeed, in a survey of ordination practices in the United Methodist Church, by far the largest mainline denomination, O'Neill found that the church ordained 71 percent of those candidates for whom psychologists had recommended that ordination be deferred, and a third of those whom they had recommended be rejected without reconsideration.

The effect of such practices, according to O'Neill, was what he called "the de-professionalization" of the clergy. He cited one study that compared students at a Protestant seminary in Chicago with students preparing for careers as doctors and nurses. That study found that early on the students in medicine adopted "a cloak of professionalism" while the seminarians did not. Seminarians were less interested in displaying the knowledge and skills of their own profession than in being "the right kind of person." In short, the ministry was becoming "a profession without authority" where the pastor as buddy, the minister as mom, were the preferred models. O'Neill attributed this transformation to the "effect of the huge increase of female candidates on the culture of Protestant seminaries." Women, he argued, are much more likely than men to create community by sharing personal information about themselves. And by the sheer weight of numbers, he added, women "are socializing the male seminarians to do the same."[11]

A great deal of what got shared was feminist resentment of religion's oppression of women. That much was clear from reading divinity school bulletin boards, where the student body's informal curricula are always on display. There I would see notices for meetings of the pro-Bible feminists, the anti-Bible feminists, the Third World and womanist groups, and lesbian caucuses. As the co-director of the Center for Religion and Women at the Graduate Theological Union in Berkeley put it: "You either come here because you are a feminist or you leave as one. You can't escape it."

In short, the formation that took place in seminaries became both highly therapeutic and relentlessly anti-authoritarian. What mattered were relationships and the authenticity of personal experience. It was in this academic environment that feminist Liberation Theology was born.

The Bible as Androcentric Text

In the form in which it first emerged, feminist theology was Liberation Theology by and for women. (Given time, it would liberate men as well.) And as in other social movements, the first voices were the most radical. If in 1963 Betty Friedan wrestled with "the problem that has no name," by the Seventies the first generation of feminist theologians—principally Mary Daly, Rosemary Radford Ruether, and Elisabeth Schüssler Fiorenza, all of them much-aggrieved Catholics—knew what the problem was and named it "patriarchy." As they defined it, patriarchy was the original sin of the Judeo-Christian tradition, one that begat all sorts of other evils: sexism, authoritarianism, a preference for hierarchy over egalitarianism, rape of the earth as well as of women, alienation in various forms, hyperrationalism, androcentrism, phallocentrism, heterosexism, mind-body dualism, idolatry, militarism, classism, etc. This litany of accusation was no different from those heard in women's studies courses, except in one respect. In feminist Liberation Theology, all of these evil isms were sanctioned by a single sacred source: the Bible.

Written, edited, and translated solely by men, the Bible could be read—and dismissed—as the religious projection of patriarchy. Indeed, by the early Eighties, Mary Daly had concluded that the Bible was beyond feminist redemption and proclaimed herself a post-Christian feminist lesbian—much to the discomfort of the Jesuit administrators at Boston College, where she was a tenured professor. Other religious feminists decamped to countercultural goddess-worship and Wicca covens in an effort to create women-centered religions. The most influential feminist scholars, however, were determined to reclaim the Bible as a user-friendly text for women's liberation.

In 1983, Ruether published *Sexism and God-Talk: Toward a Feminist Theology* and Schüssler Fiorenza published *In Memory of Her: A Feminist Theological Reconstruction of Christian Origins*. Between them, they laid out an agenda for radical reinterpretations of the Bible aimed at both validating women's religious experience and rescuing the Bible from its patriarchal bias. Theirs would not be the disinterested scholarship favored by males in the academic guild—a false neutrality, in their view, that masked patriarchal assumptions. Instead they called for an engaged scholarship of liberation for the benefit of what Schüssler Fiorenza described as "an ekklesia of women who, in the angry power of the Spirit, are sent forth to feed, heal and liberate our own people who are women."[12]

The basic feminist liberation approach to the Bible involved variations on a four-step praxis of interpretation: begin with women's long experience as "the oppressed of the oppressed"; submit biblical texts to a "hermeneutics of suspicion" (systematically question and subvert the Bible's patriarchal bias); employ a "hermeneutics of retrieval" (recover the suppressed history of women in the Bible as well as the Bible's repressed feminine images of God); and deploy the results toward the liberation of women's experience of religion. Obviously, this approach inscribed a closed hermeneutical circle that in principle brackets male experience—which may be why the men who edited the major theological journals tended to invite only women to review books on feminist Liberation Theology.

Recovering the suppressed history of women in the Bible, especially those of the Hebrew Bible (the Christian Old Testament), is a daunting challenge. Of the 1,500 or so characters named in its pages (the number varies depending on which set of canonical texts are used), only about 10 percent are women.[13] A few, like Deborah, Esther, Judith, Ruth, and Susanna—the latter four the only women with a biblical book of their own—immediately stand out as examples of courageous leadership when compared to the faith of weak and vacillating men. Even male readers can admire them. But because they were recognized by the male compilers of the Bible, these women did not yield the history of male suppression that feminist Scripture scholars wanted to uncover.

Miriam, the sister of Moses and Aaron, provides a more promising case of patriarchal suppression. In the book of Exodus she is called a prophet (as are a few other Old Testament women), which feminist exegetes took to mean that she was a serious rival to her brothers and an early example of a powerful woman leader. In Numbers, Miriam reappears in a scene where she and Aaron question Moses' authority. That God steps in and punishes her, but not Aaron, was a sign to feminist interpreters that a pro-Moses party among the Hebrew Bible's male editors deliberately excised an earlier and more positive memory of Miriam among the ancient Israelites. Thus, if feminist interpreters could prove that women as well as men once were prophets, so the argument ran, the Bible could be rescued for use by women and the conspiracy of its male editors exposed. But given that the Bible represents the only memory we possess, even the existence of Miriam—not to mention other characters in these stories—lacks corroborating evidence. Under these circumstances, the temptation to imagine what might have been remains a serious occupational hazard—one that Harvard's James L. Kugel, a renowned historian of biblical interpretation, acknowledges "has a very distinguished history going all the way back to the third or fourth century BCE."

Since much more is known about society in first-century Israel, the New Testament is less intractable for those who want to recover the roles women played in the Jesus movement. The Jesus of the Gospels is remarkably open and at ease with women. Indeed, although he chose only men for his inner circle of "the Twelve," the women in his outer circle of disciples are more steadfast. So much for titles.

Elisabeth Schüssler Fiorenza knows this material well. She was trained in Germany in the 1950s, a time when universities there were still mandarin male enclaves where women were rarely seen, much less listened to. That may partially explain why her books display so much intellectual hauteur, and also why she considers herself a "resident alien" in the guild of Scripture scholars. *In Memory of Her* was the opening salvo in a sustained effort to prove that the earliest Christians practiced a "discipleship of equals" that included women as missionaries, preachers, and leaders of house churches—in a word, that they, too, were apostles just like the men, and deserving of the same august respect.

Of these women, feminist pride of place belongs to Mary of Magdala: after Mary the mother of Jesus, she is the woman most often mentioned in the New Testament. In the Gospel According to John she is the first of Jesus' followers to experience the risen Christ and the one who informs Peter and the other male apostles of the Resurrection. For this reason, even the androcentric Christian tradition cherishes Mary of Magdala as "the apostle to the apostles."

But in feminist liberationist construction, Mary of Magdala emerges as a rival to Peter in a male-female struggle for leadership of the post-Resurrection church. Much of the evidence supporting this view comes from the "Gospel of Mary," one of several Gnostic texts that were not included in the biblical canon. Feminist scholars regard this exclusion, plus the fact that the party of Peter actually won out, as evidence that hierarchy itself is a male malformation imposed on the more egalitarian and gender-inclusive community intended by Jesus himself.

God/She

The other major quest of feminist biblical criticism has been to mine the text for feminine language and images of God. Since the ancient Israelites were alone among Near Eastern peoples in rejecting worship of female deities, the Hebrew Bible offers few examples for feminists to build on. Most are similes that analogize some aspect of God or His activity to women's experiences. But nowhere in the Bible is God referred to as "She," much less called "Mother."

There was a reason for this male monotheism, and it wasn't just a male effort to project onto God the patriarchal structure of Israelite society, as feminist theology tends to argue. The God who emerges in the Old Testament creates by verbal fiat; unlike nearly all the gods of the ancient Near East, "He" needs no female consort. This God is altogether separate from "His" creation in a way that a mother cannot be separated from the children she brings forth from her womb. He is "holy" (at root, *holy* means "separate") and he is "one"—the "Holy One" who is personal yet totally other, beyond male/female contrarieties, beyond nature—beyond, in fact, human naming. To call this God "She"—the only other pronominal option—is to evoke a range of ideas that were foreign to the Hebrew understanding of what God is and is not. These, then, are some of the reasons why Judaism, Christianity, and Islam are, even now, the only major religious traditions that do not use feminine words and images for God.

For their part, Christian feminists had to contend with the symbolism of a triune God—Father, Son, and Holy Spirit. Some early feminist exegetes claimed that within the Trinity the Holy Spirit functions as a nurturer and thus represents the feminine principle or aspect of God. But what to do with Jesus, who was indisputably male? Sandra Schneiders, a Catholic nun and seminary professor, argued that by taking flesh as a man rather than a woman, Jesus assumed the burden of "belonging to the oppressor class," which he then subverted by behaving in a nonpatriarchal way— "nonaggressive, noncompetitive, meek and humble of heart, a nurturer of the weak"—all traits Schneiders took to be feminine.[14] This rendering of Jesus as essentially feminine overlooked his aggressive, agonistic, and divisive behavior—all masculine traits. Nor did it answer Rosemary Ruether's pointed question, "Can a male savior save women?" No, it seems, if he is understood in male-only terms as the *Son* of the *Father*.

Here Ruether, Schüssler Fiorenza, and Fordham University's Sister Elizabeth Johnson proffered a bold feminist alternative. They fastened on the female figure of Sophia, from the Greek word for Lady Wisdom, a female personification found in Proverbs and other canonical and noncanonical Hebrew texts. Sophia creates, redeems, establishes justice, gives life, and protects the world. This, of course, is what God does. Thus, instead of proclaiming Jesus Son of the Father, both patriarchal terms, Christian feminists advanced the option of proclaiming him the incarnation or manifestation of Lady Wisdom. Hence, in the title of one of her books, Schüssler Fiorenza avoids the masculine altogether in naming Jesus "Miriam's Child, Sophia's Prophet." Others proffered "Creator, Redeemer, Sustainer," a Trinity of function, or "Mother, Lover, Friend," a Trinity of bonding.

All of these proposals, it should be said, were advanced through impressive displays of scholarly acumen. On that score alone they commanded—and were accorded—academic attention. As with women's studies and gender studies, feminist theology became a discipline of its own, complete with specialized curricula, academic journals, and professors occupying endowed chairs.[15]

But the purpose of feminist theology was not only to make room for the suppressed voices and experiences of women in the past. It also aimed to create a contemporary movement of "self-identified women and women-identified men" transcending denominational boundaries.[16] Without independent worshipping communities, there could be no feminist revolution in a church or synagogue no matter how many women were ordained. These communities were christened "women-church."

"The Hot Blood of Our Wombs"

Rosemary Ruether recognized early on the need for forming "autonomous feminist base communities" where liberation from sexism, racism, militarism, and other isms could be lived out as a model for what the whole church might someday become. A veteran of movement religion, Ruether had been very active in the civil rights cause, in the Catholic resistance to the war in Vietnam—one of her early books was dedicated to Daniel Berrigan—and in liberation movements in Latin America, where I first met her. For women-church she composed a handbook of liturgies that included a "Coming Out Rite for a Lesbian," a "Rite of Mind-Cleansing from the Pollution of Sexism," liturgies for celebrating the onset and cessation of menstruation, a "Liturgy of Healing for a Battered Wife," and similar rites.

Apart from operatives like Ruether, I confess I never met any self-identified women, much less women-identified men, who belonged to women-church communities. But then neither my wife nor I was an ideal recruit. The movement seemed to thrive on the margins, the last dogged expressions of the Sixties commune culture. The likeliest recruits were liberal Catholic nuns embittered by their church's denial of ordination to women and by their own inability to attract like-minded younger novices. So were members of peace and justice groups (again, mostly Catholics) for whom the oppression of women had become *the* social justice issue. Certainly, women who studied under professors like Ruether and Schüssler Fiorenza were encouraged to build their own women-church communities. By 1993, there was a women-church network large enough to attract 2,500 representatives to a third national conference in Albuquerque, New Mexico. According to a report in the *New York*

Times, "quite a few" of the attendees "were nuns, and gray hair predominated."

The idea of celebrating women-centered religious symbols and rituals found wider support among ecumenical church agencies and many mainline Protestant denominational leaders, both male and female, for whom gender as well as racial inclusiveness had become central to their Christian witness. In 1993, the World Council of Churches sponsored a Re-imaging Conference in Minneapolis, which drew several thousand women from mainline churches. Among the conference icons were reproductions of *Christa,* a bronze sculpture by artist Edwina Sandys, an American granddaughter of Winston Churchill, which displays a nude woman crucified on a cross. The sculpture, which had already been on exhibit in the sanctuary of St. John the Divine in New York, captured exactly the twin modalities of the feminist theology: woman as victim of male oppression and woman as Our Savior from the sins of patriarchy. In their worship sessions, conference participants pointedly avoided prayers in the name of Jesus, opting instead to address God as Sophia. Rituals included a closing ceremony of milk and honey and evocations of the life-giving powers inherent in "the hot blood of our wombs" and "the nectar between our thighs." Most of these women, it should be said, were proper middle-aged churchwomen from small mainline Protestant congregations in the middle of America.

Words and Music

Beyond these sometime gatherings, the deepest penetration of feminist theology into American religion was through the inclusive language movement. In the early Eighties, the National Council of Churches published an inclusive language translation of the lectionary, the scriptures used for worship services by member denominations. Masculine pronouns for God were eliminated (although, oddly enough, Satan, who is also without body, remained "he").

References to God the Father included "and Mother" in bracketed italics to retain the sense of parenthood without the patriarchal connotation. Similarly, "Son of God" became "Child of God." The pre-Resurrection Jesus kept His personal male pronoun but the post-Resurrection Christ did not—the point being that His glorified body was genderless.

To my ear, the new lectionary represented a kind of linguistic "stripping of the altars" that once again minimized the body and its symbolism. But despite considerable grumbling from the pews, most mainline Protestants seemed to tolerate this new way of hearing God's word. Singing inclusive-language hymns, however, was something else.

Hymns are the soul music of Protestant Christianity; they also constitute a prime unbroken chain of religious witness linking the individual Protestant of today to the gathered saints who preceded them. By the early Nineties, however, most liberal mainline denominations had authorized collective surgery on their hymnals, eliminating some old standards as sexist and rewriting many others to make the raised voices of the faithful conform to liberationist canons.

The New Century Hymnal, published by the determinedly inclusive United Church of Christ, went the furthest to "bring Christian hymnody and worship into the next century"—chiefly by suppressing masculine referents to God. Thus the revised "The Battle Hymn of the Republic" no longer resounded with the familiar "He." A frankly feminine medieval hymn, "Mothering God, You Gave Me Birth," replaced the frankly masculine standard, "Praise the Father Giving Life." In "Silent Night," "Son of God" was neutered into "Child of God." "Be Thou My Vision" no longer exclaimed "Thou My great father, I Thy true son / Thou in me dwelling, and I with thee one." The revised lyrics now read like a Valentine to an androgynous parent: "Mother and Father, you are both to me / now and forever, your child I will be." And so on. There could be no "Glory to the new-born King" in "Hark! The Herald Angels Sing," because kings represent male hierarchy. Indeed, after much internal debate the editors concluded, for the same reason, that no hymn should praise "the Lord"—which, of course, is what Christian hymns are all about.

Obviously, there was more than pronoun envy at work in the revised hymnals. By suppressing some symbols and introducing new ones, the hymn doctors were promoting a new form of Christianity. Or so their critics argued. The most vociferous objectors were African Americans, whose precious store of spirituals and gospel music were promptly put off-limits to ideological redactors. Indeed, the black churches had good reason to resist the whole feminist liberation project in religion.

Matriarchal Muscle

As polls routinely confirm, the most religious group in the United States is African Americans. Apart from black Muslims, nearly all of them are Protestants, and among these the largest single constituency is Baptist. Among all American clergy, black ministers are the most politically involved, a reflection of the historic importance of the church within black communities. Only about 5 percent of black clergy are women, and most of these are Pentecostal. Yet statistics show that at least 70 percent of black church members are women. If the person in the pulpit were the only measure of power in religion, then the black church, with its deep roots in the Old Testament, would be the most patriarchal form of American religion outside Mormon Utah.

But if we look inside black congregations, we can see how much patriarchs must defer to matriarchs. Here is how the late C. Eric Lincoln, one of the great scholars of black religion, distilled for me the dialectic of gender and power in the black church:

> The well-managed black church is an organization of subgroups in which women predominate and wield their own power. Women raise the money and, though men dominate the church boards of trustees, it is their wives who effectively determine how it is spent.

Among black Baptists, power belongs to "the Mothers," a group of older women who have been in their congregations for decades and constitute the heart and soul of the church. On Sundays, the Mothers dress distinctively in white and preside from a special section—opposite the "Amen corner" where the male trustees sit. The minister who has the Mothers on his side is virtually unassailable, and woe to the minister who doesn't.

Black women have sound sociological reasons for preferring men in the pulpit. Given that 70 percent of black children are born to unwed mothers and that more than half these kids will grow up without a father in the house, black mothers and grandmothers want their children to see in a pastor the disciplined father figure who is missing from their homes. This is of special importance to mothers of boys. In the inner city, where most black churches are, 60 percent of young African American males have no contact with the church—a 20 percent increase since the civil rights era. Indeed, in the black church's turf war with the black Muslims, the latter's persistent taunt is that Christianity is a religion for women.

The role of women in black Christianity flows out of a subject people's historical experience. But how different is it from the roles women play in white churches and synagogues? For that we have to look inside the local congregations.

Half the World

According to a Chinese proverb, women hold up half the world. But in American religion, women also shoulder most of the weight. As any rabbi or Christian pastor can attest, women typically outnumber men two-to-one at worship services. Moreover, since women live longer than men, in aging congregations—about a fourth of those in mainline Protestant denominations—women represent 80 percent of the adults sitting in the pews. And that is just on weekends.

From Monday to Friday, pastors live in a world bleached of men, especially in the suburbs. Even now that most mothers hold jobs outside the home, women still dominate the church committees, the prayer groups, the Sunday schools, the Bible study groups, the office staff. Women maintain the prayer chains for the sick and dying and the day-care centers for children for "working" mothers. Of the thirty thousand Catholic lay ministers created to offset the steep decline in priests, eight out of ten are women. Conversely, the hardest challenge facing most pastors in any church setting is finding ways to draw men into active participation beyond the parish finance committee and the apparently gender-specific brotherhood of church ushers. William Willimon, a longtime Methodist minister and dean of the chapel at Duke University, spoke for legions of clergymen when he said, "No one told me when I left the seminary that most of my time would be spent with women."

One reason for this is that nurture of the young is a large part of what goes on inside religious congregations. (In liberal Protestant congregations, therapeutic functions in the form of pastoral counseling and twelve-step programs for adults occupy much of the other weeknight activities.) If we ask how children typically "get religion," the answer is through the aegis of women, not men. Synagogues fairly bustle with mothers preparing the young for their bar or bat mitzvah. The same is true of Catholic parishes where nuns and (more often) laywomen prep children for their First Holy Communion and the sacrament of Confirmation. The pastor or the rabbi is the chief executive in a congregation, but to the young he is like the principal of the school: a more or less remote authority figure, depending on his personality. As with popes and saints, authority and influence are not correlative. In religion, unlike business, those who do the formation are more significant than those who run the show.

Parents, of course, are the prime conduits for passing on religious faith. But within the family, the significance of gender is reversed. Sociologists report that the best predictor of whether a child will remain religious as an adult is the piety not of the mother— for children take that for granted—but of the father, because he is not expected to be religious. That is, if the father demonstrates that religion is important to who he is and how he lives, the child—

especially the male child—is much more likely to be religious upon reaching adulthood.

From the perspective of actual congregational life, therefore, the irony of the feminist liberation movement was this: it sought to further feminize territory already dominated by women and domesticated by their interests. By the mid-Nineties, the feminist effort had produced very mixed results. On the one hand, the culture of seminaries, where half the students were women, continued to be far more relational and therapeutic than those of other professional schools. On the other hand, few clergywomen received a call or appointment to serve as chief pastors of large, "tall steeple" congregations. This "glass ceiling" suggested that many people in the pews—men and women alike—sensed that the pulpit and the altar were the last bastions of male presence in the church.

Inevitably, feminist theology went the way of the Latin American variety: it became an academic specialty. The second generation of women scholars tended to focus less on uprooting patriarchy in the Bible and more on providing women's perspectives on specific biblical texts that traditionally had been interpreted with only male experience in mind. Indeed, some feminist theologians even returned to medieval monastic sources for fresh forms of female spirituality.

For all the heat it caused at denominational conferences and seminary classrooms, the feminist assault on religious patriarchy had a spectacularly short shelf life—especially in comparison to the stunning feminist successes in Democratic Party politics and in the departmental politics of the once-patriarchal academy. Once women were granted ordination in Protestant and Jewish seminaries and moved up the clerical ladder, the only remaining issues were equal opportunity and gender parity at the top. However, the emergence of women as bishops in the Episcopal Church, for example, did not stanch its hemorrhage in membership. If anything, it has enhanced the feminization of institutional religion in this country. The Catholic Church's rejection of female ordination to the priesthood continues to rankle many Catholic women, and many priests continue to support women's ordination in the name of social justice. But neither Rome nor the Orthodox churches have witnessed mass defections of women, which some feminist organizations predicted. On the other hand, the abject failure of the leaders of Catholic religious orders to attract women to their ways of life and service has brought most religious communities of women in the United States to the brink of extinction.[17]

Feminist theology survives as a curricular option in divinity schools and remains a touchstone for various subgroups within academic associations like the American Academy of Religion. But, like gender studies in universities, feminist theology speaks to a dwindling audience among educated women. Preoccupied with texts and dependent on maintaining a steady sense of female oppression, feminist theology was never designed for mass support like other forms of movement religion. Neither could it cross the generational divide. What the baby boomers were looking for from religion had nothing to do with ancient texts, gender wars, or institutions. What they wanted was something personal, immediate, and transformative: the experience of their selves as sacred.

Part IV

CHAPTER 9

Experiential Religion

Counterculture

At the end of the 1960s, nearly half the U.S. population was twenty-five years old or younger. Whatever the young were up to or "into" was therefore of interest to more than just their parents. Those in college became the subjects of their own professors' books on youthful alienation, published at the rate of about one new title a week, or so it seemed. As potential agents of social revolution, students also became the objects of considerable ideological coaching from left-wing junior faculty who imagined them a replacement for Marx's old industrial proletariat. Inevitably, this first wave of baby boomers was much examined and celebrated by the media as well: *Time* named them its "People of the Year" in 1969, and at *Newsweek* the editors decided to devote one cover story every September to a report on the changing "mood on campus."

The first and most influential interpretation of the dissenting young on and off the nation's college campuses was Theodore Roszak's *The Making of a Counter Culture* (1969). Like Harvey Cox's *The Secular City,* which had appeared just four years earlier, Roszak's book became indistinguishable from the social phenomena it set out to describe. Far from embracing Cox's rational and coolly pragmatic "technopolis," Roszak argued, the young were rejecting the skeptical, rationalistic culture of the universities, and with it the secular humanism that had become the dominant intellectual tradition of the West. These dissident young were turning not simply to religion but to precisely those elements of religion—myth, mysticism, and ritual—that Cox had said were obsolete. "The dissenting young have indeed got religion," Roszak wrote in one of his more understated passages. "Not the brand of religion Billy Graham or William Buckley would like to see the young crusading for—but religion nonetheless. What began with Zen has now rapidly, perhaps too rapidly, proliferated into a phantasmagoria of exotic religiosity."[1]

Something like a Third Great Awakening did indeed appear to be in the offing. But this time the beliefs and practices were drawn from various schools of Buddhism, Hindu metaphysics, Sufi mysticism, Mesoamerican shamanism (the books of Carlos Castaneda were campus bestsellers), Native American vision quests, channeling the dead, the occult—anything (and virtually everything) but the Protestantism, Catholicism, or Judaism of their parents. The young thought of themselves as spiritual rather than religious, a distinction that essentially meant they wanted something to experience rather than merely something to believe, much less doctrines to uphold. They were willing to believe almost anything so long as— and *for* as long as—those beliefs fostered a sense of the self as a sacred participant in a sacral universe.

Experiential religion was the antithesis of movement religion and reflected disillusionment with protest politics and social reform. What mattered was transformation of self rather than of society; myth and metaphysics rather than morality; expanded (or altered or higher) consciousness rather than appeals to conscience. To these ends, the religions that emerged out of India, with their refined spiritual technologies of inner exploration and yogic practices of breath and body control, were more serviceable than the pious moralisms taught in Sunday school and boring weekend sermons. Before there could be a genuine political revolution, Roszak believed, there had to be a revolution in spiritual consciousness. "What is yoga, after

all," he asked rhetorically, "but a disciplined effort to find the kingdom [of God] and enter?"

At thirty-six, Roszak was still young enough to be trusted by
the young he wrote about, and just old enough to be their willing
mentor. He was also well placed. A historian by trade, he was teaching in the San Francisco Bay area, home to the Beat poets of the
Fifties, the hippies of the Sixties, and now the supersaturated center
of every countercultural quiver. Roszak's own lodestar at the time
was the visionary poet William Blake, whose eighteenth-century
Gnostic prophecies seemed to him to be unfolding in his own time
on Northern California's shores. But if the young sought, like Blake,
"To see the world in a grain of sand / And heaven in a wild flower,"
there was a good reason: experiencing the world as suffused with
the sacred was very much like a good acid trip.

Roszak's counterculture was essentially the California hippie
subculture minus drugs. But without the mediation of the drug
culture—specifically, without hallucinogens like mescaline and
LSD—it is unlikely that many of the young would have turned so
readily to Asia for enlightenment. Already in 1953, Aldous Huxley, living in Los Angeles, had tripped on mescaline and proclaimed
it a pharmaceutical shortcut to the experience of all mystics of all
ages and all religions.[2] His short account, *The Doors of Perception*
(the title is a phrase from William Blake), became a must-read
among Sixties counterculturalists. (It was also the source for the
name of Jim Morrison's popular rock band, the Doors.) Alan Watts
and Huston Smith, two influential writers on world religions who
longed to experience the bliss they read about in Asian texts, also
ingested hallucinogens as an aide to achieving cosmic consciousness. LSD was the alchemical trigger that induced the transformation of Dr. Richard Alpert, Harvard psychologist, into Baba Ram
Dass, resident counterculture holy man in San Francisco.

But it was Alpert's more celebrated Harvard colleague, Timothy
Leary, who became the high priest and chief evangelist for the transformative benefits of LSD. The one time I encountered Leary was in
1969 at an event in Greenwich Village where he took the stage with

Harvey Cox, who read from the book of Revelation; Episcopal priest Malcolm Boyd, who read from his own book, *Are You Running with Me, Jesus?*; and comedian/activist Dick Gregory, who burned his draft card at every performance. The program was called "An Evening with God," and there was no doubt that the silver-haired Leary, sheathed in a gauzy white Indian tunic and intoning his signature mantra, "Turn on, tune in, and drop out," was playing the lead role. Already in 1962, at a Hindu temple in Boston, Leary had mixed LSD with holy water from the Ganges and—according to the story he tells in one of his books—watched as members of the temple ashram were transformed into Hindu gods and goddesses. He himself was Shiva, whose symbol is the erect phallus, and a woman from the ashram readily assumed the role of Shakti, Shiva's willing consort. "I recognized that day in the temple," Leary declared, "that we are all Hindus in our essence." From a historical perspective, Dr. Leary spoke better than he knew.

Sacred Selves: The Hindu Influence

Embedded as they are in the sacred rivers and mountains and villages associated with their cults, the Hindu gods and goddesses, some 300 million in all, have never traveled well beyond the borders of Mother India as the holy land of primordial revelation. But beginning in the nineteenth century, Vedanta metaphysics, derived from the Upanishads, Hinduism's oldest wisdom literature, proved to be both portable and potable on American soil.[3]

Ralph Waldo Emerson and other New England Transcendentalists read some Hindu texts in translation and resonated with their basic metaphysical insight that Brahman—absolute reality—is identical with Atman, the transcendental and imperishable ground of the self. Although Walt Whitman was not a Transcendentalist, much less a Hindu, his great celebratory hymn to the expansive self, *Leaves of Grass*, spoke to those Americans who never accepted the Puritans' Calvinist God, and *for* those millions of Americans who always suspected that humanity was closer to divinity than either

Judaism or Christianity would allow. What these Americans lacked was a coherent philosophy to express their intimations of inherent divinity.

Enter Swami Vivekananda, the first Hindu to evangelize the West, a kind of Apostle Paul figure who set out to show Europeans and Americans that they, too, were Hindus in their essence. In 1893, Vivekananda arrived via a railroad boxcar uninvited and unannounced in Chicago. There he managed to deliver an electrifying series of addresses in English to the first World Parliament of Religions, held in conjunction with the World's Fair. His words so impressed the four thousand gathered clergy and scholars of religion that he was invited to stay and lecture across the country. Psychologist William James, who first advanced the term *experiential religion,* quoted Vivekananda at length in his *The Varieties of Religious Experience,* and Harvard University offered Vivekananda the chairmanship of its Eastern Philosophy Department.

Vivekananda's personal mission was to spread the teachings of his revered spiritual teacher, Ramakrishna, who had died in 1886. After experimenting with Christianity and Islam—as Gandhi later did—Ramakrishna had concluded that all religions provided pathways to "God realization" and should therefore be treated with tolerance. Further, all religions should promote an ethic of service to others since all human beings share a common and innate divinity. It was a message that appealed to millions of unchurched Americans of a spiritual bent.

During his American lecture tour, Vivekananda expounded the basic principles of Ramakrishna's Advaita (nondualist) Vedanta, which emphasizes spirituality as an alternative to—even the opposite of—religion. On this view, all religions are illusory insofar as they personalize the Absolute in the form of Jesus, or the Buddha, or Allah or Shiva or Vishnu. Conversely, all religions are true insofar as they lead practitioners to experience, through meditation and other yogic disciplines, their real selves as identical with the Absolute. "Would to God," he wrote, "that the whole world were advaitist tomorrow, not only in theory, but in realization." Indeed, the whole point of Vivekananda's spirituality was to overcome the illusion that there is a God to be worshipped, other than one's own transcendental self—a self that is beyond good and evil, beyond virtue and vice, beyond misery and death. As Vivekananda tersely put it, "God does not worship God."

Before his return to India, Vivekananda established a network of Vedanta societies for laity and a few monastic communities, like the one Leary would later visit, called the Ramakrishna Mission. It was at the mission in New York City, just around the corner from his parents' apartment off Fifth Avenue, that J. D. Salinger discovered the work of Vivekananda and Ramakrishna in the late Forties. Vedanta became Salinger's lifelong religious passion and a key to the otherwise baffling spiritual crises that afflict Seymour, Franny, and other members of the Glass family.[4]

Swami Vivekananda not only shaped how Hinduism would be understood by Americans in the first half of the twentieth century; he also inspired an American intellectual and spiritual tradition that deeply influenced the Sixties counterculture. One of the key links in this chain of transmission was Aldous Huxley, who in 1942 wrote a foreword to *The Gospel of Sri Ramakrishna,* and two years later published *The Perennial Philosophy,* in which he posited a universal set of mystical experiences and beliefs behind all religions, and to which organized religions perennially return. The notion of a perennial philosophy, affirming the identification of God with the self, turned up regularly in the writings of Alan Watts, Ananda Coomaraswamy, Huston Smith, Jacob Needleman, Joseph Campbell, and other academic preceptors of the Sixties revolution in consciousness.

When I joined *Newsweek* as religion editor, I never supposed that I'd have to cover Hinduism or Buddhism or any of the other "alternate" religions, as we called them then. There simply weren't enough Hindus or Buddhists in the United States to merit more than occasional notice. That began to change in 1965 when Congress lifted previous restrictions on the number of Asians allowed to migrate to this country. Among the new wave of immigrants were a number of Hindu gurus who, having watched how Christian missionaries worked in India, decided to reverse the process. Where

Vivekananda had appealed to intellectuals by presenting Hinduism as a universal philosophy, these new and often more traditional missionaries stressed precisely those cultic aspects of Hinduism that Vivekananda had deliberately left out. This was something altogether new on the American religious landscape: the introduction of devotion to Indian gods and goddesses.

Krishna Consciousness

The most improbable of these new gurus was a seventy-year-old retired Bengali businessman commissioned by his own guru to introduce Americans to the worship of Lord Krishna. A. C. Swami Bhaktivedanta Prabhupada arrived penniless in New York City in the fall of 1965 and immediately began preaching and chanting "Hare Krishna" on the streets of the Lower East Side. Rather rapidly, he attracted a following of youthful hippies, druggies, and dropouts willing to shave their heads, don saffron robes, and go about the city playing musical instruments while chanting their trademark mega-mantra a prescribed two thousand times per day. Through this musical and ecstatic form of bhakti (devotional) yoga, a Bengali tradition going back to the sixteenth-century saint Caitanya, the Lord God Krishna would become manifest to their consciousness.

Such was the California counterculture's appetite for religious novelty that within a year, Swami Prabhupada found himself the object of a fete at a Mantra-Rock Concert in San Francisco, where several thousand young people heard Timothy Leary and Beat poet Allen Ginsberg hail the highs that come with Krishna Consciousness. It wasn't Krishna the young were celebrating but yet another method of altering consciousness.

Despite his fleshy face and bodily girth, Swami Prabhupada was an ascetic who loathed what he called "show-bottle spiritualists," meaning those Westerners who extolled Indian spirituality but refused to live the austere life of a true devotee. From his own disciples, Prabhupada required monastic discipline: abstinence from meat, fish, and milk, and from drugs, alcohol, tobacco, and sex (unless they were married); submission to the common good of the community; the study of scriptures; hours of meditation; the performance of puja (sacred ritual) every morning before an image of Krishna; and, above all, complete surrender to the swami as the teacher who dispels illusion by imparting true knowledge. Such a life was best suited to rural communes where parents could raise their children from birth in tonsured devotion to Lord Krishna, where renunciates could pursue their rigorous inner path and all could worship in the communal temple.

To experience Hinduism in this way was like joining a nineteenth-century utopian community, and for a time Prabhupada's International Society for Krishna Consciousness (ISKCON) claimed at least a thousand of them in the United States and Europe. But after the swami's death in 1977, ISKCON in the United States suffered from internal rivalries, charges of brainwashing and drug trafficking, violence toward ex-members, even lawsuits and countersuits. The center of the movement eventually shifted back to India—specifically to the city of Vrindavan, where tradition says the young Krishna was raised.

TM: Meditation for the Masses

The best-known Hindu guru, and certainly the most ambitious, was the Maharishi Mahesh Yogi. He was also, in the fashion of Billy Graham and other American evangelists, the most entrepreneurial. In the early Sixties, the Maharishi relied on the brief embrace of the Beatles, the Beach Boys, and other pop celebrities to publicize the benefits of Transcendental Meditation, only to have them discard him like an old sock. In June 1968, he announced that his mission to bring happiness to the world through the practice of TM had failed. Rather than fold his tents and return to India, however, the Maharishi restructured and adopted a new, more secular marketing plan. His literature now promoted TM as "the Science of Creative Intelligence." It worked.

Under the new rubric, the Maharishi convinced administrators at Harvard, UCLA, and a few other universities to offer students courses—for credit—in the theoretical and practical applications of Transcendental Meditation. So did public high schools in Miami, Hartford, and other cities. Instead of rock stars, the Maharishi called on researchers at Harvard and Stanford to attest to the benefits of TM. More than sixty corporations invited the International Meditation Society, the largest of six organizations set up by the Maharishi, to teach TM to employees and their wives. In Connecticut and Illinois the state legislatures passed resolutions thanking the Maharishi for bringing the Science of Creative Intelligence to the United States.

By the end of 1973, the Maharishi's enterprises were flourishing. With some four thousand teachers of TM operating out of 206 centers across the country, he had a franchise system worthy of Colonel Sanders. In the fall of that year, he opened the doors of Maharishi International University in Southern California to 250 freshmen, offering a degree in "the development of consciousness" along with academic programs. While other gurus struggled to keep their ashrams afloat, the Maharishi announced a new goal: to provide one TM teacher for every one thousand Americans.

It seemed to me that if I was going to write about the Maharishi and his meditation technique I ought at least to try it myself. My wife wanted to do it, too. Our initiation, which cost a fairly steep $125 at the family rate (half to the teacher, half to the organization), took place at a TM center in a converted clapboard house in Chappaqua, New York. Incense was burning when we arrived, signaling that our initiation would take the form of a puja. We were instructed to remove our shoes. The flowers and selection of fruits we were told to bring were placed on a candlelit altar featuring a color portrait of Swami Brahmananda Saraswati, Jagadguru, Bhagwan Shankaracharya of Jyotir Math—Guru Dev, for short—who had been the Maharishi's spiritual teacher for fifteen years. Clearly we were getting the religious version of TM, not the secular version offered to universities, corporations, prison antidrug programs, and local Rotary clubs.

Our initiator, a recent Yale dropout, asked us our names, ages, and occupations. Then he turned, bent over the altar, and, chanting in what I took to be Sanskrit, offered bits of rice, salt, and sandalwood in homage to Guru Dev, whose spiritual teachings were being passed on to us. At the close of the ceremony, Betty was taken aside to receive her personal mantra. Then it was my turn. The young man bent down and whispered in my ear. "*Hair-dhign, hair-dhign,*" he repeated slowly until I had mastered the sounds myself. This would be my secret, personal mantra, which I was to recite at least twice a day for twenty minutes each. According to the TM literature, each mantra is taken from the Vedas, chosen by the initiator for the aptness of its sound in relation to the grains of personal information he has gleaned from his brief interview with, in this case, me.

"So what's your mantra?" I asked Betty as soon as we returned to the car.

"It's *personal,*" she said. "You're not supposed to tell."

"Maybe we have the same one," I suggested, but to this day she refuses to reveal hers. A month later, though, I revealed my mantra to the two million readers of *Newsweek* in a story about Transcendental Meditation. To my knowledge, I was the first to do so to the public. Over the next two weeks, I received more than a dozen letters from outraged readers—outraged because my personal mantra was theirs as well.

From a marketing perspective, the Maharishi managed to sell TM to two very different audiences. Most of his income was generated by those individuals and groups who paid to learn a simple technique that does indeed calm the autonomic nervous system, reduce stress, and help those who suffer from high blood pressure, as countless research studies in the Seventies affirmed. This was the scientific sell: TM as the healing power of positive nonthinking. But it was also a religion for those who chose to make it one. Serious meditators were expected to meditate several hours a day, and take advanced courses (for up to $1,100) on retreats with the Maharishi himself. In this way they could advance from pure consciousness—the elementary level—through "cosmic" consciousness and "God" consciousness to "unity" consciousness—TM's term for the unity of Brahman with Atman. Advanced meditators could measure their progress by the number of seconds they supposedly could bring their bodies to hover inches off the ground. The Maharishi calculated that it would take at least 73,500 minutes of very deep meditation to achieve unity consciousness, a daunting proposition for any ordinary American householder, which is why his true disciples were the few who joined the Maharishi's ashrams.

The Maharishi's embrace of science to prove the value of TM turned out to be a bargain with the devil. In 1975, Harvard psychologist Herbert Benson published *The Relaxation Response,* a study validating the health benefits of Transcendental Meditation. But Benson also showed that almost any set of melodious syllables from "Om" to "Alma Mater" would produce the same effects. In short, one did not need initiation into the Hindu spirituality of the Maharishi to reap the benefits of regular meditation. By the end of the decade, the Maharishi's American enterprises were fast fading, replaced in part by secular "wellness" centers.

I confess I was never much moved by the Swami or the Maharishi—or for that matter any of the other gurus who came here on a mission to teach self-realization. What *did* interest me were the stories I was hearing of Hindu saints, those self-realized human beings who achieve godlike status in this life and afterward, in the eyes of their devotees, are regarded as avatars of Vishnu, Shiva, or one of the innumerable Hindu mother goddesses. Maybe it was my Catholicism, but I preferred saints who had a reputation both for holiness *and* for working miracles. There were plenty of them in India, some with international reputations, but they were not the sort to board a plane and make appearances in the United States. If they would not come to me, I had ways to get to them.

Miracles of a Godman

Fortunately, *Newsweek* was an international magazine, and in New Delhi we had a wiry, quietly ironic colleague named Ramanujam who was our longtime native Indian correspondent. American correspondents came to Delhi and went, but "Ram" was the man we writers in New York relied on for files on Indian culture and religion. One of the first pieces we cooperated on was a 1969 profile of Sathya Sai Baba, a diminutive, bushy-haired Hindu "godman" in bright orange robes with an international following that included a couple of Indian Americans who worked with me at *Newsweek*. They told me stories of how Sai Baba would appear to them in dreams, and how the next morning they would find mounds of sacred ash heaped around their portraits of him. Baba's signature *siddhis* (supernormal powers) including healing, bilocation, and, more prosaically, manifesting Rolex watches and other objects out of the air. More traditional Hindu gurus dismissed such displays as cheap, show-off miracles, but the "godman" nonetheless won mobs of devotees among India's political and social elites.

In the Seventies, Sai Baba spent most of his time at his ashram at Puttaparthi, an impoverished village in southern India. When Ram alerted me that Sai Baba was going to appear at a gathering of gurus near Delhi, I sent him to report for a profile I would write. The resultant story, with on-the-spot photos, gave, I thought, a fair sense to Western readers of what a "godman" is and does without affirming or denying the miraculous powers attributed to him.

Six months later, Ram stopped by my office on a visit to New York and told me that the photos we ran were thanks to Baba's intervention. The photographer from the Associated Press he had hired to do the shoot ran out of film. Baba asked him what kind of film he used and where he bought his supplies. Then, after closing his eyes for a long moment, he told the photographer to look in his camera bag. Inside were a dozen fresh rolls of Tri-X film.

Ram smiled and watched my reaction of disbelief. There was more, he wanted me to know. When the AP photographer rotated home to San Francisco, he stopped by his photography store, where the owner told him this story: three months earlier a short Indian in an orange getup and a bush of black hair had come in, asked for a dozen roles of Tri-X, and tried to pay him in rupees. Then he disappeared.

I've been dining out on this story for decades, as a way of emphasizing the alternate universe in which Asian religions, with their emphasis on self-realization through spiritual discipline, find their coherence. The story is also a major reason why, a quarter century later, I wrote a book on the meaning of miracles in each of the five great world religions. But there was more to Sai Baba than miracles.

Long before he died of a heart attack in 2011, Sai Baba had created what is reputedly the largest private charity in India, with free hospitals and schools for the poor in most of the country's major cities. Once a village of mud huts, Puttaparthi had become a small city with its own university, airport, and stadium—all owing to its most famous son. His funeral, attended by India's prime minister, was broadcast nationally on television. Sai Baba himself left behind a trust initially estimated to be worth about $10 billion. A search of his private rooms disclosed $2.8 million in cash, plus bags of diamonds, gold, and silver valued at another $5 million. His closets contained 750 robes, an Imelda-like collection of five hundred pairs of shoes, and dozens of bottles of perfume and hair spray. The godman knew how to live.

Interviewing a Goddess

It wasn't until the summer of 1997 that I finally got to meet a genuine, self-realized Hindu saint. She was sitting cross-legged under a huge stained-glass window of Jesus inside the Universalist Church on Central Park West in Manhattan. Outside, about a thousand devotees, all of them white Americans, many of them suburban mothers with young children, were waiting to be hugged. The woman doing the hugging was a forty-four-year-old Indian known formally as Mata Amritanandamayi (Mother of Sweet Bliss) and addressed informally as Ammachi (Holy Mother). From my position directly at her back I could observe the stream of bliss-struck faces as one by one her devotees, shoeless and kneeling on mats, slowly inched up the center aisle for their individual embrace. Some brought pictures of relatives in need of healing. They gave their petitions to the orange-robed swami sitting next to Ammachi, who then translated them for her. Ammachi is illiterate and doesn't speak English. Nonetheless, she whispered something to each devotee and daubed them with consecrated sandalwood paste between their eyes, the spot identified with the seat of consciousness. When she turned her head I noticed that her eyes were turned upward, much like the eyes of exorcists I'd seen in Africa during a trance.

What was going on was not at all the sort of transmission of knowledge that takes place between male gurus and their students. To be embraced by Ammachi is to enter the spiritual force field of the Mother Goddess and receive a portion of her Shakti, or divine energy, as a jump-start on the journey to self-realization.

Like all Indian saints, Ammachi exists in and through the stories told about her; apart from them, she has no personal history or identity. Among those stories are these: At birth her skin was flush with a bluish hue, the color of Krishna, whose songs she sang spontaneously at age three, though no one had taught them to her. Beginning in childhood, she experienced states of samadhi (deep absorption) and eventually came to the realization that she was manifesting the "divine moods" of the goddess Devi. The fact that Ammachi had no education, and no initiation from a guru, is further evidence to her followers that she is a pure-born self-realized saint, with no bad karma from previous lifetimes.

The most significant story in her hagiography tells of how, after six months of living as a solitary outcast while still a youth, going without sleep the whole time and subsisting on a diet of basil leaves and water, she found that her body would assume the form of any god she meditated on—including the elephant-headed Lord Ganesha. Eventually, she manifested the power to experience all forms of life as dimensions of her divine Self. The message to competitors in India's highly crowded saint market is clear: as the realization of any and all gods and goddesses, Ammachi is able to be all things to all people because she recognizes that the divinity in everyone is indistinguishable from her own formless and eternal Self.

How Do You Interview a Formless Self?

Before Ammachi's return to India for the dry season, her handlers promised me she would reply to a few written questions. Mostly, I wanted her to tell me who or what she understood herself to be, and what significance she attached to her miraculous powers. Her replies, written and transmitted by the orange-robed swami, were notable chiefly by the absence of personal pronouns. Without them it was impossible to tell who was replying, Ammachi or the swami for her.

Right off I was informed that Ammachi does not identify with the body I had seen, which after so much hugging was round and lumpy like a beanbag chair. "Some call it Mother, some Devi or Krishna, yet others consider it to be a Buddha or a Christ," she—or he—wrote. "There are also many who like to call this body Amritanandamayi and other names. It doesn't matter what you call this body. No one can pierce the mystery of this pure Being."

On the matter of miracles she refused to speak of her own, which would be unbecoming of a saint. But she was quite critical of "man-gods" like Sai Baba who specialize in "materializing objects" and "curing diseases." That was small stuff compared to a great soul, such as herself, who "can change mortals into immortals, the ignorant into wise ones and man into God."

So there it was. This was why, on every stop on her U.S. tour, crowds like this one came to be hugged. They wanted to know that they could become immortal, and maybe even gods themselves.

Conversations with a Living Buddha

In the fall of 1999, I made my first trip to India. I was not prepared for the onrush of so much humanity in New Delhi—the beggars and the hustlers, the sidewalk swamis and gaunt fakirs standing motionless in the heat, the head-spinning mix of odors, the innumerable shrines and temples, even on commercial streets. The otherness that India imposes on the Western visitor is physical as well as metaphysical. Toward evening, when my photographer and I made our way to the train station, every flat surface in the city seemed to be occupied by people bedding down for the night: an estimated three million people, uncounted in the official census, slept outdoors there every night. On the overnight train north we shared our spartan cabin with a honeymooning couple that had splurged on first-class accommodations hoping for a little privacy. It was their wedding night and they held hands between the lower sleeping benches, giggling while the two of us above pretended not to hear or notice. They were traveling to a shrine where the groom was anxious to introduce his bride to his favorite goddess, as if the latter were his mother.

We, too, were traveling to a kind of shrine. I had come to India primarily to interview the Dalai Lama at his residence in Dharamsala, a former colonial British army cantonment high in the Himalayan foothills that is now the seat of the Tibetan government in exile. As we approached the Dalai Lama's compound, I noticed knots of elderly women circumambulating the grounds, as pilgrims do around stupas containing relics of the Buddha. It was a dramatic reminder that the man I had come to see, Tenzin Gyatso, was not just the monk or exiled head of state. To Tibetans everywhere he is also a living Buddha.

I had spoken with the Dalai Lama a number of times and in various places over the previous quarter century, but never before in his own reception parlor. "Old friend," he greeted me, wrapping my shoulders in muscular embrace. He had the grip of an athlete—a by-product of the strenuous knee bends and vigorous upper-body movements inherent in the hundreds of prostrations that, since adolescence, had been part of his daily prayer rituals. Although Buddhism stresses the ultimate insubstantiality of the self, it doesn't follow, as it does for realized Selves like Ammachi, that the body is of no consequence. Nor does the Dalai Lama, for all his previous lives, eschew the pronoun *I*.

"When we first meet?" he asked in his broken but always apt

English. Then he answered his own question: "Ah! In newspaper office."

I was astonished that this man who spends six months of every year on the road, much as the early disciples of the Buddha did (but for different reasons), had remembered such a trivial event. Actually, we first met in 1979 at the Waldorf-Astoria, a block from *Newsweek;* there he and his entourage always rented an entire floor high up in the hotel's private tower section. It was his first visit to the United States. The Dalai Lama was the first reincarnated lama I'd ever met, and certainly the first emanation of a Buddha. I asked him a lot of questions before working up the courage to ask him what I really wanted to know: "Your Holiness, do you remember anything from your previous lives?"

"No," he said. "But do have bump." Then he turned and pulled his robe away from his shoulder to show me a hardly visible lump on his back that he said he thought was caused in a former life. I think this gesture was his gentle way of answering a question that a journalist he had just met had no right to ask. In any case, I didn't know then that merit, not memory, is what a Buddhist carries over from one life to the next.

The newspaper office he remembered was the *Washington Post,* where we met again just two weeks later. Publisher Katharine Graham had agreed to host a lunch for him and asked me to come down to help move the conversation along. She was not yet the Washington party-giver and power broker she later became—in fact, she was still so insecure in those days that she bailed out of her own luncheon, sending Executive Editor Ben Bradlee to preside in her stead. "What do we say to this guy, 'Hello Dalai'?" was his opening line to us. Bradlee was notorious for caring little about foreign affairs and less about religion. So the rest of us carried the conversation. If the Dalai Lama noticed, he didn't let on.

We had time for more extended conversations in 1991 at the University of California, Santa Barbara. The Dalai Lama was there to deliver a speech at a time when I happened to be on hand as a visiting Regents Lecturer in the Religious Studies Department. No one told the university president that the Dalai Lama is a vegetarian, but sitting next him at a luncheon in his honor I noticed that he ate his broiled steak rather than embarrass his host. "Am not formal person," he said.

More than any other religious figure of his stature, His Holiness has spent an enormous amount of time on American university campuses, mostly in dialogue with faculty. He does this for at least two reasons. He is genuinely curious about what Western sciences have to teach him. But he is also concerned about whether and how Buddhism as he understands it can be faithfully transmitted to Western, postmodern cultures. For him, Buddhism is a religion, not just a psychology or philosophy, and his fear, he told me more than once, is that Buddhism will be mistaken for just another "New Age fad."

Of the estimated million or so Americans who identify as Buddhists, most are Asian Americans whose forebears brought their religion with them, just as the Romans did their household gods. Like European immigrants before them, these Buddhists created ethnic enclaves as a way of preserving both their religion and their culture, even though some now call their temples churches. But these "communal" Buddhists are not the kind who typically attend the Dalai Lama's public lectures, or his rallies for a free Tibet, or appear at his side in newspaper and magazine photographs.

Those Buddhists who do are overwhelmingly American-born and predominantly white, well educated, and well-off. Typically, they came to Buddhism in the Sixties and the Seventies, the golden age of experiential religion, as an alternative to the religion—or lack of it—of their parents. In contrast to communal Buddhism, this "designer Buddhism," as I call it, is voluntaristic, individualistic, and eclectic. Not surprisingly, in their efforts to create a Buddhism that comports with secular culture many designer Buddhists tend to elide the religious elements in Asian traditions as unnecessary cultural baggage. Indeed, in its most aggressively secular forms, designer Buddhism dispenses altogether with the bedrock doctrines of karma and rebirth. Without these metaphysical presuppositions, though, it is hard to know what Buddhist awakening and enlightenment might mean.

The one indispensable element in the non-Asian appropriation of Buddhism is meditation as the central practice. Ironically, however, most Buddhists throughout history have *not* meditated, nor have they studied the Buddhist scriptures. These practices are typically reserved for members of the *sangha* (monastic community), the only institution created by the Buddha Sakyamuni twenty-five centuries ago, and the only environment in which, after countless lifetimes, human beings can enter the path to enlightenment. In the traditional Buddhist division of labor, the role of the monks (and nuns) is to maintain a certain purity through detachment from the world by keeping more than two hundred vows. The role of lay Buddhists is to support the *sangha* with offerings of money, food, and other fruits of labor forbidden to monks. In this way, laity accumulate precious karmic capital toward a favorable rebirth. Both monks and lay Buddhists also pray and experience the Buddha through mandalas, images, and other forms of sacred art. But even within the *sangha,* meditation is only one in the arsenal of "skillful means" used to pursue enlightenment.

The novelty of American designer Buddhism is that its practitioners are laymen and -women who want to do what heretofore only some monks did—meditate and study texts—but without the communal discipline and personal renunciation required by monastic life. (In this they recapitulate the Protestant Reformers who abolished the priesthood and proclaimed the priesthood of all believers.) Instead of the monastic *sangha,* designer Buddhism is typically organized around a dharma or Zen center where a resident lama teaches meditation and Buddhist thought to groups, like an instructor in an aerobics class, or through intense one-on-one formation. The goal is to enhance life in this world, not the next. In the Seventies and early Eighties, there was no common code of ethics governing the behavior of the teacher or required of students. For instance, at the famed Naropa Institute in Boulder, Colorado, I once observed the learned Chogyam Trungpa, one of many reincarnate lamas who followed the Dalai Lama into exile and then settled on a freelance career in the United States, gulping sake straight while discoursing on the dharma. In 1987, he died bloated and disoriented from alcoholism at the age of forty-seven. More to the point, his teachings on the necessity of detachment did not preclude the formation of emotional attachments between students and himself. Nor was he alone in this regard. In the mid-Eighties, scores of Buddhist teachers, foreign-born lamas, and Zen masters, as well as Americans who had acquired those titles, were discovered to have seduced their students, male as well as female.

The scandal was further evidence to the Dalai Lama that spiritual integrity is hard to preserve in the open, unregulated, and ethically indifferent atmosphere of designer Buddhism. "Dependence on one teacher or person not good. Very purpose of meditation," he reminded me, "is to increase determination to discipline emotions and reduce afflictive ones." He was also concerned about the ways in which American designer Buddhists were selectively interpreting Buddhist ethics. They pay him heed when he talks about the environment and promotes religious tolerance. But, he noticed, this was not the case when he declared that abortion and euthanasia are violations of the Buddhist principle of "nonviolence toward all sentient beings," or when, in San Francisco (of all places), he declared that one could not be a Buddhist and have sex with others of the same gender. Despite his popularity, he said, he sometimes thinks his influence is no deeper than a "screensaver on computer."

"That's not a bad metaphor," I lightly needled him, "for the constructed and fluid self of Buddhist metaphysics."

The Dalai Lama's own practice of daily meditation begins by 4 a.m. and continues, usually, for five hours. After paying obeisance to the Buddha, he sits down on his meditation pillow to contemplate his eventual death. This is an advanced tantric exercise in which he visualizes the gradual separation of his consciousness from his senses. If, in the last moments of his life, he can remain mindful throughout this process, he will be able to steer his own death onto the path of enlightenment, rising as a Buddha in a mind of clear light. "I think I have [achieved] about seventy percent control over next rebirth," he confided. "If my spiritual development goes further, maybe I get other thirty percent." In that event, he will be free to direct his own rebirth where, how, and when he chooses, or he may decide on no rebirth at all. That would spell the end of one lineage of reincarnated personages associated with the Dalai Lamas.

But what about his other form of incarnation as the embodiment of Avalokitesvara, the god of compassion and the patron deity of Tibet? This is an ascribed identity that he is trying to puzzle out. From scraps of memory of past lives and from the study of his predecessors he finds affinities with some predecessor Dalai Lamas but less so others. "Is confusing," he said. "First Dalai Lama considered [the embodiment of the] god of Mercy, third considered god of Wisdom, fifth god of Compassion. In my case, I don't know. I am cipher."

His Holiness places great emphasis on dreams and their interpretation not only as a guide to the future but also as clues to his own past lives. "Sometimes in dream I have violence or am meeting women. Then in dream remember I am monk. Monk my core identity. Never in dream do I remember I am Dalai Lama. Dalai Lama identity not that important."

The identity of the next Dalai Lama, however, is very important to the Chinese government. Chinese authorities had already seized the latest reborn Panchen Lama, who had the approval of the Dalai Lama, and replaced him with a young man of their choosing. Earlier in 1997, Beijing announced that the next Dalai Lama would also be born in China—and therefore under their control. But His Holiness knows how to play the politics of rebirth. "If I pass away while still in exile, next Dalai Lama will appear outside Tibet and Tibetan community will choose him my successor. Very purpose of the reincarnation is to fulfill policies initiated but not accomplished in previous Dalai Lama's life."

Chief among those purposes is securing a democratic and Buddhist Tibet as a quasi-autonomous region within China. In that unlikely event, Tenzin Gyatso would dissolve his modest "Little Lhasa" like a mandala made of sand and return to Tibet tomorrow. But he would prefer to do so as a private citizen: he long ago tired of being head of state, and in 2009 he formally retired from that post.

"Am getting old, old friend," he said as an aide brought us tea. "Am already sixty-four. Have active life of maybe fifteen more years. After that, too old."

"You and I are the same age," I interrupted, "give or take a few thousand rebirths, and *I* am planning on more than fifteen years of active life."

At this he threw back his head in one of his signature hearty laughs. He possesses what the ancient Greeks called *hilaritas*—an infectious joy in living. Whether he comes by this naturally or as a by-product of monastic discipline is impossible to tell. He then went on to preview how, in fact, he has spent his remaining years. "My name, my popularity useful in other fields, like promotion of human values and harmony among world religions," he said. "Have made many friends around the world and want to continue these friendships." When at last I rose to leave I was genuinely sad to think I would never again spend an afternoon with this man the world calls the Dalai Lama. But I was pleased that Tenzin Gyatso never called me anything other than "old friend."

In his later years, the Dalai Lama spent at least a third of every year in the United States teaching, fundraising for his government-in-exile, and indulging his lifelong interest in Western science and technology. Magazines like *People* loved to publish pictures of the Dalai Lama and other Tibetan monks with electrodes pasted to their heads so scientists could monitor their brain waves during deep meditation. They were, I thought, apt images for a strange sequence in American history in which a wide range of psychologists and psychotherapists sought to provide secular alternatives to the ways that religions address the basic human questions of how we should live and what happens when we die.

CHAPTER 10

Alternatives to Religion

Triumph of the Therapeutic

In the fall of 1973, *Newsweek*'s editors asked me to assume responsibility for the Ideas column in addition to Religion. Ideas was a new section created the previous year as a place to profile intellectuals and discuss new trends, chiefly in the humanities and social sciences. It was a choice assignment for any writer, one that allowed me to come up to speed on a variety of disciplines, such as psychology and sociology, that I hadn't much liked as an undergraduate.[1] It also gave me the opportunity to get to know a number of writers and thinkers who profoundly influenced my own developing outlook. The two who taught me the most were social historian Christopher Lasch and child psychiatrist Robert Coles. Both men were at once politically liberal and culturally conservative, a confounding of intellectual allegiances that reflected my own bent. Both had a keen nose for intellectual pretense, and both imbued in me an innate suspicion of experts. Both were highly moral, genuinely humble men and both became valued friends.

Ordinarily, we do not think of the Seventies as a period fecund in new ideas or movements. Compared to the cultural revolution of the Sixties and the counter-counterculture of the Reagan Revolution of the Eighties, the Seventies—even while in progress—seemed bereft of definition or direction. But, as Nicholas Lemann astutely observed in a 1991 essay, "what was in fact going on was the working of the phenomena of the Sixties into the mainstream of American life."[2] Those among the firstborn of the boomer generation who had not dropped out permanently moved into the wider society, taking with them the mantras and mandalas of alternative religions along with their amplified music, lengthened hair, tie-dyed shirts, and, most conspicuously, their recreational drugs. Not for the first time in American history, the bohemians went bourgeois and—more to the point—the bourgeoisie went bohemian. Where the two coalesced was in the unfettered quest for personal growth, a quest that not only conditioned American religion but, in the hands of humanistic psychologists and psychotherapists, became a powerful alternative to religion itself.

Sigmund Freud anticipated that the analyst's couch would replace the confessional and other religious—and therefore outmoded—methods for the cure of souls. Indeed, he imagined the psychoanalyst as a "secular spiritual guide" who would inherit the authority previously exercised by the Christian clergy.[3] Freudian psychology appealed mainly to the nonreligious, and especially to secular Jews like Freud himself. Most of his patients were Jews, as were most of his friends, and most of his disciples in the formative years of Freudian psychotherapy were nonreligious. Even so, by the middle of the twentieth century, Freudian psychology exercised a cultural authority far beyond the long, expensive, and often inconclusive experience of psychoanalysis.

In 1966, sociologist Philip Rieff published a book with a resonantly prescient title, *The Triumph of the Therapeutic*. With the advent of Freudian analysis, he argued, a new character type, "psychological man," had replaced the "political man" of classical antiquity, "economic man" of the industrial revolution, and, more recently, "religious man" of Judeo-Christian culture. By that he meant that Western culture no longer provided the kind of moral communities and character norms by which individual selves were tempered and honed for higher and agreed-upon social purposes. With the decline of such communities, the therapeutic process had assumed a kind of cultural suzerainty with psychology "legitimizing self-concern as the highest science." In the emergent cultures of the West, Rieff predicted, "a wider range of people will have 'spiritual' concerns and 'spiritual' pursuits" in the form of self-discovery, self-realization and self-authorization.[4]

By the early Seventies, it was clear that the language and concepts of psychology and its instrumental handmaiden, therapeutic technique, had assumed the kind of cultural dominance that sociology and its activist handmaidens had enjoyed in the Fifties and the Sixties. *Time* acknowledged the shift by introducing a new section, Behavior, to its table of contents. But the emblematic magazine of the Seventies was neither *Time* nor *Newsweek*. Nor was it William Shawn's *New Yorker,* Clay Felker's *New York,* Willie Morris's *Harper's,* Harold Hayes's *Esquire,* or Gloria Steinem's *Ms.* It was T. George Harris's monthly, *Psychology Today.*

From a wobbly start-up, with 150,000 subscribers in 1968, Harris built *Psychology Today* into a fat and trendy magazine with a circulation of 1.1 million by 1976 and a total "pass-along" readership four times that number. In its pages, the general reader could follow the latest developments in everything from post-Freudian psychoanalysis, developmental psychology, and behavior modification to sexology and the newest forms of spirituality. Harris, a genial fellow journalist who called me at least once a week from his office in Southern California, really believed that the latest trends in psychology and newest therapeutic techniques would heal the ancient divisions between psyche and soma, and even those between science and religion. The success of his magazine suggested he was hardly alone. This evangelical faith in "psychological man," I want to argue, is what finally defined the Seventies' contribution to American religion and culture.

The Erikson Influence

Oddly enough, the man most responsible for psychology's rise in intellectual influence was nowhere mentioned in *The Triumph of the Therapeutic.* And yet it was psychoanalyst Erik H. Erikson, more than any other American intellectual, who refined Freud's idea that the essential struggle of human existence is not religious but psychological in nature. He did this by moving beyond Freud's emphasis on the first five years of life to focus on the lifelong process of developing an inner core of personal "identity" throughout the whole of the human life cycle. "If everything goes back to childhood," he reasoned, "then everything is someone else's fault and trust in one's power of taking responsibility for one's self may be undermined."

When I came to *Newsweek* I knew nothing about Erik Erikson other than his connection to the phrase "identity crisis"—which, by the Seventies, appeared to be something everyone, at least in adolescence, was supposed to experience. This hole in my education amazed Robert Coles, who had studied with Erikson at Harvard, and he set about bringing me up to date. During Coles's travels in the South in 1962, where he observed the black and white students who tested their idealism against the raw realities of segregation, Bob told me he regularly saw copies of Erikson's first book, *Childhood and Society* (1950), among the few objects those courageous kids carried along with Bibles into Alabama jails. A conversation with sociologist Robert Bellah backed him up: "If there is one book you can be sure undergraduates have read, it's Erikson's first one," he assured me. "You can't always be sure they've read Shakespeare, but you know they've read Erikson."

Nestled into the middle of that book was Erikson's first schematic presentation of the eight stages or "crises" in the life cycle, which became the scaffolding for a widely influential model of human development. In his formulation, each crisis requires the resolution of a psychosocial conflict that structures and restructures the "I" or subjective sense of self. For example, in infancy the conflict is between basic trust and mistrust, and the desired developmental outcome is the infant's capacity to hope. In maturity (stage seven), the conflict is between generativity and self-absorption, and the desired outcome is the capacity to care for succeeding generations. To Freud's "internal" model of psychological formation Erikson added the "external" dimensions of social, cultural, and even religious experience in a hugely ambitious effort to account for the whole of human development, conscious as well as unconscious, from birth through old age. Erikson insisted that his developmental stages were "epigenetic," meaning not only that later crises were influenced by the outcomes of earlier ones, but also that the restructuring of individual identity was an ongoing process that only ceased at death.

Like Freud, Erikson had the mind of a moralist. The conflicts that characterized his eight stages of identity formation sounded almost Calvinist and easily translated into *virtues,* a word he preferred to more psychological terms like "ego strengths." Unlike Freud, however, Erikson did not dismiss religion as an infantile illusion. On the contrary, the subjects of his two book-length "psychohistories," a genre he invented, were religious and moral revolutionaries: Martin Luther and Mahatma Gandhi. Like that quintessentially American psychologist of religion, William James, Erikson was interested in how the experience of religion, in contrast to the contents of faith, enhances or retards the formation of a healthy identity. He read deeply those theologians like Søren Kierkegaard and Paul Tillich whose efforts to transcend the boundaries of specific religious traditions and communities of faith echoed his own aversion to identities derived from mere belonging. Erikson deplored the "moralism" and "dogmatism" that he felt resulted from identities based on creed, class, sex, or nationality. He regarded these groupings as "pseudo-species" that, in extreme form, justified Hitler's genocidal pogrom against the Jews. What he hoped to foster was a "species-wide" ethic of mutuality based on his own "universal" model of human psychosocial development. In that model, all forms of identity and belonging based on ethnicity, nationality, religion, community, and family are to be transcended and subsumed. In short, the only truly human identity was at once personal and universal, and the only true community was the universal human community.

By 1970, Erik Erikson's influence on the way Americans thought about themselves, their children, and a great many other things had made him more than just a cultural icon. With his abundant white hair, limpid blue eyes, and meditative mien he looked at age sixty-eight—at least in the few photographs he allowed to be published—like a Western sage, the grandfather figure everyone could trust. In that year, Erikson won both the Pulitzer Prize in general nonfiction and the National Book Award in Philosophy and Religion, for *Gandhi's Truth*. The same year, Coles published a 440-page study of his mentor and his work. As a favor to Bob, Erikson waived his lifelong refusal to engage with journalists, which allowed me to profile him in a cover story for *Newsweek*.

"Erik Erikson: The Quest for Identity" appeared just before Christmas—a week usually reserved for cover stories on religion, which says something about the reverence accorded Erikson in the autumn of his career. Like most intellectuals, Erikson craved recognition from his peers but *not* the more popular kind the media provides. He was also highly circumspect in talking about himself. He would not allow *Newsweek* to photograph him, supplying his own photos instead. Nor did he permit me to interview him in person, so there was no way that I could register for readers my own sense of his presence off the page. I mailed my questions to him at his home in Stockbridge, Massachusetts, and over a two-week period pages of neatly typed answers appeared mysteriously under my office door. In them, Erikson offered his thoughts on rebellious youth and adult authority, his feminist critics, morality, approaching old age, and why, for him, dialogue with journalists is "a forbidding business." Altogether, his responses ran to a generous 2,300 words. But his only fleeting reference to himself was this witty closing riposte: "Let me say in conclusion, that the identity images an old man has to 'restructure' includes what he reads about himself in the press." His was the most nimble prose in the magazine that week.

Despite his circumspection with journalists, Erikson had begun to write autobiographically about his own "identity confusions," starting with his birth. He never knew his father and was never told his name. It is hard, he noted, to develop an Oedipus complex if you don't have a real father to unconsciously contend with for the affections of your mother.

The deeper family secret, never revealed while he was alive, was that Erik was born out of wedlock and that his Danish mother was sent to Germany to have her baby in order to avoid scandal to her respectable Jewish family. There she married a Jewish pediatrician,

Theodor Homberger, who adopted Erik at age three and raised him in a bourgeois German Jewish household. But unlike his parents, Erik Homberger was blond and blue-eyed and strikingly tall. "Before long," he wrote, "I was referred to as 'the goy' in my stepfather's temple; while to my schoolmates I was a 'Jew.'" As for nationality, in his youth he privately imagined himself not as a German or a Jew but as the son of a noble Danish father.

Erik's identity achieved real-life definition when, in his late twenties, he was adopted into Freud's Vienna circle. His own analysis was under Freud's daughter, Anna, who also trained him in the emerging discipline of child psychoanalysis. In lieu of any university or medical degree, this sterling psychoanalytic pedigree earned him the credentials to practice anywhere in the world as a lay psychoanalyst. While in Vienna, Erik met his Canadian-born wife, Joan, an artistic daughter of an Episcopal clergyman. With their two children they migrated to the United States in 1933, the land of new identities for immigrants and birthplace of the tantalizing myth of the self-made man. When, six years later, the Eriksons applied for U.S. citizenship, they chose a Danish and distinctly non-Jewish surname: Erikson. Erik Homberger became literally Erik son of Erik, as if he were his own self-creation.

This late-in-life revelation drew stinging criticism from some Jewish intellectuals who accused Erikson of deliberately suppressing his Jewish identity and early immersion in that community of faith. But as he produced more autobiographical essays, it became clear that Erikson understood himself to be an outsider to every circle in which he moved—a man who lived on the borders between Europe and America, the clinic and the university, science and religion without ever feeling "at home" in any of them. His whole theory of identity formation excluded the kind of concentric circles of belonging that augment the formation of personal identity in ordinary religious people like myself. To the contrary, his developmental model made psychology the arbiter of what was good or harmful in religion.

It seemed to me from his autobiographical writings that Erikson's focus on identity as the central drama of human life was as much an effort to explain himself to himself as it was to explain others to themselves. This would hardly be the first time that an intellectual breakthrough grew out of a very personal problem. But one had to question whether his theory was as "species-wide" as he claimed.

As Erikson advanced into old age, he tended to invest the achievement of a fully integrated sense of "I" with moral, prophetic, and even quasi-religious import. His last project, never completed, was to follow up his book on Gandhi with a shorter one on another historical figure whose message of "universal love" he much admired: Jesus. In it, Erikson planned to explore how Jesus' personal sense of "I" was connected to the "I Am" by which, in the story of Moses, God identifies Himself. Along the way, Erikson also intended to compare the healing techniques of Jesus (favorably, I gathered, from a preliminary essay he published in 1981) with those of Sigmund Freud.

In the early Eighties, Harvard University established a research center in the names of Erik and Joan Erikson. By then Erik had begun to acknowledge what his closest friends had long known, that from the beginning Joan had been her husband's close and indispensable collaborator in all his work. Through the mediation of the center's amiable director, Dorothy Austin, I was finally able to meet the great man and his wife in person at the center. I was particularly keen on learning more about his work on Jesus.

Erikson was in his eighties then. Age and infirmity had diminished him physically but his pale blue eyes were alert and his welcome was gracious. As we exchanged pleasantries, I complimented him on the expensive bottle of Château Haut-Brion that a prior visitor had left him as a gift. He offered to open it right then and there in a gesture that any other time would have been a gracious offer. The problem was that it came at ten thirty in the morning. Joan intervened to deftly dissuade him, and in that moment I sensed that Erik was in the early stages of dementia and that there would be no book on Jesus or any discussion of it. In our conversation, Erik could not recall his earlier collaboration with *Newsweek* or our correspondence. But Joan Erikson did. As I gradually realized, it was she who had selected the photos we had published and—more to the point—it was she who had crafted the elegant responses to my questions.

In Erikson's declining years, his wife assumed total responsibility for her husband's lifelong work, in addition to writing books of her own. Indeed, after Erik's death in 1994 Joan published a new edition of his final book, *The Life Cycle Completed,* to which she added a ninth stage of identity formation based on her experiences of her husband's struggles in his final years. Clearly, Joan Erikson wanted to leave for posterity a theory of the human life cycle with nothing left out.

Erikson's work was psychology's last great effort to create a comprehensive theory to account for the whole of human experience. Certainly it was the last psychological enterprise to influence a wide general audience beyond interested intellectuals. One measure of his influence is the nearly one hundred books eventually produced by the members of Erikson's informal summer seminars held on Cape Cod. The core group included psychiatrists Robert Coles and Robert J. Lifton, between them winners of a National Book Award and a Pulitzer Prize, plus psychologist Kenneth Keniston, historian Bruce Mazlish, and sociologist Richard Sennett—all of whom published important books that drew sustained attention from reviewers. Another, more dubious measure was the flash flood of "psychobiographies" of public figures—Richard Nixon was the most popular choice—in which authors who had never met their subjects confidently put them on the couch. Mercifully, the trend was short-lived. There were no real sequels to *Gandhi's Truth* because that book owed as much to Erikson's literary gifts as it did to his theory of identity formation.

All of Life's a Stage

Much of Erikson's appeal in the Seventies was based on the way his general model of psychological development seemed to answer a felt loss of an ordered and meaningful direction to human life like the kind religions had once provided. Influenced by Erikson, a variety of social scientists worked to fill the void. For example, at Harvard, psychologist Lawrence Kohlberg wrote books outlining six stages of cognitive moral development, to which he kept adding half and quarter stages as his theory grew ever more complex. Echoing Kohlberg, James Fowler, a psychologist of religion, developed a six-stage model for the growth of religious faith. Elisabeth Kübler-Ross's bestseller, *On Death and Dying,* identified five stages in negotiating life's closing chapter. But the bulk of the psychological stage work characteristic of the Seventies centered on calibrating the middle years of life, a period when men, especially, seemed to wake up and find themselves "lost" on the path through life, like Dante in the opening lines of *The Divine Comedy.*

The most celebrated book of this genre was journalist Gail Sheehy's *Passages,* which offered itself as a "guide to the predictable crises of adult life." It was the "predictable" that gave *Passages* its must-read cachet and kept it on the bestseller lists for two years. In it, Sheehy popularized (and to some extent appropriated) the work of researchers at Yale, Harvard, UCLA, and elsewhere who set out in the Seventies to prove that even in adulthood all of life's a stage. Yale psychologist Daniel Levinson was quite open about the youth culture's role in the genesis of their work: "Most of us who decided to study adult development did so in the late Sixties, when we were already in our mid-40s. We were sensitive to the challenges of the young, who saw our lives as stupid and empty. Some of us thought they were right."

In one of his own books, *The Seasons of a Man's Life,* Levinson argued that every adult male passes through a predictable sequence of stable and transitional periods, each lasting four to eight years, during which he builds, modifies, and rebuilds the basic structure of his life. The influence of Erikson was self-evident. But where Erikson focused on unconscious processes in the development of adult identity, Levinson stressed the conscious choices a man makes about occupation, marriage, and life goals as he forges his identity. The import seemed to be: Life is a series of sequential, age-related changes and in the end we become the sum of our choices.

. . .

This was supposed to be good news, not only for the young who feared there was no life after forty, but also for the middle-aged, who could now picture their lives as a secular Pilgrim's Progress with several transitions yet to come before Kübler-Ross's final five stages kicked in. Very shortly, however, there was a reaction from "life span" researchers who felt that the life-stage folks (I was never clear on the distinction between the two) were establishing age-related norms for how individuals should feel and act. In fact, argued Bernice Neugarten, a nationally prominent gerontologist at the University of Chicago, the United States was actually evolving into an "age-irrelevant" society—and all the better for it. "Our society," she declared, "is becoming accustomed to the 28-year-old mayor, the 50-year-old retiree, the 65-year-old father of a preschooler and the 70-year old student." That may be so, said sociologist Glen Elder Jr. But, he countered, "We have to have age norms to anchor and structure our lives. An age-irrelevant society is a rudderless society."

Be All You Can Be

As influential as it was, Erikson's developmental psychology represented only one avenue—and a very cautious and cerebral one at that—by which, in Rieff's terms, "psychological man" sought to occupy the place once held by "religious man." The bolder bid by far came from a wide assortment of theorists and therapists gathered under the broad tent of "humanistic psychology." On the one hand, humanistic psychologists rejected Freud's essentially tragic, even pessimistic view of the human condition; on the other, they rejected the stimulus-response behavioral psychology associated with J. B. Watson and B. F. Skinner. As a third way between these schools, humanistic psychology advanced a decidedly optimistic view of the individual's abilities to overcome whatever is inhibiting one's pursuit of personal well-being. In the therapeutic marketplace of the Seventies, humanistic psychology was popularly known as "the human potential" movement.

Like almost everything else from the Sixties that expanded in the Seventies, the human potential movement began as a California phenomenon. Its epicenter was the Esalen Institute, created in 1961 by a pair of Stanford graduates, Michael Murphy and Richard Price, on Murphy's former family estate overlooking the Pacific Ocean on the cliffs of Big Sur. The site had a countercultural pedigree. Before Esalen, Big Sur was known chiefly as the occasional redoubt of Beat generation writers and the final home of the pre-Beat writer Henry Miller. Coincidentally, 1961 was also the year that U.S. censors allowed U.S. publication of Miller's 1934 hard-core paean to male sexual liberation, *Tropic of Cancer.*

Initially, Esalen was an expensive but laid-back California think tank cum high-end spa where the kind of big-picture intellectuals that *Time* liked to feature on its cover—Arnold Toynbee, Linus Pauling, B. F. Skinner, Paul Tillich, Ashley Montague—gave forth in shirtsleeve seminars. In its first year alone four thousand people visited Esalen. Joan Baez, Simon & Garfunkel, Bob Dylan, and at least half the Beatles came by to perform and soak up the vibes. The site's hot mineral baths, where romping nude was encouraged, gave Esalen a sybaritic sheen.

It was here, in 1965, that Michael Murphy and former *Look* magazine editor George Leonard coined the term *human potential* and proclaimed it a movement. But it was only after Ramanujam and I teamed up for *Newsweek* on a profile of the great Indian philosopher-mystic Sri Aurobindo that I began to grasp what Esalen and the human potential movement were ultimately up to.

At a Stanford class on world religions, Murphy was introduced to Aurobindo's magnum opus, *The Divine Life,* a book of more than 1,100 pages that he would read over and over for the rest of his life. Aurobindo had studied Western science at Cambridge University in the 1920s and his book was a ponderous synthesis of Darwinian evolution and Hindu metaphysics. In it, Aurobindo envisioned an evolution of divine consciousness in the human mind and body that would eventually invite a corresponding descent of the "Supermind"—his word for Brahman—into the material universe.

The result would be the transformation of the human species into supermen, an evolutionary leap that would be signaled by the reappearance of the classic *siddhis,* or supernormal powers described in the ancient Vedic literature.

Through his own system of integral yoga, Aurobindo claimed that he himself had personally achieved this evolutionary leap forward in 1926. On the same day, he turned control of his ashram at Pondicherry, India, over to his spiritual consort, Mira Richard, the beautiful young wife of a French diplomat who had left her husband after Aurobindo recognized her as the embodiment of the "Divine Mother." Long before his death in 1950, Aurobindo identified "the Mother" as the vessel through which the ocean of divine light (the Supermind) would begin to empty into the material universe.

In 1956, Murphy arrived at the ashram, where he spent the next fifteen months meditating eight hours a day with 1,800 other devotees. On the evening of February 9 that year, the Mother announced to the ashram that she had willed the downward flow of divine light. Later, she also revealed her plans to create a new international receptacle for this downpour of superconsciousness: Auroville. With official sponsorship by UNESCO and platting by utopian city planners, Auroville was meant to be the world's first "planetary" city, built five miles away on the Bay of Bengal on land donated by the Indian government.

Like an urban Noah's Ark, Auroville hoped to attract immigrants from each of the world's nations, with a maximum population of fifty thousand. In this way, it would be a concrete realization of the eventual unity of humankind—but without any of the inhibiting conventions of less evolved societies. Citizens of Auroville were to be "free of moral and social conventions," including marriage, although couples who wished to were allowed to procreate. There would be no religious observances permitted, either, only the system of "integral yoga" created by Aurobindo. Auroville opened its doors in 1968 to a couple thousand immigrants. Two years later, *Apollo 12* astronaut Charles "Pete" Conrad reported seeing an inexplicable light "as big as Venus" flashing steadily from a point "down from Burma and east of [that country]" on his return flight from the moon. Inhabitants of Auroville, which still exists, cited Conrad's observation as proof that the Supermind was indeed descending.

Murphy's vision for Esalen was grounded in his reading of Aurobindo and his experiences at the ashram. Esalen, too, would be a place where the evolution of human nature would be advanced through a melding of Eastern spiritual practices and Western experimental science. Unlike the discipline at the ashram, however, life at Esalen would be intellectually freewheeling, wholly democratic, and sexually unbuttoned. But while others "did their thing," Murphy focused his own research on "the enlightenment of the body" as set forth in his most important book, *The Future of the Body* (1992). Murphy believed that human beings were capable of supernormal functions like seeing and traveling beyond the limits of the body if only they could find the right techniques. In his view the ancient *siddhis* defined the ultimate potential of the human potential movement.

Like Auroville, Esalen was to be a place that espoused "the religion of no religion," which meant that every exercise in mind expansion and self-transcendence, every sense-enhancing technique, every form of ritual dynamics, above all, every explanation of what life is really all about, was welcome except those derived from Bible-based religions. This made Esalen the American Mecca for mystical seekers and fleers from traditional religions, a retreat where all forms of dogma and behavioral norms—certainly anything that repressed or forbade or stigmatized—were to be checked at the door. Not surprisingly, Episcopal bishop James Pike of San Francisco became one of Esalen's most ardent supporters and a father figure to Murphy, who had been reared in the Episcopal Church.

Inevitably, this enticing surrogate for religion found a common mode of discourse in the language and concepts of humanistic psychology. In its headiest days, Esalen was headquarters for the movement's most celebrated theorists: there one could experience the self-actualization psychology of Abraham Maslow, the Gestalt psychology and "organismic integration" of Fritz Perls, the psychosynthesis of Roberto Assagioli, the encounter groups of Will Schutz, and the work of scores of other autodidacts that bespoke Rieff's triumph of the therapeutic. To Murphy, they were all welcome as pragmatic Western explorations in the service of Aurobindo's evolutionary philosophy.[5]

By the time I began writing the Ideas section, every American city with a hundred thousand or more inhabitants had its personal growth centers, forming a kind of twentieth-century Chautauqua circuit for human potential practitioners. In 1981, social researcher Daniel Yankelovich estimated that "perhaps as many as 80 percent of all adult Americans" in the previous decade were involved in a search for self-discovery, personal growth, or spiritual liberation.[6] At least 17 percent of them, he figured, were serious searchers who identified explicitly with the human potential movement.

In the fall of 1975, I began sampling some of the more popular techniques and interviewing practitioners with a view to writing a cover story. I tested techniques for enhancing my body awareness, tried a few visualization exercises with Jean Houston, who would later give advice at the White House to Hillary Clinton, and had my aura read by two different psychics. The first said it was red, the second royal blue, which indicated to me that auras, like beauty, are in the eye of the beholder. I, of course, saw nothing. I deliberately avoided more painful therapies like the deep massage of Ida Rolf and the expensive ones like Arthur Janov's primal scream therapy, which aimed at releasing repressed childhood traumas locked in the central nervous system and cost six thousand dollars for six months of treatment. According to one popular handbook on the human potential movement, there were more than eight thousand ways to "Awaken in North America," and like the tips of tree branches the movement kept throwing off new buds. Who could keep up?

As a shortcut I began attending gatherings of the Association for Humanistic Psychology (AHP), which Abraham Maslow founded as an umbrella organization for anyone who had developed a method for unlocking our hidden human potential or wanted to experience one. A third of the members were psychologists but AHP accepted anyone willing to pay the thirty-five-dollar annual fee. The conference I remember best was held in two Atlantic City hotels, where

1,600 delegates were offered 135 workshops on the growth potential in everything from adultery to Zen. The popcorn was free for those who took in the workshop on the liberating effects of watching erotic films.

This was better duty than the earnest conferences of Methodists and Presbyterians I'd attended, but a lot of the folks I met were not all that different. Many of them planned their family vacations around such meetings, like doctors, dentists, and Southern Baptists do. The conference theme was "The Human Spirit in Transition," which sounded like the credo of a creedless church. Indeed, several conferees I met in evenings at the bar said they'd first encountered the movement in the basement of their Unitarian church.

The conference grand finale was the Saturday night nude swim at one of the hotel pools. This tradition originated at Esalen, where nude bathing was a cherished form of uninhibited sharing of embodied selves. Esalen brochures featured photos of nubile naked masseuses administering vigorous after-bath rubdowns to the nude bodies of long-blond-haired men. There weren't a lot of either in evidence in Atlantic City that weekend, but still, as a reporter, I thought I ought to observe the participants at play. Problem was, I'm nearsighted. To swim without my glasses was to observe nothing but watery blurs, but to swim in a pool of naked bodies with them on was to announce myself a voyeur. My solution was to volunteer to be the person who handed out the towels, which I did from a critical vantage point behind the diving board. What I can now report is that there was no sharing of embodied selves in the pool—and certainly no erotic payoff in watching mostly pear-shaped middle-aged men and women bouncing off a board.

Re-creating Werner

By the summer of 1976, I felt that I had sampled enough of the human potential, my own and others', to put together a cover package on what I chose to call "the consciousness movement." But *Newsweek*'s new editor, Ed Kosner, wanted one last piece: a profile of

Werner Erhard, the inventor of *est*, the latest, slickest, and most lucrative package of instant self-improvement on the human potential market. In 1971, its first year in operation, Erhard had induced some 83,000 Americans to pay $250 each for the privilege of spending four fifteen-hour days on successive weekends locked inside a hotel ballroom while he and his trainers assailed them as dupes and dummies and "assholes" in a systematic attack on whatever ego structure they had managed to develop. *est* was a lowercase acronym for Erhard Seminars Training, a set of "processes" he had put together to induce others to experience for themselves the same enlightenment that, he said, had come to him spontaneously while driving on a California freeway, where, indeed, one is apt to encounter a lot of assholes behind the wheel. As the French word for "is," *est* also signified that Erhard had discovered the secret of reconciling what we want to be with what *is*.

Central to Erhard's marketing plan was the idea that *est* could best be sold by word of mouth from those who had taken the course. Journalists were encouraged to write whatever they wanted to about *est*—Tom Wolfe's famous *New York* magazine essay on the human potential movement, "The Me Decade," opened at an *est* session—but only after they had experienced *est* for themselves. Like other trainees, journalists were not allowed to take notes during sessions and pens and notebooks would be confiscated if they tried. My friend John Leo, who covered the social sciences for the *New York Times*, left after the first weekend because he didn't like Erhard's top sergeants telling him when he could eat and when he could relieve himself. I was not interested in writing about my own experience of *est* and thereby becoming part of Erhard's publicity machine. But I was keenly interested in learning what Erhard thought he was doing and why, and for that I insisted on interviewing the man himself. No interview, no profile in *Newsweek*, was my position.

Erhard had already disclosed enough about himself to make him a prime candidate for any analyst interested in identity crises. Born John Paul Rosenberg, he ended his formal education in Philadelphia when he married right out of high school and took a job selling used cars under the name Jack Frost. At age twenty-five he abandoned his wife and three children and fled to California, where he eventually married and sired four more children. There he worked as a motivator of door-to-door salesmen, among other jobs. He also changed his name again, this time to a combination of two prominent Germans he had read about in *Esquire:* the physicist Werner Karl Heisenberg and former West German chancellor Ludwig Erhard. Werner Erhard claimed he had spent eleven years exploring Eastern religions and various strategies for expanding his human potential, including Scientology, before his freeway experience when he suddenly "got it."

To reach a modus vivendi, Kosner invited Erhard to lunch at the Four Seasons, Manhattan's prime power restaurant, where he rented the private dining room for a high-level encounter. I think Kosner wanted a chance to size up Erhard for himself almost as much as he wanted to make a newsstand-friendly cover story happen. Erhard sat at the center of one side of a long table flanked by eight trusted trainers. Kosner sat opposite him with eight *Newsweek* staffers. Since I was going to write the story I sat at the end of the table to observe the interplay. Kosner and Erhard had much in common: they were about the same height and build; both were Jewish; both had experienced marital problems; both had reached career pinnacles—Kosner as the youngest editor in *Newsweek*'s history, Erhard as a multimillionaire entrepreneur—before the age of forty. For nearly three hours, the two sparred as if they were diplomats negotiating a treaty. Erhard insisted that *est* was not a set of ideas that I, as ideas editor, could grasp apart from personal experience of the training sessions. Eventually we reached an agreement: I would interview Erhard once, for as long as needed, and would forgo *est* training. But the interview had to be by long-distance phone since he was off to Hawaii the next day. Erhard would discuss anything except his personal life, but I could not quote him. That was the deal.

After listening to Erhard describe the *est* processes, I realized why you could no more experience *est* over the phone, even if it was the master on the other end, than a sinner could get saved over lunch with a revivalist. That's because *est* was structured exactly like a revival: first show the crowd the need to change their lives and then show them how to do it. In both cases, the method relied heavily on crowd psychology with its attendant shouting, sobbing, and other forms of emotional letting go.

The first set of *est* processes aimed at inducing physical exhaustion by rationing food and drink and restricting bathroom visits. The next set exhausted the mind and emotions by attacking the ego and its defenses. The whole point, said Erhard, was to dislodge everyone in the room from their "belief systems," which in *est*-speak meant the predetermined meanings the mind imposes on experience, and to force them to focus on the misery they were actually experiencing under Erhard and his trainers.

Dialectically, the second process introduced self-hypnosis, visualization exercises, and other techniques by which trainees were taught how to make their backaches, headaches, and other *est*-induced discomforts disappear. Once trainees realized that consciousness can alter bodily states, they were open to accepting one of *est*'s cardinal principles: "You are God of your own universe. You caused it." In the closing process, the crowd was shown how to create an inner "space" into which each of them could retreat and immerse themselves in their own private consciousness. Trainees were said to "get it" when they finally realized that while they cannot change other people or the rules they had to observe if they were to get along on the job, in love relationships, or in any other social situation, they *did* have the power to prevent any of these associations from affecting what was most precious in life: their personal sense of well-being or (to use another *est* term) their "aliveness." It was all a matter of self-consciousness.

est was not the first programmatic effort to psychologize the American myth of the self-made man. Nor was Erhard alone in teaching others how to recognize that they can be "perfect" just the way they are—another *est* axiom. But among human potential gurus he was certainly unique in insisting that those who worked for him learn to "re-create Werner" by executing every task precisely according to the boss's detailed instructions. Not the least of the ironies *est* embodied was Erhard's demand that those who trained others to discard their belief systems must first adopt Werner's belief system as their own.

At the height of its popularity, *est* averaged nearly six thousand graduates a month and by 1982 had trained more than three hundred thousand people, a fourth of them in California alone. Who were these people? More than half of all *est* graduates had come of age in the Sixties; nearly all were white and nearly all had gone to college but only 57 percent had graduated. Women outnumbered men. Of those who were employed, most *est* graduates held middling clerical jobs like the salesmen Erhard once had trained. More than two-thirds were either never married or divorced when they took the training. Only one in ten practiced a religion.[7] In short, they were mostly thirty-somethings who had difficulty making adult connections.

Criticism of the human potential movement was almost as plentiful as the therapies it spawned. "Narcissism" was the label most often used to decry the culture's inward turn. Among the most discerning critics was Christopher Lasch, who recognized that the widespread preoccupation with self was not a modern iteration of Narcissus's love of his own image but just the opposite: the pathology of people who lacked a sense of self-worth and so turned to experts whose therapies promised to provide a self worth having.[8] What Lasch overlooked, however, was the manifestly religious thrust behind the growing edge of the human potential movement.

Going out of Body

Inevitably, humanistic psychology begat a fourth way of probing human potential called "transpersonal psychology." This movement grew out of workshops at Esalen and, like the evolutionary mysticism of Sri Aurobindo, sought to synthesize Asian and other "ancient wisdom" traditions with Western psychology. Transpersonal psychologists took as their field of inquiry the scientific examination of out-of-body, near-death, and similar "transpersonal" experiences as evidence of the human capacity to escape the confines of the body and even transcend death itself. Most transpersonal psychologists, I was told, believed in reincarnation—as did a fourth of the American population, according to polls taken in the Seventies.

My introduction to this emergent discipline took place in Council Grove, Kansas, at the eighth annual meeting of the Association for Transpersonal Psychology, where an assortment of Native American spirit guides and shamans, Asian spiritual masters, and psychic researchers joined experimental psychologists in exploring ways in which human beings connect spiritually with others in this world and in the next. "Transpersonal psychology assumes that psychic energy is a concrete force that can be transmitted to other people," explained the conference organizer, Dr. Stuart Twemlow, a psychiatrist at the venerable Menninger Clinic in Topeka. The clinic was once famous for the way that Karl Menninger, a pious Christian, made religious midwesterners comfortable with Freud and psychoanalysis. But the mystical paths the transpersonalists were treading were precisely the sort of ventures that Freud found repellent in the psychology of his protégé Carl Jung.

By way of illustrating the power of psychic energy, a young Menninger Clinic psychologist offered his own experience as an example. Through deep meditation, he said, he was able to enter an altered state of consciousness that allowed him to travel out of body at will. In one experiment, he said, he traveled from his office to his home, observed his wife preparing dinner in the kitchen, checked the time, and returned without her noticing. "I looked in a hallway mirror while I was there and I couldn't see myself," he said. "But when I returned from the office that evening I was able to tell my wife exactly what she had done in the kitchen, and exactly when she did it."

This was not the first time I'd met someone who claimed to travel out of body. At that time, the researcher in the Science department at *Newsweek*, a young man with a BS in physics, routinely disappeared into the empty office opposite mine at lunchtime so that he could spend the hour traveling out of body to all sorts of places. But what caught my attention in the psychologist's story was his Dracula-like encounter with the mirror. What unseen part of him, I wanted to know, did the traveling?

It was, he said, the work of the subtle energy that lies coiled at the base of the spine, known in Hindu Tantric lore as the Kundalini, or "serpent power." Adepts in Kundalini yoga say they are able to activate this power through seven openings, or chakras, in the astral body connected to the physical body that we see. By activating these spiritual power centers, he explained, his expanded consciousness was able to travel without his physical body and to see without being seen.

Once again, I thought, Kansas really is the Land of Oz. "So what happens to expanded consciousness once the physical body dies?" I asked.

"That's the big question transpersonal psychology hopes to answer," he replied.

Embracing Death

Between 1968 and 1972, some 1,200 books were published on the subject of death and dying. That output matched the total number of volumes on the same subject published in the previous eighteen years. By 1976, another 800 titles were added to the list. Several of them, like psychiatrist Elisabeth Kübler-Ross's *On Death and Dying* and psychologist Raymond Moody's *Life After Life,* a study of near-death and other out-of-body experiences, were mega-bestsellers that revealed a public anxious to have empirical evidence of a new and better life beyond the grave. Even more philosophical books like Ernest Becker's brooding *The Denial of Death,* cultural studies like historian Philippe Ariès's *The Hour of Our Death,* and psychologist Rollo May's *Love and Will* made the bestseller lists along with new editions of a hardy perennial, *The Tibetan Book of the Dead,* which Americans read—erroneously—as a step-by-step guide to the afterlife.

During this same period, thanatology, the psychological and sociological study of death, dying, and bereavement, became a discrete academic discipline: Columbia Presbyterian Hospital in New York, the University of Minnesota, and Wayne State University in Detroit were among a dozen institutions with research centers in thanatology. Additionally, more than one thousand U.S. colleges, nursing schools (though not, oddly enough, most medical schools), and even high schools offered seminars on how to deal with death and dying. One high school in Minnesota went so far as to take students to a local funeral home so they could take turns lying in a casket.

In her 1963 bestseller, *The American Way of Death*, British writer Jessica Mitford had excoriated the American funeral industry for masking death by making corpses look as if they were merely in repose. Now, a decade later, Americans writers and thinkers were obsessed with putting death at the center of cultural conversation. "Death is the most important question of our time," declared psychiatrist Robert J. Lifton. The reason, he argued in his book *The Broken Connection: On Death and the Continuity of Life*, is that the threat of nuclear war had subverted traditional forms of transcending death through one's children, through lasting works of art, and through nature's cyclical renewal of the earth. Other theories were more sociological. Some experts said the cultural preoccupation with death was a reaction to increased longevity: for the first time in history, half of Americans could expect the Bible life span of three score years and ten. Eighty percent of the elderly now died in hospitals, rather than at home, and advances in prolonging life for the aged raised emotional ethical issues like who should pull the plug and when.

In the early months of 1970, I suggested to *Newsweek*'s editors that instead of the usual religion piece at Easter time we focus the cover story on the human predicament that the Resurrection narratives were meant to address: death and the hope of eternal life.[9] *Newsweek*'s top editors were not encouraging. No magazine had ever put death on its cover, they argued, and besides, the subject was too abstract for a newsmagazine. But if I wanted to go ahead and write something, they'd be willing to give it a look.

"How America Lives with Death" turned out to be one of the

most personally satisfying pieces I ever produced for *Newsweek*. Even now, I think it captured a moment in American history when death had ceased to be a metaphysical mystery or a summons from God, but rather a managerial problem for the medical and other technicians charged with supervising nature's planned obsolescence. When the deadline approached, the editors decided that death was too dour a subject to sell well on the newsstand. They replaced it with a cover story on the Gremlin, American Motors' new subcompact car, and ran my piece inside. I suspect the real reason for the switch was that our always-upbeat editor in chief, Oz Elliott, was secretly a thanatophobe.

I don't remember how many newsstand copies the Gremlin sold. But I do remember that nearly all the letters in response to that issue of the magazine were about death. I read them as evidence that a lot of ordinary Americans were indeed preoccupied with the subject. So did T. George Harris, who in a subsequent issue of *Psychology Today* invited his readership to participate in a survey on death. Thirty thousand responded, more than twice the number who had filled out an earlier survey on sex. By default, I became *Newsweek*'s resident thanatologist, reviewing books and writing several pieces on death. Indeed, it was probably death that later earned me the nod as ideas editor.

In 1978, death finally did make the cover of *Newsweek,* this time at the urging of the editors themselves. By then those in the academic and therapeutic communities concerned with death and dying had, in the fashion of the times, declared themselves activists in a new movement. The general thrust of "the death awareness movement" was to abolish the cultural taboos surrounding death, especially the institutional barriers that separated the hospitalized dying from the merely sick—a system that California's New Agey governor, Jerry Brown, denounced as "apartheid" for the terminally ill. Inspired by Cicely Saunders's hospice movement in England, one branch of the death awareness movement promoted practices such as administering morphine cocktails to lessen the pain of terminal cancer victims, group therapy for all terminal patients, and moving the dying out of hospitals and into homelike settings where they could live out their last days in the company of visiting relatives and friends. Thanks in large part to the pioneering work of Elisabeth Kübler-Ross and her attention-getting books, counseling the dying became a new and almost heroic calling among clinical psychologists.

In its more audacious efforts, the death awareness movement sought to make the approach of death less forbidding by facilitating preliminary access to the afterlife. At the Menninger and other clinics that embraced transpersonal psychology, terminally ill patients were trained to focus on out-of-body states as a way of overcoming the physical and emotional confrontation with death. In this way, psychiatrist Stuart Twemlow claimed, "patients prepare themselves for the death of the physical body, become less frightened and are able to integrate the last remaining time they have in this dimension."

One way Twemlow and others in the movement induced such experiences was by hooking patients up to a "signal generator" that used taped recordings of sound impulses to aid the separation of consciousness—or soul or astral body, depending on one's metaphysical preference—from the body. The signal generator was the invention of Robert A. Monroe, a Virginia businessman who claimed he had sent 1,400 psychologists and other people on out-of-body trips over the past seven years. On his own voyages Monroe claimed to have explored other "reality systems" where he communicated nonverbally with "very intelligent beings that know nothing of our physical-matter systems."

I regret now that I did not accept his invitation to test his invention myself, if only for the sake of this book. But I did the next-best thing: spend a day with Monroe's most celebrated trainee, psychiatrist Elisabeth Kübler-Ross, who on various out-of-body trips had befriended spirit guides of her own.

Kübler-Ross's Grateful Dead

By the spring of 1978, Elisabeth Kübler-Ross had become the Mother Teresa of the death awareness movement. Her work at the bedsides of more than a thousand terminally ill patients had earned her considerable moral capital—not to mention sixteen honorary degrees in the previous four years—which she was now spending lavishly on proving that there is life after death. At the time, Elisabeth and her husband, Manny, a neuropathologist, were living in Flossmoor, a suburb on the far south side of Chicago, where we agreed to meet. Their home was more California than Middle West—a long, low-slung house of redwood with a deck overlooking an oval swimming pool. Inside, a billiards table was set up in the dining room. At least one member of the household knew how to relax.

Elisabeth greeted me in an apron and invited me into the kitchen while she fixed us a stew for lunch. She was a short woman with a head of curly hair and spoke with a marked Swiss accent. Watching her bustle about, I immediately thought of the no-nonsense *putz-frau* on the Old Dutch Cleanser label. It was hard to imagine that this was a woman who traveled an average of 250,000 miles a year giving lectures and workshops around the world.

Elisabeth had a medical degree and had spent three years in analysis in preparation for her career. But from our conversation it was quickly apparent that she had since drunk deeply from the wells of the human potential movement. Only recently, she said, she was attending a conference on transpersonal psychology when, while walking between workshops, she suddenly experienced the full force of the Kundalini bursting through the chakras in her astral body.

"So what was it like?" I asked.

"Like a thousand orgasms all at once," she replied. These were, I recalled, the exact words that Timothy Leary had used to describe his trips on LSD. There was, I began to realize, a kind of shared language among pilgrims on the pathways of human potential, as well as a menu of spiritual peak experiences, like the Kundalini, they were all expected to master.

Our conversation turned quickly to another of those experiences: Elisabeth's personal journeys out of body. Thanks to Monroe's machine, she said, she had learned to travel "at the speed of light horizontally," change course at sharp angles, and arrive at "places where nobody probably had ever been. It felt super." She demonstrated by making an airplane of her right hand in zigzag flight over her plate of stew. On one of her flights, she said, she had met "Willie," one of three spirit guides who gave her reports on how life goes on the other side of death, which she was gathering for another book.

But the most rewarding experiences, she wanted me to know, were the occasional visitations she received from "materializations" of grateful former patients she had assisted on their deathbeds. These visitations were just some of the scientific evidence she had collected to prove that death is just a door to another dimension of life. When I asked for examples, she described how one patient, Mary Schwartz, materialized in Elisabeth's office at the University of Chicago nine days after her death.

"Were you frightened?" I asked.

"No, I just felt pleased," she said. "Mary had come to thank me and the Unitarian hospital chaplain for helping her pass over. Since the minister was no longer on staff I gave her a piece of office stationery and suggested she leave him a signed note."

With Elisabeth's help I managed to track down the minister at a hospital in Boston. He sent me a copy of the handwritten letter, which began cheerily enough:

> Hello there, Dropped in to see Dr. Ross. One of two on the top of my "list." You being the other. I'll never find or know anyone to take the place of you two. I want you to know, as I've told her, I'm at peace. . . .

For my cover story "Living with Dying," *Newsweek* replicated this portion of the letter as an illustration accompanying my sidebar on afterlife investigations. I had to think it was the first time any newsmagazine had published a letter from beyond the grave. The remarkable thing, though, was that of the four hundred or so letters to the editor we received on the cover story, not one questioned the authenticity of this written communication from the dead.

A year after my interview with Kübler-Ross, her husband filed for divorce. He had staked his wife to a forty-acre spread outside San Diego for Shanti Nilaya (Sanskrit for "Ultimate Home of Peace"), a center for investigating psychic healing and conjuring with therapeutically powerful spirit entities. There Elisabeth became embroiled with Jay Barham, the self-ordained minister of the Church of the Facet of the Divinity, who conducted séances with materialized "spirit entities." Critics later charged that the entities were actually men and women Barham hired for sex with those who attended the pitch-dark séances, though the San Diego District Attorney's investigation was dropped for lack of evidence. The scandal tarnished Kübler-Ross's reputation. She had believed in Barham's powers and claimed kinship with a number of spirit entities herself. Nonetheless, she continued to believe that death should be welcomed as a "growth" experience, and published another dozen books on death, dying, and the afterlife before her own life ceased in 2004.

During my pilgrimage along the converging paths of the human potential movement, I was reminded at every turn of a maxim often attributed to G. K. Chesterton: "A man who won't believe in God will believe in anything." In many ways, the entire project of uncovering our hidden human potential also represented the latest recrudescence of the ancient Gnostic dream of realizing one's higher, spiritual and immortal self through secret knowledge (gnosis) and esoteric practices aimed at transcending the limitations of the body, including death.

But as Christopher Lasch recognized, this modern form of Gnosticism had sociological roots as well. Lasch understood that sturdy selves could not be therapeutically engineered because they are formed through communal attachments and responsibilities.

In short, Lasch shrewdly connected the Seventies' inward turn to the disappearance of meaningful work and to the decline of institutions like the family, neighborhoods, churches, and other social networks.[10]

Lasch wasn't the only one to notice the breakdown of the family. Others, on the alienated fringes of society, noticed, too. And they were prepared to create new religious forms of belonging to take the bourgeois family's place.

CHAPTER 11

Sacred Families

In the spring of 1997, on the Friday before Good Friday, I wrapped up a cover story, "The Mystery of Prayer," that was timed to be on the newsstands during Holy Week. Like the other newsmagazines, *Newsweek* practiced "calendar journalism," which dictated that every Christmas or Easter—and sometimes both—we would feature a religion story on the cover, most often one that dealt with the latest scholarly take on Jesus. Typically, it also meant that I would be free the following week to observe the Easter Triduum, which Betty and I planned to do that year with our elder son and his family in Atlanta.

On Holy Thursday, however, I got a call from the editors in New York summoning me immediately to *Newsweek*'s Atlanta bureau. The day before in suburban San Diego, thirty-nine members of an apocalyptic cult called "Heaven's Gate" had committed suicide. As part of *Newsweek*'s cover package I was to write an essay explaining the weird religious ideology of the group's prophet, Marshall Applewhite, who had perished like the rest by swallowing a lethal pudding laced with phenobarbital and washed down with vodka. For insurance, the Gatelings then tied plastic bags over their heads and lay down on beds to await the moment when their spirits would shed their physical "containers." Applewhite had convinced them that their spirits would be rescued by extraterrestrials and transported to the next level of existence in a spaceship that, he said, was arriving in the slipstream of the approaching Comet Hale-Bopp.

Heaven's Gate's mass suicide seemed to confirm the assumptions of many grant-seeking professors of religious studies that the end of the second millennium would witness the kind of wild apocalyptic behavior that had accompanied the end of the first. Boston University, for example, established a new Center for Millennial Studies to "harvest," analyze, and archive the eruption of millennial beliefs and movements that professors there expected to see with the approach of the year 2000. But in fact there was almost nothing to record. Far from being a harbinger of millennial madness to come, Heaven's Gate turned out to be a grisly aftershock from an earlier disjointed era. Literary critic Harold Bloom, an expert on millennial foreboding, got it right: "These wretched souls are further victims of that [late Sixties–early Seventies] ferment."

As it turned out, Marshall Applewhite, the son of an itinerant Texas minister, had abandoned his wife and two children in the Sixties to join the emergent tide of spiritual seekers. The contents of his mature religious vision were like a length of countercultural flypaper: stuck to it were flecks of Mormon eschatology, the sci-fi cosmology of L. Ron Hubbard's Scientology, Buddhism's cyclical vision of time, New Age mysticism, and biblical apocalyptic. Even the collective suicide he orchestrated for his small community of followers mimicked the largest mass suicide in American history: the poisoned Kool-Aid rendezvous with death that the Reverend Jim Jones concocted in 1978 for 914 of his true believers at their commune in Jonestown, Guyana.

The American continent has long been fertile ground for self-proclaimed prophets and messiahs. They and the cults they form seem to emerge cyclically in American history, usually in periods of excessive social upheaval. The Sixties and Seventies, we have already seen, was just such a period. According to J. Gordon Melton's authoritative *Encyclopedic Handbook of Cults in America,* some 370 new religious movements were founded between 1961 and 1979 and many older ones experienced flickering recrudescence. Estimates of how many Americans actually belonged to cults varied wildly from as many as 5 million to Melton's considerably more stringent assessment of no more than 300,000. Like Applewhite, many cultists drifted in and out of various groups, making precise figures impossible to tally. At the time, though, I figured that if *Newsweek* were to publish one story a week on an emerging cult, the series would extend for more than eight years.

Sociologists of religion have offered a number of reasons for the flourishing of religious cults in the Sixties and Seventies. But no one, to my knowledge, has made the necessary connection between the cult phenomenon and a concurrent and far more consequential social phenomenon: the disaggregation of the family structure as American society's fundamental institution.

Divine Parents

Among members of my own generation, two-thirds of all marriages lasted until the death of one spouse. But as the baby boomers came of marrying age the divorce rate began a steady climb. So did the number of out-of-wedlock births and single-parent families. By the 1970s, the Fifties' culture of marriage and the family was rapidly giving way to a culture of what many sociologists blandly called "alternative family lifestyles."

One consequence of this social transformation could be seen in a single stark statistic: in the Seventies, at least a million children a year ran away from home. These weren't poor Dickensian kids who took to the streets at an early age to make their way. Nor were they midcentury Huckleberry Finns lighting out for parts unknown. Nearly all were adolescents or college dropouts from middle- or upper-class white families—and many of them ended up in religious movements that took the form of "sacred families."

Leaders of these families could be bearded patriarchs like David Berg (also known as King David, Moses David, or just plain Mo), founder-prophet of the Children of God, which morphed into the Family of Love and finally the Family International. They could also be widowed matriarchs like Elizabeth Clare Prophet, leader of the Church Universal and Triumphant. Or they could be couples who assumed the role of sacred parents. Heaven's Gate, for example, was the family formed by Applewhite and his spiritual consort, Bonnie Lu Trusdale Nettles, who had abandoned her own spouse and four children to hit the spiritual trail with him. For a while Marshall and Bonnie Lu playfully called each other "Bo" and "Peep"—co-shepherds of lost-in-the-cosmos sheep. Nettles died in 1985 and Applewhite went to his death in the belief that her eternal spirit was awaiting him and their sacred family aboard the extraterrestrials' spaceship.

One characteristic common to sacred families was the requirement that converts cut all ties to their natural families, especially if their parents opposed the cult. Even if parents did not try to intervene, new recruits were usually accompanied on short visits home by another cult member to ensure their return. Conversely, parents who did object—and even some who did not—were blocked from visiting their children.

Another characteristic of sacred families was the programmatic way in which potential members were identified and recruited. In the early Seventies, I got the chance to witness this recruitment process firsthand when one of the largest and most successful cults chose to pitch its tent virtually in my own backyard.

The Perfect Family of Dr. Moon

In 1973, the founder of the Unification Church, the Reverend Dr. Sun Myung Moon, moved from Seoul, South Korea, to a twenty-two-acre estate overlooking the Hudson River in Tarrytown, New York, just five miles south of where I lived. There he installed his decades-younger second wife, Hak Ja Han, and their seven children (she would have six more) in a twenty-five-room mansion serviced by a detachment of "Moonies," as his youthful disciples came to be called. Soon after, the church purchased a former Catholic seminary to the north in rural Barrytown, New York, where Moon established a quasi-military training center for new church recruits. And in Manhattan, Moon bought the old Columbia University Club building and transformed it into his international church headquarters— much to the chagrin of the tweedy set that frequented the Princeton and Century clubs directly across West Forty-Third Street.

At the time, no one knew exactly how the billionaire evangelist came by his fortune as a post–Korean War industrialist, only that he spent huge sums with gaudy flourish. The church took out full-page ads in the *New York Times* declaring "Christianity in Crisis," and commuters into the city encountered Moon's round, smile-button face beaming down on them from giant posters. On the streets of Manhattan, international cadres of clean-cut Moonies confronted pedestrians with urgent messages about wayward American youth, exploding drug use, and the collapse of the American family. Those who listened were invited to hear the evangelist himself at a series of lectures in Carnegie Hall—the kickoff to a twenty-one-city American "crusade" by Dr. Moon that concluded with a speech to three hundred thousand people in front of the Washington Monument.

Moon's religious revelations were contained in his book of scripture, *The Divine Principle*, which offered a novel exegesis of the Bible that placed marriage and the family at the center of salvation: the biblical characters were the same but the plotline was different. According to Moon, Adam and Eve were created to produce a perfect human family. But Satan's sexual seduction of Eve poisoned the primal marriage and produced the fall of humankind instead. So God eventually sent Jesus as the "second Adam" to restart the original plan. But again that plan was frustrated when Jesus was executed before he could find a perfect mate and sire the first perfect family. Now the "third Adam" was about to appear who would complete the plan that began in Eden. This much could be revealed about the new messiah's identity: he had already been born in Korea in 1920, which happened to be the year of Moon's birth. Modestly, Moon did not claim the mantle for himself—at least not right away. But among his followers he was hailed as "the Perfect Father" and Hak Ja Han as "the Perfect Mother."

Short, balding, well tailored, and well fed, Dr. Moon at age fifty-three made for an improbable messiah. He spoke little English, gave few interviews, and spent much of his time on his fifty-foot cabin cruiser, *New Hope,* when not tending to his business and political interests. (As a staunch anticommunist he was well received among cold war conservatives in Congress.) When Moon did appear in public, he preached for hours at a time in Korean, a language few who heard him understood, pausing every few sentences for his translator. His pulpit performance was pugilistic, his hands karate-chopping the air with an occasional kung fu kick of his leg to emphasize a point. At his rallies in Yankee Stadium and Madison Square Garden I saw seats emptying long before he finished speaking. Yet making mass conversions was really not the rallies' main purpose. The point was to give those who were already committed a demonstration of the messiah in action.

Like most other cults, conversions to the Unification Church began well offstage on college campuses or in small get-togethers with the lonely or the curious buttonholed on urban street corners. On Moonie buses the recruits I talked with were mostly older teens and twenty-somethings who seemed lost in the transition to adulthood and in need of friends and fatherly direction. It was from encounters such as these that I first began to suspect that the emergence of the cults said as much about those who joined them as it did about those who led them.

Moon's step-by step recruitment process was a textbook case on how to attract the young and disconnected. First came an invitation to an informal meal at one of the church's centers, where recruits were given a brief introduction to the church. But the main goal was to provide recruits with a circle of "brothers and sisters" a little older than themselves who encouraged their guests to discuss their hopes for the future and unburden themselves of their personal problems. In cult jargon this was known as "love bombing." In turn, the Moonies told how they, too, had felt lost until they found peace, purpose, and personal happiness as members of "the Perfect Father's family."

Next, the recruits were invited to a weekend workshop where the church provided more food and friendship plus outdoor games and small-group prayer services after six-hour lectures on *The Divine Principle*. On Sunday night, recruits were urged to sign up for a strenuous weeklong workshop that left little time for sleep and no time for reflection. At the conclusion recruits were pressed to make a decision: either become a follower of the movement, which meant spending weekends at a church center while continuing with their studies or living at home, or go all the way by becoming a full-time member of the church. Either way, Dr. Moon told me when I finally got close enough to ask, recruits had to "choose between their original faiths and our movement."

Full-time initiates were assigned to Barrytown or one of the other 150 church communes. There they were outfitted in church-issued shoes and clothes and provided with money for medicines and other basic necessities. Training lasted for up to sixteen weeks: a mix of listening to hours-long lectures taped by Dr. Moon, physical conditioning, and hours more of group prayer beseeching "the Father" for guidance in the upward path of moral righteousness. Graduates were then sent into the streets to rustle up recruits, sell flowers, candles, and other items made by the communes, or—if they were gifted—be sent off to work in one of the Father's commercial enterprises.

Within the church, men and women were segregated into dormitories. Fraternizing with the opposite sex was strictly controlled. Dating was forbidden. The church's supreme virtue was moral purity and so personal chastity was vigorously monitored and enforced. After seven years of faithful service to the church, members became eligible for marriage. Moonies could propose spouses of their choice but the ultimate decision about who married whom belonged to Moon, who liked to match men and women from different countries in furtherance of his goal of unifying all of humanity. Often as not, bride and groom had never met each other until their wedding and many couples did not even share the same language. The weddings themselves were outsize group ceremonies like the one held in 1982 at Madison Square Garden where more than two thousand Moonie couples exchanged vows.

A marriage blessed by Dr. Moon committed husband and wife

to his church as much as to each other. Only through the church could couples further "purify" themselves before procreating perfect children, who in turn would produce perfect grandchildren, and so on. Given time, Moon told them, they would collectively raise up a sinless humanity thanks to the new messiah, a title Moon formally assumed in 1992.

Parents of the spouses were forbidden to attend Moon's wedding ceremonies unless they had proven over the previous seven years that they supported their children's decision to join the church. Those who did not, Moon declared, were agents of Satan, and as such were refused contact with their children and their grandchildren. If the purpose of the Unification Church was to unite the human race under a "new Adam" and "new Eve," then previous ties to natural families as well as to traditional religions had to be severed.

Not surprisingly, Moon was attacked by Christian and Jewish groups. But the most effective anti-cult networks were formed by aggrieved parents who could not understand why their children would abandon their own families for an Asian messiah. They blamed sacred families like Moon's church, the Children of God, and the Hare Krishnas of "brainwashing" them. According to one academic expert on the Moon cult, between 1973 and 1986, at least four hundred Moonies were abducted by their parents and forcefully "deprogrammed" in an effort to restore them to the family circle.

Had Moon been a native-born George Soros, a Bill Gates, or a Jeff Bezos, we would remember him as the most messianic plutocrat in American history. At various times Moon owned or controlled a titanium plant and weapons factory in South Korea; automobile plants in China and North Korea; a publishing house and the New Yorker Hotel in New York City; a fishery in Alaska; vast tracts of land in South America; a golf course in California; a computer firm in Japan; ten newspapers in six countries, including the *Washington Times* in the nation's capital; the UPI press agency and a cable television network; a symphony orchestra and a ballet company; plus two universities.

The administrative ties and fiscal transfers among these enterprises and the church were impossible to untangle. So were Moon's ties to the South Korean government and its intelligence apparatus. Not since the Communist Party USA proliferated front groups in the 1930s had any organization created more societies of academics, scientists, and other fellow travelers devoted to world peace and human solidarity. In 1978, a subcommittee of the U.S. Congress investigated the church and its various organizations and concluded in an overwrought statement that "among the goals of the Moon Organization is the establishment of a worldwide government in which the separation of church and state would be abolished and would be governed by Moon and his followers." Three years later, a U.S. appellate judge turned down the church's application for tax-exempt status on the grounds that its primary purpose was political rather than religious. The following year Moon himself was found guilty of tax evasion on a paltry $1.6 million and sentenced to eighteen months at the federal minimum-security prison in Danbury, Connecticut. Moon claimed he was a victim of racial and religious prejudice, and I was inclined to agree.

Throughout these trials, Dr. Moon continued to insist on his messianic commission to reunite the entire world into a perfect family. But there were signs that his own children were far from sinless. In 1999, one son, aged twenty-one, committed suicide by jumping from a seventeenth-floor balcony at the Harrah's hotel in Reno, Nevada. This happened just after the wife of Moon's firstborn son and heir apparent published a book that painted the Moon clan as a rival-ridden nest of pampered rich kids spawned by absentee parents. She claimed her husband was a skirt-chasing cocaine addict who beat her regularly, including once when she was two months from giving birth.

By then most of the other sacred families had disappeared. Moon himself absorbed his church into a new, more secular-sounding organization called the "Family Federation for World Peace and Unification." But for the Perfect Parents there would be one last messianic fete. On the evening of March 23, 2004, eight years before Moon's death, three hundred guests, including a dozen members of Congress, assembled in the Dirksen Senate Office Building at the invitation of yet another Moon front group, called the Interreligious and

International Foundation for World Peace. At one point, a Democratic congressman from Illinois wearing white gloves entered the room bearing two gold crowns, which Moon and his wife placed on their heads. There followed an oration from Moon proclaiming himself "humanity's savior, messiah, returning Lord and True Parent."

The saga of Dr. Moon would not be worth recalling if it were not also a concave mirror in which we can glimpse the larger story of what was happening to the bourgeois American family in the Seventies. That story was presaged a decade earlier by developments within the African American family.

Daniel Patrick Moynihan and the Politics of the Family

In 1965, Daniel Patrick Moynihan, then an assistant secretary of state in the Johnson administration, noticed that while Negro unemployment was decreasing, the percentage of Negro women and children on welfare was increasing. This was contrary to the assumptions of social scientists like himself. In his now-famous report, *The Negro Family: The Case for Action,* Moynihan described the making of a permanent black underclass alongside a slower-growing black middle class. Moynihan attributed the former not just to poverty and discrimination but also to the persistence of mother-dominated fatherless families, reaching back to slavery and the depredations of Jim Crow. His statistics showed that nearly 25 percent of Negro children were born out of wedlock, and in some large urban ghettos the rate was double. From these fatherless families, he argued, came juvenile delinquency, school failure, crime, and welfare dependence—a "tangle of pathology" that, he told the president, would inhibit the black underclass from translating newly won civil liberties into economic progress.

Moynihan's report would prove to be prophetic, but only in the long run. Coincidentally, just days after Bill Moyers, Johnson's press secretary, leaked the report to *Newsweek, Time,* and other major media outlets, the Watts section of Los Angeles exploded in riots, fires, and looting. Other urban riots followed and their political effect was to squelch President Johnson's grand plans to make the Negro family the center of a new civil rights initiative. Even absent the riots, Johnson's new initiative probably would have remained stillborn. In a burst of black pride, spokesmen for civil rights organizations like the National Association for the Advancement of Colored People (NAACP) and CORE—themselves members of the black bourgeoisie—repudiated Moynihan's analysis. Negro poverty, they insisted, was the product of white racism, period. In a widely cited review in *The Nation,* psychologist William Ryan accused Moynihan of "blaming the victim." An entire generation would pass before scholars dared look again at poverty and the black family structure.

Other interest groups, however, quickly inflated the "Moynihan Report" into a full-blown fight over the politics of the family. Feminists defended the black matriarchal family structure as an empowering counter-example to the oppressive "patriarchal" system of the white nuclear family. Planned Parenthood's research arm published a study of black teenage pregnancy that urged more of what that organization could provide—namely, contraception and sex education taught by teachers rather than parents. In 1978, a researcher at the University of Wisconsin introduced the term "the feminization of poverty" into the national debate. It was a catchy but misleading slogan that elided the fact that it was the "single moms" *and their children* who were locked into poverty's basement, not women as such.

By the middle of the Seventies, new research on the benefits of intact families began to contradict the assumptions of the anti-Moynihan political consensus. Several studies underlined the educational advantages enjoyed by children reared in stable, two-parent homes. At a time when many states began passing no-fault divorce laws, the first of psychologist Judith Wallerstein's longitudinal studies of 131 children whose parents had divorced in 1971 detailed the psychological trauma kids experience as a result. (Follow-up studies by Wallerstein and others would find that children of divorce are less likely to marry than children from intact marriages, and that those who do marry are more likely to divorce.) Gradually, the research supporting the social benefits of enduring marriages and stable families and the deleterious effects of alternative structures became impossible to wave off.

In 1976, Jimmy Carter ran for president on a "pro-family" platform, promising to hold a White House conference on the subject. The conference became a magnet for social scientists, policy wonks, movement activists, and interest groups, all with conflicting agendas. The country was in a recession and, as political scientist William Galston, who would become a domestic policy advisor to President Bill Clinton, later put it, "Liberals talked about structural economic pressures and avoided issues of personal conduct and conservatives did the reverse. Liberals habitually reached for bureaucratic responses, even when they were counter-productive, and conservatives reflexively rejected government programs even when they would work."[1]

The basic conflict was over the definition of "family." On one side were those who wanted the conference to recognize that in addition to the traditional intact nuclear family—married heterosexual couples and their children—there was now a diversity of alternative family structures to acknowledge and in some cases even celebrate: single-parent families (usually headed by women); blended families resulting from remarriage after divorce; extended families; unwed parents with children, including teenage "children having children"; same-sex couples with adopted children; multifamily communes; and childless married couples. These variant family structures reflected alternative styles of coupling: serial monogamy (cohabitation with one partner at a time), serial marriages, "open marriages," and (my favorite) "starter" marriages contracted on the understanding that they were dry runs for more permanent unions with future spouses yet unmet.

On the other side were those who understood marriage to be an institution the primary purpose of which was the birthing and development of the next generation, for which a stable family headed by husband and wife was the best arrangement. Their main concern was to create policies that would encourage and support families of this kind. When, after several postponements, the conference finally met in 1980 the name had been changed to the National Conference on Families, with an African American "single mom" as its head. One side had to win and did. But the conflicts between them provided the crucible in which the politics of the family was transmuted into the wider "culture wars" that would shape American politics for the rest of the century.

By the time the first baby boomer president, Bill Clinton, had settled into the White House, the percentage of all children born to unmarried parents had quintupled. Unwed white women were now producing the same percentage of children as unmarried black women had when Moynihan wrote his report. Meanwhile, the percentage of black children born out of wedlock had metastasized to nearly two out of three and would eventually reach three out of four. Americans had also achieved the highest divorce rate in the world. Whereas 81 percent of American children born in the Fifties lived continuously until the age of seventeen with their biological parents, the projected rate for those born in the early Eighties was 30 percent. For African American children the rate was a paltry 6 percent. The welfare rolls swelled.

Once again, Moynihan, now a Democratic senator from New York, took note. In an essay for *The American Scholar* he summed up what, in both social and moral terms, had happened to American society since 1965. Social behavior that was once considered deviant and destructive, especially when manifested by blacks, had become tolerable as alternative lifestyles when embraced by middle-class whites. In short, Moynihan concluded, Americans had responded to family decay and its attendant social ills by simply "defining deviancy down."[2]

Defining Adulthood Up

Long before I began writing or even thinking about the American family, I began to notice peculiar behavior among parents a half generation older than myself. It was during Senator Eugene Mc-

Carthy's second run for the Democratic presidential nomination, in 1972. My wife was working the local precincts, where I was surprised to find that most of the middle-aged women working with her were wearing blue jeans. Hard to believe now, but blue jeans had become the uniform of campus rebels and symbolic of youth in general only a few years earlier. It would be another decade before jeans specially cut for women would become a fixture in women's fashions.[3] To put the matter delicately, the stiff denim jeans produced in the early Seventies were not designed to accommodate the settled bodies and broader backsides of the middle-aged, and these women had to know it. Yet there they were, moving about like stuffed Christmas stockings because—no other explanation made sense—they were determined to dress as young as the college kids who in 1968 had "come clean for Gene."

Not only did parents begin to dress like their children; they began to talk like them as well. Until the Seventies, I never heard adults routinely use expressions like "wow" and "cool" as one-syllable substitutes for real conversation. As it turned out, what I was observing were the first stages in an effort by adults to stay young beyond their years by (as Pat Moynihan might have put it) defining adulthood up. Conversely, the young were taking longer to grow up: they stayed in college longer, took more time to establish careers and longer yet to marry—in short, they were postponing adult choices and avoiding long-term commitments. Where Erik Erikson and others had sought to chart the stages of human development through adulthood and old age, there now seemed to be only one stage worth arriving at: eternal youth.

When parents refuse to embrace their adulthood and children hope to avoid it, neither generation benefits. This was the lesson I took away from an incident that occurred in Chappaqua, New York, an upscale village next to ours where Bill and Hillary Clinton would later settle. One weekend, while their parents were away, some high school kids threw a party during which pot-smoking classmates trashed their home. The parents sought a meeting with the classmates' parents. But those parents sided with their children and refused to meet the offended couple. The kids whose home was trashed were ostracized at school and eventually the family had to move out of town.

That incident so enraged me that I eventually wrote a series of stories on the family and, at the end of the decade, a book about the grandparent-grandchild bond. In 1975, *Newsweek* published a cover story that asked, "Who's Raising the Kids?" It was the first time the magazine had devoted a cover to the family and, as if to demonstrate the writer's credentials, the editors published a photo of my own young family at the top of the table of contents.[4]

The story portrayed the pathos of parents trying to raise children at a time when society no longer provided a consensus on what children should be like as young adults or how to get them there. Teenage drug abuse was on the rise, as was divorce, and suicide had emerged as the second leading cause of death among youths between the ages of fifteen and twenty-four. Divorce was approaching the now-familiar rate of one for every two marriages a year and in an increasing number of divorce proceedings, *neither* parent wanted custody of the children. In the decidedly dim view of anthropologist Margaret Mead, "[w]e have become a society of people who neglect our children, are afraid of our children, find children a surplus instead of the raison d'être of living."

So who *was* raising the kids? For the first time in American history a majority of mothers held jobs outside the home. Even some who stayed at home, one study showed, spent as little as fifteen minutes a day in actual communication with preschoolers. "Television," charged Yale psychologist Kenneth Keniston, chairman of the Carnegie Council on Children, "has become a flicking blue parent occupying more of the waking hours than any other influence— including both parents and schools." Moreover, two million children of school age were *not* in school, and another million more were "latchkey" children—kids who returned home after school to an empty house with, at best, a note from Mom taped to the refrigerator door.

To the troubled American family the Seventies produced a typically American response: a new psychotherapeutic discipline called "family therapy," augmented by new therapeutic communities like

"Families Anonymous" and "Parents Anonymous." It was a bad time for parents with a low threshold for guilt. But it was a golden time for experts on child rearing. Whereas my wife and I had had only Dr. Benjamin Spock's down-home book on child rearing to consult, there was now a flood of such books vying for the attention of anxious parents. The most pervasive was Dr. Thomas Gordon's Parent Effectiveness Training (PET), which employed nearly 8,000 instructors to conduct eight-week courses providing 50,000 customers a year with "specific parenting techniques, like golf pros do." For the first time, the noun *parent* acquired a verbal form and "parenting" achieved occupational status.

My personal views were deeply influenced by Robert Coles, who was probably the only expert on family life able to see the connections between the stress common to migrant workers' families and that of families of corporate nomads. At the time, Bob was deep into his multivolume study, *Children of Crisis,* which examined in minute detail the ways in which put-upon families, white as well as black, found ways to cope. "We can't feed our children, discipline them, select schools, books, or games for them, even it seems, have an ordinary conversation with them without consulting someone who claims to be in the know," Coles observed in a typical fit of exasperation. "This loss of self-respect and common sense is the principal reason why we turn to specialists, as if God had chosen to reveal Himself through them."

Near the end of his only term as president, Jimmy Carter was finally able to make good on his promise to convene a White House Conference on the Family. (Such was the friction among family experts that self-styled "child advocates" demanded and eventually got a White House conference of their own.) As a run-up, *Newsweek* assembled a team of twenty-nine reporters, writers, and editors to produce a special report titled "Saving the Family," which ran for eighteen pages. Even at that length the number of experts offering solutions made writing our report feel like squeezing an oversize pillow into an undersize pillowcase.

Predictably, White House conferees asked not what families can and should do for themselves but what government can and should do for families. The man in charge, Joseph Califano, had previously served as the general in charge of President Johnson's War on Poverty, but this time around, practical ways to assist poor families proved elusive. Even financial relief in the form of direct aid, vouchers, or tax credits turned out to have unintended consequences. After experimenting with income supplements to selected poor white and black families in Denver and Seattle, the federal government found that the most needy mothers were also the ones most likely to leave their husbands when given a minimum income guarantee.

Among the proposals to combat illegitimacy among poor women, the most Swiftian was put forward by Nicholas Zill of the Foundation for Child Development: create new contraceptive regimens such that poor women would have to make a conscious decision to *have* children—and then institute compulsory education on child rearing, plus state-controlled birth licenses.

Inevitably, the White House conference served the politics of the family more than families themselves. This was particularly true of the sessions devoted to the career demands versus the needs of children as experienced by middle-class families. That ideologically freighted issue elicited the only memorable remark I read. "There's a real conflict between what's good for adults and for children, and possibly even between males and females," observed sociologist Sarane Boocock. "What nurtures the family unit is in conflict with what maximizes personal development. You just can't have it both ways."

It was while I was writing about the problems of the American family that I began, almost inadvertently, to investigate a religious tradition, native to this country, whose members were convinced that they could indeed form strong families and, at the same time, maximize personal development. It was, and remains, the most complete and durable expression of the church as Sacred Family.

The Mormons' Eternal Family

Late on Thursday afternoon, June 8, 1978, word came forth from Salt Lake City that, after much prayer and beseeching of God, President Spencer W. Kimball, Prophet, Seer, and Revelator of the Church of Jesus Christ of Latter-day Saints, had received a historic revelation: henceforth the Mormon priesthood would be open to all worthy males "regardless of race or color." The revelation was historic because it negated what Brigham Young and other Mormon prophets had taught: that blacks were a cursed race descended from Adam's murderer son, Cain, and for that reason no man with even a drop of Negro blood could be allowed into the Mormon priesthood. Several of the church's Twelve Apostles who were in the room with Kimball said they all felt the power of the Holy Spirit come over them, just like Pentecost.

The revelation was good news for those Mormons who felt that the charge of racism had been lifted from their church, perplexing news for those Mormons who thought the racial ban was written on golden plates, if not stone tablets. But its timing so late in our publishing week was disconcerting news for me. I had arranged to close the Religion section early that week so that on Friday night I'd be free to watch Kenny Norton fight Larry Holmes on television for the WBC heavyweight championship. Now I had to find a way to report and write this late-breaking story without missing the "marvelous mayhem" my longtime friend, boxing maven Bert Sugar, predicted for the fisticuffs in Las Vegas.

At that point in my life, the only Mormon I had ever talked with at length was the prophet's son, Spencer L. Kimball, who taught my contracts class at Michigan Law School. So I called Charles, the church's urbane public information officer in New York City, and asked him to meet me at Reidy's, a *Newsweek* watering hole on East Fifty-Fourth Street, where the accommodating proprietor Bill Reidy had reserved a table directly in front of the television set. I wanted Charles to give me a better grasp of what the revelation would mean for black Mormons—just a little something extra for what would have to be a brief addition to the Religion section.

Charles arrived as the third round was ending, with Norton already absorbing a beating from his younger adversary's whiplash jab. He ordered a Perrier and lime, which was the drink of choice for Mormons and other nondrinkers in New York. In his blue blazer and rep tie, my guest did not look at all like a priest, but that is what he was.

So was almost every other white Mormon male, which was one reason why the new revelation was so important. Between the fourth and fifth rounds, Charles explained that virtually all Mormon males are admitted to the priesthood as adolescents. Gradually they gain the right to bless marriages and perform other "ordinances" or sacraments of the church. Moreover, although not all priests are called to temporary service as nonpaid pastors, each Mormon husband functions as a priest within his own family by leading prayers, counseling, and conferring patriarchal blessings on his children. The impact of the new revelation, then, was to make this range of privileges and responsibilities available to Negro males. No more sitting in the back of the church bus, was my automatic first thought.

By the eighth round, Norton's left hooks were slicing through Holmes's defense and the momentum of the fight had shifted. I ordered another round of drinks; the fight was getting bloody and I figured I'd learned enough from Charles. But he assured me that I hadn't. The most important thing for blacks, he wanted me to know, was that they could now enter Mormon temples and participate in the church's most sacred rites. In particular, Negro couples could now have their marriages "sealed" for all eternity, and their children with them.

"Eternity is a long time to be married, Charles," I ventured. "I don't think I'd like that, and I'm sure my wife would agree."

Charles glanced around at the adjacent tables and then lowered his voice. "You don't understand," he began. "We believe that God was once a human being just like you and me, that He married and eventually progressed to become God in the next life. We believe that the Heavenly Father produced spirit children for whom He organized this world so that we could all come here and progress just as He did. For that, we must be married as He is, either in this life or in the next."

At this point, our conversation became far more absorbing than the brawl raging on television. "You mean," I asked, "there's a Mrs. God?"

"Well, we don't call her that," he said. "We refer to her as 'Our Heavenly Mother.' We don't talk about her much, but we know she is there. Otherwise, you and I wouldn't be here."

That was my introduction to the Mormon religion.

The Latter-day Saints had been around for more than 150 years and yet I knew very little about their beliefs and practices. Christian Fundamentalists knew more about Mormonism than most other Americans because they recognized Mormons as competitors for converts and regarded their religion as a dangerous cult. But most religions begin life as a cult—the Latin *cultus* means "worship." Christianity, for example, emerged from Judaism as the worship of Jesus as messiah and soon enough as the only-begotten Son of God. In any case, Mormonism had long ago acquired the numbers, the organization, and the complexity that for sociologists distinguish churches from sects and cults. And in the mid-Seventies, the LDS church experienced an extraordinary spurt in growth overseas through a stepped-up missionary program and proliferating vernacular translations of the Book of Mormon.

As it turned out, it was precisely this global outreach, rather than domestic pressure from the civil rights movement, that had spurred the Prophet and his Apostles to seek a revelation on Negroes and the priesthood. The church had just built a temple in Brazil for sealing marriages, baptizing the dead, and all the other rituals for which priesthood is essential. But in mestizo Brazil so many Mormon converts had Negro blood somewhere in their veins that the church's patriarchs realized that no temple there—much less in black Africa—could thrive unless the church dropped its racial barriers to the priesthood. The revelation resolved that impasse.

Between 1960 and 1980, the Mormon church also experienced enormous growth here at home. One reason was that Mormon families produce significantly more children on average than other Americans. Another was the expansion of the church's domestic missionary programs. At a time when the traditional American family appeared to be self-destructing, the Latter-day Saints offered a safe haven for families under stress: a religion that sacralizes marriage and family bonds for time and all eternity. "For us, marriage becomes the highest form of religion," Truman Madsen, a philosophy professor at Brigham Young University, explained to me at the time, "because we are simply trying to imitate in our lives here the kind of experience, joy, and power that constitutes divine fatherhood."

The Mormon Myth and the Cultus *of the Family*

Every religion embodies a myth or comprehensive story that addresses life's central questions: who are we, where did we come from, why are we here, what is our purpose in life, and what must we do to achieve it? The Mormon myth is unique as a cosmic family drama linking heaven and earth.

The "Heavenly Father" worshipped by Mormons is neither the inexpressible "wholly Other" of the Old Testament, nor the intimate "Abba" whom Jesus addresses in the New. Rather, He is the fully realized "family man." Once a human just like us, He continues to possess a material body—though exquisitely refined—of flesh and bone. So does His spouse, the "Heavenly Mother." Uncountable eons ago the two of them populated heaven with a vast number of spirit children. Like all fathers, this God understood that His children must eventually leave home and make their own ways if they are to mature and become adults in the literal image of their divine parents.

At a council in heaven, God's firstborn Son proposed a "plan of salvation" for the Father's spirit children. According to that plan, the Son fashioned the earth as a place where the spirit children could acquire the mortal bodies and like their parents begin the long road to godhead themselves. The Son also saw that with free will those children would inevitably commit sins. Out of compassion, he volunteered to take on flesh himself so that he might suffer and die for those sins and make eternal salvation possible for the spirit children. In the mortal world, the Son was known as Jesus Christ.

While on earth Jesus also established a church as the sure and indispensable aid in the salvation of humankind. But shortly after his death, that church became corrupt and lost the fullness of divine truth. Christianity remained corrupt until the 1820s, when the Heavenly Father and Son chose a teenager, Joseph Smith Jr., to restore the church to its original purity. Smith did this first by translating into English the Book of Mormon, which, at the direction of the angel Moroni, he unearthed as gold plates that had been buried centuries earlier near his home in upstate New York. Together with the Bible, the Book of Mormon constituted sacred scripture for the fledgling church. To these Smith added other doctrines based on a series of revelations that lasted until his death fifteen years later.

But it was only in the final five years of his life that the Prophet revealed his most audacious doctrines and ritual practices. All of them institutionalized the family as the vehicle—indeed, the very glory and purpose—of eternal life.[5]

The most radical of these innovations was plural marriage. Smith himself had been secretly practicing polygamy for several years, eventually taking some thirty additional wives ranging in age from fourteen to fifty-six, and including two women who were sisters and at least a dozen who already had husbands. Naturally, word of the Prophet's polygamous ways caused considerable consternation among Mormons—especially Smith's first wife, Emma, who insisted after her husband's death that only she was his real wife. In 1840, the Prophet gathered his Apostles together and told them that the Father wanted them, too, to embrace the principle and practice of plural marriage. Smith invoked the precedent of Abraham and the other polygamous patriarchs of the Hebrew Bible from whom, he believed, he and his Apostles derived their authority. Three years later, in an act that would fuel the public outrage that eventually cost him his life, the Prophet dictated a revelation declaring that plural marriage was part of God's "new and everlasting covenant" that was to be embraced by all Latter-day Saints.

Polygamy was also entailed by the institution of Celestial marriage, which acquired its fullest sacerdotal expression with the completion of the Mormon temple in Navoo, Illinois, a Mississippi River city rivaling Chicago in size that Smith controlled as mayor and as head of a militia second in size only to the federal army. Unless a woman were sealed for time and eternity to an upright Mormon male, a ritual that could only be performed in a temple, she might gain personal salvation in the next life but not the eternal glory reserved exclusively for righteous Mormon spouses and their progeny. Moreover, sealing to the Prophet or one of his Apostles was particularly advantageous to a woman and her family since the Prophet and his Apostles were expected by their stature to be among the most exalted members of the Celestial Kingdom. As Smith promised the mother of one of his plural wives, their sealing would "ensure your eternal salvation & exaltation and that of your father's household & all your kindred."[6] In turn, by sealing additional families to himself through plural marriage, *every* Mormon male added to the glory that would be his in the next life, the crown of that glory being the eternal begetting of spirit children as a Heavenly Father himself.

To these radical innovations, Smith added a third: Baptism of the Dead. Although the Prophet had contradicted Jesus' teaching that marriage ends with death, he strictly interpreted St. Paul's dictum that baptism is necessary for salvation. To the first generation of Mormons this meant that none of their deceased non-Mormon forebears could join them in the afterlife. When Smith decreed that the living could be baptized as proxies for deceased family members, he provided yet another way of preserving family ties beyond the grave. Eventually the ambition of the church's proxy baptisms was expanded to include the names of everyone who ever lived— hence the church's emphasis on genealogy.

With each new latter-day revelation from their prophet, groups of Mormons left the church, usually because they could not reconcile what Smith was now saying with what they read in the Book of

Mormon—not to mention what they found in the Bible. Nowhere in either book could they find that God was once a man or that He now had a body, much less that He was married and that there always were and always will be many other gods in other worlds besides the Heavenly Father who presides over this one.

Nonetheless, the majority who remained faithful to Smith and his successor Prophets and Apostles had something more important: a sure solution to the problem of death. In the nineteenth century, many women died in childbirth and many more routinely lost children to diseases that medical science has since tamed or eliminated. But as Smith had reconfigured it, death itself was merely a brief interruption between this life and the next, much as mortal life was but a temporary phase between pre- and post-mortal existence. Eternity became a continuation of time, rather than the cessation of it, as faithful Mormon spouses moved ever onward and upward with their families toward the achievement of divinity themselves. Indeed, by imagining an eternal progression of couples toward godhead, and thus the power as divine parents to populate other planets with spirit children, Smith succeeded in "familializing the cosmos," as one contemporary Mormon scholar puts it.[7]

At Home in Zion

Shortly after my introduction to Mormonism at Reidy's pub, I made a series of trips to Utah. To be sure, there were sizable communities of Mormons in New York and Washington, D.C., but only in Utah, I felt, could I experience what was perhaps the last robust example of embedded religion outside the Baptist South.

There's no mistaking the Mormon roots of Salt Lake City. Its main thoroughfares remain extra wide, just like Brigham Young laid them out in order to accommodate wagon trains. The Beehive House, where Young kept some of his fifty-six wives, and from which he later ruled the territory that became the state of Utah, is a civic monument. And dominating the city's center is the soaring Mormon temple, mausoleum-like in its marmoreal whiteness. Young was still alive when ground was broken for the temple, which took forty years to complete. Its sheer bulk recalls the great medieval cathedrals of Europe. But whereas those soaring sacred spaces were open to noble and beggar, saint and sinner alike, the temple in Salt Lake—like LDS temples everywhere—is closed to all but properly initiated and hierarchically approved Mormons. Even the temple windows are opaque, so that no one can see in. This Masonic-like identification of the sacred with the secret is also part of the city's distinctive Mormon character.

In all other ways, however, the Mormons I met were far removed from the theocratic and communitarian separatists who had created the church's intermountain Zion. After sixty years of steady assimilation, most Mormons had avidly embraced free enterprise, capitalism, and even the Republican Party that had forced their forefathers to renounce polygamy as the price of Utah's statehood. This transformation was already well advanced in the 1950s when President Eisenhower appointed Ezra Taft Benson, a future president and Prophet of the church, as his secretary of agriculture.

By the early Seventies, the church's hierarchy—the hundred or so General Authorities who direct the church's religious and secular enterprises—were mostly men who had found success in business, the law, politics, or other professions before being called to serve the church full-time. Together they had instituted a "correlation" program that standardized church procedures and centralized decision making in the church's Salt Lake City headquarters. This in turn required the development of a corps of Mormon civil servants to run the church's energetic publishing, advertising, public relations, and other operations. In addition, the church controlled numerous secular enterprises, such as hotels and department stores, that contributed to the church's burgeoning financial empire. In Salt Lake City, I was told more than once, you did business "the Mormon way or not at all." All of which reminded me of G. K. Chesterton's famous description of the United States as "a nation with the soul of a church." In Salt Lake, it seemed to me, the midcentury saints had fashioned a church with the soul of a corporation.

The Mormon work ethic would make even an old-fashioned

Calvinist look lax. The church's doctrine of eternal progression entails a Pelagian spirit of constant striving—in the next life, where there is no rest for those who aspire to divinity, as well as in this life, where there is no room for contemplation in a church devoted to work. Every local congregation is—or is expected to be—a weeklong hive of activities. Indeed, the best story I heard from Mormon friends was about a former Mormon Prophet/president who repeatedly asked his deceased predecessor for advice on a pressing decision he had to make. After weeks of silence, the predecessor finally weighed in from the next life and apologized: "It's so busy up here with church work, I just now found the time to answer you." That the church's work of making converts continues after death is just one of the unique features of Mormon life after death.

Even so, in 1970 President Joseph Fielding Smith decreed that Monday nights should be set aside for Family Home Evening, and he directed local congregations not to hold any meetings or activities on those nights so that parents and children could spend time together in prayer, study, and addressing family issues. The immediate beneficiaries were Mormon bishops (pastoral leaders of local congregations), who spend an average of fifteen to twenty hours a week serving their congregants in addition to holding full-time secular jobs. Ironically, this meant their commitment to their own families often suffered. In short, the decree on Family Home Evening was a practical reminder that the church exists for the family and not the reverse.

The one-night-at-home decree was also designed to help young Mormon couples preserve their marriages at a time when the rising divorce rate was affecting temple marriages as well. Within five years, Family Home Evening was central to the church's promotional activities through advertising campaigns in *Reader's Digest* and other publications.

The Mission of the Mormon Family

Mormonism's most recognizable image—especially after *The Book of Mormon,* surely the American theater's most improbable long-running musical—is that of young LDS missionaries in white shirts and black pants walking two by two down the byways of the world seeking to make converts. Knocking on the doors of strangers is the coldest of cold calls, as my salesman father would have said, and for the Mormons they rarely produced converts. According to various estimates, about nine doors out of a hundred were opened to them. Lucky was the missionary elder who performed one or two baptisms a year, and baptisms recorded in foreign mission fields did not always represent lifelong conversions.

Why then does the LDS church annually send out tens of thousands of missionaries, at the cost of $15 million or more a year? Making converts is not the only or probably not even the primary reason. The real effect of the missionary program is to bind these young men (and, increasingly, young women) to the church. More than bar and bat mitzvahs for Jews, and certainly more than confirmation rites for Christians, going on mission is a rigorous rite of passage to Mormon adulthood. Missionaries learn their faith by teaching it to others—a brilliant strategy that other religions would do well to emulate. On mission, these young Mormons not only come to identify with their church as its official representatives but also to experience the rejection that their forebears knew in the hard days of building up the Mormon Zion. And when they return home at the age of twenty-two or so and resume the normal process of dating and mating, they are biologically driven as well as spiritually conditioned for the most essential rite of passage from this world to the next: a marriage sealed for all eternity in a temple rite.

But in the mid-Seventies, the church developed a more fruitful strategy for winning converts. Like many of the newer religions and cults, mission officials recognized that the best way to convert strangers is first to make them your friends. The best targets, according to a thirteen-step guide published in 1974 in the *Ensign,* an official church publication, were families new to the neighborhood with no friendship networks of their own. The first steps described ways that Mormon families could befriend these neighbors while avoiding any mention of religion. Step Seven called for inviting the newcomers over during a special Family Home Evening in the course of which the hosts would demonstrate—again without mentioning religion—how they handle child rearing and other family issues. The point was to present the host family as a model of domestic togetherness.

From there LDS families were encouraged to invite their new friends to Mormon picnics and the like, and if they then showed interest, to invite them to Sunday services at the local ward, which are not much different from mainline Protestant services. Only at Step Twelve are Mormons instructed to give personal testimony to the faith. If their friends still show interest, the last step is to arrange a home meeting with Mormon missionaries to begin learning the distinctive doctrines that distinguish Mormonism from all other faiths.[8]

In short, every Mormon family was henceforth to be a vehicle for attracting converts.

Dinner with an Apostle

My longest sojourn among the Mormons came at the invitation of the church's Department of Public Affairs, by far the largest public-relations apparatus of any American denomination. During my earlier visits to Salt Lake most of my conversations were with Mormon intellectuals and writers connected with *Sunstone* and *Dialogue,* the only two Mormon journals independent of the church. If *Newsweek* would send me back to Utah, I was promised an escorted tour of the church's facilities, a round of interviews with church operatives, and—the real inducement—a rare opportunity for face time with one of the church's General Authorities.

My escort, Steve Coltrane, the church's New York public information director, drove his own family car from Westchester County
so he could personally chauffeur me around Salt Lake, up to the
Wasatch mountain where the church stores its genealogical records
in case of nuclear attack, and to Brigham Young University to interview scholars devoted to collecting evidence in support of the ancient history found only in the Book of Mormon. All week long we
sweated together in temperatures above one hundred degrees. On
our way to Provo, Steve even stood sentry in his three-piece wool
suit on a barren rock above the small desert lake where, after asking
him to pull over, I took a skinny-dip. That brief diversion, had it been
known, could have cost me the highlight of my visit: dinner that
evening at the home of Elder Boyd K. Packer, then one of the youngest members of the church's Quorum of the Twelve Apostles—a
level of authority just below the three-person First Presidency itself.
It was quite a coup, Steve wanted me to know, since Apostles rarely
speak to journalists, much less invite them to the family table. (At
his death in 2015, Packer was second in line to become the church's
president and Prophet.)

Upon entering the Packer manse, my first thought was, My God,
he's invited me to a party. A dozen or so other guests were already
standing about, all of them elegantly dressed—including a boy of
about seven in a white shirt, tie, and blue blazer. As it turned out,
everyone there was a member of the Apostle's extensive family. All
of us fit easily around a dining table long and wide enough to accommodate Jesus and his Twelve Apostles at the Last Supper.

From the grace he said before our meal to the grace he said at
the close, it was clear that dinner with an Apostle did not include
asking him pointed journalistic questions. On the contrary, most
of the questions from around the table were directed at me: where
had I been that week with the church, whom did I talk to, what
did I learn? Unlike the other Apostles, Elder Packer had risen to a
place among the Twelve through the church's Education Department, and at one point spoke of the obligation church historians
have to respect the essentially sacred history of the Saints—a veiled
reference to the more open-minded historians I had interviewed on

previous trips to Salt Lake. He also showed me his latest project: an LDS version of the King James Bible published by Cambridge University Press, the KJV's original publisher, with footnotes, indexing, and cross-references to the Book of Mormon and other scriptures of the church. It was yet another way of demonstrating the congruity between Mormonism and the Bible rightly understood.

But what I remember most about the evening was the moment just before dessert was served when one of the Apostle's pretty married daughters put her own question to me: "Now that you have been among us for a week, do you want to become one of us?"

All eyes turned to me. "Thank you very much," I replied, "but I already have a religion, one that I find hard enough to live up to." Only then did I realize that I had been invited into Elder Packer's house in order to experience something rare: a Mormon Apostle's own Family Home Evening. It was to be the climax of a weeklong incubation in the church and for an instant I felt almost sad to disappoint at the climactic moment. Friday morning on my return to *Newsweek,* I ran into Oz Elliott, who looked at my suitcase and asked me where I'd been. "You won't believe me, Oz," I said, "but I'm just back from dinner with one of the Twelve Apostles."

In the later decades of the twentieth century, Mormons grew in confidence as participants in the nation's public square. Their solid family values and emphasis on hard work meshed well with the ethos of the emergent body of free-enterprising Evangelical Christians. Theologically, the two made strange bedfellows. But in the culture wars of the late twentieth century they found common cause in opposing abortion on demand and same-sex marriage, and on other social issues that bedeviled American politics. Evangelicals were by far the larger electoral force but, ironically, it wasn't until one of their own was elected president of the United States that Evangelicals came to dominate the opposite (Republican) political party.

Part V

CHAPTER 12

Piety and Politics: The Republicans and the Religious Right

"Born Again"

During an interview with the press in 1976, Jimmy Carter was asked by one of his supporters if he was "born again." Carter readily said he was. Everyone he knew around his hometown of Plains, Georgia (pop. 653) was born again, and not just fellow Southern Baptists. It's what got you saved.

That was news to reporters who followed Carter on the campaign trail and it soon became a campaign issue. Few of them from outside the South knew the pertinent Bible verses Christians like Carter use when talking about their conversion experience. Some political reporters thought Carter, a pious Sunday school teacher, belonged to a religious cult. Gallup did a survey and found that half of all Protestants and a third of all adult Americans (nearly 50 million) claimed to have had a born-again experience. To most members of the national media, those numbers had the force of revelation.

But rather than harm Carter's chances of winning the presidency, his born-again identity turned out to be a boon. Beginning in 1960, no Democratic candidate for president had won a majority of the white Evangelical vote. But Carter, simply by describing himself as born again, sent a linguistic signal to Southern Baptists in particular and Evangelicals in general that he was one of them.

President Gerald Ford, Carter's Republican opponent, took note. An Episcopalian and a northerner, Ford insisted that he, too, was an Evangelical Christian. Although he stopped short of calling himself born again—the term was foreign to Episcopal church-speak—he said he read the Bible daily in the Oval Office and that (like George W. Bush in the 2000 election) his life had been transformed by Jesus Christ. That sufficed for Rev. Wallie Amos Criswell, patriarch of Southern Baptist Fundamentalists, who endorsed Ford as the two of them stood on the steps of Criswell's Dallas megachurch. Carter had offended Criswell by giving an interview to Robert Sheer for *Playboy* magazine. Like other reporters, Sheer was mystified by born-again religion, and Carter, in an earnest effort to show that his secured salvation was no prophylactic against temptation—after all, he was a Navy veteran—admitted in the interview that he had committed "adultery in my heart many times." But although he condemned himself for "lusting in the heart," Carter wanted Sheer to know he was a regular guy: "That does not mean I condemn someone who not only looks on a woman with lust but leaves his wife and shacks up with somebody out of wedlock."[1] That was the quote that really stoked Crisswell's ire: it sounded like the candidate approved of adultery. But most Southern Baptists—indeed, a slight majority of Evangelicals—swung round to support one of their own.

Two weeks before the election I wrote a cover story for *Newsweek* with an emphatic "Born Again!" emblazoned on the cover and another boldface headline inside proclaiming 1976 "The Year of The Evangelicals." The purpose was to explore and explain what the editors took to be a new cultural wave with political consequences. Chuck Colson had just published his autobiography, *Born Again,* which was heading toward sales of a million copies, and celebrities from onetime Black Panther leader Eldridge Cleaver to former stripper Candy Barr were trumpeting their born-again bona fides. Whatever was going on went well beyond the entrepreneurial thrusts of Billy Graham and Bill Bright.

What the story showed, I thought, was that Evangelicals were indeed an overlooked gathering force. But I also portrayed them as a divided, fractious bunch, with various groups fighting over the "inerrancy" of the Bible and what being "born again" is or ought to mean. The leadership of the Southern Baptist Convention (SBC), in particular, wanted the world to know that they didn't need other Evangelicals—they were bigger than the rest. "A world that had thought we were an ignorant, barefooted, one-gallused lot was jarred out of its seat," said the SBC president, "when it found out that . . . our voluntary gifts in a year are approximately $1.5 billion, and that on an average Sunday our churches baptize about three times as many people as were baptized at Pentecost."

But that is not how a lot of Evangelical readers understood the story, nor how the story has been treated in subsequent history books. Evangelicals like Colson saw it as a media milestone: for the first time, Evangelical Americans were recognized as a distinct and numerous movement in American religion, right up there with Catholics and mainline Protestants. Indeed, to judge by the hundreds of letters to the editor, the mere appearance of the story was invested with all sorts of unintended symbolism. Some respondents saw it as a divinely inspired rejoinder to *Time*'s "Is God Dead?" cover story published ten years earlier. Others traced a longer historical arc. Nineteen seventy-six was the nation's bicentennial and with that very much in mind, the *Newsweek* cover was deemed almost providential—a return, at last, to what many Evangelicals believed was the nation's Christian—that is, true Protestant—roots.

The *Newsweek* story barely limned the outlines of a new parallel culture, as wide as, but a good deal less cohesive than, the Catholic culture I'd experienced growing up. Evangelicals operated not only their own colleges and Bible seminaries but also their own Christian academies and elementary schools. This was a sharp reversal from the days when they criticized Catholics for creating their own parochial schools. But in the South especially, Supreme Court decisions banning prayer and even the posting of the Ten Commandments in public classrooms—not to mention white flight—convinced conservative Protestants that the public schools were now in the hands of secularists. So, many felt, were the federal government and the Supreme Court. One answer was to circle the wagons. In cities as different as Portland, Oregon, and Miami, Florida, Evangelicals published the *Christian Yellow Pages: A Telephone Directory of Born Again Christian Businesses and Professionals*. The idea, explained a directory salesman in Atlanta, "is more or less to keep the money within the kingdom."

Given Evangelicalism's entrepreneurial thrust, it was inevitable that God's kingdom would become a marketplace mirroring the very world that Fundamentalist and conservative Evangelicals once scorned. By the late Seventies, they had their own radio and television programs; their own association of "Christian" broadcasters; their own list of Christian celebrities and entertainers, newscasters, and pundits; their own publishers, bookstores, and bestseller lists; their own "Christian" music; and, soon to come, their own "Christian" rock bands. To the two-fingered V signaling "peace" there was now the Evangelicals' raised index finger countersignaling Christ as the one (and only) way to salvation.

As both a market and a parallel culture, Evangelicals had also become a political constituency to be courted. From Billy Graham to the local preacher they were mostly conservative in politics as well as in religion. But it was a pair of Catholics and a Jew who figured out how best to exploit this opportunity for the Republican Party. And what better way to arouse an oral/aural culture than through a preacher with an established broadcast audience?

The Making of the "Moral Majority"

About the time *Newsweek*'s "Born Again" cover appeared, Richard Viguerie, a direct-mail wiz servicing conservative political causes, recognized the Evangelical subculture as ripe for political plucking. Together with Paul Weyrich of the Committee for the Survival of a Free Congress and Howard Phillips of the Conservative Caucus, Viguerie held a series of meetings with Fundamentalist preachers in an effort to move them from bystander status to full-blown political operatives. Big-time evangelists could not afford overtly partisan politics but a Fundamentalist with the right credentials could. The preacher who had the most to offer was the Reverend Jerry Falwell.

As a religious entrepreneur, Falwell possessed an impressive re-sume. In sixteen years he had built from scratch a congregation of 12,000 members, nearly a fourth of the entire population of Lynch-burg, Virginia; an auditorium-style church that seated 10,000 wor-shippers; a private Christian Academy for 612 students K through 12; a fledgling college with 1,000 students; and a fleet of 89 buses that swept a 65-mile radius to transport worshippers to Sunday services. His ministry also included a perk that even Billy Graham lacked: a 27-passenger Convair turboprop. Falwell's success was so impres-sive that I wrote a profile of him in 1972 at the urging of and with reporting from *Newsweek*'s Atlanta bureau. What most impressed Viguerie, however, was Falwell's broadcast ministry, *The Old-Time Gospel Hour,* which was beamed to four hundred television stations, carried on several hundred more radio stations, and—the pearl in this oyster—owned a coveted computerized mailing list of tens of thousands of "faith partners."

Falwell, then forty-seven years old, also carried some baggage. He had a history as a segregationist who had supported the apart-heid regime in South Africa and opposed Martin Luther King Jr. and his "non–civil rights movement," as he called it. That wasn't much of a hindrance to Weyrich, who had taken over leadership of the American Independent Party from segregationist George Wal-lace. The problem was that Falwell, a flamethrowing Fundamen-talist, had long opposed mixing religion and politics. But Viguerie and Weyrich, both Catholics, and Phillips, a Jew, shared Falwell's conviction that "secular humanists" were taking over the country. Abortion, evolution, and sex education in public schools, gay rights, the Equal Rights Amendment—these and other issues, they argued, would persuade reluctant Fundamentalists and other conservative Evangelicals to become politically active. Weyrich even found the perfect name for the movement they hoped to birth: the "Moral Ma-jority." Falwell did not need much persuasion.

Actually, I'd always felt a certain sympathy for Fundamentalist Protestants. Like them, we Catholics have always had problems with any form of humanism that sought to sequester religious faith from public thought and practice. The core Fundamentalist doctrine—

that the Bible is literally true and without error—functioned, I've always thought, much like the infallibility of the pope has: as an anchor of authority that in practice adds nothing to the content of Christian faith. The difference is that papal infallibility has been formally invoked only once, and then after wide consultation with his fellow bishops,[2] while with each sermon Fundamentalist preachers invoke a Bible presumed to be inerrant.

The 1980 Presidential Election

As a Fundamentalist, Falwell had a lot to learn about politics, and as the public face of the Moral Majority he sometimes left food on his chin. For example, at a rally in Alaska, where the Moral Majority controlled the 1980 GOP state delegation, Falwell trumpeted a story about how, at a White House meeting with selected clergy, he had sharply questioned President Carter concerning "the known practicing homosexuals" on his staff. But a transcript released by the White House showed that no such conversation took place. Falwell insisted he had not lied, though he had. Nor did he apologize until I asked him on NBC's *Meet the Press* if he had done so. "I'm doing it right now," he said. It was the first of numerous retractions and apologies Falwell would be forced to make.

In the 1980 presidential race, all three contenders—incumbent Carter, Republican nominee Ronald Reagan, and independent candidate John Anderson—described themselves as born-again Christians. Of the three, the clear favorite of the new Christian Right was Reagan. He was also the only one whose born-again faith was, at best, a recently acquired taste. Reagan rarely saw the inside of a church but when it came to religion talk, the former actor could mimic the choked-up hush of the truly pious and deliver evangelistic chestnuts like "America's hunger for spiritual renewal" as if Billy Graham had never existed. Early on, the Reagan campaign signed up the Moral Majority's executive director, Robert Billings, to serve as a liaison to the party's newly acquired constituency. The pact with the Religious Right was sealed in Dallas just five weeks before the Republican National Convention. Addressing a rally of seventeen thousand Evangelicals sponsored by the right-wing Religious Roundtable, Reagan famously declared, "I know you cannot endorse me, but I want you to know that I endorse you." At the convention, the impact of the Republicans' newest constituency was manifest in a party platform that stiffened the GOP's opposition to abortion on demand and reversed its previous stand in support of the Equal Rights Amendment, much to the displeasure of George H. W. Bush, the vice presidential nominee. As historian Steven P. Miller has written, "on social issues, at least, the pew trumped the country club."[3]

After Reagan's thumping of Carter in the 1980 election, Falwell and other leaders of the new Christian Right claimed to be the difference makers by delivering a majority of the white Evangelical voters. In fact, Reagan won majorities in virtually every social and religious category. But there was no doubt that the newly active born-again bloc of Fundamentalists and conservative Evangelicals had shown itself to be a force in American politics. What was novel was how they went about it.

Fundamentalism and Free Enterprise

Unlike mainline Protestants, born-again Christians in the 1970s did not hold places at either party's leadership table. Unlike the Catholics, they had never exerted their influence through mediating institutions like labor unions and big-city political machines. The only organization they had to work with, really, was the church. Willing pastors were trained—not always well—by groups like the Moral Majority in how to preach about politics without violating IRS rules, mostly by letting their listeners know whom they personally were voting for and why. They were also supplied with bundles of voter guides and urged to use their bus ministries to transport the faithful to Religious Right rallies and to the voting booth on Election Day.

Theirs was a church-based populism that was new to twentieth-century American politics. Conservative Protestants had watched on the political sidelines as blacks, feminists, and gays pressed their own agendas. They had witnessed the weakening of traditional institutions like marriage and the family, the collapse of public education as they had known it, the rise of drugs and violence, and a general thumbing of noses at traditional moral values. Secular humanists were responsible for this rending of the social fabric, they believed. And so, bumbling but biblically self-assured, they entered the once-forbidden arena of politics with cleats on. Liberals who valued participatory democracy were quite unprepared for the advancing horde of newly engaged church folk. By sheer force of numbers, that horde redrew the lines separating religion and politics and altered the language of political discourse.

None of this would have happened, though, without the power of religious broadcasters. If evangelism is essentially entrepreneurial, as I have argued, that trait is best seen in its hard-won dominance of religious programming. In the 1950s and '60s, the Federal Communications Commission required local stations to provide free airtime to religious broadcasters. In Omaha I had observed firsthand that those religious groups that got access were determined by local stations in cooperation with local Catholics, Jews, and mainline Protestants. Fundamentalists and other conservative Evangelicals were frozen out. So they were forced to buy airtime, create programming, and learn how to solicit funds on air. When the FCC changed its rules in the 1970s and local stations were no longer required to provide free airtime for religious programming, the born-again bloc was well positioned to button up the available paid-time program slots in radio and on television. For an essentially preached religion, the rules change seemed heaven-sent. Thus was born "the electronic church."

For Falwell, as for Oral Roberts and numerous lesser-known television preachers, broadcasting was the engine that fed their entrepreneurial ambitions. It was how they kept the money coming in, how they marketed their wares, and how they financed their building projects. Falwell, for example, was able to charge students at Liberty Baptist College (now Liberty University) half the average cost for tuition, room, and board through subsidies from his broadcasting operation.

In other words, Fundamentalists were not only free-enterprisers in religion; as broadcasters they were also wed to free enterprise in economics as well. One by one they had bought their way into radio and now television broadcasting. It wasn't only moral issues that made them natural allies of conservative, free-enterprising Republicans like Ronald Reagan.

But even for preachers, free enterprise is governed by rules and regulations. Shortly before the 1980 election, one of Falwell's financial advisors called and asked me to come to Lynchburg. There was a delicate matter he wanted to discuss but not over the phone and not in public. We would meet at his estate. Since he was being so cautious, I thought it best to stay at the home of a Notre Dame classmate in Lynchburg until we had a chance to talk. The advisor said he was concerned because Falwell was lending money from his $1-million-a-week broadcast ministry at no interest—and with no payback schedule—to help keep the Moral Majority afloat. The advisor thought this was morally wrong, economically risky, and probably illegal: tax-exempt organizations like Falwell's ministries cannot fund political action groups. Falwell was already under investigation by the Securities and Exchange Commission (SEC) for floating $56 million in unsecured bonds, and this advisor was worried about the financial impact on Liberty College. He showed me supporting documents and promised to mail a full set to me. Before I left Lynchburg I met with Falwell, who said that any money he raised was his to spend as he saw fit. There was, he showed me, a phrase in fine print in all his promotional literature that allowed him to do that.

Back at *Newsweek,* I found that the Nation section was preparing a cover story on Falwell just before the election. I could do a sidebar page but there would be no investigation into his finances. I was angry, of course, but until the promised documents arrived I couldn't make my case. They never did. Instead, I received a phone call informing me that the financial advisor had died in a mysterious accident: he was hacked to pieces, apparently after falling into the blades of his own thrasher.

Following the 1980 election, President Reagan awarded three posts in his administration to members of the Religious Right. James Watt, a conservative Pentecostal, was appointed secretary of the interior; anti-abortion physician C. Everett Koop became surgeon general; and James Billings, the former Moral Majority operative, was given a high-level position in the Department of Education. But that was it. On legislative and cultural issues dear to the Religious Right, the Reagan administration kept the movement standing tippy-toed and puckered for a serious kiss.

There were sound political reasons for this strategy. Although Reagan and House Speaker Tip O'Neill enjoyed an Irishmen's camaraderie, the Democratic-controlled lower chamber was not about to pass any laws favoring school prayer or abortion limits. Moreover, Reagan recognized that whatever the importance of the born-again vote to the party's success, the Religious Right was not endorsed by the vast majority of American citizens. Polls showed that among the 40 percent of Americans who were even aware of the Moral Majority, actual support for it and for Falwell was in single digits.

The Overreach of Jerry Falwell

Nonetheless, for the ten years of its existence, the Moral Majority, with Jerry Falwell as the face of the broader Religious Right, commanded outsize media attention. Jerry himself appeared on the cover of both *Newsweek* and *Time* and was a frequent guest on ABC's *Nightline* and other talk shows in part because he typically boosted viewership, especially among those who feared and loathed him. Brusque, pugnacious, and often outrageous in his opinions, Falwell seemed to revel in his ability to make enemies.

The key to his personality, I always thought, was his determination to make good as well as make waves. In terms of Lynchburg society, which included several first families of Virginia, the Falwells were local Snopeses from the wrong side of the tracks. His father had been a small-time businessman and sometime bootlegger who shot and killed his brother in an argument. After his born-again experience as a college sophomore, Jerry left town for a small hard-core Bible college in Springfield, Missouri. There he found not only a new identity but also a career path in the ministry that would in time make him Lynchburg's largest employer, best-known citizen, and biggest entrepreneur. The first time we met, Jerry took me to a low mountain above the town to show me the future site of an expanded Liberty University: it would be to Fundamentalists what he imagined Notre Dame to be to Catholics. His political seduction, however, nearly shattered his dream.

The burden of leading the Moral Majority made Falwell's fund-raising efforts ever more desperate. In 1981, for instance, he was caught publishing a photo of a Lynchburg bank (with the name of the bank blacked out) and passing it off as the business school of his college, and a photo of a picturesque college chapel as if it were a building on his campus. In fact, the chapel was fifty miles away on the campus of Washington and Lee University, the alma mater of fellow broadcaster Pat Robertson. A few years later, a photographer tipped me off to the fact that on his Sunday television broadcasts Falwell was soliciting funds (again, with small print saying all donations would go for this *and other projects*) to help the boat people fleeing Vietnam, more than a year after the last of them had been rescued from the waters. The real story of Jerry Falwell, I began to see, was not his politics but his reckless drive to succeed.

In the spring of 1982, Falwell's ambition peaked. He had recently published a book, *The Fundamentalist Phenomenon*, ghosted by two of his aides, which pictured the larger Evangelical establishment as a "jumbo jet" that, thanks to Falwell and the Moral Majority, had been "suddenly highjacked by Fundamentalist pilots." Fundamentalists were the only truly orthodox Christians, Falwell contended, and he appealed to Graham-style Evangelicals to "re-acknowledge your Fundamentalist roots."

It was Jerry's naked bid to replace Billy as the lodestar of American Evangelicalism. And for a time his candidacy was taken seriously. Seeing that Graham's main interest was evangelizing overseas, a dozen Evangelical leaders, including two of Graham's own appointees as editors of *Christianity Today,* invited Falwell to a secret meeting in Washington, D.C., early in 1982. It was the closest thing in Evangelical circles to a search committee and a key moment for American Evangelicalism. Falwell made his case, arguing that Evangelicals had abandoned belief in an inerrant Bible, Fundamentalism's key tenet, and that he was the man to lead them back to truth. But his listeners rejected him and his retrograde agenda. When I learned of the meeting I asked Graham about Falwell's bid to replace him. His answer, in effect, was "Jerry who?" "I've met Mr. Falwell once, for a minute at a prayer breakfast," he calculated, "and I've talked to him only once, I think, by phone." Graham's own opinion was that the Moral Majority represented no more than 10 percent of Evangelicals in America—and he turned out to be right. Far from taking over, Falwell eventually declared that he, too, was an Evangelical.

In the run-up to the 1984 election, Reagan blew a few symbolic kisses in the direction of the Religious Right. He declared 1983 the "Year of the Bible," which produced a flood of television programs and magazine articles on the Good Book, including a *Newsweek* cover story I wrote on the historical impact of the Bible, titled "The Bible in America." Under Reagan's name, the Republicans published a campaign book called *In God I Trust.* The president also chose the annual meeting of the National Association of Evangelicals as the occasion to deliver the most memorable speech of his first term, an address on foreign policy in which he famously assailed the Soviet Union as "an evil empire." But if Reagan again embraced the Religious Right, it was even more the case that the Religious Right had come to embrace what the party called the "Reagan Revolution."

Religion hung like kudzu from the stage of the 1984 Republican National Convention in Dallas. Fiery Texas evangelist James Robison offered the opening prayer and Falwell closed the convention with a benediction that proclaimed Reagan and Vice President

George H. W. Bush "God's instruments in rebuilding America." In between, televangelist Pat Robertson, who would run for the GOP nomination himself four years hence, and lesser worthies of the Religious Right shared the stage.

This riotous display of pious partisanship was further proof to Democrats and their secular supporters that the Republicans were recklessly violating the hallowed tradition of separation of church and state. The emergence and temporary triumph of the Religious Right had already produced a countermobilization of organizations such as television writer and producer Norman Lear's newly formed People for the American Way; Americans United, which (as Protestants and Others United for the Separation of Church and State) had previously targeted Catholics in politics; and the American Civil Liberties Union, which abandoned its tradition of defending social pariahs by opposing the Moral Majoritarians of the right. As it turned out, however, Reagan's landslide victory in 1984 marked the high point for the right's political preachers. And the first to feel the wages of political ambition was the overreaching Jerry Falwell.

Falwell's final entrepreneurial misadventure occurred in 1986, when he took control of the PTL (for "Praise The Lord" and later, "People That Love") television network from disgraced televangelist Jim Bakker. With it came Heritage USA, Bakker's gaudy theme park in South Carolina that was second only to the two Disney parks in the number of tourists it attracted. At the time, Bakker's annual take from his ventures was $129 million, half as much as Falwell's broadcasts produced. Bakker and his cohost/wife, Tammy Faye Bakker, were Pentecostal Christians who promised material prosperity to their donors. Most of their supporters were lower-middle-class Pentecostals who saw in the Bakkers a religious couple of their own kind who had made good. Tammy Faye's thickly mascaraed eyelids and heavily made-up face represented liberation to millions of Pentecostal women who were taught as children to abjure cosmetics and other profane adornments. A vacation at Heritage USA was, in effect, their chance to jump through the television tube and join the freed-up Jim and Tammy Faye at play in a Pentecostal version of Las Vegas. Falwell immediately invested $20 million in a water slide at the park and, descending on his back in his black three-piece minister's suit, gamely launched the slide himself. No matter. Pentecostals knew that the park's new owner was a Fundamentalist who had routinely disparaged Pentecostal practices like speaking in tongues. Very quickly, Falwell lost his customers and his shirt.

The following year, Falwell resigned from the Moral Majority, saying he was through being "a politician or a businessman" and was going "back to the pulpit, back to preaching, back to winning souls." In fact, he bowed out because of continuing financial crises at the university that needed his full attention. Indeed, it took an infusion of funds from wealthy friends, including—improbably—Dr. Moon of the Unification Church, to bail the school out.

The last time I saw Jerry Falwell was in 1988 at a Los Angeles hotel where the Religious Roundtable was holding its annual conference. As one evangelist pointed to a chart correlating the decline of American morals with the banning of prayer in public schools, I read deep unease in the face of the event's honored guest, Republican nominee George H. W. Bush, an old-school Yalie who looked as if he had been suddenly enrolled in a Texas Bible college. But Falwell looked even worse: weary, almost broken, like a boxer on his stool who knows he's already lost the fight. I myself felt like I was meeting an old adversary I'd gone too many rounds with to dislike. We even exchanged a clumsy hug, as pugilists do. Jerry was open about his problems with the university but still insistent that it would become Fundamentalism's Notre Dame. Already, he said, the university had a first-rate team in baseball, his abiding love. "But Jerry," I said, "you need a football program. That's the sport that gave Notre Dame its national identity." We were talking his second language, sports, and it was the only time we ever shared a laugh.[4]

A year later, the Moral Majority was disbanded and eight years after that Jerry Falwell, always overweight, suffered a fatal heart attack.

Channeling the Holy Spirit

In the world of entrepreneurial religion, the Eighties turned out to be a period of recurring scandals and crises. The major victims were Pentecostals, especially those who specialized in on-air miracles and healings, often amid profuse shedding of tears. Jim Bakker was caught in an adulterous affair with a church secretary, Jessica Hahn, then found guilty of twenty-four counts of fraud and conspiracy and sent to prison. Jimmy Swaggart, a shaman-like evangelist whose television trademark was his almost orgasmic reenactments of the born-again experience, was shamed off the air after revelations that he regularly paid prostitutes to disrobe and strut in front of him. His sobbing "I have sinned" admission was prime-time television news. Faith healer Oral Roberts, whose motto was "Expect a Miracle," fell from grace after he went on-air saying God would call him home unless he raised $8 million for a medical school at the university that bears his name. High-living prosperity preacher Robert Tilton (not a Pentecostal) lost his audience after ABC's *Prime Time* revealed that he never read, much less prayed over, the "prayer requests" that millions of viewers sent him along with their donations for his intercession.

"Gospelgate," as the string of scandals came to be known, was a made-for-television drama that played out nightly on programs like *Larry King Live* and Ted Koppel's *Nightline*. It was on *Nightline* that I most often encountered these fallen angels. In 1984, Richard Smith took over as editor in chief of *Newsweek*. Rick showed limited interest in religion and under him the annual number of religion stories declined by half. But at *Nightline* I found a new outlet for my reporting. Fortunately, the immensely gifted Marshall Frady, son of a Baptist preacher, had moved from *Newsweek* to *Nightline* as an on-air reporter. We agreed to share what we were learning about the unfolding scandals and if *Newsweek* wasn't interested I had an outlet at *Nightline* as a commentator.

Prophecy and Politics

The only religious broadcaster who avoided scandal in the 1980s was another Pentecostal, Myron "Pat" Robertson, though he, too, lost an estimated $28 million in contributions because of Gospel-gate. Robertson was by far religious broadcasting's best-educated and shrewdest entrepreneur. The son of a veteran Democratic senator from Virginia and a graduate of Yale Law School, Robertson had gone into business in the Fifties with his law school roommate, another student of Frank O'Malley at Notre Dame, and also served as chairman of Adlai Stevenson's presidential campaign on Staten Island. But after meeting a Lutheran minister who had undergone a Pentecostal "baptism of the Holy Spirit," Robertson enrolled in New York Bible Seminary, where he fervently sought and eventually experienced the same baptism with all its powers of revelation and prophecy. The experience forever changed the man and his politics.

Pentecostalism itself is a late bloom of American revivalism and its most ecstatic flowering. The first Pentecostal irruption to gain public notice occurred in 1906 at the Azusa Street Church in Los Angeles. Like other made-in-America religious movements, its adherents sought to recapture Christianity as its earliest disciples experienced it—specifically at Pentecost, when they began to speak "in other languages" as the sign that they had received the baptism of the Holy Spirit. Here again, the experience of divine presence is wholly verbal, though as practiced by most Pentecostals the language of "tongues"—a form of involuntary motor behavior—is incomprehensible to ordinary ears. To many in the first generation of Pentecostals, though, the outpouring of the Holy Spirit also signaled the beginning of the end-times, giving Pentecostalism an apocalyptic edge.

For the Apostle Paul, speaking in tongues was one of many gifts of the Holy Spirit, along with prophecy, healing, and miracle-working. But unlike Paul, who saw these powers as spiritual gifts for building up the church, Robertson used them to build a career as a religious broadcaster, beginning in 1960. On his daily *700 Club* program, Robertson's signature sequence was (and remains) a segment in which, head bent and eyes closed, he discerned ulcers healing, bent limbs straightening, hemorrhoids shrinking—all the ills humankind is prone to miraculously disappearing while Robertson prayed. Whether Robertson thought he was directing that power himself was never clear, though in 1985 he boasted that he had diverted Hurricane Gloria away from Virginia Beach, Virginia, where he had built his headquarters, to the sodden householders on the southern shores of Long Island, New York. But on his broadcasts Robinson never named those who were being healed while he spoke, nor did he claim healing powers for himself, as Oral Roberts and other Pentecostal preachers did. What he *did* claim on television was the power to discern what Jesus was up to here and now. These séance-like interludes on the *700 Club* were mixed in later years with sophisticated news reports, interviews with Christian celebrities, and his own conservative commentary on what soon became the satellite-beamed Christian Broadcasting Network on cable.

Although he was ordained as a Southern Baptist minister, Robertson was never a member of the Billy Graham circle. As a functioning Pentecostal, he inscribed an orbit of his own. Eventually, his ambition turned to politics. In 1978, Robertson established his own political action organization, the Freedom Council, using mailing lists from his *700 Club* and relying mainly on Pentecostal churches to organize local chapters of his Freedom Council in political precincts across the country. A decade later, these local councils became the grassroots organization behind his own campaign for the Republican nomination for president. Robertson surprised the party's elders by taking second place in the 1988 Iowa caucus—ahead of future president George H. W. Bush. But his bid ended amid serious charges that he had not seen combat as a marine in the Korean War, as his campaign literature claimed, plus revelations that (like Falwell) he had been using funds from his broadcasts to support the Freedom Council. Robertson was further embarrassed when the press discovered that his eldest child had been born months before he and his wife married. After the election, the Freedom Council was transformed into the Christian Coalition, which allowed Robertson to maintain degrees of political influence for yet another decade.

"I have always been an entrepreneur," Robertson once told me, and as a businessman he prospered mightily from CBN, buying television stations and taking his network global. Beginning in 1977, he founded a series of professional schools (thereby avoiding the financial risks of expensive undergraduate and doctoral education) that have since become Regent University, which he prophesied would endure until the Second Coming, when Christ would need well-educated Christians to help Him rule the world. Statements like that are what made Robertson's voice unique within entrepreneurial religion, bizarre but wonderful to quote. Whether offering advice to the World Bank or predicting the end of the world in 1982, or merely handicapping market futures, Robertson invoked a gnosis that only he could grasp. One never knew whether his calculations were based on empirical data or the powers he'd acquired from the Holy Spirit. I questioned him several times on television and I'm not sure he ever knew himself.

My longest personal exposure to Robertson came at a public conference on southern religion at the University of North Carolina in the Eighties. Robertson and I were the only nonacademics on the stage. In the audience was a group of Robertson student devotees who regarded him as a modern prophet. Instead of addressing our assigned topic, Robertson took the occasion to witness to his own spiritual powers. He was just back from China, he said, and among other marvels that befell him was one that occurred on the quay in Shanghai. As Robertson told it, he went out and spoke to a multilingual group of strollers who gathered round him. And, as at the first Pentecost in Jerusalem, each heard him in his or her native tongue.

I challenged that. As it happened, I had strolled out at night on the very same quay in Shanghai the previous year. As a rare American in Communist China, I also drew a crowd. I, too, spoke to them in English and I also saw them smile and nod as if they understood. "The Chinese are polite like that," I said.

"Are you calling me a liar?" Robertson demanded, though as always he never stopped smiling.

"No," I said. "I'm just saying you misunderstood what was happening."

I was calling his special powers into question and he wasn't pleased. He said he'd never speak to me again, and he never did. But it hardly mattered. Robertson was usually cagey and often cautious in an interview. On the other hand, he was never so quotable as when he was talking freely on his television show, channeling the Holy Spirit.

The 2000 Campaign: Questioning the Candidates

The Clinton presidency was a time of transition for the Religious Right. The Southern Baptist from Hope, Arkansas, who had studied at the Jesuits' Georgetown University proved that a Bible-quoting Democrat from the South could win back Reagan Democrats, including Roman Catholics, by stressing economic issues, but not the Evangelicals, who remained solidly behind Bush. During the eight Clinton years, leadership of the Religious Right passed from the old televangelists like Falwell and Robertson to the pastors of Evangelical megachurches, mostly in the South and West, and presidential candidates adjusted their weathervanes accordingly. In the Nineties, Billy Graham himself passed a symbolic baton (in the form of the hat he always wore to presidential inaugurations) to *The Purpose-Driven Life* author Rick Warren, pastor of Saddleback Church, a multi-themed worship center in Southern California, while Franklin Graham inherited his father's evangelistic association and began pushing it off his father's moderate path toward the angry far right.

Of much greater significance was the maturation of Evangelical politicos like Ralph Reed, who moved from directing the Christian Coalition to Republican Party operative. What didn't change was the quadrennial political ritual in which presidential candidates from both parties were expected to declare their religious bona fides.

No one who wants to be president nowadays would dare wave off requests for information about his or her religious convictions the way that Franklin Delano Roosevelt did when he entered the race in 1932: "I am a Christian and a Democrat and that is all they need to know," he told his aides. And so, early in the primary season leading up to the millennial election of the year 2000, *Newsweek* dispatched me to New Hampshire to probe the four major candidates about their personal religious beliefs and practices.

They were not a particularly pious bunch. Vice President Al Gore allowed that he was "a Christian, a Protestant, and a Baptist" in that order but added a distinctly Evangelical credential, saying that "none of these labels are as important as my own personal experience." Former Democratic senator Bill Bradley recalled testifying publicly for Christ as a member of the Fellowship of Christian Athletes but said that he eventually realized this fervor was inauthentic. Republican senator John McCain, a Baptist, said he attended church most Sundays. Right away he corrected himself, as if he'd just remembered that the bus we were sitting in was called "The Straight Talk Express." "Make that more like once a month," he said.

Oddly enough, the most religiously demonstrative candidate that year, Texas governor George W. Bush, was also the only one who refused my requests for an interview. The reason, I came to believe, was that he had already made his Evangelical witness a month earlier on television during a Republican candidates' debate in Iowa. When it was his turn to name his favorite philosopher and explain why, Bush immediately responded: "Jesus, because he changed my heart." Never mind that Jesus spoke as a prophet, not a philosopher. With those five words Bush signaled the party's religious base that if he were elected president God would have an Evangelical witness in the White House.

The study of religion and politics would be a lot more relevant if scholars could demonstrate a relationship between any president's policies and his religious beliefs and practices. Denominational ties, in particular, are useless in predicting how a president will govern. This was especially true of George W. Bush. A baptized Episcopalian and sometime Presbyterian, Bush eventually joined the church of his wife's choice and became a Methodist, even though the United Methodist Church's official positions on public policy were the obverse of his own conservative politics. In fact, the candidate who said his heart had been changed by Jesus was not the product of *any* church. Rather, his piety was shaped by "the small group movement," sociologist Robert Wuthnow's term for the vast network of support groups ranging from Bible study circles to twelve-step programs like Alcoholics Anonymous to hobbyists and book discussion clubs. In 1994, Wuthnow estimated that four out of ten Americans belonged to the movement, which he saw as filling a populist need for community and attracting people with an aversion to large organizations—including religious denominations.[5] Habitat for Humanity, which was founded by Millard Fuller, a pious Christian, was and remains a conspicuous example.

Like many others, Bush's small group experience was essentially therapeutic. In the 1980s, he joined a nondenominational Bible study group to help him overcome a dependence on alcohol that was wounding his marriage, and he came away with a view of religion that was personal, therapeutic, and focused on the efficacy of small, voluntary circles of caring. Why is this important? Because as I have emphasized throughout this book, *how* a person gets religion can powerfully influence the understanding of the religion he got. But it is also important if we are to understand the one policy of the Bush presidency that could be said to be motivated by his personal experience of religion.

Bush's Faith-Based Bust

Decisions a chief executive makes during the first week in office are often intended as symbols of a presidential change in direction. For example, four days into his presidency Bill Clinton celebrated the twentieth anniversary of *Roe v. Wade* by holding a televised session in the Oval Office where he issued a series of executive orders rescinding certain restrictions the Reagan and Bush administrations had placed on federal funding of national and international abortion providers. It was a pledge he had made to his feminist constituency and was reinforced at home by Hillary. George W. Bush's first act in office was a pair of executive orders establishing the Office of Faith-Based and Community Initiatives, with desks in the various branches of the federal government. The purpose was to provide federal funds to faith-based and other local community organizations on the premise that they are better placed than government bureaucracies to assess and provide social services. This, too, was the fulfillment of a campaign promise.

Politically, the faith-based initiative was meant to put flesh on the bones of "compassionate conservatism," Bush's campaign theme.[6] But it was also an application of the kind of small-group, self-help religion that had turned his own life around. Inevitably, the program generated opposition. Attorney General John Ashcroft, a devout Pentecostal, was sent out to convince those Evangelicals who feared government money would lead to government control of the services they rendered in the name of Jesus. Secular critics feared the government would wind up mixing the gin of religious proselytizing with the tonic of faith-based social services. The issue of where to draw the line was dicey since there was impressive empirical evidence, from recidivism rates for paroled prisoners, to countering gang-based violence in the inner city, that religious faith was a powerful factor in turning individuals away from the path of crime.

And yet it could be argued—indeed, was argued in a brief but adroit piece in *The New Republic*—that Bush's compassionate conservatism owed more to Catholic social thought than to any other source.[7] The new president's experience of Evangelical Christianity, with its emphasis on personal salvation, offered no principles for building a just society. But Bush's chief speechwriter, Michael Gerson, a Wheaton College graduate, had studied Catholic social teachings and he introduced his boss to several Catholics who tutored candidate Bush on the meaning of that doctrine's major concepts, like "solidarity," "subsidiarity," and "the common good." Among them was University of Pennsylvania political scientist and crimi-nologist John Dilulio, who had directed a number of faith-based projects in Philadelphia's inner city. "The last institutions to aban-don the slums," he liked to remind politicians, "are the liquor stores and the churches."

Bush chose Dilulio to direct his faith-based program, thus mak-ing him the only Catholic and only Democrat among his White House advisors. The president's plan was to provide up to $8 bil-lion in funding, but the budget never came close to that figure and eight months into the Bush administration, Dilulio became its first member to resign, later citing White House staff's indifference and focus on the politics of the program as his main reasons. Like his father, though, George W. Bush lacked what the elder Bush had dis-missed as "the vision thing." Had it been otherwise, he might have brought to the Republican Party a view of civil society in which a wide range of institutions and associational organizations enrich the gap between government and the individual citizen. It was a missed opportunity.

Throughout his eight years in office, George W. Bush wore his re-ligion openly, like Russians do their medals. As the 2004 election approached, *Time, Newsweek,* and *U.S. News & World Report,* as well as *The New Republic, Commonweal, America,* and numerous other opinion journals, analyzed what *Time* called "the faith factor" in American politics. One study that attempted to quantify pres-idential "God talk" since the rise of the Religious Right declared George W. Bush the winner over Ronald Reagan, Bush the elder, and Bill Clinton—though not by much. No one, however, found a way to measure how any of this talk influenced the governance of the country. Never mind that Bush's reelection prompted a rash of feverish articles warning of an incipient "theocracy" conceived by political "theocons."[8] The latter, it turned out, were either fringy Evangelical thinkers or Bush's Catholic advisors, who never did in-fluence his thinking.

By the close of the second George W. Bush administration, it was obvious that Evangelical Christians owned more than their share of seats at the table. As the largest and most reliable voting bloc in the Republican Party they had a major say in how that particular party's table was set, and who said grace over the meal. The party's air of acquired righteousness probably put off as many voters as it attracted. But as the Democratic Party demonstrated, in politics there is more than one way to be religious, and in religion there is more than one way to be righteous.

CHAPTER 13

Religion as Politics: The Democrats

A White House Declaration of Faith

In the culture wars that freighted American politics during the last quarter of the twentieth century, Republicans routinely charged that the Democratic Party had become the party of secularists while theirs was the party of religious believers. The most provocative thrust came from President George H. W. Bush at the start of the 1992 campaign. Addressing a gathering of Religious Right leaders, Bush declared that the Democratic platform had "left out three simple letters, G-O-D." That line provoked an editorial warning from the *New York Times* that such rhetoric threatened to "divide the nation along religious lines." The charge of irreligion also rankled the Democratic leadership. After all, Jimmy Carter, the only Democratic president during the Seventies and Eighties, was a born-again Southern Baptist and probably the most rigorously religious president since Woodrow Wilson. More to the point, Bush's opponent that year was another Southern Baptist, Bill Clinton, who enjoyed listening to preachers as much as he enjoyed hearing a good saxophonist: indeed, as candidate and as president, Clinton never found a pew he couldn't sit in.

What sort of man was it, I wanted to know, who could borrow the very words of Jesus at the Last Supper, "new covenant," for his inaugural theme? But every time I asked to interview President

Clinton about his religious views, the White House turned me down. Finally, two years into the Clinton administration I got a go-ahead. But it wasn't the president who agreed to see me at the White House. It was First Lady Hillary Rodham Clinton, already a figure of nearly equal public fascination.

A cynic would say that the White House agreed to the interview for political reasons and a cynic would probably be right. The interview was scheduled to appear a week before the 1994 midterm elections, which eventually saw the Republicans gain control of *both* the House and the Senate for the first time in forty years. But even a cynic would have to acknowledge that a religious profile of the controversial First Lady just before an election was an unnecessary political gamble unless the president were confident that a story reflecting his wife's manifest religious sincerity could only help the party's cause.

From my pre-interview research and reporting it was clear that Mrs. Clinton was one of those rare figures in public life whose political views cannot be separated from their religious convictions. Long before Hillary Rodham was a Democrat, a lawyer, or a Clinton, she was a Methodist. She can trace her family roots back to eighteenth-century England and Wales shortly after the Methodist movement began. Unlike many baby boomers, she had a deep immersion in Methodist youth organizations during high school and, unlike most college students in the mid-Sixties—especially brainy women who studied at elite women's colleges like Wellesley during the feminist awakening—she continued her involvement with the religious groups. Indeed, her political transformation from Goldwater Republican to McGovern Democrat owed a great deal to the progressive movements within the Methodist Church.

The interview took place in the White House Map Room around a makeshift folding table that looked like it had just been cleared of dishes. I placed two tape recorders on the table: one to listen to the next day and the other for transcription. I had only forty-eight hours to write a profile that editor Maynard Parker wanted as the lead story to the National Affairs section. But as soon as Mrs. Clinton arrived (black dress, string of pearls), she asked me to turn the recorders off so we could get to know each other a bit before taping began. That the First Lady seemed nervous dissolved any remaining anxiety I had brought with me to the White House.

I was surprised to learn that Hillary Clinton's religious reading habits ran toward Evangelical books and magazines about prayer and spiritual growth rather than those that provide religious arguments for progressive politics. On the other hand, she assured me that upstairs in the family area of the White House she kept the latest edition of the Methodist Book of Resolutions, which records the denomination's consistently liberal stands on a wide range of moral, social, and political issues. Piety plus politics was her message.

On two moral issues that were politically fraught in the 1994 midterm elections, Mrs. Clinton took positions that did not quite fit with those of her husband's administration. On the subject of contraception, she said she was "not comfortable" with condom distribution in public schools, which contradicted the policy of Surgeon General Joycelyn Elders. A fellow Methodist whom the Clintons had brought with them from Arkansas, Elders was known for keeping a "condom tree" on her desk. On the subject of abortion, the First Lady's view neatly captured both the contradictions of the pro-choice position and the moral ambivalence of the electorate: she allowed that abortion is morally "wrong," but not so wrong as to override a woman's right to have one. Not surprisingly, that was also the official position of her church.

As Arkansas's First Lady, Hillary Clinton had taught Methodist Sunday school and occasionally preached at church conferences. When her husband was elected president, the Methodist bishop of Little Rock declared that in Hillary the White House would have its first "theologian-in-residence." But her range of theological reading, she said, did not include much in the way of feminist theology. She knew nothing of the much-discussed Minneapolis conference (noted in Chapter 8) the previous year, in which several thousand Protestant churchwomen sang hymns to Sophia and gave thanks for the "honey in my loins" and "the perfume in my breasts." When I described the goings-on to her, her eyes widened in disbelief. "Sounds like a good thing not to know about," she said laughing.

Then, on impulse, I asked her what she *did* believe. To my surprise the First Lady cheerfully submitted to a brief examination of faith.

"Do you believe in the Father, Son, and Holy Spirit?" I asked.

"Yes"

"The atoning death of Jesus?"

"Yes."

"The resurrection of Christ?"

"Yes." The entire interview lasted about an hour and at the close I called attention to the fact that in six more years—or possibly only two—she would no longer call the White House home. "Have you ever thought of becoming an ordained Methodist minister?" I asked.

"I think about it all the time," she blurted out, but after glancing at her press secretary, Lisa Caputo, she quickly added: "But you can't use that."

"Why not?"

"Because it will make me seem much too pious," she insisted. I pleaded—I could see the headlines this would make. But then so could she. Conservatives would doubt her statements anyway and liberals would wish them away. So I kept my word—until now, when it no longer seems to matter.

It was only when the interview was over that I discovered that I never did reactivate my two tape recorders after Mrs. Clinton had asked me to turn them off. Nonetheless, in less than twenty-four hours I had a nearly complete transcript. The same White House taping system that had snared Richard Nixon had saved my butt.

That weekend, the White House ordered a load of advance copies of *Newsweek* containing my religious portrait of the First Lady. The president was flying to Israel and wanted to distribute the story to the clutch of editors from *The Christian Century* and other liberal Protestant publications whom he had invited to join him on Air Force One. Like Ronald Reagan before him and George W. Bush afterward, Bill Clinton courted only those religious figures who supported his policies. He also used them as moral focus groups for his programs. In flight, Clinton asked his guests for their reactions to my piece. I don't know what they said but I do know that the president strongly objected to one quote, a wry but knowing comment by Hillary's former youth minister in Park Ridge, Illinois: "We Methodists know what's good for you." The reason he objected, I suspect, is that it echoed criticism of Hillary for what many thought was her I-know-best attitude as head of the president's (failed) commission on health-care reform.

"We Methodists know what's good for you"—to me this was the most revealing quote in the entire article. It captured not only the righteous ethos of American Methodism but also the politics of moral righteousness that had characterized the Democratic Party since its transformation under another prominent Methodist politician.

McGovern and the Transformation of His Party

In *The Irony of American History,* published in 1952 when the cold war with the Soviet Union was at its frostiest, Reinhold Niebuhr wrote: "All men are naturally inclined to obscure the morally ambiguous element in their political cause by investing it with religious sanctity." Twenty years later, with the nation deeply divided over the war in Vietnam, there was no appetite on either side for irony, much less moral ambiguity. Within the Democratic Party, especially, the antiwar movement had developed the single-mindedness of a religious crusade. In 1972, the movement's most outspoken U.S. senator, George McGovern of South Dakota, captured the party's presidential nomination, vowing to end what he regarded as the "criminal, immoral, senseless, undeclared, unconstitutional catastrophe" in Vietnam. In his campaign McGovern called for the creation of a "coalition of conscience" not only to end the war but also to "reorder" the basic institutions of American society.

In terms of campaign strategy, McGovern's rhetoric was aimed at attracting younger, affluent, mostly suburban and better-educated voters who were more interested in "cultural" than economic issues. Together with blacks and members of the emerging women's movement, they were projected as the constituents of a new, more activist, and more secular Democratic Party. As it turned out, McGovern's coalition of the morally convicted excluded several pillars of the old New Deal coalition—chiefly blue-collar workers, Catholics, and the traditional trade union leaders, an overlapping constituency—that had helped elect Presidents Roosevelt, Truman, Kennedy, and Johnson. Without these traditional Democrats, McGovern lost every state but Massachusetts and the District of Columbia.

To be sure, the old coalition was already fractured. In the mid-Sixties, as President Johnson foresaw, passage of his administration's passel of civil rights legislation ensured the loss of the party's conservative (and largely segregationist) white Southern Protestant wing. Then came the street battles outside the riotous Democratic National Convention of 1968, in which antiwar demonstrators and activists representing a host of countercultural causes fought the Chicago police of Mayor Richard J. Daley while the entire nation watched on television. As Bill Clinton later observed in the first volume of his memoirs, Vietnam was only one point of contention in what was really a wider clash between generations, social classes, and moral cultures: "The kids and their supporters saw the mayor and the cops as authoritarian, ignorant, violent bigots. The mayor and his largely blue-collar ethnic police force saw the kids as foul-mouthed, immoral, unpatriotic, soft, upper-class kids who were too spoiled to appreciate authority, too selfish to appreciate what it takes to hold a society together, too cowardly to serve in Vietnam. . . ."[1]

But an equally consequential event at the 1968 Democratic convention occurred inside the convention hall and virtually escaped media notice. That was the delegates' approval of a new Commission on Party Structure and Delegate Selection, with McGovern as chairman. The goal was to replace the old nominating system, in which big-city bosses and state party chairmen (a great many of them Catholic) determined who would run for the party's presidential nomination, with a more democratic procedure based on state primaries and caucuses, which advantaged the new breed of party activists. Over the next four years the McGovern Commission, as it came to be known, pushed through a sequence of reforms ensuring that, culturally as well as politically, the delegates to the 1972 convention would resemble the activists who had rallied outside the 1968 convention more than those who had been seated inside. Republican strategists were delighted. In *The Emerging Republican Majority,* published in 1969, Kevin Phillips accurately predicted, "The Democratic Party is going to pay heavily for becoming the party of affluent professionals, knowledge industry executives, social-cause activists and minorities of various sexual, racial, chronological and other hues."[2]

For the 1972 convention, the Democrats did in fact establish an informal quota system for women, racial minorities, and youths that, by 1980, became a mandate that half of every state delegation *must* be women. As proof that the times were indeed "a-changin'," the convention's credentials committee rejected an elected Illinois state delegation controlled by Chicago's Mayor Daley in favor of a nonelected delegation headed by civil rights leader Jesse Jackson.

Another sign that the Democratic Party was assuming a left-wing ideological character could be seen in the party platform. In a key section on "Rights, Power and Social Justice" the platform announced: "We can no longer rely on old systems of thought. . . . It is time to rethink and reorder the institutions of this country so that everyone—women, blacks, Spanish-speaking, Puerto Ricans, Indians, the young and the old—can participate in the decision-making process inherent in the democratic heritage to which we aspire." This was an endorsement of identity politics, wrapped in the moral rhetoric of the junior faculty lounge.

But there was more: "We must restructure the social, political and economic relationships throughout the entire society in order to ensure the equitable distribution of wealth and power." To that end, the platform proposed that the federal government guarantee a job for every worker. To the working class of the old coalition, this sounded like socialism. Two of the new classes of citizens whose rights were in need of protection were "children" and "youth." And among the new rights were a number of novel ones, including "the right to be different" and "the right to the lowest possible cost on goods and services in the market place." And all of these rights, the platform asserted, were to be enforced by expanding the authority and reach of government agencies.

Apart from editorial writers, political junkies, and opposition leaders, few Americans actually read twenty-five-thousand-word party platforms. But on television everyone could witness the fierce debates over the platform that made the 1972 convention as contentious as the one that preceded it. A plank commending forced busing of students in order to achieve racial balance in public schools survived challenge but a minority plank in favor of gay rights did not. On the second night of the convention, Eleanor Holmes Norton and other feminist leaders fought until 4 a.m. for a minority plank recognizing "reproductive freedom," a euphemism for abortion on demand, as a basic human right. Concerned that the abortion plank would cost them the election, the McGovern campaign worked the hall to defeat it and even allowed a speech from a pro-life congressman. The plank failed, but it was the last time the party would allow any pro-life Democrat to address its national convention.

The last night of the convention devolved into political farce. Delegates insisted on nominating their own candidates for vice president to compete with McGovern's choice, Missouri senator Thomas Eagleton. Still smarting from the previous night's defeat, feminists mounted a campaign for Frances "Sissy" Farenthold, then the only woman in the Texas House of Representatives. Gloria Steinem gave the nominating speech despite the fact that she was not even a convention delegate. In the final ballot, Farenthold did well against a field of seventy-seven that included prankish votes for CBS Television's Roger Mudd, China's Mao Zedong, Yippie Jerry Rubin, and Archie Bunker, the central character of television's *All in the Family*. The prolonged exercise pushed McGovern's acceptance speech back to 2:48 a.m., well beyond the bedtime of most Americans in the continental United States—and even of those on ships at sea.

National conventions normally give presidential candidates an initial boost, but the 1972 convention pushed McGovern farther down in the polls. Even after McGovern replaced Eagleton (following revelations that he had been hospitalized three times for depression and had undergone shock therapy) on the ticket with Sargent Shriver, John F. Kennedy's ebullient brother-in-law and the clan's most ardent Catholic, President Nixon went on to win 59 percent of the Catholic vote—a record for Republican presidential nominees. Nixon also carried 55 percent of blue-collar voters. Altogether, 37 percent of Democrats cast their ballots for the Republican ticket, a crossover never seen before. As McGovern later put it with his typically self-deprecating wit, "I opened the doors of the Democratic Party and twenty million people walked out."

The transformation of the Democratic Party had several long-term consequences, two of which I want to emphasize. First, it dislodged the Catholic vote from its traditional moorings in the Democratic Party, paving the way for the Reagan Democrats of the 1980s and the emergence of Catholics as the nation's largest swing vote. Second, by expanding the concept of individual rights (with no corresponding concept of responsibility) into the domestic sphere of marital and family relationships—thus echoing Steinem's resonant axiom that "the personal is political and the political is personal"— the party planted its flag in the emerging culture wars firmly on the side of hyperindividualism. In doing so, the Democrats virtually ensured the emergence of the Christian Right a decade later.

The Democrats' Methodist Moment

Politics is a secular pursuit but George McGovern was not a secular man. The son of a Methodist minister, McGovern grew up in a small-town pastor's manse. His first calling was to the pulpit. After graduating from Dakota Wesleyan, a Methodist college, he studied for the Methodist ministry at Garrett Theological Seminary in Evanston, Illinois, and spent a summer preaching in Chicago churches. Changing course, he earned a doctorate in history at Northwestern and returned to Dakota Wesleyan to teach before accepting a call to rebuild the state's moldered Democratic Party. In his run for president, McGovern came across as an earnest, upright prairie preacher—one reason why, I always thought, even the most ardent Democrats among urban Catholics and Jews were reluctant to accept him as their party's standard-bearer. He just didn't sound like the typical Democratic politician. That's because he wasn't.

The reform of the Democratic Party that began under the aegis of George McGovern gave birth to what I call the party's "Methodist moment." If the party became a vehicle for secular liberalism, as conservative critics argued, it also became a mirror image of the United Methodist Church, echoing many of the social policies adopted by the nation's largest mainline Protestant denomination, suffering similar internal conflicts, and, above all, projecting the same ethos of moral high-mindedness. Indeed, over the last three decades of the twentieth century it was often hard to distinguish the righteous politics of the Democratic Party from the political righteousness of the Methodists and their mainline Protestant allies.

Four months before the Democratic convention of 1972, for example, the United Methodist Church held its quadrennial General Conference, the denomination's highest legislative body. There a thousand delegates updated the church's social principles and adopted positions on a panoply of issues ranging from U.S. foreign policy toward various countries to city planning to the regulation of products advertised on television. A review of the Methodists' 1972 Book of Resolutions reveals an extraordinary symmetry between the party platform subsequently adopted by the Democrats and the positions approved by the church. Both documents opposed the war in Vietnam and called for immediate withdrawal of all American troops. Both saw the nation's economic ills as "systemic" and therefore proposed wholesale transformation of economic and social institutions.

Methodists didn't need McGovern or the Democratic Party to tell them that society was rife with social discrimination. Appropriating the moral authority of the civil rights movement—as would the party—the church called for recognizing new rights for an expansive list of Americans perceived as victims of families, schools, and other putatively repressive institutions. In many cases the church went well beyond what even the most liberal party loyalists could wish for. Among the "Rights of Children," for instance, the Methodists included the right "to a full sex education, appropriate to their stage of development." In a statement on the "Rights of Youth," aimed mainly at universities, the church demanded an end to "discrimination" against young people and urged their inclusion in unspecified "decision-making processes." Affirming the "Rights of Women," the Methodists called for equality with men in "every aspect of our common life" and demanded elimination of "sex-role stereotypes." To counter overpopulation, the convention recommended the distribution of "reliable contraceptive information and devices." Writing less than a year before *Roe v. Wade,* the church urged the "removal of abortion from the criminal code," but stopped short of approving abortion on demand.

Like the McGovern Commission, the 1972 General Conference embraced "inclusiveness," eventually establishing racial/ethnic quotas for membership on the church's national boards and agencies. Even though a bare 6 percent of United Methodists were nonwhite (African Americans established their own Methodist denominations in the early nineteenth century), long-serving white members of the church's activist General Board of Church and Society were fired on short notice—at Christmastime, yet—in order to reserve 30 percent of seats for nonwhites.[3]

There's no question that McGovern had a hand in shaping the Democrats' 1972 party platform. But then so did other party activists of different, indifferent, or no religious faith. As a church, Methodists could and did appeal to Scripture in support of their social and political policies. For the party, it was enough to claim the high moral ground of enlightened conscience in framing its platform. In other words, a Democrat did not have to be a Methodist to think and act like one. Indeed, history shows that the vein of moral righteousness in American politics owes as much or more to Methodism as it does to any other religious or secular tradition.

Piety and Social Reform

Methodism's drive to reform others goes back to its origins in eighteenth-century England as a revivalist movement within the Anglican Church. After experiencing the "assurance" that he had truly been reborn as a child of Christ, founder John Wesley, an Anglican priest and Oxford don, formed a network of like-minded lay preachers organized into small, itinerant evangelistic societies. Like Ignatius Loyola, who had founded the Jesuits two hundred years earlier, Wesley provided his disciples with detailed methods of prayer, repentance, self-examination, and Scripture study—all with the aim of perfecting personal holiness in this life. Opponents sneered at him and his hymn-composer brother Charles for being too methodical—hence the term "Methodists," which was hardly a compliment. Early on, Wesley also devised precise rules for assisting the poor, founding schools, and carrying out other forms of Christian benevolence, which he saw as the natural fruit of anyone who has experienced a "New Birth" in Christ.

After the United States won independence from England, Wesley organized American Methodists into an independent church. Through the waves of evangelist revivals that swiftly followed, Methodism spread rapidly across the western frontier through the energy of its circuit-riding preachers. By the middle of the nineteenth century, Methodists represented a third of all churched Americans, making their church not only the "the largest religious body in the nation," according to historian Nathan O. Hatch, but also "the most extensive national institution other than the Federal government."[4]

After the Civil War, Methodists made common cause with other English-speaking Protestants in promoting revivalism, perfectionist piety, and moral reform. Through domestic and foreign missions, they sought to create a righteous empire that would hasten the return of Jesus Christ and the establishment of God's kingdom on earth. Before the end of the century, however, the churches divided into what historian Martin Marty has called "two-party Protestantism": a private party (the larger) that stressed personal transformation through evangelization and individual conversion, and a public party that focused on transforming the sinful social structures created by the rapid industrialization and urbanization of postbellum America.[5]

Both parties faced a daunting task. Between 1840 and 1890, the nation's urban population increased thirtyfold: Chicago alone grew from a town of 5,000 to a metropolis of 1.1 million. Most of the newcomers were immigrants from south and central Europe who, together with domestic migrants from rural America, lived in urban squalor and worked at the whim of capitalists in the nation's new industrial sweatshops. In 1908, Methodists adopted Protestant America's first "Social Creed," which put Wesley's heirs firmly behind the Social Gospel of the Progressive Era. But while public-party Protestants lectured the nation's elites on structural reform, private-party Protestants—a mix of Methodists, Pentecostals, and Fundamentalists—founded churches in dirt-poor farming communities and inner-city slums.

As if to emphasize Protestantism's role as custodian of the nation's social conscience, the Methodist Church in 1924 moved its most powerful national agency, the Board of Temperance, Prohibition, and Public Morals, from Topeka, Kansas, to a brand-new Methodist Building overlooking the U.S. Capitol and the U.S. Supreme Court. There the church became landlord to Washington lobbyists from the other mainline Protestant churches, an ecumenical collectivity that, by its lights, was called to proclaim the will of God to the federal government and—not incidentally—form a Maginot Line against the growing influence of Catholics in national politics.

Thirty years later, in the small towns and cities like the one where I grew up, the local Methodists still fought for Sunday blue laws and against gambling and other threats to public morals. In the next decade, Methodist bishops and church boards also provided much of the Protestant leadership in support of civil rights, the Equal Rights Amendment, and other progressive causes. After McGovern's disastrous run for president, Methodism's Washington representatives realized that prophetic witness alone was insufficient to influence national politics. They also had to master the arts of influencing legislators and assisting in getting specific bills passed. Although they had little access to the White House between the Johnson and Clinton administrations, Methodist and other liberal Protestant lobbyists worked closely with liberal Democrats, whose party controlled both houses of Congress. For example, staffers on the Methodist Board of Social Concerns, successor to the old Temperance Board, teamed with the office of Senator Ted Kennedy in his persistent efforts to pass a universal health-care bill. The election of Bill Clinton in 1992 made liberal church lobbyists West Wing players again, and in Hillary Rodham Clinton the Methodists had their own in-house advocate. When Bill appointed Hillary to lead the party's charge on health-care reform, she could draw on fourteen years of Methodist position papers—plus the pious assurance that Methodists know what's good for the nation.

Of Rights and Righteousness

By the time the Clintons took up residence in the White House, the transformation of both major parties was complete. There was no longer a liberal wing to the Republican Party nor a conservative wing among the Democrats. Eventually, this ideological realignment would make it virtually impossible in Washington to assemble bipartisan teams to advance legislative projects.

The Republicans' mix of piety and politics was dictated by the party's need to expand its southern base, the most religious sector of the country, and to establish its image as the party of "family values." In need of new constituencies to replace the ones they had jettisoned in 1972, the Democrats expanded McGovern's original "politics of righteousness" by making their own the burdens and grievances of all those who felt oppressed by sexual, racial, class, and economic oppression. To McGovern's coalition of conscience the party sought to add a coalition of the excluded. Hence the rebirth of the Democratic Party as the party of "inclusion."

How do you include the excluded? Beginning in the Sixties, it was done by appealing to state and federal legislators—and especially to the courts—to recognize, defend, and advance an ever-widening range of individual rights for American citizens. With amazing alacrity, our political discourse was subsumed under the legal and moral language of rights: the rights *of* racial and sexual minorities, of women, of children, of the handicapped, the poor in general, and immigrants in particular, to name just a few. And with these was a range of rights *to:* health care, jobs, housing, education, and other social and economic goods.

In some instances, reliance on rights talk has led to real advances in social justice. But just as often it has issued in competing abstract claims, hardened ideologies, and, more recently, stale and stagnant politics. As sociologist Robert Bellah and his colleagues pointed out in their farsighted 1991 study, *The Good Society,* "To cast a social question in terms of rights tends to make the answer to it an all-or-nothing affair. . . . The most troubling problem with 'rights' is that everyone can be said to have them and when rights conflict, the rights language itself offers no way to evaluate competing claims."[6]

The Social Offspring of Roe v. Wade

The most consequential demonstration of the limits of rights language was *Roe v. Wade,* the 1973 Supreme Court case that established a woman's absolute right to abortion on request through the first two trimesters of pregnancy while asserting a very limited state interest in regulating abortion after viability, which occurs in the third trimester. The plaintive was Norma McCorvey, a twenty-year-old Dallas waitress who found herself poor, unmarried, and pregnant in a state that permitted abortion only to save the life of the mother. To make her case more dramatic she claimed that she had been gang-raped, a story she later admitted was false. Although Justice Harry Blackmun, who wrote the 7–2 majority opinion, denied that the decision "entitled a woman to terminate her pregnancy at whatever time, in whatever way and for whatever reason she alone chooses," that was in fact the effect of the ruling. That's because, under *Roe,* the child in the womb has no right to legal protection before viability and very little afterward. As Blackmun argued, "The word 'person' as used in the Fourteenth Amendment does not include the unborn."

Feminist groups, abortion providers, and civil liberties organizations hailed *Roe* for establishing a woman's constitutional right to "control her own body," as the slogan had it, but it was much more: women now had the unprecedented right to decide who shall be allowed to live and who shall not based on whether the unborn child was "wanted." Exponents of the sexual revolution like the editors of *Playboy* and *Penthouse* magazines also applauded the decision: after all, abortion is a far simpler and cheaper way to deal with a lover's unwanted pregnancy than to support a child into adulthood— especially since men do not have to undergo abortions themselves. But some prominent legal scholars were more critical. Constitutional law professor Laurence Tribe of Harvard Law School, though personally pro-choice and pro-*Roe,* chided the court for "reaching beyond the facts of the case to rank the rights of the mother categorically over those of the fetus, and to deny the humanity of the fetus. . . ." He also regretted that Blackmun did not show "a more cautious sensitivity to the *mutual* [emphasis his] helplessness of the mother and the unborn that could have accented the need for affirmative legislation to moderate the clash between the two."[7] Another critic at Harvard Law School, Professor Mary Ann Glendon, contrasted *Roe*'s absolutist rights position with the ways in which various societies throughout Western Europe fashioned "compromise statutes that gave substantial protection to women's interests without completely denying protection to developing life."[8]

The immediate effect of *Roe v. Wade* was to remove the abortion issue from the political process at a time when several states were moving toward more liberal abortion statutes. But the long-term effects, as Justice Ruth Bader Ginsburg observed four decades later, was to stimulate the "right-to-life" movement, divide the country, and pollute American politics.[9] Henceforth, as Ginsburg herself could attest, abortion became a not-so-hidden litmus test for Supreme Court nominees, producing a great deal of disingenuous questions from their congressional interrogators and evasive answers in response.

To an even greater depth, *Roe v. Wade* poisoned party politics. It could do so because Americans themselves—especially women—were so deeply divided over the morality of abortion. In her pioneering study of California women active in the pro-choice and pro-life movements, sociologist Kristin Luker found in 1984 that the former tended to be highly educated, well-paid careerists with few children, with little or no ties to religion and a strong vested interest in their work roles. The pro-lifers, by contrast, tended to be practicing Catholics with large families, with no or low-paying outside jobs, whose self-esteem derived from their maternal roles. For the first group, loss of the right to abortion would threaten their place in the work world and hence their self-identities. For the second, the very notion of abortion called the value of their self-defining role as mothers into question. For the first, motherhood was an option and children a project. For the second, motherhood was a calling and children a gift.[10]

Post-*Roe*, Democratic Party platforms came to reflect the values and fears of the first group of women, the Republicans' the second. But since there is no way to overturn *Roe* except through the Supreme Court or—even less likely—a constitutional amendment—abortion politics produced a lot of pious dissembling by politicians from both parties. Neither Ronald Reagan nor George H. W. Bush was pro-life until the party's marriage to the Religious Right forced them to reconsider their stance. Even then, the GOP remained sufficiently elastic to support dissenters, like Senator Arlen Specter of Pennsylvania and New York mayor Rudy Giuliani, who—if only for their support of abortion rights—were labeled Republican "moderates" by the media.

Even after *Roe*, the Democratic Party was for a time more pro-life than the GOP, largely because there were so many Catholics in positions of leadership. Any number of the party's liberal Catholic members of Congress could have written the sort of letter that Senator Ted Kennedy sent to a constituent who asked where he stood:

While the deep concern of a woman bearing an unwanted child merits consideration and sympathy, it is my personal feeling that the legalization of abortion on demand is not in accordance with the values which our civilization places on human life. Wanted or unwanted, I believe that human life, even at its earliest stages, has certain rights which must be recognized—the right to be born, the right to love, the right to grow old.[11]

The Democratic Party and the Catholic Dilemma

At the time of the *Roe* decision, opposition to abortion was widely regarded in both religious and political circles as an essentially Catholic position. Most mainline Protestant denominations accepted *Roe* largely because of the Reformation principle of liberty of conscience, though they generally opposed abortion for purely therapeutic purposes. Partly because the Bible does not explicitly mention abortion, and partly because they were not inclined to make common cause with Catholics on *any* front, most Fundamentalist and Evangelical leaders ignored the abortion issue until 1979, when a revered Fundamentalist sage, Francis Schaeffer, produced a book and (with Dr. C. Everett Koop, later Reagan's surgeon general) a video series both titled *Whatever Happened to the Human Race?* In them Schaeffer urged reluctant Christian Fundamentalists and other conservative Christians to join Catholics in "co-belligerency" against abortion, euthanasia, and infanticide. Jerry Falwell, Tim LaHaye, and psychologist James Dobson, founder of Focus on the Family, all cited Schaeffer as the goad who helped move them to political action as leaders of the Religious Right.

But the Catholic Church was big enough and experienced enough in addressing issues of public policy that its leaders were prepared to go it alone. The American bishops could draw on a long line of papal teaching that condemned abortion as the deliberate taking of a human life—and therefore mortally sinful—but also on a secular tradition of social justice in which killing the unborn is seen as a violation of the very basis of all human rights—namely, the right to life itself.

But a decade after *Roe,* Catholic and other pro-life Democrats had to answer to a different magisterium. By then the party's position on "reproductive rights," as the pro-choice argument now was reframed, was firmly under the control of the party's extensive feminist apparatus. Particularly in presidential election years, the party depended heavily on the National Abortion Rights Action League, Emily's List, Planned Parenthood, and similar organs of the nation's sprawling abortion lobby to turn out the vote by raising the specter of *Roe*'s reversal and even of threats to access to contraception if the Republicans should win.

By then it was clear that no Democratic senator or congressman who did not support abortion rights could expect support from the party's coffers or appointment to select legislative chairmanships. They certainly couldn't run for the nation's highest office with the party's backing. Thus, formerly pro-life politicians like the Reverend Jesse Jackson, Edward Kennedy, Joe Biden, Christopher Dodd, Dennis Kucinich, John Kerry, and Mario Cuomo quietly joined the pro-choice ranks.

Caught between the church's absolutist position that abortion is always evil and the party's equally absolute insistence that abortion is every woman's right, Catholic Democrats aspiring to high office adopted a common posture: though personally opposed, they were obliged by *Roe* to uphold a woman's right to abortion. Going into the presidential election season of 1984, this seemed like a tenable way to make the Democratic Party politically safe for personally pro-life Catholic candidates or—alternatively—to make publicly pro-choice Catholic Democrats acceptable to their church. Except it wasn't. Which is the main reason why many American Catholics remember a former governor of New York.

The Political Conscience of Mario Cuomo

The first time I met Mario Cuomo the first words out of his mouth were "Teilhard de Chardin."

It was early September 1984 and *Newsweek*'s editors had invited the governor of New York over for an off-the-record lunch. Cuomo's rousing keynote address to that year's Democratic National Convention (though he was out-roused that night by Jesse Jackson) had vaulted him onto the party's list of possible future presidential candidates. *Newsweek* was preparing a cover package on religion and the presidential race for which I was to write the concluding essay. We were waiting at the elevator on the fortieth floor for Cuomo, and when the doors opened the name of his favorite Catholic theologian were the first words *any* of us heard from his lips.

It appeared as if the governor had been having a deep discussion with his two aides on the ride up from the lobby. But my own surmise was that Cuomo had timed his opening words to impress his *Newsweek* hosts. Teilhard's daring theological interpretation of evolution had been the rage when Cuomo and I were both undergraduates, and the governor had every reason to believe that *Newsweek*'s editors knew nothing of the long-deceased Jesuit's work. My instinct told me that the governor, who relished his reputation as an intellectual Catholic, wanted to throw the editors off their game and begin our noontime conversation with the ball firmly in his own court.

Sure enough, the lunch began with Cuomo going on about Teilhard for five minutes before Editor in Chief Rick Smith could turn the discussion toward politics. I waited until the main course was served before telling Cuomo, as politely as I could, "Governor, I think you've got Teilhard's theory wrong." Cuomo shot me a quick glower, the kind reporters in Albany who criticized him often saw, and the conversation moved on. At the end, the governor announced that he would be giving a major lecture at Notre Dame in a few days and invited me to ride with him in his official plane. With the cover package on Cuomo nearing deadline I had to decline, but I promised to read his every word.

In the run-up to the 1984 presidential election, every aspirant had a religious card to play. Rev. Jesse Jackson's bid for the Democratic nomination was launched, funded, and sustained by black churches—"Big Church," he called it—with nary an eyebrow raised by the IRS. Jackson finished third behind former divinity student Gary Hart and nominee Walter Mondale, who was the son of a Methodist minister and married to the daughter of another Methodist minister. The Republican National Convention featured an address by Rev. Jerry Falwell who, as noted, blessed President Ronald Reagan and his running mate, George H. W. Bush, as "God's instruments for rebuilding America." A great many American Jews felt so perplexed by all the God talk that the first audience Mondale and Reagan jointly addressed was a convention of B'nai B'rith, whose members wanted to hear their views on the proper role of religion in public life. As it turned out, neither party's candidate's views on the relationship of religion to politics mattered as much as those of Mario Cuomo, who appropriated that issue for himself.

Going into the convention, Mondale made it clear that he wanted to make history by having a "minority"—meaning a woman, an African American, or a Hispanic as a running mate. The National Organization for Women got behind New York congresswoman Geraldine Ferraro and Mondale chose her with the hope of attracting women's votes and winning back some of the white ethnic and Catholic voters who had flocked to Reagan in 1980. Ferraro was the first woman and the first Italian American to run for the vice presidency on a major party ticket. She was also the first Catholic on either party's ticket since *Roe v. Wade* and thus occasioned the first national test of the personally-opposed-but-publicly-in-favor position on abortion rights.

Shortly after the convention, Pope John Paul II selected John J. O'Connor to be the new archbishop of New York. An admiral in the Navy and former head of military chaplains, the garrulous O'Connor noted on arrival in New York that unlike politicians he had been appointed to his post, not elected. His political naiveté soon became evident during a locally televised Sunday morning press conference not long after Governor Cuomo had signed rather than vetoed a bill providing state Medicare funding for elective abortions. His rationale was fairness: the poor should not be denied a service that the rich can afford. Asked for his own views, O'Connor replied, "I don't see how a Catholic in good conscience can vote for a politician who explicitly favors abortion." Asked whether such a politician ought to be excommunicated, the archbishop demurred: "I'd have to think about that," he said.

O'Connor's comments were quickly forgotten until, two months later, Governor Cuomo summoned a *New York Times* reporter to his office and accused the archbishop of telling Catholics how they should vote. The way Cuomo inflated the importance of O'Connor's words, one might have supposed the archbishop had issued a pastoral letter ordering Catholics not to vote for any pro-choice candidate. Cuomo's rebuttal prompted the president of the U.S. Conference of Catholic Bishops to issue a statement saying that the hierarchy does not take positions on political candidates, and O'Connor himself released a press release saying that at no time had he said Catholics could not vote for any candidate. Even so, the verbal jousting between Cuomo and O'Connor continued in the New York media.

Why had Cuomo decided to create a public controversy where none before existed? The reasons range from the purely political to the patently psychological to the traditional ethnic conflict between Irish and Italian Catholics, and all of them were probably true. Tim Russert, at the time Cuomo's administrative assistant, thought the governor felt snubbed at O'Connor's inaugural mass when he gave a pulpit shout-out to Cuomo's party rival, Mayor Ed Koch—"How'm I doin', Mr. Mayor"—but not to Cuomo. The major reason, I believe, was that invitation to speak at Notre Dame. For an Italian grocer's son from Queens this was an opportunity as big in its own way as his invitation to keynote the Democratic convention. And what better way to ensure the attention of the national press than to pick a fight with the archbishop (and soon-to-be cardinal) of New York? Hence his invitation to me to come fly with him to Notre Dame.

Cuomo's speech was by turns humble and self-assured, professorial and prosecutorial, with enough caveats about the relationship between personal and public morality to make even a medieval casuist wince. At the core of his argument was the right of any politician to exercise his own prudential judgment on issues of public morality. On the issue of abortion, his own conscience told him that there was no way to reverse or even limit the effects of *Roe* that would be both reasonable and fair given the country's morally pluralistic polity. Nor should Catholic politicians try. "We know," he warned his Catholic audience, "that the price of seeking to force our beliefs on others is that they might someday force theirs on us."

Then, as now, I found Cuomo's line of argument fraught with pious dissembling. First, he mischaracterized the church's teaching on abortion as simply one "belief" among others that loyal Catholics like himself accept on faith—in other words, a plank in a sectarian belief system imposed by the bishops as official church teachers. The clear implication was that if Cuomo belonged to some other church that found no evil in aborting the life of an unborn child, his personal belief as a loyal member would be just the opposite. Nowhere did the governor argue that he, Mario Cuomo, like millions of other Americans who are not Catholic or even religious, had through any kind of moral intuition or reasoning of his own concluded that abortion was morally abhorrent in and of itself. Instead, his argument inadvertently resurrected the hoariest of anti-Catholic slurs—namely, that "loyal" Catholics do not think for themselves.

But of course the governor did regard himself as a man who thinks for himself on matters of right and wrong; otherwise he would not have been invited to speak at Notre Dame. Well before the American hierarchy did, Cuomo had come to the conclusion that the death penalty is immoral and that the state had no business inflicting such a penalty even for the most heinous of crimes. This personal moral conviction was one of the reasons why Cuomo lost his bid to become mayor of New York City in 1977, a time when street crime made even an evening out in Manhattan dangerous. Even so, as governor he continued—as a matter of personal conscience—to push for a state ban on the death penalty, despite the opposition of the majority of New York's legislators and, according to the polls, a majority of its citizens.

On abortion, however, Cuomo argued precisely the opposite. Because there was no public consensus on the morality of abortion—indeed, as he pointed out, polls showed that Catholics barely differed from the rest of Americans in their opposition to a constitutional amendment outlawing abortion altogether—it would be both politically futile and morally wrong for any Catholic politician to work to limit the reach of *Roe v. Wade.*

This, the second of his faulty assumptions, clearly begged the question. Those same opinion polls also showed that throughout the Seventies and Eighties a majority of adult Americans supported limiting abortion rights to the "hard" cases—rape, incest, and immediate physical harm to the mother—and rejected the right to abortion upon demand as enshrined in *Roe v. Wade.* In short, most Americans rejected the reasons why nine out of ten women sought abortions in the first place. This was clearly a consensus that a master politician like Cuomo might nurture to legislative effect—if he so chose. Indeed, the governor allowed that he could, "if so inclined, demand some kind of law against abortion not because my bishops say it is wrong, but because I think that the whole community, regardless of its religious beliefs, should agree on the importance of protecting life—including life in the womb, which is at the very least potentially human and should not be extinguished casually."

This wink and nod in the pro-life direction led many of those in the audience to assume that down the line and if the political conditions were right Cuomo would do as he said he could. I took him to mean that the choice was his to make and that bishops like O'Connor should get off the backs of pro-choice Catholics like Geraldine Ferraro and himself.

Notre Dame, of course, was pleased to be the site of the only memorable speech given during the 1984 campaign. But one person in the audience with wider political experience than Cuomo could claim was not impressed by his arguments. Father Theodore Hesburgh, Notre Dame's longtime president, had served on the U.S. Civil Rights Commission under four presidents, two Democrat and two Republican, among many other presidential appointments. He had seen John Kennedy pushed into proposing civil rights legislation when there was no consensus to support it, and he had seen Lyndon Johnson twist arms in order to pass his landmark civil rights legislation knowing it would cost his party the South. Still, Hesburgh was willing to cut Cuomo some slack. "His position on abortion is part of a whole climate of opinion in New York State, New York City and the New York *Times*," he ventured. "If he were from a Prairie state he could take a different line."[12]

In fact, Cuomo rarely traveled outside his home state and never stayed long when he did. He had not come to South Bend to address the locals but looked immediately to see how his speech played back east and in the national media housed there. It played very well, especially among secular intellectuals who could read it for themselves in the *New York Review of Books*. But neither Cuomo nor Ferraro was of help to Mondale in the November election. President Reagan won the women's vote, the Italian American vote, and a record 55 percent of the Catholic vote. Mondale set a record, too: he garnered the fewest number of Electoral College votes in the history of presidential elections.

In 1986, Cuomo was reelected governor in a landslide and there was talk among New Yorkers that he could be the first president from their state since Franklin Roosevelt. There was a biography in the works, with publication slated to coincide with the 1988 election. Seeing this, *Newsweek* again put Cuomo on its cover in March 1986 with a package that examined him from four angles: as governor, as potential candidate, as an Italian American, and (my contribution) as a Catholic. He was the only major politician of his era whose ethnicity *and* religion were considered integral to his public persona.

When I arrived at his Manhattan office to interview him, the governor reminded me of what I had missed by not flying with him to Notre Dame. A storm had rocked the plane so severely that one of his aides—probably Russert—pulled out his rosary beads and the governor himself was moved to nervous prayer. "You should've come," he said. With that opening I recited poll data, mentioned above, and asked him why he couldn't build on that consensus of limitation to create public policies that would reduce the number of abortions, which had reached more than a million a year. "I don't believe in polls," he said—an odd statement since Cuomo maintained a full-time pollster on his staff. "There is no consensus. You can't describe it. Cardinal O'Connor can't describe it, even the Jesuits with all their subtleness can't."

The fundamental issue, he went on to say, was personal liberty, and reading from another speech he'd given, he said that "only when liberty intrudes on another's right, only when it does damage to another human being, only when it takes or hurts or deprives or invades may it be limited."

"But surely abortion damages another human being." I interjected."

"Not everyone agrees on when human life begins," he shot back. "Even theologians can't say when the soul enters the body."

"Come on, Mario," I said, getting into the shoot-back mood myself, "all you have to do is wait 266 days and see what you get. A human embryo does not turn out to be a cat or dog." And so it went.[13]

It was obvious we had reached an impasse on the subject. The governor was not about to waste any of his political capital on aligning his public with his private conscience. But then neither was any other Catholic running for the Democratic nomination. Cuomo eventually opted not to run in 1988 but another Catholic who did, former governor Bruce Babbitt of Arizona, praised Cuomo for providing moral cover on abortion. "Geraldine [Ferraro] got in trouble on the issue because she didn't have her facts straight," he told a press conference. "Mario got it right."

Bob Casey and the Politics of Inclusion

The last time I heard Mario Cuomo speak in person was at the 1992 Democratic National Convention, at Madison Square Garden. Bill Clinton chose him "as our best orator" to give the first nomination speech. A major convention theme was the party's inclusiveness—what the Democratic National Committee called "the big tent," which in contrast to the Republicans' welcomed Americans, as Cuomo put it, "of whatever color, of whatever creed, of whatever sex, of whatever sexual orientation. . . ." Down on the convention floor, where I spent my time, there were waves of placards identifying Native Americans, Hispanics of assorted Latin American backgrounds, African Americans, at least a dozen feminist groups, lesbians, transsexuals, bisexuals, plus a parade of whooping, placard-waving gays. (The sexual alliance signified by the initialism *LGBT* had yet to congeal.) I bought a selection of campaign buttons for my children and noticed that in every delegation I passed there was a clutch of women wearing a button for the National Abortion Rights Action League (NARAL). But hands-down the most provocative button featured Pennsylvania's two-time governor Robert Casey Sr. dressed as the pope.

Bob Casey was probably the most progressive governor in the country and programmatically far more successful than either Cuomo or Clinton. He created a model school-based child-care program that offered infants and preschoolers—including poor children—full-day services so that teenage parents could stay in school and impoverished adults could work with the assurance that their children were safe. He pushed for universal health care for Pennsylvania residents. When that failed, he secured passage of a bill that provided health insurance for children whose parents could not afford it but whose incomes were too high to be eligible for public assistance. Casey also appointed the first black woman anywhere to a state supreme court and more female cabinet members than any other Democratic governor. In his first five years in office, state contracts to female- and minority-owned firms increased by more than 1,500 percent. In short, he was a model liberal Democrat.

But unlike Governors Clinton and Cuomo, Casey was also a pro-life politician who found ways to limit the sweep of *Roe,* a stand that made him a target of NARAL, Planned Parenthood, and other pillars of the party's pro-choice base. In 1989, he helped push through the Pennsylvania legislature a law that limited access to abortion in four ways. It required doctors to inform women about the health risks of the procedure; it required minors to get consent from a parent or guardian prior to having an abortion; it imposed a twenty-four-hour waiting period before obtaining an abortion; and it required wives planning an abortion to give their husbands prior notice. In response, the Republicans ran a pro-choice woman against Casey, which indicated that on the abortion issue, at least, the GOP had the bigger tent. Casey won by a million votes, thereby proving—contra Cuomo—that being pro-choice was not a political necessity for every Democratic politician.

That was the message Casey took to the party platform hearings, where his views were summarily dismissed. In the run-up to the convention, Casey asked to present the delegates with a minority report on abortion. The DNC did not bother to reply. Instead, the committee invited six women to speak on abortion rights. Among them was Kathy Taylor, a pro-choice Pennsylvania Republican who had helped thwart Casey's progressive tax reforms. At that point, I began to search out Casey for a comment. It wasn't easy since the DNC had seated the Pennsylvania delegation in the Garden's equivalent of the bleachers. I arrived there just before Kathy Taylor did, trailed by a camera crew sent by the DNC to film the expected confrontation. But the governor had been tipped off to the vindictive ploy and had left the convention before either Taylor or I could speak to him. Thus was an honorable man dishonored by his fellow liberals. Clearly the party's inclusiveness excluded pro-life Democrats.

In his run for president in 1992, Bill Clinton pledged to make abortion "safe, legal, and rare." He was as good as his word on the first two. As noted earlier, one of Clinton's first acts as president was a series of executive orders nullifying several Reagan-era rules prohibiting federal funding of abortions. Three years later, he vetoed a bill passed by both houses of Congress that would have banned "partial-birth abortion," a late-term procedure in which the live fetus is partially removed from the mother, exposing the head so that the skull can be pierced and crushed. Democratic senator Daniel Patrick Moynihan aptly described partial-birth abortion as "the

closest thing to infanticide," but a bill banning the ghoulish procedure would not be passed until 2003, under Republican president
George W. Bush with the support of a minority of Democrats in
both houses.

Abortion and the New American Way of Life

By the time of Bill Clinton's second term, a new generation of Americans had come of age since the passage of *Roe v. Wade*. By then
abortion rights were essential to a new social fabric woven by the
sexual revolution, the decline of the family as an institution, the postponement of marriage among the college educated, and the increase
of cohabitating couples at all socioeconomic levels. Already in 1988,
a nationwide survey of women who had had abortions, conducted
by the Guttmacher Institute, the research arm of Planned Parenthood, the largest abortion provider in the United States, showed
that most women decided to abort for a mix of three reasons: giving
birth would interfere with school, work, or other responsibilities;
lack of financial support; and "relationship problems" with the unborn baby's father.[14] These were not irrational reasons. But they also
were not the usual reasons put forward in defense of abortion rights,
which is why the Guttmacher Institute never—to my knowledge—
repeated the survey.

In May 1997, *U.S. News & World Report* did something that
neither *Newsweek* nor *Time* dared do. Editor James Fallows published a cover package on who gets an abortion and why and gave
it a provocative title: "Was It Good for Us?" At the time, politicians
from President Clinton on down were expressing concern for teenage mothers—"babies having babies," as they were called. But as the
magazine reported, more than half of children born out of wedlock
were to women in their twenties, compared to 22 percent to teenagers. Moreover, more than half of the abortions performed each year
in the United States were also to women in their twenties, most of
them unmarried. In other words, this was a cover story about abortion as a social consequence of sex among unmarried young adults,

and it went on to note the almost total silence on this subject from any pulpit, in the White House or in churches. The main reason for this silence was evident from the magazine's own poll: three out of four respondents regarded nonmarital sex between consenting adults as never or almost never wrong.[15]

Development of sonogram technology augmented both pro-life and pro-choice positions. Ultrasound images of the developing fetus can and do cause some women to reconsider a planned abortion. On the other hand, sonograms can also detect fetal abnormalities as well as the sex of the fetus, information that a mother can use to decide whether to abort or give birth. For example, nine out of ten babies identified as having Down syndrome are now aborted. But since not all fetal abnormalities are as easily detected, some gynecologists as well as feminist theorists argued that because a newborn baby is wholly dependent on its mother, mothers ought to have a grace period of at least a month after birth to have their babies thoroughly checked out for undetected defects. In this way, the right to choose was expanded to include the right to reject the less than perfect.

The effects of *Roe v. Wade* extended well beyond politics. Language was one of the first areas to register the cultural divide over abortion. The *New York Times* and other liberal publications studiously avoided normal usages such as "unborn baby" or "unborn child" because, one gathers, these terms suggest that abortion involves the destruction of a human being. Instead they used the word *fetus*, which is at once more "scientific" and nonrelational, or evasive abstractions like "conceptus" or "contents of the womb." When the debate over "partial-birth abortion" arose, the *Times* disallowed use of the term by its reporters and headline writers because it had first been used by opponents of the procedure, thus saddling the paper's copy desk with vague and awkward neologisms like "a form of late-term abortion" and "a procedure that opponents call 'partial birth abortion.'"[16]

John Kerry and the Politics of Abortion

The abortion issue emerged in yet another form during the 2004 election, when Democratic senator John Kerry of Massachusetts became the first Catholic since John F. Kennedy to be nominated by either party for president. Like fellow Massachusetts senator Edward M. Kennedy, Kerry owned a perfect record in support of abortion rights, including six straight votes against bills banning partial-birth abortion. Coming from a liberal state where most Catholics are baptized into the party as well as into the church, Kerry naively assumed that taking a personally opposed but politically pro-choice position was a safe political bet. After all, hadn't Cuomo's Notre Dame speech settled that issue for Catholic politicians? Kerry's commitment to abortion rights as one of the Democrats' nonnegotiable "core values" surfaced early when he floated the idea of asking his Senate friend and fellow Vietnam War veteran John McCain, a pro-life Republican, to be his running mate. The prospect of a bipartisan ticket excited many leading Democrats, especially after early polls showed such a ticket would trump Bush-Cheney by 14 points. The deal carried only one caveat. "Senator McCain would not have to leave his party," Kerry explained. "He could remain a Republican, would be given some authority over selection of cabinet people. The only thing he would have to do is say, 'I'm not going to appoint any judges who would overturn *Roe v. Wade.*'"[17] McCain refused the gambit.

Kerry's high-profile embrace of abortion rights vexed the bishops of his church. The previous November they had formed a task force on Catholics in Public Life and agreed not to release their guidelines until after the 2004 election, lest they be accused of trying to influence its outcome. But this restraint did not apply to individual bishops as heads of their own dioceses, and a half-dozen (out of 194) published guidelines of their own. The archbishop of Newark, New Jersey, issued a pastoral letter asking all pro-choice politicians not to present themselves for Holy Communion at any of the churches under his jurisdiction. Another in Missouri directed his priests specifically to refuse Communion to candidate Kerry if he campaigned in the state. A third bishop in Colorado Springs, Colorado, went even further: in a pastoral letter he directed Catholics who knowingly vote for candidates supporting abortion rights, euthanasia, same-sex marriage, or embryonic stem-cell research to confess their sins before returning to the Eucharist. But these were outliers. The majority of the nation's Catholic bishops opposed, as Cardinal Theodore McCarrick of Washington, D.C., put it, "a confrontation at the altar rail with the sacred body of the Lord Jesus in my hand."

This intra-Catholic squabble probably embarrassed the bishops more than it did Kerry, who could and did argue that on the other social and economic issues dear to the Catholic hierarchy he and his fellow Democrats were closer to the bishops than the Republicans were. And like Ted Kennedy and other patrician Catholics in the party, Kerry exuded an air of confidence that in due time the bishops would catch up with the party's more enlightened views on abortion as well. In the meantime, though, Kerry became the first Catholic presidential candidate to lose the Catholic vote, and with it a close election.

Abortion was not the only or even the most consequential issue for what pollsters identified as "values voters." Same-sex marriage, an issue new to a presidential election, was far more prominent, and in all six states where measures supporting such unions were on the ballot the initiatives were defeated. Nor were Catholic bishops the only religious voices heard. At least fifty organizations—some of them secular, most of them religious—worked to advance the moral agenda of one or the other major parties. Indeed, in the morning-after judgments of many liberal *and* conservative pundits, Bush won on the back of a zealous and intolerant Fundamentalist Christian horde that Garry Wills likened in an Election Day essay in the *New York Times* to Al Qaeda. In fact, postelection analysis showed that Bush marshaled a coalition of constituencies, any one of which could claim to have ensured his narrow victory over Kerry.

The Retro Campaign of 2012

How important, then, is the religious vote? According to political scientist John Green, the acknowledged dean of studies on the faith factor in American politics, religion typically turns out to be a more powerful variable than gender, age, income, or class in predicting how a citizen will vote in a presidential election.

It wasn't always thus. Prior to the McGovern revolution in the Democratic Party, the *Roe v. Wade* decision, and the rise of the Religious Right, most white Protestants voted Republican and most Jews and urban Catholics voted Democrat. It was only in the late Seventies that moral issues like abortion and same-sex marriage began to rival and at times supersede issues of domestic and foreign policy, thus making religion a factor to reckon with on Election Day.[18] Until then, as Senator Eugene McCarthy (the only theologically sophisticated Catholic who ever ran for president) liked to say, only two kinds of religion were tolerated in a presidential election: "vague beliefs strongly affirmed and strong beliefs vaguely acknowledged." McCarthy's witticism bespoke the genial religiosity of presidents like Dwight Eisenhower (vague expression) and Ronald Reagan (vague beliefs), but for different reasons it also characterized the candidates for president in 2012.

Republican Mitt Romney was the candidate with strong beliefs. He was not the first Mormon to run for president of the United States: that honor belongs to the Mormon Prophet himself, Joseph Smith Jr., who mounted a brief and little-noticed independent campaign in 1844 before his murder a few months later. At the outset of the 2012 campaign season, a poll by the Pew Research Center found that 51 percent of Americans said they knew very little or nothing at all about Mormonism, and Romney chose to keep it that way. He referred all reporters' questions about his religious faith to the church's public information office. To talk openly about his religious convictions would certainly have led to a distracting public discussion of the deep differences between Mormonism and the biblical beliefs of the party's core religious constituency. Which was too bad, I thought, because the story of his polygamous grand-father's flight from the law, his hazardous new life in Mexico, and the family's return to the United States and eventual prosperity was just as compelling as Barack Obama's family narrative. In any case, Romney's strategy worked, even though he lost. Right after the election, a second Pew poll showed that 51 percent of Americans *still* knew little or nothing about the LDS church.[19]

Barack Obama's religion problem was the opposite. As in the 2008 election he had to convince skeptics, including a majority of Democrats, that he really is a Christian. The president was not raised in a church. Indeed, having grown up in a Muslim country (Indonesia) and with Hussein as a middle name, Obama went into the final three months of the campaign with at least 20 percent of registered voters thinking his religious commitment was to Islam. Nor did it help that, like George W. Bush, the president and his family chose to worship out of public view at the nondenominational chapel at Camp David.

But what kind of Christian is he? The more Obama mentioned "our Lord and Savior Jesus Christ," the more obvious it became that he is uncomfortable with Evangelicalism's emphasis on personal witness. Perhaps his most forthcoming statement came in 2008 at a faith and politics forum sponsored by Rick Warren, where Obama declared, "My Bible tells me that when God sent His only son to earth, it was to heal the sick and comfort the weary and feed the hungry and clothe the naked and befriend the outcast and redeem those who had strayed from righteousness." The language was right out of the nineteenth-century Social Gospel movement and in perfect key with the Democratic Party's Methodist moment.

Who's Got a "God Problem"?

Just before Obama's first run for president, John Green published a study of voting patterns that vindicated the view that the Democrats have a "God problem." According to his analysis of survey data, those voters who say they attend religious services once a week or more, or pray frequently and regard religion as important or very important in their lives, most often vote Republican. Conversely, those who rarely or never attend worship services, seldom or never pray, and say religion is of little or no importance in their lives typically vote Democrat. Moreover, Green found, this new "religion gap" cut through the various communities of faith, whether Evangelical or Catholic, Jewish or African American, Mormon or mainline Protestant. The key to the religious vote was not just religious identity but the intensity of a voter's religious commitment.[20]

Yet the question remains: in a presidential election, how significant is the vote of those who are serious in their practice of religion? More recent survey data finds that at most one voter in four fits this description. We're not talking about Mother Teresas here, just ordinary religiously convicted voters whose moral and spiritual values are important factors in deciding how to vote. On the other end of the spectrum are the 23 percent of Americans who identify as either atheists or agnostics (about 6 percent) or who simply do not identify with any religious institution or tradition. Two-thirds of these non-affiliated voters are millennials who, unlike previous generations, no longer feel constrained to claim a religious identity just because they were baptized or sent to church as children. As of 2014, the nonaffiliated represented 24 percent of the Democratic vote—a constituency larger than the African American, feminist, or any other of the party's core constituencies. What these numbers suggest is that while religion may still be a significant factor in congressional elections, Democrats do not need to capture the "religious vote" in order to win the White House. Republicans, on the other hand, cannot win without it. In politics, that may be the real God problem.

Epilogue

Goodbye to All That ... Almost

Early in 2002, *Newsweek* offered the latest in a series of buyouts, each one slightly less generous than the one before, and I elected to take it. That summer, Betty threw a surprise retirement party at our home that included our grandchildren as well as neighbors, old friends, and several of my *Newsweek* colleagues. The magazine's editor, Mark Whitaker, and his wife, Alexis Gelber, an assistant managing editor, were in on the secret and drove up from the city to present me with the company's equivalent of a gold watch: a framed *Newsweek* cover with my face on it. And then it was over. Almost.

Managing Editor Jon Meacham offered me a contract as a contributing editor, which gave me a title to put after my byline wherever my work appeared, and an unmarked office I could drop into whenever I wished. By then either early buyouts, retirement, or death had taken away most of my longtime colleagues, and with them much of the magazine's institutional memory. I particularly missed Jack Kroll, *Newsweek*'s legendary arts editor and critic, who had been my lunch partner most days of the week. For years after his death in 2000, Jack's disheveled office with its floor-to-ceiling hedgerow of books remained undisturbed as a kind of homage to this icon of *Newsweek*'s glory days. It was that kind of place.

Meacham's promotion to editor of *Newsweek* in 2006 was historic, and not just because he was only thirty-seven years old: he was the only top editor in the magazine's history who also functioned as the de facto religion editor when cover stories of that kind were to be written. This made sense because no one else on staff could match his knowledge of the field or enthusiasm for the subject. Jon is a graduate of the University of the South (Sewanee) and his immersion in the traditional Anglican liturgy, theology, and piety of southern Episcopalianism was as deep as mine was in midwestern Catholicism. Had the Anglican Communion established its own version of the Jesuits, I've always thought Jon would have made an ideal candidate.

During his brief tenure, Meacham tried to transform *Newsweek* into a magazine of essays and other long-form journalism. He had, he said, always admired eighteenth-century English publications like *Tatler* and *The Spectator*. "I'm not sure the future of *Newsweek* is with Addison and Steele," I ventured when he told me of his plans. Jon lost his gamble—the odds it would pay off were always long—and the magazine was sold to *The Daily Beast*. Tina Brown tried to reanimate *Newsweek* digitally and in print but the later version disappeared in November 2012. The brand, which was all that was left of the magazine, eventually migrated to its present owners, but not the *Newsweek* we experienced as an established set of journalistic norms and practices. *That* newsmagazine belongs to history.

The truth is, *Newsweek,* as well as *Time* and *U.S. News & World Report,* had been continuously "reinventing" the newsmagazine for decades in a protracted battle first with television and then with the Internet and the advent of the 24/7 news cycle. But you couldn't really hear the death rattle until management began to close its news bureaus around the world. A newsmagazine doesn't need paper to survive but it cannot exist without its own reporting. Much of what passes for news on digital imitations of a newsmagazine are stories first reported by others elsewhere and aggregated by editors whose main contact with the world is confined to the computer screen in front of them.

The Recent Present

History is useful in discerning patterns in the past, and I hope this book is helpful in understanding how—in the relationships between religion, culture, and politics—we got to where we are. History can provide comparisons with the past and offer perspectives on the present, but even recent history cannot tell us what will happen next. If, as I have argued, the religious volatility of the last half of the twentieth century is best understood as a reaction to social, cultural, and political upheavals, then the first decade and a half of the new millennium should have witnessed similar echoing effects. But it did not.

The unprecedented terrorist attacks of September 11, 2001, which killed more than three thousand Americans in the fiery destruction of the World Trade Center's twin towers in lower Manhattan, the destruction of part of the Pentagon, and a plane crash in Pennsylvania, made all Americans realize that their homeland was no longer invulnerable. Fortunately, the assault by Muslim terrorists brought the nation together—and with it an outpouring of national prayer as well as national mourning. Unlike the previous century, there were no doomsday cults, no millennial forebodings, no retreats to rural—and presumably safer—communes.

Most Americans also supported the following month's invasion of Afghanistan, followed in turn by President George W. Bush's far more questionable decision in 2003 to invade Iraq, a military excursion into the quagmire of the Middle East that has kept Americans at war for the longest period in the nation's history. (And despite various troop withdrawals, U.S. military involvement in the Middle East is again increasing.) But these military ventures, while accompanied by some voices of dissent, did not produce the kind of movement religion that accompanied the war in Vietnam. The main reason was that students were not subject to military duty, and so could ignore the war, nor were Americans at home called upon to make wartime sacrifices. As before, those who volunteered to fight alongside career soldiers came mostly from that portion of the population with few other career options. Our "brave fighting men and women" were other Americans' proxies.

And then, in December 2007, the $8 trillion housing bubble burst, setting off the worst recession since the Great Depression. The following year saw the near collapse of overleveraged investment banks, necessitating a federal bailout of the very financial institutions whose reckless practices had precipitated what became a global financial crisis. More than eight million workers lost their jobs, the average family income plummeted, and the number of Americans living in poverty rose to a post–World War II high. But unlike the 1960s, there were no poor people's marches on Washington, perhaps because an African American was in the White House; no prophetic voices from the pulpits, perhaps because there were no longer any nationally prominent pulpits or prophets to fill them; no pastoral letter on the economy from the U.S. Catholic bishops, as in 1986, probably because they recognized their lack of competence in the intricacies of global finance. In sum, no religious mobilizations of any kind, because there was no one of sufficient stature to do the mobilizing. Yet racial tensions remain combustible in cities like Baltimore and Chicago, the gulf between the very rich and the rest of Americans has widened, and the cultural views and values of the American people (as registered by traffickers in the new, unfiltered "social" media) are more segmented than ever.

The New Religious Landscape

This segmentation is readily apparent in American religion. Recall the map of religious America I described in the first chapter of this book. There we saw that in the 1960s half the counties in the United States were dominated by citizens who identified with one or another Christian denomination, and that between them, Baptists and Catholics alone accounted for 40 percent of the American population. Today, the map's chromatics would have to include a generous portion of white—a noncolor—to identify the religiously nonaffiliated who now represent the largest single "denomination" in nineteen states and nearly a quarter of the population. A contemporary map would also have to be shaded to indicate levels of commitment within those areas where one denomination still dominates. In Massachusetts, for example, Catholics still outnumber other religious groups, yet only 17 percent of them regularly attend Sunday Mass. As a visual, the contours of a current map of religious America would resemble a mound of ice in midsummer: still rather thick down the middle and across its (southern) base but rapidly melting at its (coastal) edges.

The unanticipated surge in the nonaffiliated has bolstered the view that the United States, long considered a religious outlier among the advanced societies in the West, was in fact treading the same path as Europe toward secularization, albeit after a delayed start and—until now—at a slower pace.[1] The likelier explanation is that institutional religion is experiencing a long-overdue winnowing effect. American "belongers-but-not-believers" and the vague "believers-but-not-belongers" are properly self-identifying as Nones. That's clarifying. I think John Green is right in estimating that only one in four adult Americans put religion at or near the center of their lives.

We are also witnessing a generational slide as older and typically more religious Americans die off and are replaced by younger generations for whom religion has become progressively less relevant to their own self-identity. *But the more encompassing fact is that most young Americans between the ages of eighteen and thirty do not readily identify with any institutions—political, civic, academic, or religious.* This weak identification with basic social institutions is what makes the experience of growing up today sharply different from the experience of those who came of age in the 1950s and early 1960s. You don't have to be a social scientist to recognize the difference. It's enough to be a grandparent.

A Different Social Script

At the outset of this book I located my youthful self at the center of concentric circles of belonging: family, yes, and outlying relatives, and the town that we felt we owned even more than it owned us. But just as significant were the schools whose teachers understood that their role was to form as well as to inform their students, and the church that seemed to be everywhere I chose to be. Even now, I abide in these institutions, much like readers do their favorite books, as they abide in me. As George P. Fletcher has argued, "historical selves" (of the kind I invoked in the first chapter of this book) are not built on the personal choices of autonomous individuals; rather, they are rooted in the rich historical loom of relationships based on mutual bonds of loyalty, obligation, and trust.[2]

But in their journey toward adulthood most young Americans now follow a different social script. Rather than defining themselves through relationships formed within family, neighborhoods, churches, schools, and teachers, the young imagine—and culturally are encouraged to believe—that the point of growing up is to discover, nurture, and express an inwardly derived, original, and authentic self—independent of institutionally structured relationships with others. Already in 1997, philosopher Charles Taylor observed that successive generations of young Americans, many of them now parents themselves, have embraced an ethics of self-authorization, self-fulfillment, and personal choice. Selves so conceived lack a social history and a capacity for self-criticism and self-restraint. Nonetheless, as Taylor points out, they remain heavily dependent on outside recognition and affirmation. Indeed, recognition denied is often considered "a form of oppression."[3]

Every new generation inhabits social structures created by their elders. If the young no longer understand themselves in relation to these inherited social institutions, neither do these institutions support, in the ways they once did, basic social needs. We acknowledge that basic institutions like families and schools are failing the poor, especially African American youth. But anyone interested in the future configurations of American faith, culture, and politics must begin by looking at how young Americans of the striving middle classes experience marriage, family, neighborhoods, and schools.

Fractured Families, Fading Neighborhoods

For the four thousand years that humankind has been known to exist, children have typically been raised by tribes, clans, and variously extended networks of kin. In the long view of history, therefore, the intact nuclear family (mom, dad, and the kids) is a recent social arrangement, one that is fraught with its own set of economic, emotional, and psychological problems.[4] The family is still the primary institution through which children acquire a sense of self and of belonging. But over the last half century, progressive public acceptance of cohabitation, single parenthood, and no-fault divorce has profoundly compromised marriage and family as foundational social institutions. Across all social classes, marriage has become one lifestyle choice among others, rather than a set of governing cultural norms that places restrictions and expectations upon the married as well as the unmarried. More than 40 percent of new mothers are unmarried and at least half of all American children can expect to live at least part of their lives in a single-parent household. Despite the heroic efforts of many single parents, fractured families are inherently less stable than intact ones. For children growing up in these circumstances, marriage and family acquire a decidedly tentative character. And, we know, children of divorce are far more likely than others to eventually divorce themselves, thus extending the cycle of institutional instability.

Even so, children have never been more dependent on parents for achieving later success. Parents who see that that homework gets done and school assignments turned in on time are a child's single most valuable education asset, regardless of teachers and classroom size. If children see their parents socially engaged, politically involved, or religiously convicted, chances are that when they arrive at adulthood they will be, too. With the advent of the two-paycheck family, parental stress has intensified. The same smartphone that allows parents to stay connected with their children also allows bosses and clients to contact them at any time. From arranged "playdates" for their children, to mandated attendance at weekend soccer games and after-work trips to the grocers, parental time is measured by an endless series of schedules to be met. Making them mesh is now a discipline all its own. The leisure of unencumbered weekends that even blue-collar workers once enjoyed is history. The Sabbath as a day of rest is a reliquary concept now found only in the Bible.

Neighborhoods as wider social spaces for childhood being, doing, and belonging have changed, too. The specific social gravity of any neighborhood can be measured by the number of people down the street, on the next block, or at the local stores who can greet kids by name and feel free to help or scold if necessary. But in many inner-city neighborhoods, gangs, guns, and drug dealing make out-of-doors a perilous place to be. Even in upscale neighborhoods, fearful parents keep kids on a short tether because drugs and danger can be found in every community. It is rare to see kids roaming unattended or squads of bicycling preteens freewheeling down suburban streets. Rarer yet is the sight of teenagers cutting neighbors' lawns, delivering newspapers, shoveling snow, stocking store shelves, caddying, or pumping gas. As late as the 1980s, working jobs like these was not only a way of earning spending money but also a way of relating to adults within the larger community.[5] Today, all these jobs are performed by adults trucked in from elsewhere. For a great many young Americans, the real neighborhood is now the nearest shopping mall, a social destination where youthful selves are tutored in the techniques of consumerism.

Forty years ago, social historian Christopher Lasch argued that the authority and competence of the family had been undermined by outsourcing the socialization of the young to teachers, experts, and social planners. In this way, he said, "the apparatus of mass tuition" had become "the successor to the church in a secularized society."[6] Lasch, who died in 1994, did not live long enough to witness the latest iteration of a process that he traced to the 1930s. Back then, the interventions of educators and social planners were aimed mainly at immigrants with the goal of "Americanizing" them. Today this form of socializing the young extends across the economic spectrum, beginning with day care for infants as young as six months, through preschool to primary school, with after-school "enrichment" programs. To be sure, many of these programs are designed to give children from disadvantaged families a much-needed "head start" in developing learning and social skills. But in upscale suburbs and city neighborhoods they function primarily as places to keep children occupied and safely off the streets until parents arrive from work to fetch their children home.

Despite the increase of mothers who work full-time outside the home, recent surveys tell us that today's parents actually spend *more* time interacting with the children than did parents in the less hurried 1950s. In part this is because children are no longer allowed to be on their own, as I have noted. But another reason is that parents in the striving middle classes are more intent on giving their children a competitive edge in the race for higher-income jobs in later life. Unlike the Fifties, there are few manufacturing jobs awaiting high school graduates, few family businesses like insurance agencies and retail shops to pass on to children—no upward mobility at all without the certification that comes with a college degree or better. Since degrees in engineering, law, or business are not inheritable, parents who are ambitious for their children invest a great deal of time preparing them for the higher-education credentials chase.[7]

Thus, early in their high school years today's adolescents learn that if they are to "make something of themselves" their immediate task is to assemble a resume—their first exercise in self-branding—that will get them into a proper college. That means not only working up a worthy grade-point average and taking Advanced Placement courses, but also engaging in a mix of school-sponsored athletics and extracurricular activities in order to attract the attention of college admissions officers. For most adolescents, this means no time for goofing off and little time for a full night's sleep. Proof of service to the community is also necessary for building an attractive resume, although time spent cooking for an aged aunt or wheeling an infirm grandparent to the park does not earn service points. The contradiction inherent in coerced altruism should be self-evident. Lasch, I think, would recognize it as the last bureaucratic bow toward the old Protestant principle that public schooling ought to build character.

College: Neither Alma nor Mater

The most important rite of passage for young Americans today is their transition to college. Now, as in the past, college is where our adolescents go—or are sent—to prepare themselves socially and intellectually for adulthood. But over the last half century, student aspirations have changed dramatically. In 1967, 86 percent of incoming freshmen said their aim was to develop "a philosophy of life." Fifty years later, the same percentage cited "being financially successful" as their goal—a major reason why humanities departments are withering on the academic vine.[8]

Today, most college students and their parents take a decidedly instrumentalist view of higher education, and who can blame them? The gaudy sticker prices (up to three hundred thousand dollars for four years at a college or university) and the prospect of many years paying off student debts raise legitimate questions about value received. For starters, today's undergraduates need fewer credit hours than were required of students in the 1950s to acquire the same bachelor's degrees. That translates into a full semester *less* of classroom instruction, yet students now pay many times the price in inflation-adjusted dollars.

Although the undergraduate population has expanded exponentially since the baby boomers came of age, it's not the students who have changed so much as the institutions most of them attend. American universities have come to resemble huge youth preserves, with as many as sixty thousand students at large state campuses, where students are comfortably fed and housed, provided with contraception, state-of-the-art gyms and fitness centers, seasonal spectacles of intercollegiate sports, and a menu of touring entertainers. But in matters like academic rigor, curriculum coherence, love of learning, adult supervision, and mentorship, students are left to their own devices. Date rape is just one of the consequences of treating adolescents as if they were adults. As education critic Albert Delbanco observes, the most obvious change in undergraduate education is the expansion of student freedom—"not just sexual freedom but what might be called freedom of demeanor, and deportment, freedom of choice as fields and courses have vastly multiplied, and, perhaps most important, freedom of judgment as the role of college as arbiter of values has all but disappeared. . . . Except in the hard sciences, academic failure, especially in the elite colleges, is rare and cheating, except in the military academies, tends to be treated as a minor lapse."[9] This is college that is neither *Alma* nor *Mater.* On the contrary, observes sociologist Christian Smith, author of several books on American youth, "it's like putting a bunch of novice tennis players together on the court and expecting them to emerge later with advanced skills and experience."[10]

Criticism of undergraduate education has mounted over the last decade and the evidence produced by researchers is sobering. Two features stand out. First, college students are routinely awarded high grades—in fact, the most common grade (43 percent) is A—for little effort. By comparison, in the 1960s, when students in each class were still graded on a curve, only 15 percent were awarded A's.[11] B is now the gentleman's C for students who are just passing time in college. More than a third of students, according to one major research sample, reported spending fewer than five hours a week studying alone. For that they were rewarded with a grade-point average of 3.2. Over the course of their undergraduate studies a preponderance of students showed little improvement—in some cases none at all—in fundamental skills like writing, creative thinking, and analytic reasoning, based on Collegiate Learning Assessment scores.[12] At graduation, those students who drift through college are rewarded with Wizard of Oz degrees that tell prospective employers only where they spent the last four to six years.

The second feature is lack of student interaction with adults during their undergraduate years. Typically, students neither seek out their professors for conversation outside the classroom nor are sought after by their teachers. Most, in fact, are taught by teaching assistants or adjunct professors their first two years, while tenured professors appear only for lectures. Assignments are given, received, and graded via email and Internet posting. Nor are undergraduates interested in the adult world outside the campus. They very rarely read a newspaper, in print or online, and very rarely discuss current events with family or friends.[13]

Morality: Who's to Judge?

The minority of young Americans who arrive on campus aiming to develop a "philosophy of life" discover soon enough that neither the curriculum nor the student culture encourages reflection on the good life, much less on how to wrestle with the moral choices they personally face in the freedom that college life confers. The reigning ethic is moral self-authorization and nonjudgmentalism: what is right for me may not be right for you but no one has the right to judge anyone else. Nor should anyone be required to justify their actions. In fact, most students lack a moral vocabulary for doing so.

In the most searching studies we have of the moral lives of American collegians, sociologist Christian Smith found that many of the students he and his colleagues studied either could not identify a moral problem they had recently faced or misidentified a problem that was not moral at all. Asked what made something right, an all-too-typical response was this: "I mean for me I guess what makes something right is how I feel about it, but different people feel different ways, so I couldn't speak on behalf of anyone else as to what's right and what's wrong."[14] This soft-core moral relativism is part of what Smith calls the "the dark side" of emergent adulthood, but it is also the prevailing moral context against which students with a sturdier sense of right and wrong must defend themselves in and out of classrooms.

Religion with a Shrug

In a pair of companion studies, Smith and his colleagues at the University of Notre Dame provide similar assessments of young Americans' attitudes toward religion as they moved through high school and college. Regardless of religious background, their studies found that the majority of young Americans hewed to what they call a "new de facto religion: moralistic, therapeutic deism." The basic beliefs of MTD are easily summarized:

> First, a God exists who created and orders the world and watches over human life on earth. Second, God wants people to be good, nice and fair to each other, as taught in the Bible and other world religions. Third, the central goal in life is to be happy and to feel good about oneself. Fourth, God does not need to be particularly involved in one's life except when God is needed to resolve a problem. Fifth, good people go to heaven when they die.[15]

If moralistic, therapeutic deism sounds terribly abstract and anemic, that's because it is. It's religion with a shrug.

Adulthood Can Wait

Since the 1970s, the transition of young Americans from adolescence to adulthood has expanded into a genuinely new phase of the American life cycle that social scientists have variously labeled "delayed adolescence," "adultolesence," youthhood," and "emerging adulthood." The causes are many but the cumulative effect has been the postponement by a dozen years or more of the standard responsibilities that mark adulthood: a real career, a stable residence, marriage, and parenthood. For the disciplined, talented, and ambitious, these transition years provide time for further education, for creative exploration of career options, and for learning—often for the first time—how to budget money and time.

But for a great many others it's a time of drift—a continuation of adolescent college habits like binge drinking, sexual hookups, intellectual stagnation, and, for more than a third of them, extended dependence on parents for money and housing. Whatever their living arrangements or degree of economic success, most emergent adults continue to inhabit same-age social enclaves. They remain relatively isolated from adults who could be their mentors, still uninvolved in civic, political, or religious organizations and the concerns, constraints, and social practices these institutions entail. I think this goes a long way toward explaining why, despite the turbulent early years of this century, young Americans have been so unconcerned and politically quiescent. Life's on hold; adulthood can wait.

Given what we are learning about emergent American adults and the social structures they inhabit, there are no good reasons to believe that the immediate future will be any different. Their widespread inability to think through moral problems or even recognize them, even more the unwillingness to hold themselves accountable to anyone but themselves, should disturb us deeply. So should their inurement to values that transcend consumerism and "being well-off."

The social history of the next half century will depend in part on how—and how many—young Americans overcome the limitations of their protracted coming-of-age. Can they build for their own children more responsible social institutions than those they themselves experienced? The future of American faith, culture, and politics may not be all that hangs in the balance.

But the young cannot do this alone. In his study of the human life cycle, Erik Erikson described the challenge of those who live into old age—*a stage that I honestly if reluctantly acknowledge to have reached*—as one that pits the temptation to terminal self-absorption against the opportunity to exercise continued care and concern for those generations moving behind us. Which may be the real reason I have written this book.

One of the blessings of old age is the clarity with which diminishing energy of mind and body allows us to see what has been our human lot all along—namely, contingency, transience, and finitude.

We cannot control what may happen to us. Nothing lasts forever. We must die. These hold true for believer and nonbeliever alike. They are the existential facts of life that all religions in different ways address.[16] In reply, Christians like myself are called to abide in Faith, Hope, and Love. What matters is that God's grace is everywhere.

Acknowledgments

For a longer and more detailed account of my experience of and interview with Mata Amritanandamayi, see Kenneth L. Woodward, *The Book of Miracles: The Meaning of the Miracle Stories in Christianity, Judaism, Buddhism, Hinduism, Islam* (New York: Simon & Schuster, 2000, 377–82).

Finally, I want to thank all the good folks at Penguin Random House, especially my editor, Gary Jansen, who asked to see the manuscript of this book and patiently guided it through the shoals of the publication process. A fine writer himself, Gary is the sort of editor who understands the difference between a push and a shove.

Notes

Chapter 1: Embedded Religion

1. For an updated map of the kind I used and much more useful historical information on religion and geography see Edwin Scott Gaustad and Phillip L. Barlow, with the special assistance of Richard W. Dishno, *New Historical Atlas of Religion in America* (New York: Oxford University Press, 2001).
2. For a broader account than just my own see Howard P. Chudacoff, *Children at Play: An American History* (New York: New York University Press, 2007), 126–53. Chudacoff describes the period 1900 to 1950 as "The Golden Age of Unstructured Play."
3. Robert D. Putnam, *Our Kids: The American Dream in Crisis* (New York: Simon & Schuster, 2015), 1–9. For a nuanced discussion of an African American ghetto in Chicago in the Fifties and its achievement of "community because of adversity," see Alan Ehrenhalt, *The Lost City: Discovering the Forgotten Virtues of Community in the Chicago of the 1950s* (New York: Basic Books, 1995), 140–89.

Chapter 2: A Fusion of Faith, Culture, and Politics

1. David Halberstam, *The Fifties* (New York: Villard Books, 1993), x.
2. I think it fair to say Eisenhower would never have invaded Cuba, as Kennedy did in 1961, and would have been warier of being drawn into a land war in Vietnam.
3. Fred Siegel, *The Revolt Against the Masses: How Liberalism Has Undermined the Middle Class* (New York: Encounter Books, 2013), 112–13.
4. For instance, as late as 1994 the United States Information Agency published in print and online *An Outline of American History,* which led off a section on the culture of the 1950s with this summation: "During the 1950s, a sense of uniformity pervaded American society. Conformity was common, as young folks and old alike followed group norms rather than striking out on their own." 202.194.48.102/englishonline/kwxx/mrmy/yj/ . . . /ooah/ooah11.asp.
5. "Khrushchev Visits Iowa Farm; Says 'God Is on Our Side,'" Associated Press, September 24, 1959, *Daily Illini,* 1.

6. Martin E. Marty, *Righteous Empire: The Protestant Experience in America* (New York: Dial Press, 1970), 259.

7. W. H. Lawrence, "G.O.P. Chiefs Push Eisenhower Draft; He Merely Smiles," *New York Times,* February 18, 1955, 1.

8. "The Lonely Crowd at Prayer," *Christian Century,* May 30, 1956, 663.

9. Will Herberg, *Protestant-Catholic-Jew: An Essay in American Religious Sociology,* with an introduction by Martin E. Marty (1956; reprint, Chicago: University of Chicago Press, 1983), 260.

10. Ibid., 83.

11. Ben Wattenberg, "How the Suburbs Changed America," *The First Measured Century,* http//www.pbs.org/fmc/segments/progseg9.htm.

12. William H. Whyte, *The Organization Man* (1956; reprint, Philadelphia: University of Pennsylvania Press, 2002), 287.

13. Ibid., 367.

14. Martin E. Marty, *The New Shape of American Religion* (New York: Harper & Brothers, 1958).

Chapter 3: Mediating Religion

1. David F. Wells, *Revolution in Rome* (Downer's Grove, IL: Intervarsity, 1972), 117, cited in Mark Noll and Carolyn Nystdrom, *Is the Reformation Over?* (Grand Rapids, MI: Baker Academic, 2005), 60. This brief book records an important historical transformation in Evangelical attitudes toward Roman Catholicism as a result of Vatican Council II.

2. James M. O'Toole, ed., *The Faithful: A History of Catholics in America* (Cambridge, MA: Belknap Press of Harvard University Press, 2008), 200–201.

3. A summary of my testimony can be found in John F. Hunt and Terrence R. Connelly, *The Responsibility of Dissent* (New York: Sheed & Ward, 1969), 136–37.

4. On the fortieth anniversary of the publication of *Humanae Vitae,* the always candid Cardinal Francis George, then president of the U.S. Conference of Catholic Bishops, said of the encyclical and the dissent it generated: "It was the occasion for a direct conflict between many people's experience as they expressed it and the authority of the church. We have then the beginning of the dissolution of the teaching authority of the church, with consequences we still live with." See Daniel Burke, "Forty Years Later, Contraception Ban Colors US-Vatican Ties," Religious News Service, 2008, undated.

Chapter 4: When the Secular Was Sacred

1. Ralph Clayborne Carson, Ralph E. Lucker, and Penny A. Russell, eds., *The Papers of Martin Luther King, Jr.,* vol. 1, *Called to Serve, January 1928–June 1957* (Berkeley: University of California Press, 1992), 1.

2. Jesus as "the man for others" never caught on as a slogan. But after Father General of the Jesuits Pedro Arrupe, S.J., heard it mentioned by his American assistant general, Vincent O'Keefe, S.J., he directed that "men for others" should be the motto for the spiritual formation given to Jesuit high school students throughout the world. It still is.

3. Harvey Cox, *The Secular City* (New York: Macmillan, 1965), 17. It is interesting that in the first revised edition, published in 1966, Cox removed what he judged

"the more egregious overstatements" of the first edition. Among the excised passages were the original subtitle I cite—it was replaced with a quote from a *Newsweek* review—and the phrase I cite.

4. William Hamilton, "The New Optimism—From Prufrock to Ringo," in Thomas J. J. Altizer and William Hamilton, *Radical Theology and the Death of God* (New York: Bobbs-Merrill, 1961), 164.

5. Joan Didion, *The White Album* (New York: Simon & Schuster, 1979), 57–58.

6. Ibid., 54.

7. William Stringfellow and Anthony Towne, *The Death and Life of Bishop Pike* (Garden City, NY: Doubleday, 1976), 262.

8. James Cone, *A Black Theology of Liberation* (Philadelphia: Lippincott, 1970), 50.

Chapter 5: Entrepreneurial Religion

1. Nancy Gibbs and Michael Duffy, *The Preacher and the Presidents: Billy Graham in the White House* (New York: Hachette Book Group, 2007), 91. For fuller accounts of this incident see Carol V. R. George, *God's Salesman: Norman Vincent Peale and the Power of Positive Thinking* (New York: Oxford University Press, 1993), 195–210; Shaun A. Casey, *The Making of a Catholic President: Kennedy vs. Nixon 1960* (New York: Oxford University Press, 2009), 123–50. Casey's account makes clear that the most obdurate anti-Catholic of the group was Harold Okenga, pastor of historic Park Street Church in Boston, Kennedy's hometown. For Billy Graham's brief account, in a late-in-life autobiography put together by his longtime editorial assistants, see Billy Graham, *Just as I Am* (New York: HarperCollins, 1997), 390–92.

2. George Marsden, "Is Religion Dead?" *Notre Dame Magazine,* Autumn 1995, 25. See also George Bigelow, "Let There Be Markets: The Evangelical Roots of Economics," *Harper's Magazine,* May 2005, 33–38.

3. How many of these books were actually written by Graham will probably never be known. But certainly the most recent volume, *Where I Am: Heaven, Eternity and the Life Beyond,* published in 2015 when Graham was ninety-six years old, deaf, enfeebled, and nearly blind, might best be described as an entrepreneurial effort by the BGEA, under the presidency of his son Franklin, to milk the brand. Given that the views expressed therein are at odds with Billy's mature theological views, some critics might also consider it elder abuse.

4. Grant Wacker, *America's Pastor: Billy Graham and the Shaping of a Nation* (Cambridge, MA: Belknap Press of Harvard University Press, 2014). I am indebted to Wacker's book for many facts and insights, but I disagree with his judgment on Graham's role in the Peale-led effort to prevent the election of John F. Kennedy as president.

5. Robert N. Bellah, "The Civil Religion in America," in *Beyond Belief: Essays on Religion in a Post-Traditional World* (New York: Harper & Row, 1970), 174.

6. Marshall Frady, *Billy Graham: A Parable of American Righteousness* (Boston: Little, Brown, 1979).

Chapter 6: Movement Religion

1. Coretta Scott King, "The Legacy of Martin Luther King, Jr.," *Theology Today* 65, no. 1 (April 2008): 8–12.

2. Quotes cited from both newspapers can be found in Michael B. Friedland, *Lift Up Your Voice like a Trumpet: White Clergy and the Civil Rights and Antiwar Movements, 1954–1973* (Chapel Hill: University of North Carolina Press, 1998), 183.

3. Eberhard Bethge, *Dietrich Bonhoeffer* (New York: Harper & Row, 1970), 380.

4. The return from Berrigan was so swift and polished that I have the feeling it was something he had already written—he was always writing because he was as committed to the writing life at least as much as to the life of an antiwar activist—but I was no less grateful for his sending it to me.

5. Kenneth L. Woodward, "A Guru on the Ramparts," *New York Times Book Review,* February 21, 1988.

6. Richard J. Neuhaus, *The Catholic Moment: The Paradox of the Church in the Postmodern World* (New York: Harper & Row, 1987), 283.

7. Richard John Neuhaus, *The Best of "The Public Square": Book Three* (Grand Rapids, MI: Eerdmans, 2007), 138.

8. Edward K. Kaplan, *Spiritual Radical: Abraham Joshua Heschel in America, 1940–1972* (New Haven, CT: Yale University Press, 2007), 377–78.

Chapter 7: Religion and Revolution

1. Francine du Plessix Gray, *Divine Disobedience: Profiles in Catholic Radicalism* (New York: Knopf, 1970), 311–12.

2. Christian Smith, *The Emergence of Liberation Theology: Radical Religion and Social Movement Theory* (Chicago: University of Chicago Press, 1991), 53. Although it began life as a doctoral dissertation in social theory, Smith's book is by far the best book on Liberation Theology as a movement and its various consequences.

3. Ibid., 230.

Chapter 8: Women's Liberation and the Feminization of Religion

1. Christopher Lasch, *Women and the Common Life: Love, Marriage, and Feminism,* edited by Elizabeth Lasch-Quinn (New York: Norton, 1997), 116. This is a collection of pieces written before his death in 1994.

2. Caroline Walker Bynum, Stevan Harrell, and Paula Richman, eds., *Gender and Religion: On the Complexity of Symbols* (Boston: Beacon Press, 1986), 15–16.

3. Rodney Stark, *The Rise of Christianity: How the Obscure, Marginal Jesus Movement Became the Dominant Religious Force in the Western World in a Few Centuries* (Princeton, NJ: Princeton University Press, 1996).

4. Anne Braude, "Women's History *Is* American Religious History," in Thomas Tweed, ed., *Retelling U.S. Religious History* (Berkeley: University of California Press, 1997), 87–107.

5. David G. Hackett, "The Prince Hall Masons and the African American Church," in David G. Hackett, ed., *Religion and American Culture: A Reader* (New York: Routledge, 2003), 316.

6. Mark Oppenheimer, *Knocking on Heaven's Door: American Religion in the Age of Counterculture* (New Haven, CT: Yale University Press, 2003), 145.

7. Ibid., 168.

8. *Origins: CNS Documentary Service* 24, no. 4 (June 9, 1994): 1.

9. Some of the material presented here on seminaries first appeared in Kenneth L.

Woodward, "Gender and Religion: Who's Really Running the Show?" *Commonweal* 123, no. 20 (November 22, 1996): 9–24.

10. Elaine Justice, "Influx of Women Students Changing Seminaries, Churches," *Emory Report*, October 30, 1995, http://www.emory.edu/EMORYREPORT /erarchive/1995/October/ERoct.30/10.95influx.of.wom.html. For a feminist seminary program for women and for men who identify with the feminist project, see Rebecca S. Chopp, *Saving Work: Feminist Practices of Theological Education* (Louisville, KY: Westminster John Knox Press, 1995).

11. Joseph P. O'Neill, "Character Disorders and Cultural Dissonance Among Mainline Catholic and Protestant Clergy," a presentation to a group of clinical psychologists and pastoral counselors who screen candidates for ordained ministry, June 1994. A draft copy of this presentation was provided to me at that time by the author. The tenor of his conclusions can be seen in the following lines from William Butler Yeats's "The Second Coming," with which he prefaced his presentation: "The best lack all conviction, while the worst / Are full of passionate intensity."

12. Elisabeth Schüssler Fiorenza, *In Memory of Her: A Feminist Theological Reconstruction of Christian Origins* (New York: Crossroads, 1983), 346.

13. Actually, the Catholic biblical canon contains many more and more interesting, more powerful women than the Jewish or Protestant biblical canons because the Catholic canon includes the so-called Deuterocanonical texts that, for various reasons, the creators of the Jewish and Protestant canons excluded.

14. Sandra Schneiders, I.H.M., "Women and the Word: The Gender of God in the New Testament and the Spirituality of Women," 1986 Madeleva Lecture, delivered at St. Mary's College, Notre Dame, Indiana, April 17, 1986.

15. During all my years at *Newsweek* I can recall few articles in the theological journals I read in which feminist theologies were criticized, except by other women. But of course I am not a member of the theological guild and may have missed some. Nor was I ever alerted to a theological symposium in which men were invited to critique the feminist theological project. Early on, male theologians (most of them married laymen) seemed anxious to avoid the line of fire. Now that so many academically accomplished women are teaching theology in seminaries and universities, perhaps their male colleagues have concluded that—as in a good marriage—some arguments are not worth having. An exception is Francis Martin's *The Feminist Question: Feminist Theology in the Light of Christian Tradition* (Grand Rapids, MI: Eerdmans, 1994).

16. Elisabeth Schüssler Fiorenza, *Bread Not Stone: The Challenge of Feminist Biblical Interpretation* (Boston: Beacon Press, 1984), xiv.

17. There are many sociological reasons for this. Among them is the failure of the Leadership Conference of Women Religious (LCWR), a national organization of the heads of most religious congregations in the United States, to provide any leadership, responsibility, or proposals for attracting Catholic women to the religious life, or for studying what the various congregations—and the LCWR itself—might be doing that actually discourages new vocations. They seem to have a martyr's death wish.

Chapter 9: Experiential Religion

1. Theodore Roszak, *The Making of a Counter Culture: Reflections on the Technocratic Society and Its Youthful Opposition* (Garden City, NY: Doubleday, 1969), 138–39.
2. Jeffrey J. Kripal, *Esalen: America and the Religion of No Religion* (Chicago: University of Chicago Press, 2007), 129.
3. Vernon Ruland, *Imagining the Sacred: Soundings in World Religions* (Maryknoll, NY: Orbis Books, 1998), 65.
4. Kenneth Slawenski, *J. D. Salinger: A Life* (New York: Random House, 2010), 231–32, 252–53.

Chapter 10: Alternatives to Religion

1. Fortunately, my colleague Phyllis Malamud had an advanced degree in social science and graciously taught me what and whom to read and personally introduced me to many of the experts I would eventually study, quote, and get to know.
2. Nicholas Lemann, "How the Seventies Changed America," *American Heritage,* July–August 1991.
3. Philip Rieff, *The Feeling Intellect: Selected Writings,* edited and with an introduction by Jonathan B. Imber (Chicago: University of Chicago Press, 1990), 131–32.
4. Philip Rieff, *The Triumph of the Therapeutic: Uses of Faith After Freud,* introduction by Elizabeth Lasch-Quinn (Wilmington, DE: ISI Books, 2006), 19–20.
5. It is worth noting that these and other theorists of the human potential movement who clustered at Esalen were not Americans but European immigrants, part of the mass migration of intellectuals from Central Europe to England and then to the United States that historian H. Stuart Hughes describes in his 1975 study, *The Sea Change: The Migration of Social Thought, 1930–1965* (New York: Harper & Row, 1975).
6. Daniel Yankelovich, *New Rules: Searching for Self-fulfillment in a World Turned Upside Down* (New York: Random House, 1981), 3.
7. Steven M. Tipton, *Getting Saved from the Sixties: Moral Meaning in Conversion and Cultural Change* (Berkeley: University of California Press, 1984), 180–81.
8. This theme runs throughout Lasch's work. See especially his *The Culture of Narcissism: American Life in an Age of Diminishing Expectations* (New York: Norton, 1978).
9. The book that gave me the idea of doing a cover story on death in America was John S. Dunne's superb study of death and immortality in Western culture: *The City of the Gods: A Study in Myth and Mortality* (New York: Macmillan, 1965). Dunne, a Catholic priest, was the only theologian among the Erik Erikson circle that gathered annually on Cape Cod, Massachusetts.
10. In particular, see Christopher Lasch, *Haven in a Heartless World: The Family Besieged* (New York: Basic Books, 1977).

Chapter 11: Sacred Families

1. William A. Galston, "Home Alone: What Our Policymakers Should Know About Our Children," *New Republic,* December 2, 1991, 41.

2. Daniel Patrick Moynihan, "Defining Deviancy Down," *American Scholar* 62, no. 1 (Winter 1993): 17–30.

3. For a history of jeans and their meanings, see James Sullivan, *Jeans: A Cultural History of an American Icon* (New York: Gotham Books, 2006).

4. In his 2006 memoir, *It's News to Me: The Making and Unmaking of an Editor*, Ed Kosner characterized "Who's Raising the Kids?" as a "bland offering," sandwiched between two hard-news cover stories on Squeaky Fromme, who tried to kill President Gerald Ford, and on another violent radical young woman, Patty Hearst. These were the first three cover stories Kosner published after his ascension to *Newsweek*'s top editorial post. As it turned out, that "bland offering" sold as well as the other two on the newsstand—newsstand sales being one of the ways the industry determines which newsmagazine editor has the best editorial instinct—and won for *Newsweek* its first and only National Media Award from the American Psychological Foundation.

5. A succinct formal articulation of this foundational Mormon doctrine is by Joseph F. Smith, sixth president of the church (1901–18), nephew of founder Joseph Smith Jr. and last church president to have known the Prophet: "Men and women may be saved singly, but men and women will not be exalted separately.... The family is the foundation of eternal glory, the nucleus of a kingdom without end. The husband will have his wife, the wife her husband, parents their children forever, provided they secure them in the manner prescribed by him [the Heavenly Father] whose right it is to regulate all things pertaining to his kingdom." See *The Teachings of Presidents of the Church: Joseph F. Smith* (Salt Lake City, UT: Church of Jesus Christ of Latter-day Saints, 1998), 176–77.

6. Richard Lyman Bushman, *Joseph Smith: Rough Stone Rolling* (New York: Vintage Books, 2007), 439.

7. Samuel Morris Brown, *In Heaven as It Is on Earth: Joseph Smith and the Early Mormon Conquest of Death* (New York: Oxford University Press, 2012), 278. In the same paragraph Brown makes another equally insightful point: "[T]he Latter-day Saints saw Jesus as the way not just to God but to Godhood, their guide to maturity as members of the species Ahman [Adam]." Brown is a Mormon, a physician by training, and is writing here of early Mormonism, not necessarily Mormonism today. A brilliant exercise in historical analysis.

8. The thirteen steps are summarized by sociologist Rodney Stark in Reid L. Nilson, ed., *The Rise of Mormonism* (New York: Columbia University Press, 2005), 79–82.

Chapter 12: Piety and Politics: The Republicans and the Religious Right

1. Robert Scheer, "The Playboy Interview: Jimmy Carter," *Playboy*, November 1976, 63–86.

2. That occurred in 1950 when Pope Pius XII proclaimed the bodily assumption of the Virgin Mary into heaven—a belief that had been popularly held for more than a millennium—as a dogma to be affirmed by all faithful Catholics.

3. Steven P. Miller, *The Age of Evangelicalism: America's Born-Again Years* (New York: Oxford University Press, 2014), 61.

4. Liberty has yet to play Notre Dame in football but on February 22, 2008, Liberty's baseball team defeated Notre Dame 6–2 at an invitational in Clearwater, Florida. Jerry would have been ecstatic.

5. Robert Wuthnow, *Sharing the Journey: Support Groups and America's New Quest for Community* (New York: Free Press, 1994), 4.

6. One could also see it as an iteration of his father's "A Thousand Points of Light" initiative.

7. Franklin Foer, "Spin Doctrine: The Catholic Teachings of George W.," *New Republic,* June 5, 2000, 18–20.

8. See, for example, Damon Linker, *The Theocons: Secular America Under Siege* (New York: Doubleday, 2006). A somewhat similar argument is made by Kevin Phillips in *American Theocracy: The Peril and Politics of Radical Religion, Oil, and Borrowed Money in the 21st Century* (New York: Viking, 2006). I found both unpersuasive.

Chapter 13: Religion as Politics: The Democrats

1. Bill Clinton, *My Life* (New York: Knopf, 2004), 133.

2. Quoted in Howard Chua-Eoan, "The American Quixote: The Death of George McGovern (1922–2012)," *Time,* October 21, 2012.

3. Steven M. Tipton, *Public Pulpits: Methodists and Mainline Churches in the Moral Argument of Public Life* (Chicago: University of Chicago Press, 2008), 76.104. I owe a huge debt—as on many other occasions in my career—to Tipton for the encouragement he gave me in looking at the Democratic Party through the lens of modern Methodism, though he is of course not responsible for what I have written.

4. Nathan O. Hatch, "The Puzzle of American Methodism," in Nathan O. Hatch and John H. Wigger, eds., *Methodism and the Shaping of American Culture* (Nashville, TN: Kingswood Books, 2001), 27.

5. Martin E. Marty, *Righteous Empire: The Protestant Experience in America* (New York: Dial Press, 1970), 177–87.

6. Robert N. Bellah, Richard Madsen, William M. Sullivan, Ann Swidler, and Stephen M. Tipton, *The Good Society* (New York: Knopf, 1991), 127–28.

7. Laurence H. Tribe, "The Abortion Funding Conundrum: Inalienable Rights, Affirmative Duties, and the Dilemma of Dependence," *Harvard Law Review* 99, no. 1 (November 1985): 330, cited in Mary Ann Glendon, *Rights Talk: The Impoverishment of Political Discourse* (New York: Free Press, 1991), 59.

8. Ibid., 58.

9. Jason Keyser, "Ruth Bader Ginsburg: Roe v. Wade Ruling Flawed," Associated Press, May 20, 2013.

10. Kristin Luker, *Abortion & the Politics of Motherhood* (Berkeley: University of California Press, 1984).

11. Letter quoted in William McGurn, "Bob Casey's Revenge," *First Things,* January 2005, 7.

12. After the debate, Hesburgh told a *Newsweek* reporter that he tried to bring ten Catholic bishops and ten Catholic politicians, including Cuomo, together to discuss their differences out of public view. Most of the bishops were willing but most of the politicians were not, realizing that word of the meeting would eventually leak out.

13. Cuomo was not a public intellectual in the manner of his fellow New York Democrat, Daniel Patrick Moynihan, though he did not deter those of his admirers who claimed otherwise. But he was, arguably, his era's most celebrated public

sophist. In dialogue with a gathering of Protestant, Catholic, Jewish, and secular academics, in which he discussed the principles behind his Notre Dame speech, Cuomo declared: "When I speak against the death penalty, I never suggest that I consider it a moral issue. I seldom talk in terms of moral issues. I am against the death penalty because I think it is bad and unfair. It is debasing. It is degenerate. It kills innocent people." For the full text of his remarks, and respondents' criticism, see E. J. Dionne Jr., Jean Bethke Elshtain, and Kayla M. Drogosz, eds., *One Electorate Under God? A Dialogue on Religion and American Politics* (Washington, D.C.: Brookings Institution Press, 2004). My own one-on-one exchange of opposing essays with Cuomo was published just before the 2004 presidential election in the September 24 issue of *Commonweal* under the collective cover title "Personally Opposed. But . . . ," which was the position Democratic presidential nominee John Kerry took.

14. Aida Torres and Jacqueline Darroch Forrest, "Why Do Women Have Abortions?" *Family Planning Perspectives* 20, no. 4 (July–August 1988): 169–76.

15. A week later I called Fallows to compliment him on the cover story—and on his guts for doing it. His voice sounded like a thin smile: I was, he said, one of a handful of readers and the only fellow journalist who admired the cover package. Even members of his own staff, he said, thought it reeked of "old-fashioned moralism."

16. Kenneth L. Woodward, "What's in a Name—*The New York Times* on Partial-Birth Abortion," *Notre Dame Journal of Law, Ethics & Public Policy* 19, no. 2 (2005): 427–42.

17. Sheryl Gay Stolberg and Jodi Wilgoren, "The 2004 Campaign: The Political Calculations; Undeterred by McCain Denials, Some See Him as Kerry's No. 2," *New York Times*, May 15, 2004, 1, http://www.nytimes.com/2004/05/15/us/2004 -campaign-political-calculations-undeterred-mccain-denials-some-see-him .html.

18. John C. Green, *The Faith Factor: How Religion Influences American Elections* (Westport, CT: Praeger, 2007), 77–79.

19. "Americans Learned Little About the Mormon Faith, but Some Attitudes Have Softened," Pew Research Center Forum on Religion and Public Life, December 14, 2012, http://www.pewforum.org/2012/12/14/attitudes-toward-mormon -faith/. For a fuller analysis, see Green, *The Faith Factor*.

20. John C. Green, "Religion and the Presidential Vote: A Tale of Two Gaps," Pew Research Center, August 21, 2007, http://www.pewforum.org/2007/08/21/religion -and-the-presidential-vote-a-tale-of-two-gaps/.

Epilogue

1. David Voas and Mark Chaves, "Is the United States a Counterexample to the Secularization Thesis?" *American Journal of Sociology* 121, no. 5 (March 2016): 1517–56.

2. George P. Fletcher, *Loyalty: An Essay on the Morality of Relationships* (New York: Oxford University Press, 1993), 23–24. Fletcher's essay is an argument against liberal—that is, individualistic—rights-based morality.

3. Charles Taylor, *The Ethics of Authenticity* (Cambridge, MA: Harvard University Press, 1991), 48–50. The idea that nonrecognition is a form of oppression is not

limited to the young. Gloria Steinem, the most recognized (and recognizable) feminist icon in the United States, had this to say last year at the age of eighty-one in a published conversation with Supreme Court justice Ruth Ginsburg: "I think Ruth is better at getting along with people with whom we profoundly disagree. I feel invisible in their presence because I am being treated as invisible." See "Ruth Bader Ginsburg and Gloria Steinem on the Unending Fight for Women's Rights," *New York Times,* November 15, 2015, ST1, ST3.

4. Arthur Kornhaber, MD, and Kenneth L. Woodward, *Grandparents, Grandchildren: The Vital Connection* (Garden City, NY: Anchor Press/Doubleday, 1981), xix–xx.

5. Drew DeSilver, "The Fading of the Teen Summer Job," Pew Research Center, http://www.pewresearch.org/fact-tank/2015/06/23/the-fading-of-the-teen-summer-job/.

6. Christopher Lasch, *Haven in a Heartless World: The Family Besieged,* op cit., 18.

7. I owe the insights of this paragraph wholly to an op-ed essay by Bloomberg View economics writer Megan McArdle, "Kids These Days—and Their Rich, Anxious Helicopter Parents," *Chicago Tribune,* December 2, 2015, 27.

8. Mark Bauerlein, "What's the Point of a Professor?" *New York Times,* May 10, 2015, SR5.

9. Andrew Delbanco, *College: What It Was, Is, and Should Be* (Princeton, NJ: Princeton University Press, 2012), 19–20.

10. Christian Smith, with Kari Christoffersen, Hilary Davidson, and Patricia Snell Herzog, *Lost in Transition: The Dark Side of Emerging Adulthood* (New York: Oxford University Press, 2011), 234.

11. Stuart Rojstaczer and Christopher Healy, "Where A Is Ordinary: The Evolution of American College and University Grading, 1940–2009," *Teachers College Record* 114, no. 7 (2012): 1–23.

12. Richard Arum and Josipa Roksa, *Aspiring Adults Adrift: Tentative Transitions of College Graduates* (Chicago: University of Chicago Press, 2012), 37–40.

13. Ibid., 99.

14. Smith, *Lost in Transition,* 22.

15. Christian Smith, with Patricia Snell, *Souls in Transition: The Religious and Spiritual Lives of Emerging Adults* (New York: Oxford University Press, 2009), 154.

16. I owe this triadic formulation of the existential facts of life to theologian David Tracy, who has been addressing them throughout all his books.

Bibliography

Abelman, Robert, and Stewart M. Hoover, eds. *The Electronic Church: Controversies and Conclusions*. Norwood, NJ: Ablex, 1990.

Allitt, Patrick. *Catholic Intellectuals and Conservative Politics in America, 1950–1985*. Ithaca, NY: Cornell University Press, 1995.

———. *Religion in America Since 1945: A History*. New York: Columbia University Press, 2003.

Altizer, Thomas, and William Hamilton. *Radical Theology and the Death of God*. New York: Bobbs-Merrill, 1966.

Amato, Paul R., Alan Booth, David R. Johnson, and Stacy J. Rogers. *Alone Together: How Marriage in America Is Changing*. Cambridge, MA: Harvard University Press, 2007.

Anderson, Katherine, Don Browning, and Brian Boyer, eds. *Marriage: Just a Piece of Paper?* Grand Rapids, MI: Eerdmans, 2002.

Arum, Richard, and Josipa Roska. *Academically Adrift*. Chicago: University of Chicago Press, 2011.

———. *Aspiring Adults Adrift: Tentative Transitions of College Graduates*. Chicago: University of Chicago Press, 2014.

Bellah, Robert N. *Beyond Belief: Essays on Religion in a Post-Traditional World*. New York: Harper & Row, 1970.

Bellah, Robert N., Richard Madsen, William M. Sullivan, Ann Swidler, and Stephen M. Tipton. *The Good Society*. New York: Knopf, 1991.

Berger, Peter, and Richard John Neuhaus. *To Empower People: The Role of Mediating Structures in Public Policy*. Washington, DC: American Enterprise Institute for Public Policy, 1977.

Berryman, Phillip. *Liberation Theology*. New York: Pantheon, 1987.

———. *The Religious Roots of Rebellion: Christians in Central American Revolutions*. Maryknoll, NY: Orbis Books, 1984.

Bethge, Eberhard. *Dietrich Bonhoeffer*. New York: Harper & Row, 1970.

Beuka, Robert. *Suburbia Nation: Reading Suburban Landscape in Twentieth-Century American Fiction and Film*. New York: Palgrave Macmillan, 2004.

Bloom, Harold. *The America Religion: The Emergence of the Post-Christian Nation.* New York: Simon & Schuster, 1992.

———. *Omens of Millennium.* New York: Riverhead, 1997.

Bowman, Matthew. *The Mormon People: The Making of an American Faith.* New York: Random House, 2012.

Brown, Samuel Morris. *In Heaven as It Is on Earth: Joseph Smith and the Early Mormon Conquest of Death.* New York: Oxford University Press, 2012.

Bushman, Richard Lyman, with the assistance of Jed Woodworth. *Joseph Smith: Rough Stone Rolling.* New York: Knopf, 2005.

Bynum, Carolyn Walker. *Jesus as Mother: Studies in the Spirituality of the High Middle Ages.* Berkeley: University of California Press, 1984.

Bynum, Carolyn Walker, Stevan Harrell, and Paula Richman, eds. *Gender and Religion: On the Complexity of Symbols.* Boston: Beacon Press, 1986.

Campbell, David, ed. *A Matter of Faith: Religion in the 2004 Presidential Election.* Washington, DC: Brookings Institution Press, 2007.

Caplow, Theodore, Louis Hicks, and Ben J. Wattenberg. *The First Measured Century: An Illustrated Guide to Trends in America, 1900–2000.* Washington, DC: AEI Press, 2001.

Carson, Ralph Clayborne, Ralph E. Lucker, and Penny A. Russell, editors. *The Papers of Martin Luther King, Jr.,* Vol. 1, *Called to Serve: January 1928–June 1957.* Berkeley: University of California Press, 1992.

Casey, Shaun A. *The Making of a Catholic President: Kennedy vs. Nixon 1960.* New York: Oxford University Press, 2009.

Castronovo, David. *Beyond the Gray Flannel Suit: Books from the 1950s That Made American Culture.* New York: Continuum, 2004.

Chappell, David L. *A Stone of Hope: Prophetic Religion and the Death of Jim Crow.* Chapel Hill: University of North Carolina Press, 2004.

Chaves, Mark. *American Religion: Contemporary Trends.* Princeton, NJ: Princeton University Press, 2011.

Chopp, Rebecca S. *Saving Work: Feminist Practices of Theological Education.* Louisville, KY: Westminster John Knox Press, 1995.

Chudacoff, Howard P. *Children at Play: An American History.* New York: New York University Press, 2007.

Clecak, Peter. *America's Quest for the Ideal Self: Dissent and Fulfillment in the 60s and 70s.* New York: Oxford University Press, 1983.

Clinton, Bill. *My Life.* New York: Knopf, 2004.

Coalter, Milton J., John M. Molder, and Louis B. Weeks, eds. *The Mainstream Protestant "Decline."* Louisville, KY: Westminster John Knox Press, 1990.

———. *The Presbyterian Predicament: Six Perspectives.* Louisville, KY: Westminster John Knox Press, 1990.

Coffman, Elesha J. *The Christian Century and the Rise of the Protestant Mainline.* New York: Oxford University Press, 2013.

Coles, Robert. *Erik H. Erikson: The Growth of His Work.* Boston: Atlantic–Little, Brown, 1970.

Cone, James. *A Black Theology of Liberation.* Philadelphia: Lippincott, 1970.

Coontz, Stephanie. *The Way They Never Were: American Families and the Nostalgia Trip.* New York: Basic Books, 1992.

Cox, Harvey. *The Secular City.* New York: Macmillan, 1965.

Decter, Midge. *Liberal Parents, Radical Children*. New York: Coward, McCann & Geoghegan, 1975.

Didion, Joan. *The White Album*. New York: Simon & Schuster, 1979.

Dionne, E. J., Jr. *Souled Out: Reclaiming Faith and Politics After the Religious Right*. Princeton, NJ: Princeton University Press, 2008.

———. *Why Americans Hate Politics*. New York: Simon & Schuster, 1991.

Dionne, E. J., Jr., and John J. Dilulio, Jr., eds. *What's God Got to Do with the American Experiment?* Washington, DC: Brookings Institution Press, 2000.

Dionne, E. J., Jean Bethke Elshtain, and Kayla M. Drogosz, eds. *One Electorate under God? A Dialogue on Religion and American Politics*. Washington, DC: Brookings Institution Press, 2004.

Domke, David, and Kevin Coe. *The God Strategy: How Religion Became a Political Weapon in America*. New York: Oxford University Press, 2008.

Dunne, John S., CSC. *The City of the Gods: A Study in Myth and Mortality*. New York: Macmillan, 1965.

Eck, Diana L. *A New Religious America: How a "Christian Country" Has Become the World's Most Religiously Diverse Nation*. New York: HarperSanFrancisco, 2004.

Ehrenhalt, Alan. *The Lost City: Discovering the Forgotten Virtues of Community in the Chicago of the 1950s*. New York: Basic Books, 1995.

Ellwood, Robert S. *The Fifties Spiritual Marketplace: American Religion in a Decade of Conflict*. New Brunswick, NJ: Rutgers University Press, 1997.

———. *The Sixties Spiritual Awakening: American Religion Moving from Modern to Postmodern*. New Brunswick, NJ: Rutgers University Press, 1994.

Elshtain, Jean Bethke. *Democracy on Trial*. New York: Basic Books, 1995.

Erikson, Erik H. *Childhood and Society*. 2nd ed., revised and enlarged. New York: Norton, 1963.

———. *Identity Youth and Crisis*. New York: Norton, 1968.

———. *The Life Cycle Completed*. Extended version with new chapters on the ninth stage of development by Joan M. Erikson. New York: Norton, 1997.

Fiorenza, Elisabeth Schüssler. *Bread Not Stone: The Challenge of Feminist Biblical Interpretation*. Boston: Beacon Press, 1984.

———. *But She Said: Feminist Practices of Biblical Interpretation*. Boston: Beacon Press, 1992.

———. *In Memory of Her: A Feminist Theological Reconstruction of Christian Origins*. New York: Crossroads, 1983.

Fletcher, George P. *Loyalty: An Essay on the Morality of Relationships*. New York: Oxford University Press, 1993.

Fowler, Robert Booth, and Allen D. Hertzke. *Religion and Politics in America: Faith, Culture, and Strategic Choices*. Boulder, CO: Westview Press, 1995.

Fox-Genovese, Elizabeth. *Feminism Without Illusions: A Critique of Individualism*. Chapel Hill: University of North Carolina Press, 1991.

Frady, Marshall. *Billy Graham: A Parable of American Righteousness*. Boston: Little, Brown, 1979.

Friedan, Betty. *The Feminine Mystique*. Introduction by Anna Quindlen. New York: Norton, 2001.

Friedland, Michael B. *Lift Up Your Voice like a Trumpet: White Clergy and the Civil Rights and Antiwar Movements, 1954-1973*. Chapel Hill: University of North Carolina Press, 1998.

Fuller, Robert C. *Spiritual but Not Religious: Understanding Unchurched America.* New York: Oxford University Press, 1991.

Gandhi, Kishore, ed. *Contemporary Relevance of Sri Aurobindo.* New Delhi: Vivek, 1973.

Gaustad, Edwin Scott, and Phillip L. Barlow, with the special assistance of Richard W. Dishno. *New Historical Atlas of Religion in America.* New York: Oxford University Press, 2001.

Gelb, Arthur. *City Room.* New York: Putnam, 2003.

George, Carol V. R. *God's Salesman: Norman Vincent Peale and the Power of Positive Thinking.* New York: Oxford University Press, 1993.

Gibbs, Nancy, and Michael Duffy. *The Preacher and the Presidents: Billy Graham in the White House.* New York: Hachette, 2007.

Gilligan, Carol. *In a Different Voice: Psychological Theory and Women's Development.* Cambridge, MA: Harvard University Press, 1982.

Gleason, Philip. *Keeping the Faith: American Catholicism Past and Present.* Notre Dame, IN: University of Notre Dame Press, 1987.

Glendon, Mary Ann. *Rights Talk: The Impoverishment of Political Discourse.* New York: Free Press, 1991.

Graham, Billy. *Just as I Am.* New York: HarperCollins, 1997.

Green, John C. *The Faith Factor: How Religion Influences American Elections.* Westport, CT: Praeger, 2007.

Guth, James L., John C. Green, Corwin E. Smidt, Lyman A. Kellstedt, and Margaret M. Paloma. *The Bully Pulpit: The Politics of Protestant Clergy.* Lawrence: University Press of Kansas, 1997.

Gutierrez, Gustavo. *A Theology of Liberation: History, Politics and Salvation.* Translated and edited by Sister Caridad Inda and John Eagleson. Maryknoll, NY: Orbis Books, 1973.

Hacker, Andrew, and Claudia Dreifus. *Higher Education? How Colleges Are Wasting Our Money and Failing Our Kids—and What We Can Do About It.* New York: Times Books, 2010.

Hackett, David G., ed. *Religion and American Culture: A Reader.* New York: Routledge, 2003.

Halberstam, David. *The Fifties.* New York: Villard Books, 1993.

Hall, David D., ed. *Lived Religion in America: Toward a History of Practice.* Princeton, NJ: Princeton University Press, 1997.

Hamilton, Richard. *Restraining Myths: Critical Studies of U.S. Social Structure and Politics.* New York: Wiley, 1975.

Hansen, Klaus J. *Mormonism and the American Experience.* Chicago: University of Chicago Press, 1981.

Hatch, Nathan O., and John H. Wigger, eds. *Methodism and the Shaping of American Culture.* Nashville, TN: Kingswood Books, 2001.

Hempton, David. *Methodism: Empire of the Spirit.* New Haven, CT: Yale University Press, 2005.

Herberg, Will. *Protestant-Catholic-Jew: An Essay in American Religious Sociology.* Chicago: University of Chicago Press, 1983.

Heschel, Abraham Joshua. *God in Search of Man: A Philosophy of Judaism.* New York: Farrar, Straus & Giroux, 1955.

Hoge, Dean R., Benton Johnson, and Donald A. Luidens. *Vanishing Boundaries: The*

Religion of Mainline Protestant Baby Boomers. Louisville, KY: Westminster John Knox Press, 1994.

Hollinger, David A. *After Cloven Tongues of Fire: Protestant Liberalism in Modern American History.* Princeton, NJ: Princeton University Press, 2013.

Hughes, H. Stuart. *The Sea Change: The Migration of Social Thought, 1930–1965.* New York: Harper & Row, 1975.

Hunt, John F., and Terrence R. Connelly, *The Responsibility of Dissent.* New York: Sheed & Ward, 1969.

Hunter, James Davidson. *Culture Wars: The Struggle to Define America.* New York: Basic Books, 1991.

Jenkins, Philip. *Mystics and Messiahs: Cults and New Religions in American History.* New York: Oxford University Press, 2000.

Kaiser, Robert Blair. *The Politics of Sex and Religion.* Kansas City, MO: Leaven Press, 1982.

Kaplan, Edward K. *Spiritual Radical: Abraham Joshua Heschel in America, 1940–1972.* New Haven, CT: Yale University Press, 2007.

Kaplan, Fred. *1959: The Year Everything Changed.* Hoboken, NJ: Wiley, 2009.

Kelley, Dean M. *Why Conservative Churches Are Growing: A Study in Sociology of Religion.* New York: Harper & Row, 1972.

Kenniston, Kenneth, and the Carnegie Council on Children. *All Our Children: The American Family Under Pressure.* New York: Harcourt Brace Jovanovich, 1977.

Kornhaber, Arthur, M.D., and Kenneth L. Woodward. *Grandparents, Grandchildren: The Vital Connection.* Garden City, NY: Anchor Press/Doubleday, 1981.

Kosner, Edward. *It's News to Me: The Making and Unmaking of an Editor.* New York: Thunder's Mouth Press, 2006.

Kripal, Jeffrey J. *Esalen: America and the Religion of No Religion.* Chicago: University of Chicago Press, 2007.

Kripal, Jeffrey J., and Glenn W. Shuck, eds. *On the Edge of the Future: Esalen and the Evolution of American Culture.* Bloomington: Indiana University Press, 2005.

Larsen, Lawrence H., and Barbara J. Cottrell. *The Gate City: A History of Omaha.* Enlarged edition with a new conclusion by Harl A. Dalstrom. Lincoln: University of Nebraska Press, 1997.

Lasch, Christopher. *The Culture of Narcissism: American Life in an Age of Diminishing Expectations.* New York: Norton, 1978.

——. *Haven in a Heartless World: The Family Besieged.* New York: Basic Books, 1977.

——. *Women and the Common Life: Love, Marriage, and Feminism.* Edited by Elizabeth Lasch-Quinn. New York: Norton, 1997.

Leinberger, Paul, and Bruce Tucker. *The New Individualists: The Generation After the Organization Man.* New York: HarperCollins, 1991.

Lerner, Gerda. *The Creation of Patriarchy.* New York: Oxford University Press, 1986.

Linker, Damon. *The Theocons: Secular America Under Siege.* New York: Doubleday, 2006.

Lotz, David W., Donald D. Shriver, Jr., and John F. Wilson, eds. *Altered Landscapes: Christianity in America, 1935–1985.* Grand Rapids, MI: Eerdmans, 1989.

Luker, Kristin. *Abortion & the Politics of Motherhood.* Berkeley: University of California Press, 1984.

Marini, Stephen. *Sacred Song in America: Religion, Music, and Public Culture.* Champaign: University of Illinois Press, 2011.

Marlin, George J. *The American Catholic Voter: 200 Years of Political Impact.* Introduction by Michael Barone. Rev. ed. South Bend, IN: St. Augustine Press, 2006.

Marsden, George M. *Understanding Fundamentalism and Evangelicalism.* Grand Rapids, MI: Eerdmans, 1991.

Marsh, Charles. *The Beloved Community: How Faith Shapes Social Justice, from the Civil Rights Movement to Today.* New York: Basic Books, 2005.

Martin, Francis. *The Feminist Question: Feminist Theology in the Light of Christian Tradition.* Grand Rapids, MI: Eerdmans, 1994.

Martin, William. *A Prophet with Honor: The Billy Graham Story.* New York: William Morrow, 1991.

———. *With God on Our Side: The Rise of the Religious Right in America.* New York: Broadway Books, 1996.

Marty, Martin E. *Modern American Religion.* Vol. 3, *Under God, Indivisible: 1940–1960.* Chicago: University of Chicago Press, 1996.

———. *A Nation of Behavers.* Chicago: University of Chicago Press, 1976.

———. *The New Shape of American Religion.* New York: Harper & Brothers, 1958.

———. *Righteous Empire: The Protestant Experience in America.* New York: Dial Press, 1970.

Mauss, Armand L. *The Angel and the Beehive: The Mormon Struggle with Assimilation.* Urbana: University of Illinois Press, 1994.

McClory, Robert. *Turning Point: The Inside Story of the Papal Birth Control Commission, and How* Humanae Vitae *Changed the Life of Patty Crowley and the Future of the Church.* New York: Crossroad, 1995.

McDermott, Robert, ed. *The Essential Aurobindo.* New York: Schocken Books, 1973.

Michaelsen, Robert S., and Wade Clark Roof, eds. *Liberal Protestantism: Realities and Possibilities.* New York: Pilgrim Press, 1986.

Miller, Steven P. *The Age of Evangelicalism: America's Born-Again Years.* New York: Oxford University Press, 2014.

Mills, C. Wright. *The Power Elite.* New York: Oxford University Press, 1959.

———. *White Collar: The American Middle Classes.* New York: Oxford University Press, 1956.

Mouw, Richard J., and Mark A. Noll, eds. *Wonderful Words of Life: Hymns in Protestant History and Theology.* Grand Rapids, MI: Eerdmans, 2004.

Neuhaus, Richard J. *The Best of "The Public Square": Book Three.* Grand Rapids, MI: Eerdmans, 2007.

———. *The Catholic Moment: The Paradox of the Church in the Postmodern World.* New York: Harper & Row, 1987.

The New World Hymnal. Cleveland: Pilgrim Press, 1995.

Nilson, Reid L., ed. *The Rise of Mormonism.* New York: Columbia University Press, 2005.

Noll, Mark A., and Carolyn Nystrom. *American Evangelical Christianity: An Introduction.* Malden, MA: Blackwell, 2001.

———. *Is the Reformation Over?* Grand Rapids, MI: Baker Academic, 2005.

Novak, Michael. *The Open Church: Vatican II, Act II.* New York: Macmillan, 1962.

Oppenheimer, Mark. *Knocking on Heaven's Door: American Religion in the Age of Counterculture.* New Haven, CT: Yale University Press, 2003.

Orsi, Robert A. *Between Heaven and Earth: The Religious Worlds People Make and the Scholars Who Study Them.* Princeton, NJ: Princeton University Press, 2005.

O'Toole, James M., ed. *The Faithful: A History of Catholics in America.* Cambridge, MA: Belknap Press of Harvard University Press, 2008.

———. *Habits of Devotion: Catholic Religious Practice in Twentieth-Century America.* Ithaca, NY: Cornell University Press, 2004.

Phillips, Kevin. *American Theocracy: The Peril and Politics of Radical Religion, Oil, and Borrowed Money in the 21st Century.* New York: Viking, 2006.

Podhoretz, Norman. *Doings and Undoings: The Fifties and After in American Writing.* New York: Farrar, Straus, 1964.

Popenoe, David. *Life Without Father: Compelling New Evidence That Fatherhood and Marriage Are Indispensable for the Good of Children and Society.* New York: Free Press, 1996.

Putnam, Robert D. *Our Kids: The American Dream in Crisis.* New York: Simon & Schuster, 2015.

Reichley, A. James. *Faith in Politics.* Washington, DC: Brookings Institution Press, 2002.

Reuther, Rosemary Radford. *Sexism and God-Talk: Toward a Feminist Theology.* Boston: Beacon Press, 1983.

Rieff, Philip. *The Feeling Intellect: Selected Writings,* edited and with an introduction by Jonathan B. Imber. Chicago: University of Chicago Press, 1990.

———. *The Triumph of the Therapeutic: Uses of Faith After Freud.* Introduction by Elizabeth Lasch-Quinn. Wilmington, DE: ISI Books, 2006.

Riesman, David, with Nathan Glazer and Reul Denny. *The Lonely Crowd: A Study of the Changing American Character.* Abridged by the authors. New York: Doubleday, 1953.

Robertson, David M. *A Passionate Pilgrim: A Biography of Bishop James A. Pike.* New York: Knopf, 2004.

Roof, Wade Clark. *Spiritual Marketplace: Baby Boomers and the Remaking of American Religion.* Princeton, NJ: Princeton University Press, 1999.

Roszak, Theodore. *The Making of a Counter Culture: Reflections on the Technocratic Society and Its Youthful Opposition.* Garden City, NY: Doubleday, 1969.

Ruland, Vernon. *Imagining the Sacred: Soundings in World Religions.* Maryknoll, NY: Orbis Books, 1998.

Schor, Judith B. *The Overworked American: The Unexpected Decline of Leisure.* New York: Basic Books, 1991.

Shannon, Christopher. *A World Made Safe for Differences: Cold War Intellectuals and the Politics of Identity.* New York: Rowman & Littlefield, 2001.

Shipps, Jan. *Sojourner in the Promised Land: Forty Years Among the Mormons.* Urbana: University of Illinois Press, 2000.

Siegel, Fred. *The Revolt Against the Masses: How Liberalism Has Undermined the Middle Class.* New York: Encounter, 2013.

Slawenski, Kenneth. *J. D. Salinger: A Life.* New York: Random House, 2010.

Smith, Christian. *American Evangelicalism: Embattled and Thriving.* Chicago: University of Chicago Press, 1998.

———. *The Emergence of Liberation Theology: Radical Religion and Social Movement Theory.* Chicago: University of Chicago Press, 1991.

Smith, Christian, with Kari Christoffersen, Hilary Davidson, and Patricia Snell Herzog. *Lost in Transition: The Dark Side of Emerging Adulthood.* New York: Oxford University Press, 2011.

Smith, Christian, with Patricia Snell. *Souls in Transition: The Religious and Spiritual Lives of Emerging Adults.* New York: Oxford, 2009.

Smith, Christian, Kyle Longest, Johnathan Hill, and Kari Christoffersen. *Young Catholic America: Emerging Adults in, Out of, and Gone from the Church.* New York: Oxford University Press, 2014.

Stark, Rodney. *The Rise of Christianity: How the Obscure, Marginal Jesus Movement Became the Dominant Religious Force in the Western World in a Few Centuries.* Princeton, NJ: Princeton University Press, 1996.

Steinfels, Peter. *A People Adrift: The Crisis of the Roman Catholic Church in America.* New York: Simon & Schuster, 2003.

Stricherz, Mark. *Why the Democrats Are Blue: Secular Liberalism and the Decline of the People's Party.* New York: Encounter, 2003.

Stringfellow, William, and Anthony Towne. *The Death and Life of Bishop Pike.* Garden City, NY: Doubleday, 1976.

Sullivan, James. *Jeans: A Cultural History of an American Icon.* New York: Gotham Books, 2006.

Swanberg, W. A. *Luce and His Empire.* New York: Charles Scribner's Sons, 1972.

Taylor, Charles. *The Ethics of Authenticity.* Cambridge, MA: Harvard University Press, 1991.

The Teachings of Presidents of the Church: Joseph F. Smith. Salt Lake City, UT: Church of Jesus Christ of Latter-day Saints, 1998.

Tipton, Steven M. *Getting Saved from the Sixties: Moral Meaning in Conversion and Cultural Change.* Berkeley: University of California Press, 1982.

———. *Public Pulpits: Methodists and Mainline Churches in the Moral Argument of Public Life.* Chicago: University of Chicago Press, 2008.

Tipton, Steven M., and John Witte, Jr., eds. *Family Transformed: Religion, Values, and Society in American Life.* Washington, DC: Georgetown University Press, 2005.

Toolan, David. *Facing West from California's Shores: A Jesuit's Journey into New Age Consciousness.* New York: Crossroad, 1987.

Turner, John G. *Bill Bright and Campus Crusade for Christ: The Renewal of Evangelicalism in Postwar America.* Chapel Hill: University of North Carolina Press, 2008.

Tweed, Thomas, ed. *Retelling U.S. Religious History.* Berkeley: University of California Press, 1997.

Wacker, Grant. *America's Pastor: Billy Graham and the Shaping of a Nation.* Cambridge, MA: Harvard University Press, 2014.

———. *Early Pentecostals and American Culture.* Cambridge, MA: Harvard University Press, 2001.

Wallerstein, Judith S., Julia M. Lewis, and Sandra Blakeslee. *The Unexpected Legacy of Divorce: A 25 Year Landmark Study.* New York: Hyperion, 2000.

Whyte, William H. *The Organization Man.* Philadelphia: University of Pennsylvania Press, 2002.

Williams, Daniel. *God's Own Party: The Making of the Christian Right.* New York: Oxford University Press, 2010.

Wilson, James Q. *The Marriage Problem: How Our Culture Has Weakened Families.* New York: HarperCollins, 2002.

Wolfe, Alan. *The Transformation of American Religion: How We Actually Live Our Faith.* New York: Free Press, 2003.

Wuthnow, Robert. *After the Baby Boomers: How Twenty- and Thirty-Somethings Are Shaping the Future of American Religion.* Princeton, NJ: Princeton University Press, 2007.

———. *After Heaven: Spirituality in America Since the 1950s.* Berkeley: University of California Press, 1998.

———. *The Restructuring of American Religion.* Princeton, NJ: Princeton University Press, 1988.

———. *Sharing the Journey: Support Groups and America's New Quest for Community.* New York: Free Press, 1994.

Yankelovich, Daniel. *New Rules: Searching for Self-fulfillment in a World Turned Upside Down.* New York: Random House, 1981.

Index

ABOUT THE AUTHOR

KENNETH L. WOODWARD, a scholar as well as one of the nation's most respected journalists, served as *Newsweek*'s religion editor for nearly forty years, reporting from five continents and contributing more than seven hundred articles, including nearly one hundred cover stories, on a wide range of social issues, ideas, and movements. He is the author of *Making Saints: How the Catholic Church Determines Who Becomes a Saint, Who Doesn't, and Why* and *The Book of Miracles: The Meaning of the Miracle Stories in Christianity, Judaism, Buddhism, Hinduism, and Islam.*